CONTENTS

ᢒᵔᵄ

THE CAMBRIDGE COMPANION TO

THE ROMAN REPUBLIC

The Cambridge Companion to the Roman Republic examines many aspects of Roman history and civilization from 509 to 49 B.C. The key development of the republican period was Rome's rise from a small city to a wealthy metropolis and the international capital of an extensive Mediterranean empire. These centuries produced the classic republican political system and the growth of a world empire. They also witnessed the ultimate disintegration of this system under the relentless pressure of internal dissension and the boundless ambition of its leading politicians. In this Companion volume, distinguished European and American scholars present a variety of lively current approaches to understanding the political, military, and social aspects of Roman history as well as its literary and visual culture. Designed to be accessible to the general reader and to students, *The Cambridge Companion to the Roman Republic* will invite further exploration of a vital formative period of Roman history and its later influence.

Harriet Flower is associate professor of classics at Princeton University. The author of *Ancestor Masks and Aristocratic Tradition in Roman Culture*, she has written on aspects of Roman history and drama as well as Latin epigraphy.

The Cambridge Companion to

THE ROMAN REPUBLIC

Edited by

HARRIET I. FLOWER

Princeton University

CAMBRIDGE
UNIVERSITY PRESS

CAMBRIDGE UNIVERSITY PRESS
Cambridge, New York, Melbourne, Madrid, Cape Town, Singapore,
São Paulo, Delhi, Dubai, Tokyo, Mexico City

Cambridge University Press
32 Avenue of the Americas, New York, NY 10013-2473, USA

www.cambridge.org
Information on this title: www.cambridge.org/9780521003902

© Cambridge University Press 2004

First published 2004
8th printing 2010

A catalog record for this publication is available from the British Library.

Library of Congress Cataloging in Publication Data

The Cambridge Companion to the Roman Republic / edited by Harriet I. Flower.
p. cm.
Includes bibliographical references and index.
ISBN 0-521-80794-8 – ISBN 0-521-00390-3 (pb.)
1. Rome – History – Republic, 510–30 B.C. I. Flower, Harriet I.
DG235.C36   2003
937'.02 – dc21   2003048572

ISBN 978-0-521-80794-4 Hardback
ISBN 978-0-521-00390-2 Paperback

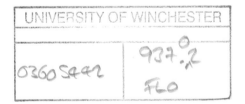

ILLUSTRATIONS AND MAPS

CONTRIBUTORS

JEAN-JACQUES AUBERT (Chair of Latin Language and the Classical Tradition, University of Neuchâtel, and currently Directeur de l'Institut des sciences de l'Antiquité) received his Ph.D. from Columbia University in 1991. He has published *Business managers in ancient Rome: A social and economic study of institores 200 B.C.–A.D. 250* (Columbia Studies in the Classical Tradition, Leiden, 1994) and an edited volume titled *Speculum iuris: Roman law as a reflection of economic and social life* (Ann Arbor, 2002).

T. COREY BRENNAN (Associate Professor of Classics, Rutgers University) is especially known for his treatment of Roman magistrates during the Republic, on which he has written a number of articles. His two-volume work on the praetorship titled *The praetorship in the Roman Republic* was published by Oxford in 2000. Professor Brennan taught for ten years at Bryn Mawr College.

PHYLLIS CULHAM (Professor of History, U.S. Naval Academy) has worked on many aspects of republican history, including the history of literacy in antiquity. She has published numerous articles in journals such as *AJAH, Historia, Glotta, Classical Philology*, and *Classical Antiquity*. She is also editor (with J. Lowell Edmunds) of *Classics: A discipline and profession in crisis* (Lanham, 1990). She has written a series of articles reviewing the evidence and scholarship on ancient women in *Arethusa* (1978) and *Helios* (1987). Her article "Did Roman women have an empire?" in *Inventing ancient culture: Historicism, periodization, and the ancient world*, edited by M. Golden and P. Toohey (London, 1997), won the Women's Classical Caucus prize for the best article on ancient women that year.

ELAINE FANTHAM (Professor Emerita, Princeton University) is a distinguished authority on Latin literature in its historical context. Her publications include *Comparative studies in republican Latin imagery* (Toronto, 1972); *Seneca's Troades: A literary introduction with text, translation, and commentary* (Princeton, 1982); *Roman literary culture: From Cicero to Apuleius* (Baltimore, 1996); *Lucan. De bello civili. Book II* (Cambridge, 1992); and *Ovid. Fasti. Book IV* (Cambridge, 1998).

HARRIET I. FLOWER (Associate Professor of Classics, Princeton University) has published on Roman social and cultural history, both in the republican and imperial periods. Her most notable contribution is her book *Ancestor masks and aristocratic power in Roman culture* (Oxford, 1996; paperback, 1999). She is currently working on a new book on sanctions against memory (*damnatio memoriae*), which will be the first to treat this subject thoroughly for the Republic.

ERICH S. GRUEN (Professor of History, University of California, Berkeley) has probably published more than anyone else in North America on the Roman Republic. Works of special note include *Roman politics and the criminal courts* (Cambridge, Mass., 1968); *The last generation of the Roman Republic* (Berkeley, 1974); *The Hellenistic world and the coming of Rome*, 2 vols. (Berkeley, 1984); *Studies in Greek culture and Roman policy* (Berkeley, 1990); and *Culture and national identity in republican Rome* (Ithaca, 1992).

KARL-JOACHIM HÖLKESKAMP (University Professor of Ancient History, University of Cologne) is the author of one of the most influential recent books on the Roman political élite, titled *Die Entstehung der Nobilität: Studien zur sozialen und politischen Geschichte der römischen Republik im 4. Jhdt. v. Chr.* (Stuttgart, 1987). His findings have also appeared in English, notably as "Conquest, competition and consensus: Roman expansion in Italy and the rise of the *nobilitas*," *Historia* 42 (1993) 12–39, and "The Roman Republic: Government of the people, by the people, for the people?" *Scripa Classica Israelica* 19 (2000) 203–23. He also regularly publishes in the history of archaic Greece, especially on the early *polis*, lawgivers, and written law.

ANN L. KUTTNER (Associate Professor of Art History, University of Pennsylvania) is one of the leading art historians to work on the art of the Republic, as well as that of the Empire. She has published *Dynasty and empire in the age of Augustus: The case of the Boscoreale cups* (Berkeley, 1995) and has edited (with A. Payne and R. Smick) *Antiquity and its interpreters* (Cambridge, 2000). Among her publications relevant to this project are "A third century B.C. Latin census on a Praenestine cist," *MDAI(R)* 98 (1991) 141–61; "Some new grounds for narrative:

Marcus Antonius' base (the "Altar of Domitius Ahenobarbus") and republican biographies," in *Narrative and event in ancient art*, edited by P. Holliday (Cambridge, 1993), 198–229; "Hellenistic images of spectacle, from Alexander to Augustus," in *The art of ancient spectacle*, edited by B. Bergman and C. Kondoleon, Studies in the History of Art vol. 56, 97–122; "Culture and history at Pompey's museum," *Transactions of the American Philological Association* 129 (1999) 343–73; and "Looking outside inside: Ancient Roman garden rooms," *Studies in the history of gardens and designed landscapes* 1 (1999) 7–35. She is currently completing a book that reexamines the influence of the Greek art of Asia Minor, especially Pergamum, on Roman art during the Republic.

JOHN F. LAZENBY (Emeritus Professor in Ancient History, University of Newcastle upon Tyne) has research interests in ancient warfare, particularly warfare in classical Greece and the Punic Wars, and in the history of ancient Sparta. He has undertaken research on the First and Second Punic Wars, Persian strategy at the time of Salamis, and the conspiracy of Kinadon, and he is currently engaged in a military study of the Peloponnesian War. His principal publications on the Roman Republic include *Hannibal's war* (Warminster, 1978, reprinted Norman, Okla., 1998); *The First Punic War: A military history* (London, 1996); "Was Maharbal right?" in *The Second Punic War: A reappraisal*, edited by T. J. Cornell, B. Rankov, and P. Sabin (Bulletin of the Institute of Classical Studies supp. 67; London, 1996); and several entries on ancient warfare in *The Oxford classical dictionary*, edited by S. Hornblower and A. J. S. Spawforth (3rd ed.; Oxford, 1996).

KATHRYN LOMAS (Research Fellow, Institute of Archaeology, University College London) is widely known as an expert on Roman Italy. She has research interests in Greek colonial history in the western Mediterranean, the history and archaeology of Roman Italy, ethnicity and acculturation in the ancient world, and the origins and development of the ancient city, and she has a particular interest in interdisciplinary research using both historical and archaeological material. For several years she has been engaged in a large-scale project investigating the origins and development of urbanism in pre-Roman and Roman Italy, and she has recently begun work on a project to investigate the development of literacy in archaic Italy. Other current projects include research on ethnic and cultural identity in Italy and Greece, acculturation in Sicily, and the Italian municipal elites in the age of Cicero. She has published *Rome and the western Greeks: Conquest and acculturation in Southern Italy*

(London, 1993) and *Roman Italy 338 B.C.–A.D. 200: A sourcebook* (London, 1996). She has edited (with T. J. Cornell) *Urban society in Roman Italy* (London, 1995) and (with E. Herring) *The emergence of state identities in Italy in the 1st millennium B.C.* (London, 2000). A volume of papers entitled *Greek identity in the western Mediterranean* was published in 2003.

STEPHEN P. OAKLEY (Professor of Latin in the Department of Classics, the University of Reading) counts Livy, the topography of pre-Roman Italy, and the tradition of classical texts as among his special interests. He has published *The hill-forts of the Samnites* (London, 1994) and *A commentary on Livy, Books VI–X*, vol. 1 and 2 (Oxford, 1997 and 1998).

DAVID POTTER (Professor of Classics, University of Michigan) is an expert on all aspects of Roman history from early times to late antiquity. He has published a number of articles and the following books: *Prophecy and history in the crisis of the Roman Empire: A historical commentary on the thirteenth Sibylline oracle* (Oxford, 1990); *Prophets and emperors: Human and divine authority from Augustus to Theodosius* (Cambridge, Mass., 1994); *Literary texts and the Roman historian* (London, 1999); and (with D. Mattingly) *Life, death, and entertainment in the Roman Empire* (Ann Arbor, 1999).

JÖRG RÜPKE (Professor of Comparative Religion at the University of Erfurt in Germany) includes among his areas of research ancient polytheistic religious systems, the sociology of religion, and the history of scholarship on ancient religion. He is best known for his books *Domi militiae: Die religiöse Konstruktion des Krieges in Rom* (Stuttgart, 1990) and *Kalender und Öffentlichkeit: Die Geschichte der Repräsentation und religiösen Qualifikation von Zeit in Rom* (Berlin, 1995). He has also written numerous articles. His introduction to Roman religion (Munich, 2001) will be published in English in 2004 (Polity Press). He is currently working on a complete prosopography of the priests of traditional cults in the city of Rome as well as on a long-term study of religion in the Roman provinces.

MORTIMER N. S. SELLERS (Director of the Center for International and Comparative Law, University of Baltimore School of Law) teaches legal history, legal theory, and comparative constitutional law. Educated in law and history at Harvard and at Oxford, he is the author of *American republicanism: Roman ideology in the United States Constitution* (New York,

1994) and *The sacred fire of liberty: Republicanism, liberalism, and the law* (New York, 1998).

JÜRGEN VON UNGERN-STERNBERG (Chair of Ancient History, Basel University) teaches both Greek and Roman history and has published widely in both fields, as well as on the classical tradition. He is especially noted for his two books *Untersuchungen zum spätrepublikanischen Notstandsrecht*: senatusconsultum ultimum *und* hostis-*Erklärung* (Munich, 1970) and *Capua im Zweiten Punischen Krieg: Untersuchungen zur römischen Annalistik* (Munich, 1975). He edited (with H. Reinau) *Vergangenheit in mündlicher Überlieferung* (Stuttgart, 1988). He has also published on the fall of the Republic, notably: "Die Legitimitätskrise der römischen Republik," *Historische Zeitschrift* 266 (1998) 607–24.

PREFACE

I am most grateful to all the contributors for their willingness to participate and their enthusiasm for and support of the project as a whole. I owe special thanks to the following for comments on individual sections and for encouragement along the way: Corey Brennan, Eve D'Ambra, Michael Flower, Dean Hammer, Karl-Joachim Hölkeskamp, John Marincola, Chris Pelling, and Kathy Spencer. This book would never have been published without Beatrice Rehl of Cambridge University Press, whose tact and good humour saw it through to completion. I also owe a special debt of gratitude to Judith Chien for her expertise and patience in helping me put this volume together. The volume was edited during the year 2002, first at the School of Historical Studies of the Institute for Advanced Study in Princeton, New Jersey, and then at Franklin and Marshall College in Lancaster, Pennsylvania. Both institutions afforded invaluable support that made it all possible.

INTRODUCTION

Harriet I. Flower

☙

The historical period covered by the Roman Republic is a long one, comprising almost five hundred years of varied political, military, and cultural change. The central aspect of the Republic was Rome's rise from a small city, virtually indistinguishable from others in central Italy, to a metropolis, the capital of an extensive Mediterranean empire. These centuries produced the classic republican political system, marked by its culture of spectacle and performance. They also witnessed the ultimate disintegration of this system under the relentless pressure of internal dissention and the boundless ambitions of its leading politicians.

It was the Roman Republic that created the characteristic Greco-Roman culture, the result of a melding of Greek influences and native Italian and Roman traditions, which would be spread by the Romans throughout the Mediterranean world. This culture of fusion, a hallmark of the republican ethos, can be traced in literature, art, architecture, law, rhetoric, philosophy, and everyday life. Latin literature in all genres of prose and verse also emerged during the time of Rome's imperial expansion. Above all, the vast changes between the early fifth century and the mid first century B.C. are reflected in the growth and adornment of the city of Rome itself. By the time of Augustus (the first emperor), the city numbered over a million inhabitants, a population that would not be matched until London reached such a size in the late eighteenth century. The image of Rome's republican politics and growing empire captured the imagination of later ages, from Plutarch and Tacitus to Shakespeare, the thinkers of the European Enlightenment, and the American Founding Fathers. Readers who are new to the study of Roman history may be more familiar with the history of Rome under the emperors, but it is the Roman Republic that modern American and European political culture has the greatest affinity with and that is arguably more relevant to the political problems and challenges of our own times.

I

The very term "republic," so familiar in Western political thought, can cause confusion because it is used in so many different senses. The English word comes from the Latin *res publica*, itself a multivalent expression for both the community and its characteristic political culture. Literally, *res publica* means "the public thing," which could be the state itself, its constitution, or its common interest. In the latter sense the term is equivalent to "commonwealth" or "common good." It is typical of the Romans that they actually did not have a separate name for their political system; it was simply equated with the community itself and its best interests. Political life consisted of involvement with this community of shared concerns and values. Rome's origin as a small town with limited territory would have made such a political vocabulary natural, perhaps especially at the time when the kings were driven out (509 B.C.) and their powers divided among annually elected magistrates, as was happening in other communities in Italy at about the same time. In modern times the term "republic" has come to describe many political systems and parties that looked back to Rome without necessarily reproducing faithfully either its institutions or political culture.

Modern historians use "Republic" to describe various aspects of the Roman past. The two primary uses are to denote a time period (traditionally 509–49 B.C.) or to designate the Roman constitutional system itself. However, both of these uses are problematic. Unlike many other historical periods, the almost five hundred year stretch is really too long to represent a significant body of shared experiences and lifestyles. Modern periodization has tended to obscure the characteristic Roman energy for innovation and the complex interplay between inherited tradition and bold invention. Similarly, it is misleading to imagine that the Roman constitution was created at some particular moment, let alone at the beginning of the Republic, and then remained essentially unchanged. Rather the "constitution," or set of political rules and norms, had to evolve and change, even as the city and empire expanded.

In both the constitutional and the chronological sense, it is difficult to find an end point for the Republic, nor did Roman authors themselves agree on this issue. Many would name Caesar's invasion of Italy in January of 49 B.C. as the overthrow of the Republic, whereas other studies represent the Battle of Actium in 31 B.C. as the final establishment of a system of one-man rule under Caesar's adopted son and heir Octavian (Tac. *Hist.* 1). But soon after, when Octavian took the name "Augustus" in 27 B.C., he claimed, however speciously, to be restoring the traditional system of Roman government (*res publica restituta*; cf. *Res Gestae* 34). Tacitus, writing in the early second century

A.D., identified the deaths of Brutus and Cassius at the Battle of Philippi in 42 B.C. as the end of the Republic in the traditional sense of the term, since the last truly republican army had been defeated (*Ann.* 2.1). The historian Cremutius Cordus had been prosecuted in A.D. 25 for his eulogistic treatment of Brutus and Cassius as the "last of the Romans" (*Ann.* 4.34). Yet during the last generation of the Roman Republic itself, Cato the Younger had declared that it was the political alliance between Caesar and Pompey (and Crassus) in 60 B.C. that had been the first and greatest evil for the city, not their subsequent quarrel (Plut. *Pomp.* 47.2–3), and Asinius Pollio chose this same year for the start of his history of the civil wars (Livy *Per.* 103; Vell. Pat. 2.44.1; Luc. 1.84–86; Hor. *Carm.* 2.1). There can be little doubt, however, that the example of Sulla, who marched on Rome with his army and "restored" the "Republic" in 82–79 B.C., influenced men such as Caesar and Pompey to see themselves as entitled to operate outside the traditional confines of republican norms. Obviously, like the term "Republic" itself, the perspective as to when the Republic ended is a shifting one.

And yet it was during the Republic that Rome acquired an empire. This fact may appear self-evident, but it illustrates what is only the most obvious difficulty with terming the subsequent age the "Roman Empire." In fact, in many ways Rome's republican political culture was synonymous with the desire to expand in each generation, first in Italy and then beyond. The Republic was thus an imperial one at home and abroad and in all levels of society. In modern times, the study of this "republic" has often consisted of analyzing its fall, especially in the age of Pompey and Caesar, with some attention paid to the civil unrest and turmoil under Marius and Sulla. Such a focus, however fascinating and complex, tends inevitably to be coloured by the bias of hindsight and especially by the typical nostalgia, both nuanced and intense, that the Romans themselves felt for their past. There is clearly much more to the Republic than its fall. Moreover, the end can itself be fully understood only when seen against the wider background of generations of remarkable success and stability enjoyed by Rome's traditional political culture.

Beyond the individual interlocking chapters to be found in this volume, a number of overarching themes emerge as essential to any investigation and understanding of Roman life and culture during the Republic. These include most notably the following eight areas of the Roman experience: the chronological progression of events; the geographical space dominated by Rome; the changing conception of Roman identity in terms of citizenship; the development of a codified set of laws together with a system of courts to enforce those laws; the evolving economy and material conditions of life; the emergence of a high culture of writing, art, and spectacle; the Roman political system itself; and ultimately the transformation of Rome into the capital of a Mediterranean empire. These fundamental topics are connected to each other, while also being independent fields for study and analysis, like a series of windows opening onto the past. Each reveals the intricate interplay of continuity and change as Roman society was transformed by the acquisition of an empire. That acquisition was accompanied by untold riches, sophisticated outside influences, and a characteristically Roman sense of anxious comparison of the present with the simpler life of an increasingly idealized earlier age, as if the Romans were frequently glancing back over their shoulders. I will now discuss each of these themes in turn.

The Roman calendar, as well as the Romans' experience of time and past history, were very different from our own. Yet certain patterns emerge as basic features of the Republic. Although the surviving literary sources from the earliest period consist of legends rather than historically preserved records, these legends, as preserved especially by Livy, contain outlines of events and individuals, even where imperfectly understood by later ages. Their complexity and variant versions reflect the Romans' own evolving debates about the origins of their community. The Romans did not write formal histories of their own until about 200 B.C., and much early material, both artifacts and records, had been destroyed when the Gauls sacked the city in 390 B.C. A culture of memory created by the political élite flourished from the late fourth century until the very end of the Republic, although it may have distorted and embellished the past as often as it preserved it.

The political system of the mature Republic emerged in the late fourth century from the civil strife of the "Conflict of the Orders." Reliable facts begin to emerge only during the period of the First Punic War (264–241 B.C.). The impetus to write history seems to have arisen, as with the Greeks, in the context of a great struggle against a foreign power, in Rome's case Carthage during the Second Punic War (218–201 B.C.). Rome's bitter fight for sheer survival in the face of Hannibal's devastating war in Italy in the third century serves as a complete contrast to the events of the second century, which was characterized by Rome's seemingly effortless expansion throughout the Mediterranean as the Hellenistic kingdoms collapsed like so many houses of cards before Rome's legions. In another complete reversal, the first century was marked by civil war and increasing lawlessness as politics came to be controlled by a few powerful generals and as the institutions of traditional government became largely ineffectual or stretched beyond their capacities.

The overarching patterns created by periodization can be enlightening, but they also have limits. For example, as almost any treatment will assert, the deaths of the Gracchi brothers (in 133 and 121 B.C.) mark the beginning of what we call the end of the Republic, a period of recurring crises that would last for over seventy years. However, these men were themselves products of the prosperous second century and of the highest ranks of the old nobility. Their own stories can be obscured by the role they came to play as forerunners of later events that went well beyond what they themselves could ever have imagined. Times of great innovation repeatedly alternated and overlapped with typically Roman phases of conscious archaism and of the (re)invention of traditions. Similarly, each age can be understood in its own right as a time of transition, as every generation tended both towards the strengthening and towards the undermining of traditional republican norms and practices. Meanwhile, Roman historiography portrayed the consequences of imperial expansion in terms of moral decay and the corruption introduced into Roman society by outside influences.

The growth of Rome's empire in the time of republican government was dramatic. Early Rome, a city that shared in a common Italian culture and was heavily influenced by Etruscans, Greeks, and others, stands in sharp contrast to the late republican city that dominated the Mediterranean. The change seems to start slowly after the capture of Veii in 396 B.C. It is articulated by bold moments of decision, such as the Roman people's vote to take a Roman army overseas for the first time (to Sicily in 264 B.C.) or the even more fateful choice of war with Macedonia immediately after the defeat of Hannibal at the end of a whole generation of conflict with Carthage. By the middle of the second century, Rome was the only remaining great power in the Mediterranean. Its own view of its central position within this world is most dramatically illustrated by the destruction of two famous ancient and beautiful cities, Carthage and Corinth, both wiped off the map by Rome in 146 B.C.

The physical space of Rome's world is vital to any understanding of its role and image, both at home and abroad. Significantly, the Romans were slow to annex extensive territories and to subject them to direct control; instead, Rome initially sought hegemony as a means of pursuing its actual goal; international stature and recognition. Despite Rome's aggressive actions, the rhetoric of Roman imperialism, especially in the wake of the Second Punic War, tended to be couched in terms of self-defense and security. Its power was articulated by a series of expanding spheres of influence and areas of operation rather than defined by fixed frontiers of the sort that would be termed an "empire" in a colonial or postcolonial sense. This gradual change is reflected in the Latin language. *Provincia* initially meant a sphere of operations assigned to a general and his army; only later did it come to designate a foreign territory under direct Roman rule. The highly developed skills of Roman surveyors were honed by constant practice in measuring and (re)assigning conquered lands. Eventually, the first publicly displayed, permanent map of the Roman world was put up as a legacy of the general Agrippa in Rome in the time of Augustus, serving as a symbol of the republican achievements that Augustus claimed to be completing.

The growth of Rome's power and ambition was accompanied by a developing sense of what it meant to be "Roman" and what Roman culture consisted of. Roman citizenship came to be seen as a coveted and privileged status but one that the Romans themselves were increasingly willing to share, with allies, friends, and a growing number of people who had been conquered by them, including freed slaves. As a result, the benefits of citizenship were extended outward from the city, first to municipal élites in Italy and then to all inhabitants of the peninsula after the Social War (91–87 B.C.). In addition, citizenship was extended, in various degrees, through colonization in Italy. By the time of Caesar, colonies of Roman veterans could also be found abroad. The characteristically Roman concept of an ever expanding citizen body not defined by ethnicity, religious belief, or social origins proved to be a powerful tool of control but also of assimilation. The Latin language and Roman customs spread to dominate first Italy and then many provincial areas. However, the Romans' sense of their own identity was equally affected by this process: Livy's early Roman history demonstrates the importance of the idea that the Romans were a diverse people made up from the earliest times of many immigrants from different backgrounds.

Rome's legal system, while not especially old in Mediterranean terms, emerged as the foundation of the western legal tradition. Although first codified in the Twelve Tables of the mid fifth century, the legal system actually developed in the second century B.C., which saw the establishment of a series of permanent courts and of a drive, however unsuccessful at times, to subject even the most powerful in society to legal norms and regulations, even in regard to their conduct abroad as commanders of armies and as provincial governors. The expectation that magistrates would be accountable, at least to their fellow senators, for their use of official power was fundamental to the Republic. In Roman thought, freedom and citizenship were defined largely in terms of a body of individuals who were all subject to the same legal sanctions and who enjoyed the legal privileges of due process and the right of appeal to their peers. A sense of legalism and of conformity to accepted norms permeated Roman society and culture, both secular and religious.

The legal system itself, however, was a reflection of the Republic's political practices and its changing economic life. Rome had its origins in a very simple agricultural society with an ideal of self-sufficiency shared at every level of the community. The Republic saw a complete change to a society of vast wealth, much of it imported, and to an economy heavily based on slave labour, itself the product of empire. While the traditional identification with life on the land and with an agricultural calendar endured, the intense focus of the élite on warfare and politics perpetuated the drive to expand the empire and precipitated the economic changes that inevitably followed. Warfare had become a money-making concern for the Romans, even as the wealth that flowed into the city changed the life of all its inhabitants.

The spoils of empire, initially controlled by the conquering general, were not equally distributed within Roman society, and vast differences in material and cultural life emerged within the citizen body. The conservative tendency to invest money in land led the wealthy to buy more land and to create extensive estates (farmed for profit by slave labour) at the expense of the independent small farmers, who had formed the traditional backbone of Roman society and of its citizen army. Meanwhile, the economic opportunities created by the empire included lucrative government contracts for buildings, roads, and supplies as well as tax farming of new provinces. Since the senators, as a social order, were legally barred from exploiting these opportunities or other commercial ventures, a new class of wealthy merchants and publicans (tax collectors) of equestrian rank emerged to amass vast profits and to develop their own political aspirations, thereby affecting the balance of power in the Republic. Similarly, the newly arrived slaves, especially those employed in Rome, changed the face of the city through their ubiquity, their diversity, and their skills and education, and ultimately through the ability of many to acquire citizen status and voting rights.

Roman culture had always been open to outside influences, as can be seen in the impact of Etruscan and Greek customs even in the archaic period. The empire created more established and regular exchanges of ideas and customs, which could be imported as easily as slaves and goods. Rome's ambition to be a world power expressed itself especially through its emulation of Greek culture, in literature, art, architecture, and through the life of leisure cultivated by its educated élite. At the same time, Roman society experienced the conflicts and tensions created by rapid changes of lifestyle and material goods. Many Romans felt nostalgia for the past, even as they developed an idealized picture of that past and of the simple rustic life and values of their ancestors. Repeated but largely ineffective sumptuary legislation attempted to limit the display of personal wealth, which could cause social tensions, and the temptations to conspicuous consumption, which could lead to financial ruin. Societal changes tended to be viewed as indications of moral decay, revealing risks of corruption associated with the cultures of conquered peoples. Hence, the dynamic creation of Latin literature and the assimilation of Hellenistic visual and performance culture took place in a context fraught with debate and anxiety over the loss of traditional lifestyles and over the very nature of Roman values. These tensions, at the same time, gave rise to an atmosphere of tremendous creativity characterized by the constant interplay of accepted norms (some old, some relatively recent creations) with innovation or transgression.

The classic republican political system flourished specifically within the context of empire. The nobility of office that emerged after the end of the Conflict of the Orders, which relied for promotion on merit rather than birth (the criterion of the old patrician élite), justified its preeminence by means of conquest, military glory, and the acquisition of conquered territory, first in Italy and then abroad, that could be used to better the position of Romans from every background. The success of these *nobiles*, along with their ethos of bravery and public service, helped perpetuate the desire to expand overseas once Rome had come to dominate the Italian peninsula. The image of that success, based on material profits and on a religious concept of manifest destiny, had a powerful impact on Roman ambitions. The Republic was characterized by tremendous vitality and creativity but also by boundless rapacity and cruelty. It had grown out of a regal system based on a royal family with a dynastic succession. To avoid collapsing back into this earlier model, the Republic was designed with a complex system of checks and balances supported by collegiality in office, the inherently conservative power of the veto, and the right of appeal shared by all citizens.

The eventual destruction of the Republic at the hands of its overambitious generals and armies ought not to obscure its central aspect,

namely, the success and prosperity created by its ability to find an enduring balance between competition and cooperation over many generations, despite and perhaps because of the extraordinarily high demands
and risks inherent in its system. Recognition by the community and the
promise of posthumous fame offered by a culture of memory centered
on great men made politics the most attractive sphere for the ambitious
and gifted. Traditional republican politics was defined as satisfying and
rewarding the aspirations of even the most successful and distinguished.
Constant expansion required a basic consensus at home. Continual rotation between times in office and periods of private life further increased
the need for accommodation between politicians. The principle of debate amongst peers and a sense of community (or communality) was
developed and maintained by the senate. At the same time, frequent
elections created a dynamic dialogue between the political élite and the
people, while they maintained the rhetoric of interaction inherent in
Roman politics and society. The sense of a shared set of values was cultivated for a surprisingly long time, despite radical changes. Meanwhile,
war was a virtually constant condition of Roman life, and a military
ethos permeated society both internally and in its dealings with others.

The creation of Rome as an imperial capital from what had originally been no more than a collection of small villages on hills over
swampy ground was perhaps the most visible expression of the aspirations and achievements of the imperial Republic. Yet this development
was largely piecemeal and rarely followed any general plan. Julius Caesar
eventually conceived such a plan, at the very end of the Republic, but he
did not live to implement it. The topography of the city itself reflected
the daily interaction between the monuments of the past and an ever
increasing number of new buildings, whether public structures funded
by booty money (temples, basilicas, arches) or the expanding houses of
the wealthier citizens, whose domestic staff alone might number over
fifty by the late Republic. The multiplication of cults and temples could
in itself serve as an index of expansion, especially after the end of the
Second Punic War. The center of the city at the Forum also evolved,
as butcher's shops and fishmongers were replaced by bankers, and the
great basilicas were built to accommodate the complex legal and commercial life of the metropolis. The Tabularium, next to the Forum, was
designed to house official archives and records. Honorific statues, war
memorials, arches, and collections of art brought from all over the empire decorated and redefined communal areas. The 50s B.C. saw Rome's
first great stone theatre, technically part of a shrine to Venus, built by

Pompey to complement the older, more traditional performance spaces of the Circus Maximus and Circus Flaminius. The city itself, therefore, still defined Romanness to the end of the Republic, but it also reflected the many changes that had occurred, both by design and by chance, as a result of the political, social, economic, and cultural effects of imperial expansion and hegemonic ambitions.

The contributions to this volume are grouped thematically under four headings but are essentially parallel and could easily be read in different combinations. Many themes cut across several chapters and can be pursued in a variety of ways. For example, the economy receives its own treatment but is also featured in the discussions of the lives of Roman women, Rome's expansion in Italy, and the factors leading to the fall of the Republic. Religion is inseparable from Roman politics and was as integral to the life of the army in the field as to that of women at home. The expansion of Rome's empire is highlighted in the chapters on Italy and on the Greek East, but it forms the essential background to virtually every topic. The descriptions of cultural developments in the chapters on art, literature, and spectacle complement the more formal discussion of Rome's political institutions. Similarly, since the household formed the basic unit of society, it is set alongside the constitution and the religious establishment to evoke the structure of Roman society. The military ethos of the Republic is explored in the chapters on the army and navy, the battles of the Punic wars, and the military character of many Roman spectacles in the city. Separate chapters give special attention to the beginning and end of the Republic as frames for the remaining discussions. As is the case for so many historical periods, the sources for the Republic are dominated by images created by and for men of the senatorial class. Yet the study of women and members of the lower orders (including slaves) by the latest generation of scholars has created a fuller and more genuine picture of life in Rome.

This Companion aims to provide an introduction to the Republic that tries not to privilege a particular time period or point of view. It offers instead a guide to a variety of areas, fields of study, and possible approaches that are currently being explored by leading scholars in America, Britain, and Europe, who are at various stages in their careers and who have been educated in different classical traditions. The goal is to suggest the richness of the ancient sources and the debates they are currently raising, without offering a formal history of scholarship or a definitive statement of results. It is not possible to be comprehensive within the format of this modest volume, nor is it necessary to reproduce a narrative of the main events, which can be found elsewhere. It is hoped that this Companion will be used to accompany and elucidate the ancient sources that bring the Romans alive for us amidst the changing concerns of each new generation. The Companion invites further reading and discussion and so should serve as a starting point for contemplating republican Rome rather than an end.

PART I

❧

POLITICAL AND
MILITARY HISTORY

1: THE EARLY REPUBLIC

Stephen P. Oakley

⁌

Origins will always fascinate. By 264 B.C. Rome was already governed by means of most of the constitutional arrangements that are familiar to us from the 'classical' period of republican history;[1] in that year it both completed the subjugation of peninsular Italy by capturing Volsinii (modern Orvieto) and began the process of Mediterranean conquest by sending its legions across the Straits of Messina into Sicily. Yet *c.* 509 B.C. it was just a large city in Latium with a constitution as yet undeveloped after emergence from a long period of monarchical rule. This chapter considers the origins of the Roman Republic and attempts to explain how the Latin city transformed itself into a nation ready and willing to grasp the prize of empire.

Before we begin, we must confront briefly the greatest problem in the study of early Rome, the notorious unreliability of our sources.[2] They are almost entirely literary, and among them Livy, the only surviving writer to present a detailed narrative of most of the period, is preeminent.[3] The reasons for this unreliability are easily explained: the Republic began *c.* 509 B.C., whereas Fabius Pictor, the first Roman historian, wrote *c.* 200; he and his successors in the second century B.C. had only very incomplete evidence, especially for the early period; many of Pictor's successors distorted what little material they had by reconstructing the history of early Rome so that it read like a history of their

This chapter deals with the history of the Republic between 509 and 264 B.C. The literature on the relevant topics is enormous, and each note cites only one or two recent and reliable discussions in English of the topic under consideration. The two fullest recent treatments in English of the early Republic are Walbank et al. (1989) and Cornell (1995); reference will not be made again to these works, but they should be consulted via their indexes for almost all the topics discussed in this chapter. My own views on many of the matters discussed here are expounded at greater length in *A commentary on Livy, Books VI–X* (Oakley, 1997–2004).

own times; and Livy unfortunately based his account on these writers rather than on the original evidence. Most scholars now agree that as a result of this process the details of Livy's political and military narrative are unreliable, amounting to reconstruction or plausible invention by Livy himself or by his sources. Yet many also believe that, once this reconstruction and invention has been stripped away, one is left with references to events that really did happen (e.g., the passing of a law or the agreement of a treaty or the capture of a town). To take a simple example, Livy (5.19–23), supported by other writers dependent on similar sources, gives a long description of how the Romans captured Veii in 396; few, if any, scholars doubt the fact that Veii fell to Rome in that year, but likewise few accept the historicity of all the legends with which the tale is embroidered in Livy and others. There remains much disagreement about what in Livy and others was transmitted reliably from the fifth, fourth, or third centuries and what was invented in the third, second, or first, but most scholars believe that our evidence gets better the further away the event in question is from 509 B.C. and that our evidence for the years after 300 B.C. is notably better in quality than that even for the period 350–300 B.C.

From all this it follows that much of what Livy and others say has been disbelieved or modified by modern scholars. Although few of the individual arguments that follow are very controversial, readers should always remember how uncertain the whole subject is.[4]

In Rome, as in all ancient and many mediaeval and modern states, public life may be seen in retrospect (even if it was not always apparent at the time) to have been dominated by three issues: how to divide the wealth of the state, how to determine who was to administer the state, and how best to secure the state against attack from those outside it.

Political conflict, what the Greeks called *stasis*, was as endemic in early Rome as it was in many cities of the Greek world, and it is important to be clear about what was at the heart of such conflict. The ancient economy was based on agriculture.[5] This is not to deny that some men and women devoted most of their working hours to other activities (e.g., labouring in a factory to make armour). Most families, however, owned land, in a society in which wealth and to a large degree social status were in proportion to the amount of land owned. It is a familiar fact that a member of the Roman élite of the first century B.C. is likely to have owned a large amount of land but is unlikely to have done much farming in person. In 500 B.C. the situation was very different: the landholdings even of the richest Romans will have been much smaller, and the owners themselves will have taken part in farming them. Only towards the end of our period is it likely that aristocrats began to be more detached from the day-to-day running of their farms.

In Livy and other ancient sources, the internal politics of the early Roman Republic are dominated by a dispute between two groups, the patricians and the plebeians; modern scholars have termed this the 'Conflict of the Orders'.[6] In the traditional narrative, after the expulsion in 510/9 B.C. of Tarquinius Superbus, the last king of Rome, the government fell into the hands of a group of aristocratic families (the patricians), who elected from their number two annual magistrates called 'consuls' and occasionally in time of crisis appointed a dictator to take sole charge of military affairs. Other magistracies were few in number: the most important was the censorship, established in 443 and held at irregular intervals by two men in order to enrol citizens into the correct class for the purposes of military service. Between 494 and 287, patrician rule and dominance was challenged by plebeian agitation, which forced from the patricians at first concessions and then the granting of an equal share in power. The key disturbances and legislation in this period, as they are recorded in our sources, may be summarized as follows:

• In 494, in protest against patrician treatment of those in debt-bondage (the Romans called this bondage *nexum* and those in it *nexi*), the plebeians went on strike and withdrew to a hill outside Rome; this episode is commonly known as the First Secession of the Plebs. In a conciliatory response, the patricians granted them the right annually to elect their own leaders, who were called tribunes of the plebs; initially these were two in number, later ten. The tribunes were regarded as sacrosanct; that is, the plebeians took an oath to take vengeance on anyone who violated the person or obstructed the actions of a tribune. Thereafter the plebeians had their own assembly (the *concilium plebis*), to which patricians were not admitted but in which they were occasionally tried for crimes against the plebeians.

• In 451 and 450, a board of ten (*decemviri*) was appointed to publish a codification of Roman law, known as the Twelve Tables.[7] Henceforth it was easier for those who were not patricians to know exactly what was specified by the law. A notorious provision of the eleventh table forbade intermarriage between patricians and plebeians. Legend had it that the *decemviri* of 450 were different from those of 451 and were removed from office only by a Second Secession of the Plebs.

• In 449, a law was supposedly passed that guaranteed the right of appeal to the people (the technical term was *provocatio ad populum*) against scourging or capital punishment by a magistrate. This reaffirmed a law supposedly passed in 509, the first year of the Republic.[8]

• In 449, a second law was passed that made plebiscites binding on the whole communty, patricians and their followers as well as plebeians.

• In 445, the law forbidding intermarriage between patricians and plebeians was repealed.

• Between 444 and 392, consuls were often replaced by three, four, or six military tribunes with consular power (consular tribunes) and in all years between 391 and 367 by six consular tribunes. According to Livy, plebeians as well as patricians were eligible for election to this office.

• In 367, the consular tribunate was abolished by a *lex Licinia Sextia* ('Licinio-Sextian law'), and the consular constitution was reestablished for 366; henceforth plebeians were eligible for election to one of the consulships, and in more than half the years between 366 and 342 a plebeian was elected. A third magistracy, the praetorship, was also established in 367.

• Another *lex Licinia Sextia* passed in 367 limited the amount of public land that could be held by an individual to 500 *iugera*.[9] It seems that some patricians had been holding far more than this amount.

• A third *lex Licinia Sextia* passed in 366 alleviated plebeian indebtedness. Similar laws are said to have been passed in 357, 352, 347, and 342.

• In 356, the first plebeian dictator (Gaius Marcius Rutilus) was appointed.

• In 351, the first plebeian censor (the same Marcius) was elected.

• In 342, a *lex Genucia* seems to have guaranteed the right of a plebeian to one of the consular posts in any given year.[10]

• In 339, the plebeian dictator Q. Publilius Philo passed several progressive measures, one of which, supposedly repeating a measure of 449 and anticipating one of 287, made *plebiscita* ('plebiscites' or 'decrees of the plebs') binding on the whole people and not just the plebeians.

• Another *lex Publilia* stipulated that henceforth one censor should be plebeian.

• In 336, Q. Publilius Philo became the first plebeian praetor.

• In 300, plebeians won the right to hold places in two of Rome's priestly colleges (the pontiffs and the augurs), both of which were enlarged.

• In 300, in a separate measure, the right to appeal to the whole people (*provocatio ad populum*) against decisions of consuls and other magistrates was guaranteed; this law was said to have reinforced earlier laws of 509 and 449.

• In 287, the plebeians seceded again, in part because of the problem of indebtedness. A law was passed reaffirming that all citizens were to be subject to plebiscites.

Even summarized as briefly as this, the traditional account of escape from patrician dominance is not likely to be completely correct. For instance, although it is certain that in the fourth century B.C. the patricians tried to monopolize the holding of magisterial office and were challenged by another group who called themselves plebeians, it is less certain that these two groups had existed without much change from the 490s. In particular, scholars have questioned, largely on account of certain nonpatrician names in our lists of the earliest consuls, whether at the beginning of the Republic the patriciate was quite the exclusive band that it had become by the time of the decemvirate. They have questioned, too, whether all those who were not patricians were always known as plebeians or whether the plebeian organization grew from being a small pressure group to become the dominant voice of opposition to the patricians in the generation before the passing of the Licinio-Sextian laws.[11]

Nor can we be certain that our information about the consulship is accurate. First, many of the names of those who are said to have held the office before the 440s may be unreliable;[12] second, the original name of the office may have been not 'consul' but 'praetor'.[13] As for the consular tribunate, it is one of the great enigmas of early Rome.[14] Livy knew of two explanations for it: one was political and held that it was established to allow plebeians a share in Rome's chief magistracy, the other was military and claimed that it was established to allow Rome more commanders in the field. Neither explanation is satisfactory. The first fails because few men who were not patricians were elected to the post, the second because dictators were still appointed in years of military crisis. All that can be safely said about these officials is that for sixty years it suited the Romans to have them rather than consuls running the state. Finally, our sources are full of duplication, as in the case of the three laws on *provocatio* and also the three laws guaranteeing the validity of plebiscites for the whole people, which are noted in the preceding list. That before 300 B.C. there were laws guaranteeing *provocatio* is generally disbelieved, and in 449 plebiscites can hardly have been binding on the whole people. However, it is conceivable that Livy's account of the *lex Publilia* of 339 regarding plebiscites is fundamentally reliable and that the law of 287 was merely a reinforcement or modification of it.

Despite all these difficulties, it is possible to make some generalizations about the course of Roman political history in this period. First, the power of the patricians was steadily eroded so that by *c.* 300 B.C. the political advantages of being a patrician were slight. This raises the important question of how the patricians were able to cling to so much power for so long. That they were supported by their clients and retainers seems clear; otherwise their numerical inferiority to the combined forces of the other citizens of Rome would have made it impossible for them to withstand political opposition. It is also very likely that patrician power was rooted in possession of land and maintained by appropriation to themselves of a disproportionately large share of land that had accrued by conquest to the Roman state. The power of patricians probably declined in part because patrician families were unsuccessful in reproducing themselves but also in part because patricians were less successful in forcing their will on their retainers.

As for the plebeians, it has long been obvious that the interests of their leaders, who were probably men of substantial property, were very different from those of the masses. These leaders wished to be able to fulfil their political aspirations and to have a share in the government of the state from which they were excluded simply by birth. Most of the reforms and legislation mentioned were in their interest and struck blows at patrician exclusivity: plebeians were eventually allowed to marry patricians and vice versa; they may have been allowed election to the post of consular tribune; and they were successively allowed to become consuls, dictators, censors, praetors, pontiffs, and augurs. By 300 B.C. the plebeian élite had largely achieved equality with the patricians.

Less progress was made in helping the poorer plebeians. These desired an amelioration of the conditions in which they lived. To this end laws were passed that helped debtors, and finally debt-bondage was abolished. The massive programme of colonization undertaken by Rome in the late fourth and early third centuries suggests, however, that there was still a substantial number of plebeians attracted by the prospect of escape from their current conditions and by the lure of pastures new. How far even this programme led to a significant reduction in debt is uncertain, since we are told that it was one of the causes of the third and final secession of the plebs, in 287. Despite various attempts in various epochs, the Roman Republic was never able to rid itself of its poor.

For many of the years about which Livy wrote in his history, the Conflict of the Orders is described in such violent terms that it seems a wonder that the Roman state survived at all in face of the numerous external foes that beset it. Doubtless his account is exaggerated, but we shall see that it was only after 366, a turning point after which the conflict between patricians and plebeians moved into a less violent phase, that Rome began to make significant conquests abroad. During the most violent phase of the conflict, the plebeian organization, led by the tribunes of the plebs, had functioned almost as a state within a state. The final years of the struggle are marked by the increasing integration of the plebeians and their tribunes into the management of the state. First there were plebeian consuls. Then, after a mechanism had been found in 339 whereby the decrees of the plebeian assembly could be made binding on the whole state, the senate – which consisted of ex-magistrates, priests, and other leading men of the state and which *c.* 339 would still have been dominated by patricians – began to work in harmony with the tribunes to introduce new measures. Livy (8.23.12, 9.30.3–4) records such measures for 327/6 and 311, and in the later years of the Republic this was to become the most common method of introducing legislation, the revolutionary instincts of tribunes being harnessed to the collective will of the aristocracy. However, the tribunate never lost its role as protector of the plebs and remained apart from all other magistracies. It is noteworthy that, when a magistrate failed in his duty (often in command of an army), he was liable to be prosecuted by a tribune.[15]

The opening up to the plebeian élite of the senior magistracies and the more important of the priestly colleges led to the creation of a new nobility that replaced the old patrician aristocracy. The values of these nobles, dominant among which were the desire for military repute, the advertisement of one's own achievements and those of one's family, the refusal to allow any one member of the governing class to become preeminent for too long, and a suspicion of outsiders, were probably not strikingly different from what had gone before. What was different was the success of this new nobility in maintaining a dominant position in the state, which it did from 287 (at the latest) more or less until Caesar crossed the Rubicon in 49 B.C. The most interesting Latin inscription to be written in this period comes from the tomb of Lucius Cornelius Scipio Barbatus, who was consul in 298. Its words illustrate very well the ideology of the Roman nobility in the early third century:[16]

> Cornelius Lucius Scipio Barbatus, born with Gaius as his father, a brave and wise man whose appearance was equal to his bravery, who was your consul, censor, and aedile, captured

Taurasia and Cisauna from Samnium (?), subdued all Lucania
and took away hostages from it.

Note here the references to the dead man's family, his aristocratic appearance, his record in office holding, and his achievements in war.[17]

Everyone knows that the language spoken by the Romans was
called Latin. It is less well known that originally Latin was not spoken
all over ancient Italy but was the native tongue only of those dwellers on
the splendid plain that is bounded by the Tiber in the north, the Monti
Lepini in the east, and the peninsula of Circeii in the south. Other
Latin towns were Antium, Ardea, Aricia, Cora, Lanuvium, Lavinium,
Nomentum, Pedum, Praeneste, Satricum, Tibur, and Velitrae. All these
were united with Rome in the Latin League; they played a significant
role in early Roman history, and in the regal period Rome was hardly
more than their equal.

Whether Rome was still only their equal in 509, the traditional
date for the beginning of the Republic, has been much debated. For
those scholars who believe that the city was already large and dominant
in Latium, a prime witness is the Greek translation of Rome's first treaty
with Carthage, incorporated by Polybius into his history (3.22.4–13).
A reasonable interpretation of the treaty suggests that Rome had hegemony over several Latin cities, including Antium and distant Tarracina.
Those who deny such power to Rome argue that Polybius was either
taken in by a forgery or misdated the treaty.[18] But whether Rome was
dominant in Latium in 509, it is clear that any dominating power that
it may have possessed did not continue long; in either 499 or 496 it had
to fight the other members of the Latin League at Lake Regillus. The
literary tradition claims that Rome was victorious, but the subsequent
course of fifth-century history provides no great evidence that Rome
reasserted the control over the Latins implied in the first Carthaginian
treaty, and it is better to regard this battle and the Cassian treaty (*foedus
Cassianum*) that followed it in 493 as laying the foundations for the stable
relationship between the Romans and the Latins that was maintained
for the next hundred years. Some modern scholars think that Rome
and the Latins were equal partners in this league, others that Rome
was once again just one among several Latin cities that were members
of it; all agree that Rome and the other speakers of Latin combined
forces for many wars and together founded colonies with the intention
of protecting their territory against common foes.[19]

This stable relationship with the Latins was much needed. For in
the early fifth century, both Rome and the Latins came under acute

pressure from the Aequi and Volsci, dwellers in the mountains inland from the Latin plain. They raided Roman and Latin territory and even invaded the Latin plain, taking over Latin settlements at Satricum, Antium, and Tarracina. Rome's other principal foe in the fifth century was the Etruscan city of Veii, with whom Rome often clashed. If the other Latin cities were more affected by the incursions of the Aequi and Volsci, it was Rome that was exposed most to Veii.

Rome and its Latin allies made few advances during the fifth century, although they established some colonies, most notably at Norba and Setia, hilltop towns that stand on the foothills between the Monti Lepini and the Latin plain and at which one can still see the magnificent Latin defences. They drove back the Aequi, who posed much less of a threat after their defeat at the Algidus Pass in 431; they kept the Volsci at bay; and in the 430s and 420s they (or perhaps Rome alone) wrested Fidenae, a small town that was just nine kilometres from Rome and overlooked a crossing of the Tiber, from the control of Veii. But at the beginning of the fourth century there were two victories of consequence: the Volsci who lived on the Latin plain were defeated, and some land was clawed back from them. More importantly, Veii was captured by Rome in 396 (apparently without Latin aid), and all her territory was incorporated into the Roman state. Rome's stature and power in Latium were thereby increased.

Then in 390 a band of marauding Gauls marched south from the valley of the Po, defeated the Romans at the battle of the river Allia (a stream just north of Rome), and sacked Rome itself. Only three things are certain about this episode: that it happened, that it left Rome with a long-lasting fear of Celts, and that virtually everything that our sources say about it is unbelievable. Following the departure of the Gauls, Rome faced further difficulties: in 389 some Latin cities threw off their alliance, and Rome found itself fighting the Aequi, Volsci, and Etruscans. Yet it survived, and by 366, when the Conflict of the Orders had begun to abate, it was ready to expand. Doubtless the territory of Veii, on which a new generation of soldiers had grown up, played a key role in this.

The next century saw Rome expand from being the dominant power in Latium to being the mistress of Italy. The speed and comprehensiveness of this conquest are best evoked simply by listing in chronological order the more important of the wars that Rome fought:

- the Hernici in the valley of the Sacco (366–358);
- the Etruscans, especially Tarquinii (359–351);
- the Latin League, especially Tibur and Praeneste (358–354);

- the Volsci on the Latin plain (358–357, 346);
- Sora, the Volscian town in the middle valley of the Liris (345);
- the Aurunci (345);
- the Samnites (343–341, a war started after Rome had gained control of Capua and its satellite towns in 343);
- the Latins (340–338, this being the last Latin war);
- the Campani, Sidicini, Aurunci (all in alliance with the Latins [340]);
- the Aurunci and/or Sidicini (337–334/3);
- Acerrae, a city neighbouring Capua (332);
- Fundi and Privernum (330–329);
- Neapolis (327–326);
- the Samnites (it was during this war [326–304] that Rome, though ultimately victorious, suffered her celebrated defeat in the Caudine Forks);
- the Marsi and other tribes of the central Abruzzo (312–298, intermittently);
- the Etruscans (311–308);
- the Umbrians (310–308);
- the Hernici (307–306);
- the Aequi (304–298);
- the Umbrians (303–295, intermittently);
- the Etruscans (302/1–292, intermittently);
- the Samnites (298–290);
- the Sabines (290);
- the Etruscans (very intermittently from 283 to 264);
- Tarentum, the Samnites, the Lucanians, and the Bruttians (282–272);
- the Picentes (268);
- Sarsina (267); and
- the Sallentini (267–266).

Add to this, first, several campaigns against the Gauls (initially on or near Roman territory [361, 360, 358, 349, 329] but then further north [especially in 296–295 and 283]) and, second, the battles against King Pyrrhus of Epirus, the famous ally of Tarentum (281–278, 275).[20]

For anyone interested in stories of battles and heroism, Livy and our other sources for the wars of conquest in Italy provide tales aplenty. However, it is the task of the historian to stand back from these details and analyse the process as a whole.[21]

In this long series of wars, two decisive turning points present themselves. The first is the settlement after the last Latin war ended in 338. In this settlement, Rome organized its juridical relationship with the Latins and other peoples whom it had conquered in such a way that they fell into the following three categories:

• The old Latin League was disbanded. Henceforth all Latin states would look to Rome for leadership. Several Latin states (e.g., Aricia, Lanuvium, Nomentum, and Pedum) were forcibly incorporated into the Roman state. Although they each continued to be governed locally, their citizens were full Roman citizens and enjoyed all the privileges and were expected to fulfil all the duties of Roman citizenship.

• A few Latin towns (e.g., Tibur and Praeneste) were left as independent states; however, now surrounded by Roman territory, they were no longer able to have any meaningful foreign policy of their own.

• Several large tracts of territory (especially Capua and its satellite towns) were incorporated into the Roman state, but in such a way that their citizens, although liable or eligible for other duties or privileges, could not vote (they were *cives sine suffragio*, 'citizens without the vote'). In other words, their citizenship was defective.[22]

Although the context of this settlement was one of aggressive Roman imperialism (something that would have been quite clear to those Campanians who suddenly found themselves Romans), the settlement was successful in providing a secure juridical framework within which Rome could dictate limits to the freedom that these defeated states now enjoyed. Further, the settlement, for the first time in Roman history, established on a large scale the concept of 'municipality' – the idea that a man or woman could have dual citizenship (be a citizen of both Rome and a provincial town) and that a provincial town could enjoy its own local government but at the same time be wholly part of the Roman state.

Another important feature of the settlement was that the concepts of 'Latin' and 'citizen without the vote' were to prove dynamic and capable of further development. In 334, when it sent a colony to Cales (modern Calvi) on the borders of Campania, Rome reestablished the concept of Latin colonization – colonization in which members of other Latin towns as well as Rome could take part – and showed that it was prepared to found colonies far from old Latium itself. Numerous other Latin colonies were to follow, both before and after the First Punic War, and the success of the idea can hardly be overestimated. These colonies were the fetters by which the Samnites and the other recalcitrant tribes of Italy were bound, since any revolt was difficult for a people who had a large settlement of Latins placed in their midst. When Italy blazed in revolt and Roman power crumbled after Cannae (216 B.C.) and in the Social War (91–89 B.C.), these colonies held firm and proved to be Rome's salvation. They fulfilled an important economic role (see below), and they were also instrumental in spreading the Latin language and culture throughout Italy, thus helping to pave the way for the spread of the Latin rights throughout the Roman empire. Interestingly, several are still provincial capitals, including Beneventum (modern Benevento), established in 268, and Aesernia (modern Isernia), established in 263. Whether at first the burghers of Aricia and Nomentum liked their incorporation into the Roman state we cannot know, but the settlement with the Latins worked, bringing a stability to Roman and Latin relations that proved the bedrock on which the rest of the conquest of Italy was founded. With the Latins securely by its side, Rome had a larger pool of manpower on which to draw, and to the east and south its territory was now cushioned by that of its allies.

The concept of citizenship without the vote was also capable of further use. In 333, Acerrae (modern Acerra), a neighbour of Capua on the Campanian plain, was incorporated on these same terms, as was Arpinum (modern Arpino, later to be the birthplace of Cicero and Marius) in 303. However, this concept proved less successful than the expansion of the Latin name; some of the states incorporated were unhappy with their second-class status and loss of sovereignty (most famously, Capua rebelled in 216 B.C., after Cannae), and others pushed for upgrading (granted to Arpinum in 188 B.C.).

Not all states with whom Rome had dealings during its conquest of Italy were incorporated as *civitates sine suffragio*: some (e.g., Camerinum, modern Camerino) were prudent enough to make an alliance at an early date and enjoyed a favourable treaty; others (e.g., the Samnites) made terms only after fighting and had a less favourable treaty. For many states, the juridical relationship to Rome is uncertain, but it is possible that some had no formal treaty, being simply Rome's 'friends'. A map of the states of Italy in 264 compiled on the basis of their juridical relationship to Rome looks like a rather confusing mosaic but displays one striking feature: an unbroken strip of Roman territory ran from Ostia to the Adriatic, separating Rome's old foes in northern and southern Italy from each other and giving a solid territorial base to its power. By the battle of Telamon, fought at the very latest in 225 against a massive army of invading Gauls, and perhaps as early as the First Punic War, the states that Rome had conquered provided it with manpower. These troops were the basis of the army that Rome used for conquest of the Mediterranean.

The other great turning point was the battle of Sentinum (Sasso-Ferrato), fought in 295 B.C. in the further reaches of Umbrian territory. Although even after this year Rome was to fight many difficult battles, it was never again confronted with so powerful a coalition of enemies as that comprising the Samnites, Etruscans, Gauls, and Umbrians who ranged themselves against it in that year. Defeat at Sentinum could have altered the course of history in Italy and put a permanent check on Rome's ambitions. As it was, after that year the Italian states were able to resist Rome effectively only when they had outside help from a Pyrrhus or a Hannibal.

The Pyrrhic War was not exactly a turning point in Rome's fortunes (Rome was already in control of most of peninsular Italy when the war began), but it, too, deserves comment. For the first time it brought Rome face to face with a Hellenistic foe, and the fact that Rome finally emerged victorious announced to the Hellenistic kingdoms, the Greek cities, and Carthage that there was now a new power in the western Mediterranean. Eleven years after the end of the war, Rome was to fight Carthage for the first time.

A remarkable feature of the process by which the Romans conquered Italy is that between 343 and 241 they went to war in almost every year. The exceptions are 331, 328, 288, 287, and 285 (but our sources for the last three of these years are very poor, and we should not rule out the possibility that fighting occurred in some of them). A pattern of this kind must have encouraged the expectation that in any given year the Romans would go to war, and it must have proved a powerful spur to conquest.

Rome profited very greatly from her successful warfare. First and most important, a large amount of land was confiscated from the states that it defeated. Much of this land was put to use in Rome's programmes of colonization. The colonies (mostly Latin but also some smaller settlements consisting almost entirely of Roman citizens) allowed those who were impoverished the chance to make a new life. This in turn led to an improvement in social conditions in Rome, and it may be no accident that between 342 and 287 we hear little about indebtedness and social unrest in the city. Land taken from defeated foes could also be acquired or leased by Romans of the upper class, who used it to increase their own wealth and standing.

Slaves were another reward of successful warfare. The abolition of debt-bondage in either 326 or 313 should not be ascribed merely to a new humanity emergent in the Roman governing élite. Rather, warfare had produced an abundant supply of slaves who could be put to work on the estates of the rich. That Roman agriculture in the late Republic was heavily dependent on the labour of slaves is well known, but it is not always appreciated that this phenomenon has its origin in the fourth century B.C.

Booty and money were yet another reward, both for individuals, who could invest it in land or elsewhere, and for the central treasury, which could use it to finance further warfare. Cash acquired in this way financed the construction of a remarkable series of temples built in the years around 300 B.C. (e.g., the temple of Bellona, vowed in 296, and the temple of Jupiter Victor, vowed in 295). These increased the splendour and prestige of the city and provided employment for the urban poor. Still larger in scale was the construction of the Appian Way and Appian Aqueduct by the censor Appius Claudius Caecus in the years immediately after 312 B.C. All this construction encouraged the growth of the city of Rome, providing employment for immigrant labour and attracting more of it. Soon the city was to be a dominant force not just in the politics and warfare of Italy but also in the economy.

Another impulse to expand was provided by the competitiveness of the emerging patricio-plebeian nobility. Prestige depended upon election to office, and in the bellicose society of Rome there was no greater source of prestige than success in warfare. It is easy to see that the prospect of success will have encouraged many Roman generals to campaign more adventurously than might have been expected at the beginning of their year in office. Whether one wishes to apply the label 'imperialistic' to Rome in the hundred years before the First Punic War is less important than understanding the potential rewards of warfare and the long-term effect that they had on the Roman economy. Yet when we make conjectures about the intentions of the Romans, both as individuals and collectively, it is hard to imagine that they conquered Italy by accident.

Individuals have barely been featured in this chapter, and indeed our sources give us no secure idea of the personality of any Roman who lived before the Second Punic War.[23] It may be helpful, however, to end with a glance at Manius Curius Dentatus, who at the time of his death in 270 was unquestionably the most famous Roman of his day and whose career illustrates many of the themes of this account of the early Republic. Curius was a 'new man': no ancestors of his are known to have held magistracies (and, it may be added, no descendants of his are known). If a notice in Cicero (*Brut.* 55) is reliable, as tribune of the plebs in an unspecified year *c.* 300, he prevented the election of two patrician consuls, a move that would have reopened the Conflict of the Orders. He himself went on to be consul three times (in 290, 275, and 274), thereby illustrating the opportunities open to plebeians. In his first consulship, he incorporated a vast tract of Sabine territory into the Roman state, its occupants being made citizens without the vote. In no other year in this period is the fundamentally aggressive nature of Roman warfare more obvious; in no other year after the incorporation of Capua was the institution of citizenship without the vote employed on so large a scale. In his second consulship, he defeated Pyrrhus at the battle of Beneventum, thereby securing his place in the pantheon of great Roman military leaders. In his censorship (272–271), he oversaw the construction of Rome's second aqueduct, which brought water from the river Aniene, a tributary of the Tiber, into the city. Like its predecessor, the Appian Aqueduct, this huge work of construction was emblematic of the way in which the city had changed during the great wars of conquest, revealing both the vast expansion of the city, which now had difficulty providing water for itself, and the vast resources now available to it. When Curius was born, probably *c.* 330, Rome had barely begun its struggle with the Samnites; when he died, most of the classic institutions of the middle Republic, as described by Polybius in the second century, were in place.

NOTES

1 See Chapter 2.

2 In this chapter, there is very little citation of sources. The relevant material is discovered most easily by consulting Broughton (1950–1986) for the year in which something is said to have happened.

3 Books 1–10 of Livy's history take the story of Rome from its foundation to 293 B.C., Books 11–20 are missing, and Books 21–45 continue the story from 218 to 167 B.C.

4 The most interesting treatment of the Roman historical tradition that lies behind Livy is Wiseman 1979. For a more conservative view of the sources, see Cornell 1986a and 1986b. Badian 1966 is still a useful introduction to the Roman historical tradition before Livy.

5 See Chapter 7.

6 For this conflict, see especially the essays collected in Raaflaub 1986.

7 For the Twelve Tables and the society for which they were designed, see Watson 1975.

8 The origins and nature of *provocatio* have been endlessly disputed; contrast the views of, e.g., Lintott 1972 and Cloud 1998.

9   A Roman *iugerum* was about two-thirds of an acre.

10   Livy (6.35.5, 7.42.2) actually says that the law of 367/6 stipulated that one consul had to be plebeian and that according to the law of 342 both consuls could be plebeians; the readjustment given in the text represents the view adopted by most modern scholars after the first clear statement of it by Richard (1979).

11   For further discussion of these matters, see Cornell 1983.

12   A classic example is provided by L. Junius Brutus, who is said to have been consul in the first year of the Republic; surprisingly, the next Junius to hold the office was D. Junius Brutus Scaeva in 325.

13   The best evidence for this view is provided by Livy (7.3.5).

14   On the consular tribunate, see, e.g., Staveley 1953; Adcock 1957.

15   For the attitude taken by the Romans to defeated commanders, see Rosenstein 1990.

16   The inscription is no. 309 in Degrassi 1957–1963.

17   On this and other inscriptions from the tombs of the Scipios, see Flower 1996, 159–84.

18   Prominent among the sceptics is Alföldi (1965), most of whose book is devoted to the thesis that our sources have misrepresented the power of Rome *c.* 509.

19   For Rome's relations with the Latin League, see, e.g., Sherwin-White 1973, 3–37. For colonization in which Rome took part, both in the fifth century and later, Salmon (1969) is a good introduction.

20   Our best source for this war, about which many doubtfully reliable legends cluster, is Plutarch's *Life of Pyrrhus*.

21   For the process of Roman conquest and its dynamics, see in general Harris (1979) and Oakley (1993), the latter with particular reference to the period before 264 B.C.

22   In English there is no entirely reliable full treatment either of citizenship without the vote or of the settlement of 338 as a whole, but see Salmon (1982, 40–72); Sherwin-White (1973) underestimates the aggressiveness of the Romans. Humbert (1978), written in French, remains the best study of the topic.

23   Perhaps, as is often held, Ap. Claudius Caecus may count as an exception, but in truth we know more about his policies than his character.

2: POWER AND PROCESS UNDER THE REPUBLICAN "CONSTITUTION"

T. Corey Brennan

⟨ornament⟩

Republican Rome had no written constitution. It did, however, have an array of remarkably tenacious continuing institutions (in the broadest sense of the term), some of which were or at least seemed virtually primeval. And at all times it had men who were willing to make confident assertions – as senators, magistrates, priests, or specialists in jurisprudence, or in more than one of these roles at once – about what was legally possible under an often fuzzy and ever evolving political and administrative system. A few went a bit further than ad hoc pronouncements. Certainly by *c.* 200 B.C. the Roman élite was taking an academic interest in the city-state's legal history.[1] In the developed Republic, at any rate, some important colleges of priests maintained books of precedents; the senate's past decrees could be consulted in written form. Cicero's *On Laws*, to single out just one of his contributions to political philosophy, actually contains a short (idealizing) constitution, a theoretical piece that treats Rome's magistracies and some aspects of the state religion. One must add that a well-connected outsider, the Greek

---

This chapter in good part distills some of the main arguments in Brennan (2000). That book does not take into consideration Finer (1997, 385–441), an important recently published study of republican political processes; nor does it engage the detailed synoptic treatment of Lintott (1999, 1–15, 27–190). Lintott (1999, 16–26, 191–255) and especially Millar (2002) are essential reading for political speculations on the republican constitution from the ancient through modern periods. For an admirably succinct overview of the main attributes of the political system in the late Republic, see Rawson ([1975] 1983, 323–5). The Appendix to this chapter attempts to present some of Rome's main political institutions in outline form. Here I discovered that my student lecture notes from P. A. Brunt served as a valuable model and guide and that the table of Roman assemblies in Taylor (1966, xx–xxi) can hardly be bettered. Of course, all errors in this chapter are my responsibility.

Polybius, writing in the mid second century B.C., left us an invaluable, though frustratingly selective and overschematic, sketch of the Roman state as he saw it.

But, again, the Romans of the Republic never made a comprehensive attempt to formalize their public law. It may be worth considering, if only for a moment, why not. One basic reason is that the people most likely to draft such a document – the leading members of Rome's senatorial establishment – were in all periods fully conscious that writing things down served only to cut into their own class prerogatives and influence. Another factor is that, by the time a Latin legal literature was first developing (say, *c.* 200 B.C.), the political system was even in its essentials too vast to take in as a whole. For some centuries, each successive year at Rome had seen the complicated interplay of individual (mostly annual) magistrates and quasi-magistrates with each other and with a number of strong but hardly monolithic corporate entities – most vitally, the senate (the body that advised the magistrates), the people (i.e., Latin *populus*, patricians and plebeians together) and plebs (the body of nonpatricians) in their several organized and even unorganized forms,[2] and various boards of priests. In the later Republic, the knights (or *equites*) – the wealthy non-office-holding arm of the Roman ruling class – added themselves to this heady mix. Indeed in all periods the shifting dynamics of Rome's profoundly hierarchical society (about which we shall say something below) influenced institutional processes.[3] So involved and ingrown became political Rome that the rationale for some aspects of its system, such as the procedure for electing certain high-ranking magistrates, escaped even the curious.[4]

Of course, concurrent with Rome's annual pattern of political give and take was its seemingly inexorable growth in power. New military and administrative challenges periodically threatened to stretch the old, inherited city-state institutions to their breaking points. That in turn forced the innately conservative Roman governing class to accept innovation and sometimes even permanent reform in the political system. The fact that Rome's administrative machinery constantly needed to adapt to new circumstances militated against any visionary's drafting a constitution that would last for long. But the dilemmas that arose out of the state's steady expansion in influence gave the experts much material for comment. The more authoritative of such statements resulted in implementation – for instance, the senate almost automatically accepted the findings of major colleges of priests on public law questions that fell within their competence – and so cumulatively went some way toward shaping the *res publica* in its pragmatic aspects.

A LECTURE ON LEGITIMATE POWER

We have a particularly succinct formulation of constitutional basics, one that introduces us to additional attributes of the republican system, from the twilight years of the Republic. It is a passage from Cicero's 13th *Philippic*,[5] delivered in the senate in March of 43 B.C. Here the orator addresses the disaffected and dangerous commander Marcus Aemilius Lepidus, who was then in charge of two armed western provinces (and before the end of the year was to establish the triumvirate with Antony and Octavian). Legitimate power, Cicero admonishes Lepidus, is what is allowed by positive laws (*leges*), ancestral custom (*mos maiorum*), and accepted precedent (*instituta*). Those who want to get and wield power are further circumscribed by a general societal expectation for self-restraint. "What an individual can do is not necessarily permitted to him; nor, if nothing stands in the way, is it for this reason also permitted."

Cicero then shifts to the personal. Lepidus' circumstance as a *nobilis* – the élite status that derives from having one of Rome's eponymous chief magistrates as an ancestor in the male line – introduces additional considerations, Cicero implies. So does his year-old position as the most important priest in the state religion, head of the board of *pontifices*. If the commander spontaneously should abandon the notion that he is entitled to do as much as he is able to do, says Cicero, and interpose his considerable personal authority (*auctoritas*) in the day's fluid political situation without use of force, "you are truly Marcus Lepidus, Pontifex Maximus, the great-grandson of Marcus Lepidus, Pontifex Maximus [in the years 180–153/152 B.C.]." Such self-restraint, we are told, is in the grand tradition of the Aemilii Lepidi. (We happen to know that Lepidus took considerable pride in his great-grandfather.)[6] But in the last resort, to check undue ambition, Rome had strong formal institutions in place. Though Lepidus had considerable personal authority, Cicero stresses that at that moment the senate was never "more dignified, more determined, more courageous." The upshot for Lepidus and his command? "You will obey the senate and the people if they see fit to transfer you to some other task."

One wonders what the elder Marcus Aemilius Lepidus would have thought of Cicero's mini-lecture on power and authority. A patrician "noble" who was regarded as the handsomest man of his day, Lepidus had the good fortune to find himself honored by the senate with an equestrian statue on the Capitol before he even started his political career in earnest.[7] Though his keen sense of entitlement led the people to hand him an initial defeat for the consulship (i.e., the paired annual magistracy that headed the state) of 188 B.C., he reached the office the next year and then again in 175 – the first man since the towering figure of Scipio Africanus (consul II, 194) to hold it twice.

But it was the accumulation of further distinctions that gave Lepidus, in the words of the greatest modern historian of Rome's political families, "truly princely status."[8] The year 179 alone saw Lepidus as *pontifex maximus*, as one of the two censors (the censorship was a magistracy that involved some especially important sacral and civic duties), and, using his censorial powers for self-appointment, as ranking senator (*princeps senatus*). Lepidus was able to hold those last two posts – in other words, the superintendancy of the state religion and a presumptive right to speak first in the senate – until his death in late 153 or 152 B.C. From time to time he combined these imposing positions of authority with other roles, including his second consulship.

Notwithstanding what Cicero implies in the *Philippics* passage, this Lepidus showed little hesitation in exercising his considerable powers to the fullest when he saw fit. For instance, in 178 as *pontifex maximus* he indemnified his daughter Aemilia, the chief priestess in the service of Vesta, for letting the sacred fire of her goddess go out – a deeply serious religious infraction – after personally scourging one of her Vestal assistants for the same offense. Now, in practically every generation of the classical Republic we find individuals with overlapping competences who freely drew on their personal influence to supplement their legitimate authority in the political and religious spheres. For the later Republic, of course a long series of names come readily to mind: Sulla, Pompey, Caesar, Antony, Octavian, and (as we have seen) the younger Lepidus. But it is not going too far to say that the elder Lepidus' lasting institution-based authority, which involved so many vital aspects of Roman public life and stretched over a span of almost three decades, most closely prefigures what Augustus ultimately achieved.

To illuminate further some of the modalities of power in the political organism called the *res publica*, there may be a particular advantage in an introductory survey such as this to focus on the magistracy, the aspect of the republican government about which we are arguably the best informed. And in examining the magistracy, it might make sense to look first and most closely at Rome's officials outside the city. It is not just that here individuals' powers (both legitimate and aggrandized) can be seen in their fullest expression. There is the added fact that, throughout the entire republican period, the problems inherent in having officials serve outside Rome in progressively more challenging military contexts served as a particularly potent catalyst for institutional change across the system.

Cicero took that as self-evident: "I will not mention here that our ancestors have always yielded to precedent in peace, but expediency in war, and have always arranged the conduct of new policies in accordance with new circumstances."[9] This is a passage from his speech supporting the Manilian law of 66 B.C. and arguing in favor of granting a special eastern command to Pompey.[10] One could go further. Not only the exigencies of war but even problems such as the simple realities of transit to and from various territorial commands and the difficulty of ensuring smooth transitions between successive generals forced the Romans again and again to reshape their conception of *imperium*, originally the unlimited and (basically) undefined power enjoyed by the Roman kings. Magistrates, priests, the senate, and the people and plebs in assembly all play their part in this centuries-long story, making the evolution of *imperium* an excellent case study in the processes of constitutional innovation and institutionalization at Rome.

From a general survey of developments that shaped magisterial power especially (but not exclusively) in the field, we may then turn to an illuminating study of ambition and power in the city of Rome in the mid second century B.C. More particularly, we will examine the improbable careers of two relatives who turned conspicuous public failure in the military sphere into domestic political success, albeit in varying degrees. The interrelated tales of the cousins Lucius and Gaius Hostilius Mancinus (who served as consul in 145 and 137 B.C. respectively) invite close analysis, for they open a welcome window on the republican political and legal process in its three dimensions. Here once again we find Rome's formal institutions – magistrates, senate, priests, and popular assemblies – intersecting in complex process. But in the story of the two Mancini we also get to see how class hierarchy and family connections, personal prestige, charisma, showmanship, historical memory, emotionality, and chance might work in republican Rome as very real historical forces.

THE UNOFFICIAL EXERCISE OF OFFICIAL POWER

To gain a notion of the effective power a magistrate could possess in the developed Republic, look no further than the Roman noble L. Licinius Crassus. Cicero in one of his dialogues has this famous orator tell how he received very little formal rhetorical instruction as a youth. However, Crassus claims he did pick up a bit after serving as quaestor in the East; on his journey back from the Roman province of Asia *c.* 110 B.C. he stopped at Athens, where, as he says, "I would have tarried longer, had I not been angry with the Athenians, because they would not repeat the [Eleusinian] mysteries, for which I had come two days too late."

The quaestorship was an entry-level office; it had limited powers, and in this period was usually held around age 30. Indeed, Crassus technically will have been superseded as an Asian quaestor when he swaggered into Athens and demanded a repeat performance of the mysteries – and with it (surely) his own initiation at Eleusis.[11]

Now in the Republic, magistrates who took up provincial appointments still had a full right to function as magistrates in Rome before departure. They also retained their full powers until they came back to Rome. We know this latter fact from a variety of literary sources and now from an important inscription, first published in 1974, that will figure below ("New Boundaries on Legitimate Power, 171–59 B.C."). Yet it still seems amazing that a low-level superseded magistrate could show this level of entitlement on his return journey to Rome and (to trust Cicero) exhibit no special self-consciousness in later recounting the episode to his peers. In this case, the Athenian officials stood up to the young Crassus. But there must have been countless instances in which Roman magistrates – or even nonmagistrates acting in an official capacity[12] – managed to cow the locals.

We have seen Cicero offering a lecture on how magistrates should restrain themselves from exercising their formidable powers to the fullest extent. Indeed, the political system of the Republic was predicated on this basic understanding. Most magistrates chose to obey this principle, to a remarkable degree, right down to the late 50s – in the city, that is. Outside Rome was a different matter. For there commanders did not face nearly as many restrictions on their official powers, and subordinates might often find themselves in semi-independent positions, without effective oversight. Before considering this dual state of affairs, however, we need to arrive at an understanding of what the Romans themselves meant by magistrates functioning "at home" and "abroad."

THE THEOLOGY OF *IMPERIUM*

For the Romans, the story of legitimate power started on 21 April 753 B.C., give or take a year. Ancient tradition is unanimous that the auspication (literally, bird watching) undertaken by Romulus on the day of the city's foundation – and confirmed by Jupiter through his sending of 12 vultures – in essence activated what are known as the "public auspices" (*auspicia publica*). Possessing the auspices of the Roman people entailed the competence to request, observe, and announce Jupiter's signs regarding an important act and then to complete what was intended. Since auspication preceded every major action taken on the state's behalf, it formed the basis of regal and then, in the Republic, magisterial power. Hence patricians – an élite class that closed their ranks to new members *c.* 500 B.C., soon after the expulsion of the Tarquins – long sought to monopolize that right as exclusively their own.[13]

The augurs – the priests who interpreted the rules surrounding the auspices – gave a spatial distinction to the spheres where public auspices were exercised. In the historical period (and perhaps well before it), the sacral boundary formed by the circuit of the old city wall (*pomerium*) delimited the urban public auspices; that area was known as *domi* ("at home"). Outside the city (*militiae*, "in the field"), another set obtained, the "military" auspices.

The term *imperium* is the standard shorthand way our ancient sources denote the king's power. The term is generally thought to derive from *parare* ("to prepare, arrange, put in order"), in which case it would have originally been a military term.[14] The greatest modern historian of Rome, Theodor Mommsen, (correctly) thought of *imperium* and the public auspices as largely overlapping concepts: "They express the same idea considered under different points of view."[15] He considered *imperium* to be an absolute power that entitled the king to do whatever he thought fit in the public interest. It was not simply a bundle of specific competences. Since *imperium* was vested originally in the person of the king alone, it was indivisible, and its power would have been no less on one side of the city boundary than on the other. Yet kings need some consent to rule effectively. Our sources report their consultation with an advisory body (*consilium*) of aristocrats, Rome's "senate." And presumably in some cases, especially those involving the making of peace and war, Rome's kings also sought the (well-organised) approval of the people in assembly (*populus*), as the ancient tradition unanimously holds.

After the expulsion of King Tarquin the Proud from Rome (customarily dated to 509 B.C.), two magistrates – later to be known as consuls – were chosen from among the patricians. Each of the consuls received full public auspices and undefined *imperium*. But they differed from the kings in that their office involved collegiality (in case of conflict, the negative voice prevailed) and annual succession. And now both the senate and (especially) the people grew in importance. Tradition held that, in the first year of the Republic, the consul P. Valerius Publicola introduced further restrictions. A Roman citizen now generally had the possibility of appeal (*provocatio*) to the people against a consul who exercised his power in the area enclosed by the *pomerium* plus one mile beyond. (Commanders in the field did not have their *imperium* thus restricted until the "Porcian Laws" sometime in the second century B.C.)

Valerius also allegedly stipulated that, in the civil sphere, only one consul at a time should have the capacity for independent action, symbolized by 12 attendants bearing the emblematic ax and bundle of rods known as the *fasces*; the *imperium* and auspices of the other consul were to be dormant, except for obstruction.[16] In special circumstances, the power of both consuls might fall dormant, with the initiative falling to a *dictator* appointed to hold *imperium* for a period of six months, notionally the length of a campaigning season. Through these means the Romans cleverly made the most of the executive branch of their government while mitigating the potential for conflict within it. Yet soon (after 494 B.C.) the powers of the plebeian tribunes would encroach further on the consuls' exercise of *imperium*. Indeed the tribunes had the power of veto against all regular magistrates, but only in Rome itself.

By the mid fifth century, it became apparent that two consuls, with the possibility of a dictator in time of crisis, were not enough to look after Rome's ever increasing administrative and military needs. On the other hand, though they were often fighting wars against hostile neighbors on multiple fronts, the Romans at this point were reluctant to give *imperium* and, with it, full public auspices to too many men. One compromise attempt at a solution to the leadership crunch was the institution of the so-called military tribunes with consular power (*potestas*), first seen in place of the pair of actual consuls for 444 B.C. Now, every republican magistrate had *potestas*, that is, the legitimate and legitimizing power that was inherent in and peculiar to one's magistracy. Here the Romans devised a college of up to six magistrates who had the consular "power" to lead an army yet who did not have *imperium* and whose auspices were deficient in some way. (For instance, we know they could not celebrate the much prized ceremony known as the triumph.) The idea perhaps was to keep members of the plebeian class – who were eligible for the office – away from the highest public auspices. Yet the consular tribunate was an awkward institution, as it irregularly alternated with consular pairs on the basis of an ad hoc decision taken each year. What is more, each of a year's consular tribunes had veto power over other individual members of his college.

Social conflict between plebeians and patricians, as well as a prolonged military struggle with the Gauls (who had sacked Rome in 390 B.C.), forced the Romans to abolish the consular tribunate in 367. Under what is known as the Licinio-Sextian legislation, they finally let plebeians into the consulship (or rather into one of the two consular slots) and introduced a new patrician magistrate, the praetor (either now or later known as the "urban praetor"), to serve as a colleague of the consuls. To create the praetorship, the Romans put a bold new construction on regal power. The praetor was to hold the king's auspices as well as an *imperium* defined as of the same nature as the consuls' *imperium* but *minus* ("lesser") in relation to theirs. As a magistrate with this type of *imperium* and auspices, the praetor could do all that the consuls could do, save hold elections of consuls and (somewhat illogically) other praetors and celebrate the Latin Festival at the beginning of each year. All other activities of the consul were open to the praetor, unless a consul stopped him. But a praetor could not interfere with the consuls.

Though it had some precedents, the invention of two grades of *imperium* – one lesser than that of the two chief regular magistrates – marked a real innovation. For the first time, the Romans were able to reconcile in a proper magistracy the concept of permanent subordination with what was essentially regal *imperium*. This in turn more or less permanently solved the problem of excessive conflict in command. A second praetor, called *inter peregrinos* ("over foreigners"), was added *c.* 247 B.C., in the context of the First Punic War. It may well be that the first such praetor was the original governor of Sicily, which was created as Rome's first permanent territorial province in 241. Sicily and Sardinia each received their own praetors *c.* 228, followed by Iberia (divided into Nearer and Further Spain) in 197. But after that, despite the accumulation of new administrative commitments, the Romans long resisted raising the number of praetors beyond six, apparently to keep competition for the consulship (for which the praetorship had become a prerequisite *c.* 196 B.C.) at acceptable levels.

Within a short period after the Licinio-Sextian legislation, other administrative developments come to our notice. In 327 B.C., it was decided that *imperium* could be extended beyond the year of the magistracy by popular ratification. This process came to be known as "prorogation" (*prorogatio*). A prorogued consul is known as a *pro consule* ("in place of a consul"), a prorogued praetor as a *pro praetore*. Such extended magistrates were expected to operate exclusively in the field; indeed, they lost their *imperium* if they stepped within the city boundary without special dispensation.

By the year 295 B.C., we see that a consular commander could delegate *imperium* – at the *minus* grade – in the field to a nonmagistrate for activities outside Rome. Livy provides the background for the first attested case.[17] A consul was departing from his military command in the most literal sense, in that he was ritually sacrificing ("devoting") himself to the enemy in battle. Before charging to his death, he handed over his insignia of office to an ex-consul who was by his side, who then fought (significantly) *pro praetore*. The emergency years of the Second Punic War (218–201 B.C.) show the Romans coming up with other ways to give out *imperium* to private citizens, including popular legislation and even (for a special grant of consular *imperium* in 210 B.C.) pseudo-election in the centuriate assembly. After 197 B.C., the dispatch of praetors endowed with consular *imperium* to hold command in the Spains became a regular feature of the Republic; later, other distant provinces as they were created also received "enhanced" praetorian commanders (Macedonia and perhaps Africa from 146 B.C., Asia starting in 126, Cilicia *c.* 100). And by the last third of the second century, we find that a consular commander could delegate *imperium* to a subordinate even while himself remaining in his assigned theater. Foundations such as these gave Rome the flexibility to build up its republican empire.

It so happens that we have from the late Republic an exposition of the theological underpinnings of *imperium* that is based on an excellent source, distilling some centuries of innovation and rationalization. Aulus Gellius, writing in the second century A.D. but drawing on expert commentary by the augur M'. Valerius Messalla (who was consul in 53 B.C.), discusses how the public auspices were divided into grades.[18] Consuls and praetors possessed auspices of the highest level (*auspicia maxima*), which were "stronger than those of others [magistrates]." One can extrapolate some important principles from this statement alone. It seems that auspices of the highest grade are a necessary prerequisite of *imperium*, though the two are not equivalent. Dictators, consuls, and praetors, all of whom had "highest auspices" both inside and outside the city boundary, held *imperium*. The situation of censors, who also had highest auspices (according to Messalla), was different. The censorship was a high-ranking magistracy created originally for patricians in 443 B.C. to enable them to take over some important consular sacral duties, no doubt so that the newly created consular tribunes (some of whom might be plebeian) could not touch them. Censors had highest auspices only in the civil sphere and did not have *imperium*.

Eventually, alongside the consuls, praetors, and censors, there emerges a sprawling third class of individuals who must have had a type of highest auspices. Some of these we have discussed above: prorogued consuls and praetors, nonmagistrates appointed in the city (i.e., by a special law) to important military commands, and men granted *imperium* in the field through delegation by someone of consular rank. To these one can add a few stray categories, such as certain commissioners elected with special powers to assign lands or found colonies. Yet all these individuals lack the highest civil auspices. Such men, for instance, cannot convene assemblies of the people, inside or outside the *pomerium*, or function as representatives of the state in any other significant activity in the city.

Our sources suggest a further technical point. An ancient organization known as the curiate assembly passed a law that seems to have validated the military auspices of new consuls and praetors. That this was the effect of the law has been disputed. But one good proof of this interpretation is that the people followed the election of censors in the centuriate assembly with the passage of a law, not in the curiate assembly, but in the centuriate assembly as well, exceptionally of all senior magistrates. Cicero is probably only guessing when he states this double vote for censors was taken "so that the people might have the power of rescinding its distinction, should it have second thoughts."[19] The procedure of a centuriate law presumably was meant to restrict the censors' powers and to ensure that they did not consider themselves colleagues of the consuls, nor think they had military auspices. As Messalla tells us, the augurs in fact deemed the censors' highest auspices to be of a different (i.e., lesser) grade (*potestas*) than that of the consuls. These magistrates could obstruct the actions only of their proper colleagues. But uncertainties as to the specific force of the curiate law must remain.

Following the passage of a curiate law on his behalf, the magistrate would activate the military aspect of his *imperium* through taking special auspices of departure to lead an army. Then, crossing the sacral boundary of the city, the commander and his lictors changed into military garb. The main evidence on these routines (as in so many other spheres of Roman political and social life) comes to us though negative examples. By the late Republic, we hear of tribunes vetoing the commander's curiate law, formally cursing the commander at his departure, and the like.

If a magistrate then had to cross back over the *pomerium*, his military *imperium* lapsed and had to be renewed. If a prorogued magistrate or a private citizen with *imperium* reentered Rome, he lost his military auspices for good. Cicero is eager to emphasize that C. Verres (praetor in

74), after his formal departure for his province of Sicily as promagistrate, violated his military auspices by tracking back – repeatedly – to the city of Rome to make nocturnal visits to his mistress. That in turn (it is clearly implied) vitiated anything he did of worth in his province.[20]

The one significant exception in the matter of recrossing the city boundary has to do with the *imperator*, that is, the commander whose exploits have earned him his soldiers' (ideally) spontaneous acclamation. A vote in the senate followed by popular ratification entitled such an individual to enter the city through Rome's triumphal gate, which was in essence a hole in the augural space. A general who properly entered through it was entitled to retain his military auspices in the city for a single day so as to make a formal procession to the Temple of Jupiter on the Capitol. In the late Republic, we see commanders waiting outside Rome for periods up to almost five years in the hope of obtaining the requisite vote for that privilege, which brought lofty lifelong status. Their *imperium* remained valid in the meantime, even without explicit prorogation.

MAGISTRATES IN COLLISION

With consuls and praetors as direct heirs (each to their own degree) of the old regal *imperium*, it would be natural for many of them to feel the temptation to throw their weight around. But when push came to shove, in the city at least, members of the same college almost never used *imperium* to check *imperium*. One outstanding exception is found for 95 B.C. In this year the consul Q. Mucius Scaevola vetoed the decree of the senate (*senatus consultum*) that granted his consular colleague – L. Licinius Crassus, whose entitled conduct at Athens was noted earlier – a triumph for fighting some undistinguished tribes in Cisalpine Gaul.[21] The two men had not been political enemies. It may be that Scaevola simply did not want to see Crassus benefit from the prestige of triumphing in the year of his magistracy. Thanks in part to the logistical problems posed by Rome's ever expanding empire, this had become a difficult feat even by the mid second century B.C. There are only about a dozen instances of such triumphs in the years 166–47 B.C., with the exceptional figures of Marius (in 104 and 101) and Sulla (in 81) accounting for three of them.

The power relationship between consuls and praetors had its complexities. The augur Messalla made it clear that consuls had the praetors as their colleagues, albeit lesser ones. After all, they were elected (at least originally, before the number of praetors swelled) on the same day in the same session of the centuriate assembly and thus under the same auspices. That said, occasionally we see consuls using their superior brand of *imperium* against individual praetors, curbing their activities in the realms of law, both civil (115, 77, and 67 B.C.) and criminal (57 B.C.), or in the matter of convening the senate (91 B.C.). Yet on one of these occasions (that of the year 67) we find a remarkable show of praetorian solidarity in the face of a distinctly "uncollegial" show of consular power. When a consul smashed a praetor's ceremonial chair for not rising in his presence, this praetor and his praetorian colleagues effected a "work slowdown" for the rest of the year, giving judgments only on routine legal matters.[22]

It is significant that for the later Republic we do not have a single secure instance of a praetor in the city using his *imperium* to veto a current colleague's actions, even in the realm of civil law.[23] Litigants who did not like a praetor's actual decision customarily appealed, not to another praetor of the year, but to a tribune of the plebs, sometimes a consul. In cases where magistrates fail to show self-restraint on a larger scale, it is the tribunes or senate that might step in, usually in a reactive way. That sometimes even gave rise to a law circumscribing a behavior deemed offensive. A show of consensus by Rome's ruling establishment often was an effective brake on those magistrates who insisted on exercising their full powers in the city – though of course that became less and less true in the last generations of the Republic, until we finally get to a situation such as that of 43 B.C., which we glimpsed earlier ("A Lecture on Legitimate Power").

Let us leave aside for the moment the question of dynamics between magistrates outside the city and the senate and people. In the field, even in periods of relative stability, there was plenty of opportunity for mixed signals and conflicts just between Roman officials and their staffs. And when things heated up, neither tribunes nor senate were on the spot to intervene. One problem was that some provinces normally could not even be reached without trampling on others. A land march in the later Republic to Further Spain demanded transit across two Gallic provinces and Nearer Spain. Bithynian and Cilician governors did not absolutely need to cut across part of Roman Asia, but they commonly did so anyway. When military glory was at stake, the chances of collision or noncooperation between ambitious magistrates and their staffs rose dramatically. This could lead to major military disaster, as the events of the year 105 B.C. show.[24] But even subsequent to this fiasco, the battle of Arausio, reluctance on the part of Roman commanders to fight joint campaigns is amply documented.

Livy offers us an example of another variety of magisterial conflict in the field. In 195 B.C. a certain praetor named M. Helvius was marching out of Further Spain after two inactive years in that province. His successor had given him a legion as a bodyguard for safe passage. However, Helvius is said to have taken over this force, fought a major battle against the native Celtiberians, and then put all the adults of a nearby town to death. On his return to Rome, he then asked for a triumph. That the senate denied him "because he had fought under another's auspices and in another's province" – that is, in his successor's province or in transit through Nearer Spain (the geography of the incident is unclear).

Yet, surprisingly, Helvius – despite his dubious technical claim and not particularly elevated social status – somehow managed to get an ovation, a lesser form of triumph. How did he do it? Perhaps he threatened to celebrate a protest triumph solely by virtue of his *imperium* on the Alban Mount (27 kilometers southeast of Rome), as a disgruntled consul had done in 197, Helvius' own magisterial year.[25]

New Boundaries on Legitimate Power, 171–59 B.C.

Twenty-five years after the Helvius incident, the senate was in a less compliant mood. In 171 B.C. the consul C. Cassius Longinus crossed out of his proper province of "Italy" to attack Macedonia (though the war there had been allotted to someone else). The senate sent three legates to catch up with the consul, now on the move. The members of the embassy were not particularly distinguished, but whatever message they delivered obviously gave the consul Cassius quite a fright. He stayed as a military tribune in the East at least through the year 168, surely to avoid disciplinary action at Rome.

This incident crystallized a principle evident already in the Helvius episode: that a magistrate or promagistrate was expected to confine his activities to his assigned theater (*provincia*) except in emergencies or by special permission. That would seem to be a basic restraint essential to the smooth functioning of the Republic.[26] But as it happens, our first clear example of the senate's micromanagement of provincial commanders comes also from the year 171 B.C. It has to do with a praetor's stern treatment of two pro-Macedonian towns in Boeotia that had surrendered to him. The senate instigated a fact-finding commission on the matter and soon passed at least one decree critical of the praetor's conduct in the field. He later was condemned for these actions after his magistracy, a condemnation that led to his exile.

The case is important. The senate of course had some long-standing rights simply by established custom. One understandable formality was for magistrates departing for the field first to obtain the senate's vote for funds and equipment. If a magistrate was travelling to his province by sea, the senate might circumscribe the route to be taken. (The return trip generally carried no stipulations regarding route or speed.) Or the senate might instruct the magistrate in his province or on the move, whether coming or going, to carry out special duties.

However, commanders in the general period of the middle Republic were very rarely successfully prosecuted for offences committed in the field – otherwise only for "treason" (*perduellio*) after major losses of Roman troops. The prejudicial decree of 171 B.C. is in fact an apparently unprecedented example of the encroachment of the senate on a magistrate's (originally absolute) powers of *imperium* within his province. There was a similar case in the next year, also concerning the East. The first provincial extortion trial came in the year 171. Soon afterward (169 B.C.) we find senatorial regulation even of the requisitions of magistrates in a theater of war.[27]

It was not only the magistracy that lost ground to the senate in Rome's "constitution" at this time. As it happens, in roughly this same period, the senate seems to have stopped submitting its decisions regarding extension of magistrates in Rome's organised territorial provinces (Sicily, Sardinia, the Spains) to popular vote, as it scrupulously had done down to at least the mid 190s B.C. Henceforth the senate acquired, in addition to its long-standing power of specifying magisterial provinces, sole right of "prorogation" – now a misnomer, since there was no *rogatio* (Latin for "legislative bill") in the process.[28] Still, the term *prorogatio* persisted in official contexts down through the Republic – a good example of the sometimes confusing conservatism of Rome's administrative language.

It is a pity that we lose Livy's continuous account in 166 B.C., before we can adequately trace developments like these further. But by the year 100 we know for a fact that there existed a small forest of regulations concerning administration not just in the territorial provinces but also in transit to and fro. We owe that knowledge to the discovery of a major inscription from Knidus in southeastern Asia Minor – a substantial fragment of a previously known pirate law – that dates to the year 101 or 100 B.C.

45

In the Knidus text we learn that even in case of abdication the commander was empowered, until his return to Rome (and so outside the assigned province), "to investigate, to punish, to administer justice, to make (legal) decisions, to assign arbitrators or foreign judges," and to handle sureties, restitution of properties, and manumissions in the same way "just as in his magistracy it was permitted." Apart from the surprising – indeed, paradoxical – point about abdication, this last section of the text offers a good summary of some of the attributes of *imperium* and the activities a commander might be expected to perform in his province and in transit. Yet the Knidus inscription also mentions limitations under a "Porcian law" – apparently new – on the movements of the commander and his staff.[29] Without a decree of the senate, the commander is not to lead a military expedition outside his province. He must prevent members of his staff from doing so, too.

Quite possibly the M. Porcius Cato who passed this bill (a praetor, although his precise identity and date are disputed) had taken over an old prohibition on a commander's marching beyond his province – we have seen that the issue had been a burning one about three-quarters of a century earlier, in 171 B.C. To make his law, he simply added a new proviso, namely, the extension of the prohibition to a general's staff. In truth, it probably had long been a recognized principle that a commander was liable for the public actions of his travelling companions. But to turn that principle into law is another thing, for it gave the senate a particularly effective handle on the conduct of commanders in the field. Cicero, for instance, in prosecuting C. Verres on his return from Sicily in 70 B.C., made much of the rule that a commander had vicarious liability for underlings.

The comprehensive law on treason (*maiestas*) passed by L. Cornelius Sulla as dictator in 81 B.C. really marks a watershed in the history of this type of restrictive legislation.[30] What details we can expressly assign to the law mostly have to do with ensuring orderly succession in the provinces, necessary for the smooth working of a new administrative system that Sulla had set up. For instance, Sulla demanded that a promagistrate spend at least one full year in his territorial province. That must be new, since we know that one governor of Asia of the mid 90s B.C. left his province after a mere nine months, with no personal repercussions. And under Sulla's law a commander had to quit the province thirty days after succession. Before that law, some commanders were presumably hanging on for more than a month. One of the most significant things about Sulla in general was the scale on which he sought to transform the restraints of ancestral custom into positive law. The provisions on succession nicely illustrate the point.

Yet in the decades after Sulla we find others who are even more pessimistic about a Roman magistrate's capacity for self-restraint. Cicero's letters to his brother Quintus as governor of Asia in 60 and 59 B.C. are a mine of information on the formal and informal rules that now restricted a magistrate in his province. The end result of the process was Caesar's hyperdetailed extortion law of 59 B.C., so comprehensive (and so severe) that it remained in effect all the way to the days of Justinian in the sixth century A.D. Among other things, Caesar even legally limited the number of the commander's travelling companions, his "cohort of friends." What is more, Sulla's treason law remained in effect down to the end of the free Republic, alongside Caesar's extortion measure.

Yet for all the creep of legislation, Roman commanders were highly skilled at finding the loopholes. The overarching impression we get is that it was no easy thing to call magistrates to account in the late Republic, especially if they were well connected. Furthermore, it is ironic that the same society that had such an appetite for legislation concerning provincial administration also acquiesced in the creation of any number of special mega-commands in which a single commander simultaneously held multiple provinces over a duration of several years. The most unusual of these was the five-year Spanish command Pompey received in his second consulship (55 B.C.), since he did not like the notion of actually going to Iberia. "His plan," says one source, "was to let legates subdue Spain while he took in own hands affairs of Rome and Italy."[31] And that is what he did, allowing two senior legates to hold Spain down through 49 B.C. There were precedents of sorts for this (most notably a consul of 67 who exercised control over Transalpine Gaul from Rome). But it was Pompey's example that Augustus later seized on and expanded when he was seeking ways to place himself firmly at the center of his imperial system of government.

"ENHANCED" IMPERIUM, SUCCESSION, AND DELEGATION

Pompey, in his third consulship (52 B.C.), instituted a thoroughgoing reform of Rome's administrative system. Now, Sulla as dictator in 81 had introduced a scheme in which both consuls and all the praetors – he had brought their number to eight – were normally to remain in Rome for the year of their magistracy, to tend to civil affairs and the various standing courts. They then theoretically went as ex-magistrates to fight Rome's wars and govern the various territorial provinces. Whether ex-consul or ex-praetor, Sulla gave each enhanced (i.e., consular) *imperium*, including those assigned to nearby Sicily and Sardinia.

Pompey modified some of these features. In an attempt to stem electoral bribery (and stymie his rival Caesar, should he win a second consulship further down the road), there was now to be a five-year gap between magistracy and promagistracy. Pompey also attempted to fix a curious built-in structural flaw of the Sullan system. Oddly, Sulla had allowed that an ex-consul or ex-praetor could refuse a territorial province after he had drawn a lot for it in the mandatory sortition. Pompey reversed the "voluntary" aspect of Sulla's system and compelled previous refuseniks, such as Cicero (consul in 63 B.C.), to fill vacant provincial slots. The Pompeian law on provinces had one additional important feature: under this law, only ex-consuls were to receive consular *imperium*; ex-praetors got praetorian *imperium*.

At the time of Pompey's reforms, Rome had fourteen territorial provinces: Sicily (acquired in 241 B.C.), Sardinia (238), Nearer and Further Spain (organized in 197), Macedonia and Africa (acquired in 146), Asia (bequeathed to Rome in 133 and secured by 129), Cilicia (acquired *c.* 100, no doubt to keep wealthy Asia safe from piracy), Transalpine and Cisalpine Gaul (acquired in the mid 90s), Cyrene (acquired soon after 67), Crete (acquired in 66 or 65), and Bithynia (with Pontus) and Syria (organized in 61). Our evidence suggests that, by the late Republic, the majority of commanders in armed provinces received the charismatic appellation *imperator* – and quickly, too. Where we can check – and this is one place where the numismatic evidence comes in handy – they invariably were designated *imperator* within a few months of arrival, no doubt as a hedge against supersession. For down to the year 146 B.C., the senate seems, whenever and wherever feasible, to have aimed at a policy of annual succession, though prorogation of commanders into a second year proved positively necessary for distant provinces like the Spains. Even after 146 – when an increase in the number of provinces outstripped the number of available magistrates with *imperium* (see "The Theology of *Imperium*" above) – the senate apparently kept plum provinces like Sicily and (later) Asia "annual."

The pressure to maintain a strict policy of succession unquestionably came from within the ruling class itself. Properly elected magistrates no doubt resented the bottleneck that resulted when a previous commander in a coveted post was prorogued for one or more years. But annual succession made for a lot of to-ing and fro-ing by Rome's provincial governors. It guaranteed plenty of transitions too. In any given year in the mid second century, six provinces (permanent or provisional) were changing hands; in the late Republic, the number in rotation more than doubled.

It is remarkable that the system worked at all. For the governors, there were (notionally) short commands, sometimes long and dangerous journeys, and no permanent adminstrative support in the provinces for bureaucratic continuity. One thing that made a province particularly hazardous – leaving aside military threats – was a hostile lame-duck governor. Cicero explains the psychology of one nasty *decessor* (the technical Latin word for an outgoing commander) leaving Sardinia in the mid 50s thus: "He wished all possible failure to [the new governor], in order that his own memory might be more conspicuous. This is a state of things which, so far from being foreign to our habits, is perfectly normal and exceedingly frequent."[32] Several months before himself taking up a consular province in 51 B.C., Cicero found himself writing to this very man – Appius Claudius, now holding Cilicia – begging him to make the transition easy.[33] This Appius did not do, instead tarrying in the province and holding a competing circuit court. It could (and did) get much worse.[34]

So how to ease succession outside the city? One increasingly common answer in the later Republic was for a commander not to wait for supersession but to delegate his authority to a subordinate and start home early. The practice was too convenient to attract much critical notice, as far as we can tell. Indeed, in contrast to the delimitation of *imperium* seen in the preceding section, delegation is one area where over time we can detect a definite broadening of the magistrate's powers.

During most of the republican period, it seems certain that an individual could not delegate *imperium* at his own level. We have seen that principle from our case of 295 B.C. (in "The Theology of *Imperium*"), where a departing consul made his subordinate (merely) *pro praetore* to lead his army. In fact there is no instance of a special consular command granted by a consul in Rome or in the field. A consul could give out only praetorian *imperium*. And despite what seems to be a universally held notion, there is no strong positive proof that the urban praetor – or any holder of praetorian power – had the ability to delegate his *imperium* at all. However, on instructions of the senate, he could choose a suitable individual and secure for him in a legislative assembly a special grant of *imperium*.

49

At some point, praetors (or even nonmagistrates) with enhanced (i.e., consular) *imperium* could start making men *pro praetore*. This was obviously a major development. Indeed, it may be that one of the major factors behind the decision to institutionalize grants of consular powers to praetorian commanders for distant provinces (see "The Theology of *Imperium*") was precisely to empower them to delegate *imperium*. In the Spains, Macedonia, Africa, Asia, and Cilicia, the seamless succession of proper governors was not easy to achieve, and praetors or quaestors might find themselves in sole charge of a large province for longish stretches.[35] Starting in the late second century B.C., this type of delegation by praetors is reasonably well attested. We can suppose that the practice grew only more common after Sulla took the step of generalizing consular *imperium* for promagistrates in all the territorial provinces. But a startling thing happened after Pompey, in 52 B.C., modified Sulla's system by completely divorcing the magistracy from the promagistracy and then restoring praetorian *imperium* as the standard grade for praetorian governors. We now find for the first time men who were *pro praetore* delegating *imperium* at their own level.[36] One wonders whether the college of augurs had occasion to comment on the practice. Though doubtless convenient – even necessary, after Pompey's overhaul of the administrative system – it is hard to see how it makes doctrinal sense.

BEHIND THE INSTITUTIONS: FURTHER DYNAMICS OF GETTING AND WIELDING POWER AT ROME

To have held *imperium*, received the charisma-enhancing acclamation of *imperator*, and celebrated a triumph conferred almost incalculable prestige on a Roman. But for an ambitious politician under the Republic, a little *comitas* ("affability") at times also might go a long way. Take Lucius Hostilius Mancinus, who as a legate in the Third Punic War held the technical distinction of being the first Roman officer to breach the walls of Carthage, though almost destroying himself and his force in the process. Once extricated (and dismissed from the theater), Mancinus managed quickly to win a consulship for the year 145 B.C. against formidable competition. How? On his return he had set up in the Forum a detailed painted representation of the siege of Carthage; standing at hand, we are told, he charmed onlookers by personally explaining the painting's (presumably self-aggrandizing) particulars. This bold exercise in self-rehabilitation infuriated the great Scipio Aemilianus, who had saved Mancinus' skin in 147, sent the legate packing, and then actually captured Carthage in the year that followed. Mancinus' presentation undoubtedly made no more favorable an impression on an electoral competitor, Q. Caecilius Metellus, who in a praetorian command had just conquered and organized Macedonia for the Romans, earning a triumph and (uniquely for a subconsular magistrate in the Republic) a triumphal sobriquet from the senate for his achievements. But Metellus "Macedonicus" had a nasty reputation for harshness of personality (*severitas*). This evidently counted for something even in the eyes of the wealthy citizens who dominated the voting units in the relevant electoral body for higher magistrates, the centuriate assembly. For Metellus came up empty-handed at these elections and for the year that followed, winning the consulship with difficulty only for the year 143.[37]

This lesson in the value of public relations was not lost on L. Mancinus' cousin Gaius, who experienced a positively disastrous consulship in 137 B.C. His story is an intricate one[38] but seems worth telling in detail, for it illustrates unusually well some of the intangibles at work behind Rome's political institutions. Fighting an unpopular war in the province of Nearer Spain, C. Mancinus and his army found themselves defeated and trapped before the small but powerful city of Numantia. The consul felt that his only recourse was to have his quaestor, Ti. Sempronius Gracchus (the future reforming plebeian tribune of 133 B.C., who had his own inherited Spanish connections), hammer out a surrender treaty with the Numantines. The junior staff officer's truce won safe conduct for the army. But those back in Rome wanted no part of it, especially since just two years previously the consul Q. Pompeius had contrived and then reneged on an unconditional surrender to this same Spanish people. Mancinus was recalled (most unusually) during his year of office, and a serious investigation and public debate ensued.

An embassy from Numantia arrived to urge ratification of the treaty; Numantines had been in Rome as recently as 138 B.C., to complain against Pompeius, but we are told that that man's vigorous self-defense and personal influence (*gratia*) allowed him to escape punishment.[39] Mancinus had to walk a rockier road. In his case, some hardliners in Rome drew parallels with a notorious episode from a fourth-century war against the Samnites and demanded that all the officers who had sworn to the unauthorized agreement, as after the Caudine Forks affair of 321 B.C., be handed over to the enemy. In the end, the senate advised and the people approved a compromise solution on the motion of both consuls of the year 136 B.C., almost certainly in the centuriate assembly. The treaty was to be rejected. And to expiate the state for its action, the new commander for Spain (a consul of 136) and one of the specialized Roman priests of military ritual known as the *fetiales* were to hand over only the disgraced former general, stripped and bound, to the Numantines. Significantly, as the commander at the Caudine Forks is said once to have done, Mancinus himself had argued before the Roman people in favor of his own surrender.

But in a dramatic and consequential turn of events, the Numantines refused to accept Mancinus. The Roman force in Celtiberia then brought back the ex-consul with due ritual into its camp, and he returned from there to Rome (it was probably now 135 B.C.), thinking that was that. He even unhesitatingly tried to take up again his proper place in the senate. It seems that the current pair of censors – whose first task of their eighteen-month term would have been to draw up the album of senators – had upon entering office in 136 included the ex-consul in the list despite his disgrace. These individuals, Ap. Claudius Pulcher and Q. Fulvius Nobilior, may have been especially sympathetic to Mancinus. Pulcher (consul in 143) was father-in-law to the quaestor Ti. Sempronius Gracchus, and Nobilior, as consul in 153, had suffered a serious reverse at the hands of the Numantines, after which he was trapped in the same spot as Mancinus.

Much less generous in spirit toward Mancinus was a certain P. Rutilius, one of the ten tribunes of the plebs in the year of Mancinus' return. Appealing to established precedent (generally or specifically, we do not know), he ordered that the ex-consul be led out of the senate on the grounds that, after his ritual surrender, he was no longer a citizen. Apparently, this took Mancinus by surprise; if the tribune held public meetings (*contiones*) on this matter, as was customary to build support for actions on contentious issues, he did so only after standing in the way of the ex-consul. In fact, the legal question whether the tribune was justified in ejecting Mancinus from the senate as if a foreigner, and no doubt the manner in which he did it, sparked massive dissension in the city. Eventually (so it seems) the issue came to a trial, and the opinion prevailed that Mancinus had indeed lost his citizenship – and with it his freedom and legal personality, not to mention his place in the senatorial album.

Mancinus may have started a press for rehabilitation immediately, perhaps even before Scipio Aemilianus, elected to a second consulship for 134, went on to level Numantia. We are told by a late source that Mancinus managed to have his citizenship restored by popular law. He also must have reentered the senate, for two late sources state that he attained high office again, namely, a (second) praetorship. This marks a *volte-face* on the part of the people, who in 135 B.C. had been willing to surrender Mancinus as a scapegoat. One other detail of Mancinus' later career has come down to us: he dedicated a statue of himself in the same guise in which he had been handed over at Numantia, stripped and bound.[40] It is a shame that we cannot date that last item with precision. Presumably he set up the statue after the law (passed by the people or conceivably the plebs) that reinstated him as citizen. It is a reasonable guess that the statue was an emotionally manipulative artistic creation that showed his physical person to maximum effect and that he aimed for it to help him in an electoral bid, whether for a junior office that might qualify him for the senate, for his second praetorship, or even for another consulship. (One remembers the acumen of his cousin L. Mancinus, who used his visual presentation skills to gain a consulship for 145.) Although Mancinus never did return to his former full consular status, he did win something that arguably counts for even more, namely, favorable assessments from later writers (including Cicero and Plutarch).

That in its basics is the story of the consul C. Hostilius Mancinus. Probe a bit deeper and glimpses of the extra-institutional political processes of Rome's Republic present themselves at practically every juncture. The first oddity concerns an ostensibly sacred ritual, the sortition of provinces. Plutarch comments how the quaestor Ti. Gracchus had drawn as his lot to campaign with C. Mancinus, "not a bad man, but the unluckiest Roman commander."[41] Leaving aside the issue of Mancinus' luck, it certainly was an amazing coincidence that Gracchus, the eldest son and namesake of a man who as a praetor for Nearer Spain in the early 170s had forged a peace with the Numantines, was allotted that very theater as his quaestorian sphere of responsibility (*provincia*). Too amazing a coincidence, we surely must surmise. As it turns out, the Romans had a quasi-technical term for the patently manipulated assignments that might fall to the well-connected: the *sors opportuna*, or lucky draw of the lot.[42]

Personal considerations surely also influenced the relationship of the enemy Numantines to Rome. As we have seen, they inflicted a great deal of damage and shame on a series of Roman forces in the field, in the end capturing Mancinus' camp and its contents. Yet Plutarch tells the story that they graciously acceded to Ti. Gracchus' request that they restore to him his quaestorian account books – based on the trust and friendship that arose from his inherited personal connections (*clientela*) – and that they would have given him anything else he wanted. Matters soon grow fuzzier for the modern observer. When the Numantine ambassadors followed Mancinus back to his city, Dio (fr. 23.1) tells us that they were met (as was customary for enemies) outside Rome's walls: the Romans wanted to show that they denied a truce to be in effect. But the Romans – that is, the senate, the competent body for dealing with foreign embassies – still made sure to send them ceremonial gifts, "since they did not want to deprive themselves of the opportunity to come to terms." So even at this stage senatorial opinion was not hardened regarding the conduct of the war in Spain. And the Numantines, for their part, are said to have spoken in the public debate against the notion of sacrificing Mancinus and the members of his staff who had formally sworn to the treaty. Thus it is reasonable to think that by the time Mancinus argued in favor of his own ritual surrender, he had grown confident of his own personal safety vis-à-vis the Numantines[43] and perhaps even envisioned a soft landing in Rome to follow.

The quaestor Ti. Gracchus had developed his own set of élite presumptions by the time of his return to the city. Dio says he had come back to Rome expecting to be positively rewarded for his conduct of the negotiations. Instead, he ran the risk of being delivered up with Mancinus to his own foreign clients. Gracchus, of course, escaped that fate, but he still had to endure the rejection of the Numantine treaty and the blow to his reputation for good faith (*fides*) that it entailed. Ancient writers, most notably Cicero and Plutarch, are adamant that it was this that alienated Gracchus from Rome's senatorial establishment and impelled him to take up his reformist course as plebeian tribune in 133 B.C. Indeed, Plutarch details Gracchus' frustration with Scipio Aemilianus, who despite his prestige (and, we may add, relationship as cousin and brother-in-law) did not press for the ratification of the controversial truce. Nor, continues Plutarch, did Scipio Aemilianus try to save C. Hostilius Mancinus. But it really is too much to expect that Aemilianus would do much for the cousin of the man who tried to steal his thunder in the consular elections for 145 B.C. Indeed, it seems that in the investigation at Rome it was Gracchus who played a dubious part. Quaestors were magistrates of the Roman people and as such, strictly speaking, responsible for their own actions. (Legates and holders of purely delegated powers were different.) Our sources say nothing to indicate that Gracchus made an eloquent or forceful speech to advocate his treaty. Rather, they hint that he quickly distanced himself from his commanding officer when he found that he enjoyed greater support in Rome than Mancinus – and saw the Caudine-style penalty proposed. In all probability, Gracchus had been co-opted into the college of augurs by this time. One wonders, therefore, whether he was the ultimate source for the reports that Mancinus persisted in sailing to Spain despite a series of three adverse omens[44] – reports so prevalent in our tradition and obviously meant to supply a theological explanation for the disaster at Numantia.

The tribune P. Rutilius, of course, provided yet another nasty twist amid these turns. His motivation? On the face of things, he was acting in a traditional tribunician role, as guardian of constitutional propriety, applying precedent as he found it. Furthermore, it seems that tribunes had only recently gained ex officio membership in the senate;[45] it would be natural for them to police perceived usurpers of this prerogative. But in Rutilius' blocking of Mancinus, personal factors may again have been paramount – factors not all that directly connected with the ex-consul. It so happened that in 169 B.C. a relative (also named P. Rutilius, probably an uncle) as plebeian tribune had come into serious conflict with the censors of the year. Those censors, as chance would have it, were the fathers of the censor of 136, Ap. Claudius Pulcher, and our quaestor Ti. Sempronius Gracchus; they retaliated with their formal powers just days after the tribune left his office and the immunity it offered. So for the younger P. Rutilius, the citizenship issue was an elegant way to settle a score now a generation old.[46] In blocking Mancinus, he simultaneously impugned the censors of 136 and the compilation of their senatorial album as well as (indirectly) the quaestor who had started the whole chain of affairs by negotiating the Numantine truce. There may be even more to Rutilius' action, but as so often for almost all periods of the Republic, our sources allow us to go only so far.

CONCLUSION

The question of how much power should reside in the hands of individual magistrates in relation to central governing bodies is obviously central to any constitution, written or not. How well did the Romans of the Republic grapple with this conceptual challenge? One test is to ask how far their system succeeded in curbing its authorities when they went astray. Now, the *res publica* granted its magistrates (especially the senior ones) formidable powers. It allowed individuals the possibility of cumulating certain important posts. It tolerated to a remarkable degree the open exercise of personal influence in the political and even religious and military spheres. The senate put up with noisy and sometimes prolonged conflict among its members (within limits). Failed magistrates, even those who had suffered serious military defeats, had surprisingly (at least to us) ample scope for rehabilitation and reintegration into the ruling establishment.

Yet there was a rough system of informal and formal checks and balances in place that worked well enough over a period of some centuries to make figures such as Sulla and Caesar outsized exceptions. The simple principle that the empowered should observe a measure of self-restraint in the interest of political harmony (*concordia*) operated as a surprisingly efficacious force down to the end of the Republic. If magistrates ignored this tacit understanding or broke with what was accepted as precedent, the negative power wielded by tribunes – even the threat of its implementation – was often enough to make even senior magistrates back down.[47] That was especially the case if an individual perceived that he did not have the necessary backing in the senate for what he was doing. Indeed, the senate itself was a most authoritative arbiter of what was or should be legal under the republican "constitution." Its recommendations (*senatus consulta*) might give rise to a consular investigation, such as we see in 136 B.C. in the Mancinus affair. Or they might prompt specific controlling legislation, passed by the people or (most quickly and conveniently) the plebs. It was in the last resort, it seems, that a magistrate of the Roman people might see fit to block directly another – usually lower – magistrate. As we have seen, members of the same magisterial college were loath to veto each other. To use one's full magisterial power against a colleague was, at the least, construed as a serious affront to his personal dignity. In an extreme situation, it could seriously breach the *concordia* that bound together Rome's governing class.

It was precisely to avoid such potentially destructive conflict that so much of Roman political power, in all periods, tended to direct itself through noninstitutional channels. Indeed, especially in the mid Republic, the reformer who wanted to define or otherwise delimit those channels might get quite a tussle if he placed élite prerogatives at risk. For example, Cicero reported a heated public debate in the mid 180s between the senior consul M. Servilius Geminus (consul 202) and a M. Pinarius (Rusca, surely as tribune) over a law that attempted to regulate the career path (*cursus honorum*) by stipulating minimum ages for candidacy for various magistracies. The senatorial establishment, here as on previous occasions, was on the side of an unregulated *cursus*: the fewer electoral restrictions, the more scope for the free use of patronage and private influence. (In 180 B.C., however, another tribune finally pushed through a *lex annalis* that held force in its essentials until *c.* 46 B.C.) The ballot laws of the latter part of the second century B.C. also regularly saw stiff opposition, including the *lex Cassia* of 137, C. Mancinus' consular year, which introduced secret voting to most popular trials. Yet with the accumulation of regulations like these, élite resistance apparently softened over time. In 67 B.C. the tribune C. Cornelius passed a law compelling praetors to follow their own edicts. The tribune's aim probably was to prevent praetors' ad hoc deviations in the administration of civil (perhaps also provincial) law prompted by favoritism or spite. We are told that many (i.e., many in the senatorial establishment) opposed the Cornelian law, but (significantly) they did not dare to speak openly against it.[48]

Let us turn to the institutional history of legitimate power. Here our investigation shows two parallel processes. The first had a "liberalizing" effect. To make their republic work, the Romans had to invent and exploit legal fictions such as prorogation, grants of *imperium* to nonmagistrates, and "enhanced" *imperium* for praetors. These particular innovations mostly had their origin in acute military crises, particularly those of the period down to *c.* 200 B.C. But they eventually found their way into the mainstream of administrative practice. Sulla's and then Pompey's constitutional reforms in the late Republic also brought qualitative changes to *imperium*. Pompey's measures may even have attracted the attention of the augurs and required their approval. For once a *pro praetore* had the capability of delegating his official power to a subordinate of his choice in one of fourteen regular territorial provinces – and this is the situation we find after 52 B.C. – we really are quite far away from the notion of *imperium* as the united civil and military power held by the old kings as heads of state.

Yet the Romans of the middle and late Republic also sought to bring their commanders under closer control, curbing the originally absolute prerogatives of military *imperium* by incrementally transmuting what was accepted custom into positive law. In a way, this can be viewed as an attempt to project the situation of the city – with the rough-and-ready checks and balances afforded by collegiality, class consensus, and tribunician intercession (seen powerfully at work against C. Mancinus in 135 B.C.) – onto the unruly field, where there was at stake not just the orderly succession of commanders per se but also Roman lives, reputation, security, and wealth. The process culminated in Sulla's treason law and the extortion law of Caesar, but it demonstrably had started some years before.

It would seem that the Second Punic War facilitated the development of explicit formal restraints on commanders. The senate's leadership was never questioned in the seventeen years of this war, which was virtually one continuous state of emergency. There is good reason to think that after Rome's victory the senate started to capitalize on the immense prestige it had accrued. As early as the 170s, it may have acquired the sole right to "prorogue" – to determine how long commanders could hold territorial provinces – taking away that important prerogative from the people and plebs. By the time of the Third Macedonian War (171–168 B.C.), the senate clearly was dictating to commanders what they could do inside their military theaters, again bypassing the people in the process. What governors did outside their province also became at this time no less a cause for anxiety for the ruling establishment. We can speculate that it is this very period (or one soon afterward) that generated the first attempts at comprehensive rules circumscribing magistrates' activity – rules that seem to have had uneven practical results, despite much subsequent elaboration.

NOTES

1   For a brief sketch of what is known of early Roman specialized legal literature, see Honoré 1996, 838.
2   For these latter two items, see Cic. *Leg.* 3.6–11.; Polyb. 6.11–58.
3   On the varieties of popular involvement in the *res publica*, see Millar (1998), which argues for the centrality of the city populace in the political system, especially in the years *c.* 79–55 B.C.
4   For an example from Cicero's day (presidency of praetorian elections), see Brennan 2000, 120–1, and cf. 55–6 on the censorship, on which see also the section "The Theology of *Imperium*" in this chapter.
5   *Phil.* 13.14–15.
6   Lepidus used the outstanding details of his great-grandfather's career to advance his own; see the coin issues collected in Crawford 1974, 443–4, no. 419 (61 B.C.).
7   For this and what follows on the elder M. Lepidus, see Klebs 1893, coll. 552–3 (basic sources), and especially Münzer [1920] 1999, 158–65; cf. Ryan 1998, 180–1.
8   Münzer [1920] 1999, 158.
9   *Imp. Pomp.* 60.
10   See the general discussion of this passage by Lintott 1999, 4–5.
11   Cic. *De or.* 3.75 (cf. 1.45); on this incident, see also Habicht 1997, 294.
12   For nonmagistrates overawing provincial communities, it is hard to top Cicero's colorful description of the young C. Verres in transit as a commander's legate to the Roman province of Cilicia: see especially *Ver.* 2.1.44–6, 49–54, 60–1, 86, 100. Other examples (from a large selection): Polyb. 28.13.7–4 (169 B.C.); and cf. Cic. *Div. Caec.* 55 and *SIG*³ 748 (74–71 B.C.).
13   See in general Jocelyn 1971, 44–51; Linderski 1995, 560–74, 608f. There is good reason to believe that the plebeian assembly and the tribunes eventually developed some complementary auspical process; see Badian 1996a, 197–202.
14   Bleicken 1981, 37, and n. 38.
15   Mommsen 1887, 90.

16 On the *auspicia* and *imperium* of the consul without *fasces* as "dormant," see Linderski 1986, 2179, n. 115. When in the field together, the consuls rotated the auspices every day.

17 Livy 10.29.3.

18 Gell. 13.15.7.

19 *Agr.* 2.26.

20 Cic. *Ver.* 2.5.34; cf. 2.2.24.

21 Cf. Cic. *Inv.* 2.111 with *Pis.* 62; also Asc. pp. 14–15 Clark.

22 Dio Cass. 6.41.1–2.

23 On an alleged instance of 74 B.C. (Cic. *Ver.* 2.1.119), see Brennan 2000, 447.

24 On which see the sources collected in Broughton 1951, 555.

25 On Helvius, see Livy 34.10.1–5, with the further references in Broughton 1951, 341. Alban triumphs are recorded for the years 231 (the first), 211, 197, and 172. After that last instance, it seems to have become something of a joke, or illegal, or both; see Brennan 2000, 148–9.

26 See Livy 43.1.10–12, 44.31.15; cf. Badian 1996b, 1265.

27 See Brennan 2000, 172–3, 213–4; cf. Lintott 1993, 98–9.

28 See Brennan (2000, 187–90) for speculation on how precisely the senate managed to aggrandize itself in this way.

29 The relevant passages are Crawford 1996, 12, Kn. IV, lines 31–9, and Kn. III, lines 1–15.

30 For what follows, see Brennan 2000, 399–400.

31 Dio Cass. 39.39.1–4.

32 Cic. *Scaur.* 33.

33 Cic. *Fam.* 3.3.1.

34 For an egregious example of noncooperation, consider the father of the great L. Licinius Lucullus (consul 74 B.C.), who fought as a praetorian commander in Sicily in 103 (Broughton 1951, 564, 568; also Alexander 1990, 35–6, no. 69), or Cn. Pompeius Strabo, who is said to have killed the consul who came to succeed him in an Italian command of 88 B.C. (references in Broughton 1952, 40), and also the actions of his son, Pompey the Great, in the East in 67 (Dio Cass. 36.19.1–2, 45.1–2) and 66 B.C. (on which see especially Plut. *Pomp.* 31.1, *Luc.* 36.1, 4–7; Dio Cass. 36.46.2).

35 Apparently, the earliest evidence for the practice of "praetorian delegation" has to do with the orator M. Antonius, attested as *quaestor pro praetore* in the province of Asia in (probably) 113/112 B.C. (*IDélos* IV 1 1603).

36 Apparent from *IGRom* IV 401; cf. Joseph. *AJ* 14.235.

37 For sources on L. Mancinus, see Broughton 1951, 462 (especially cf. n. 3 with Plin. *NH* 35.23 on his presentation in the Forum). For Q. Caecilius Metellus Macedonicus as consular candidate, see Broughton 1991, 8–9. The tribal assembly (*comitia tributa*), where the predominant organizing principle for the voting units was place of residence rather than property qualification, was also attuned to the personalities of candidates who sought election to lower offices; cf. Val. Max. 7.5.2 (precise date uncertain, but possibly *c.* 144 B.C.) with Broughton 1991, 40–1.

38 Full sources in Broughton 1951, 484, 486–7; 1986, 104. The most expansive recent discussion of this man's consulship and the aftermath is Rosenstein 1986. See also Brennan (1989, 486–7) for some of the legal questions involved.

39   Cf. App. *Hisp.* 79.343–4 with Cic. *Rep.* 3.28, *Off.* 3.109, and Vell. Pat. 2.1.5.

40   For these details of Mancinus' later career, see *Dig.* 50.7.18 (citizenship and second praetorship), *De vir ill.* 59.4 (the praetorship), and Plin. *NH* 34.18 (his statue).

41   *Ti. Gracch.* 5.1.

42   On systemic cheating in the sortition – a phenomenon that some recent studies of the lot at Rome minimalize – see Brennan 2000, 758–63.

43   On this basic point, see Badian 1968, 10–11.

44   On these religious aspects, see Rosenstein 1986, 239, and n. 28; see also Broughton (1951, 495–6) on the composition of the college of augurs in this general period.

45   On the probable date of the *lex Atilia* that gave tribunes this right (*c.* 160 B.C.), see Badian 1996a, 202–6.

46   Sources on the troubles of 169 B.C. are collected in Broughton 1951, 424–5. The Rutilii (not a large family) had a history of adversarial behavior. See Livy fr. 12a (from Book 20) on the third-century M. Rutilius, who is said on personal grounds to have stirred up a popular riot so severe "that the senators in fright fled for refuge to the Capitoline."

47   Tribunes, no doubt at least partly to impress their constituency, might even imprison the most recalcitrant magistrates: see Millar 1998, 126. For an extended examination of the unwritten conventions of *concordia* in Rome, especially in the general era of Tiberius Gracchus, see Badian 1972.

48   M. Pinarius: Cic. *De or.* 2.261; cf. Broughton (1951, 388) on the *lex Villia Annalis* of 180 B.C. Ballot laws: see sources in Broughton 1951, 485 (137 B.C.), 526 (119 B.C.), 551 (107 B.C.). C. Cornelius in 67 B.C.: Broughton 1952, 144.

Appendix: Select Republican Political Institutions

SENATE. The senate was the main *consilium* ("advisory body") of magistrates and consisted mainly of ex-magistrates (300 before 81 B.C., 600 until 45 B.C., then 900 until Augustus reduced it again to 600). The most senior magistrate available in Rome usually presided but could step aside for others. What the senate decided (a *senatus consultum*, abbreviated *sc*) was strictly only a recommendation to magistrates. But in actual fact, the senate long guided state administration and policy in almost all matters, including wars, allocation of provinces, (eventually) all extensions of *imperium*, triumphs, the state religion, and finance; it also engaged in preliminary discussion of legislative bills. A *senatus consultum* could be vetoed (by a consul acting against his colleague or by a tribune), in which case it was called a *patrum auctoritas*. The *senatus consultum ultimum*, first passed in 121, was employed in cases of extreme crisis, but again technically it was no more than advice.

ASSEMBLIES: POPULUS. The *populus* was composed of both patricians and plebeians (nonpatricians).

Curiate Assembly (*comitia curiata*)	The curiate assembly gave "military auspices" to consuls and to praetors once they were elected by the centuriate assembly, and also to dictators and nonmagistrates *cum imperio*. It validated in some way the powers of lower magistrates (aediles, quaestors). Its president was a consul (or sometimes, apparently, a praetor); in Cicero's day, the assembly met merely in skeletal form, with a lictor symbolically representing each of the 30 voting *curiae* ("wards") of the city.

Centuriate Assembly (*comitia centuriata*)	Originally, the centuriate assembly was simply the army, which had *centuriae* as its constituent units. *Equites* ("cavalry") and *pedites* ("infantry"), the latter divided into five classes ranked by census wealth, totalled 188 centuries; added to those were five unarmed centuries. A majority of these 193 voting units, not a majority of individual votes, determined decisions. Under a consul (or, theoretically, a praetor), the assembly passed important legislative bills (*rogationes*) into law (*lex*, plural *leges*) and voted on war and peace. Under a consul (or dictator, interrex, or consular tribune), it elected consuls, praetors, and censors. Under a consul or praetor (after the assembly was convened, "lending" auspices to the tribune of the plebs), it conducted popular trials if the penalty was death.
Tribal Assembly (*comitia tributa*)	After 241 B.C., there were four tribes in Rome itself and thirty-one around the city. New territory, as added, was incorporated administratively into existing tribal units; freedmen, however, were restricted to the four urban tribes. Consuls and praetors presided in this assembly, where individuals had equal votes within their tribes and a majority of tribes determined decisions. The assembly voted on legislation, elected minor magistrates, and conducted some popular trials if the penalty was a fine. Under the *lex Domitia* of 104 B.C. (suspended 81–63 B.C.), seventeen tribes chosen by lot elected members of the principal colleges of priests.

ASSEMBLIES: THE PLEBS (*concilium plebis*). Tribunes of the plebs presided over this assembly, which elected tribunes and plebeian aediles and passed the bulk of routine legislation, usually following the senate's initiative. Bills passed were termed "plebiscites" (or, nontechnically, *leges* or "laws"). The *lex Hortensia* of 287 B.C. definitively gave plebiscites the same binding force as the people's *leges*, even without *patrum auctoritas* ("authority of the senate").

Consul	There were two consuls, each a patrician down to 366, when the office was opened to plebeians. The praetorship was a prerequisite for the consulship from *c.* 196; the qualifying age for the office was set at 42 in 180 B.C. Consuls were elected in the centuriate assembly and possessed *imperium* (*maius* against that of praetors) and *maxima auspicia*. Heads of state, consuls gave their names to the year. A suffect might be elected to replace a dead consul. They had precedence over all magistrates except (by custom) the dictator. Either consul could veto the other (but rarely did so in actual practice). A consul presided over assemblies of the people and, when available, served as senate president; he also could let out contracts in default of censors. Consuls fought Rome's major wars and (by the first century B.C.) held commands in the more important regular territorial provinces.
Praetor	There was one praetor (*urbanus*) from 366 to *c.* 247 B.C. With the addition of a *praetor inter peregrinos*, there were two praetors from *c.* 247 to 229, four for the period 228–198, six for 197–81, eight for 80–47, ten for 46; fourteen for 45, and sixteen for 44 B.C. The praetorship was originally a patrician office, and the first plebeian praetor was elected for 336 B.C. A law of 180 B.C. set the qualifying age at 39; the quaestorship as a prerequisite was confirmed in 81 B.C. Praetors were elected in the centuriate assembly, following the election of consuls and originally on the same day (and thus under the same auspices). A dead urban or peregrine praetor might be replaced by a suffect. Holding *imperium* (*minus* against that of consuls) and *maxima auspicia*, a praetor could do all that a consul could do except (most importantly) name a dictator, hold elections of magistrates with *imperium*, and conduct the Latin Festival. Any praetor could perform a colleague's tasks, though by custom the urban praetor had precedence in the city. Praetors had significant responsibilities in the Roman legal system (including supervising civil law and, after 149 B.C., presiding over standing criminal courts) as well as in the military/provincial sphere.

Quaestor	There were eight quaestors in the mid third century B.C. and twenty after 81 B.C. (the interim numbers are unknown). Sulla fixed the qualifying age at 30 and first gave quaestors ex officio membership in the senate. Quaestors were elected in the tribal assembly under a consul's presidency. They evidently held some auspices, and on taking office, quaestors had a curiate law passed on their behalf. Two quaestors had charge of the *aerarium* ("treasury") in Rome; others had certain minor responsibilities in Italy and acted as assistants, especially though not exclusively financial, to commanders in the field.

MAGISTRACIES: SOME OFFICES OUTSIDE THE *CURSUS*

Dictator	The office of dictator disappeared after *c.* 200 B.C., only to be revived by Sulla (81) and Caesar (49, then multiple times through 44). Traditionally, a dictator was given a six-month term though Sulla in late 82 B.C. was named dictator for an indeterminate time (he occupied the office down through at least 81 B.C.) and Caesar, in 48 B.C., held the office for one year. Properly a consul named the dictator under (apparently) civil auspices; the dictator then named an assistant, the Master of the Horse (*magister equitum*). Dictators held *imperium* and by custom had the right of initiative over all other magistrates; surely they also held *maxima auspicia*. But by the late third century dictators were subject to citizens' appeal and tribunician veto.
Interrex	This magistrate had to be a patrician senator. Given a five-day term, an interrex was designated when the administrative year started without elected consuls. The interrex had *imperium*, but the first *interrex* of a series did not have full (civil) auspices to convene the centuriate assembly; those that followed did. There was no curiate law.

Censor	The office was instituted in 443 B.C. There were two censors, and they held office (notionally) for five years (a *lustrum*). Originally a patrician office, after 339 one censor had to be a plebeian. By custom, censors were ex-consuls. They were elected in the centuriate assembly. They held *maxima auspicia*, confirmed – and delimited – by a centuriate law. The office, which had an eighteen-month term, could not be held by just one member of a college. Censors conducted the *census* of citizens, made up the roll of the senate (*lectio senatus*) and the list of "knights with a public horse" (*equites equo publico*), and let out contracts for a broad range of activities.
Aediles	Two plebeian aediles were elected by the plebs under the presidency of a tribune. Election of two curule aediles (originally alternating between patricians and plebeians each year, until perhaps *c.* 99 B.C.) took place in the tribal assembly under the presidency of a consul. In the late Republic, 36 was the customary minimum age of candidature for this office. Aediles supervised certain public buildings and places (e.g., markets at Rome, roads, and brothels) and had some powers of jurisdiction. They also put on (increasingly expensive) games.
Tribunes of the Plebs	Traditionally, the office seems to have been held after the quaestorship. There were ten tribunes, the candidates were all plebeians, and they were elected by the plebs under the presidency of a tribune. Physically sacrosanct, they had a personal right to give assistance (*ius auxilii*) to citizens against magistrates but only within one mile of the city. By extension, they had the right of veto (*intercessio*) with regard to any official act, including all legislative bills, even (unless a *lex* barred it) decrees of the senate, and elections (except for elections of tribunes). Tribunes proposed bills to and conducted noncapital trials before the plebs; on petition to a senior magistrate they conducted capital trials in the centuriate assembly; and occasionally they acted as default presidents of the senate, even before they became ex officio members of that body through a *lex Atinia* (perhaps *c.* 160).

3: THE ROMAN ARMY AND NAVY

David Potter

❦

MILITARY REVOLUTION

I n the last decades of the fifth century B.C. and the first decades of
the fourth, the army of the Roman *res publica* could lay claim to
the unenviable title "least efficient military establishment" of any
major state in the Mediterranean world. Despite advantages conferred by
population and location, Rome had trouble controlling the other states
of the Latin plain and was locked in a struggle with the much smaller
city of Veii to its north. In the course of the fifth century, it managed
to add only about 200 square kilometers of land to the territory that it
controlled. By 290, it was the dominant state in peninsular Italy, and its
army was the most effective military force in the Mediterranean world.

The transition of the Roman army from ineptitude to lethal efficiency was the result of one of the most significant military revolutions
in European history. A military revolution is defined by the transformation of a state's military and civilian administration to enable a high
degree of coordination between the two.[1] Such structural change is
often accompanied by significant developments in military equipment
and doctrine that make the revolutionary state superior, for some period
of time, to its rivals. Changes of this sort took place in fourth-century
Rome, and the Roman military revolution was so profound that it
shaped the course of the history of the Mediterranean, Europe, and the
Near East for six centuries.

This chapter owes much to discussions that I have had over the years with friends at
the University of Michigan, especially Christopher Barnes, John Dillery, Brian Harvey,
Rosemary Moore, John Muccigrosso, and Nigel Pollard. My interest in the topic was
sparked many years ago by conversations with Peter Derow and George Forrest. I am
very grateful to the editor of this volume for the invitation to write this chapter and
acknowledge debts of long standing. All dates are B.C. unless otherwise indicated.

The Roman military revolution began with the reformation of the political system in the middle of the fourth century. Domestic reform was accompanied by the growth of an efficient system of alliances that enabled Rome to take advantage of the military potential of states that it defeated, a new tactical doctrine based on the effective use of combined arms, and a switch from dependence on infantry armed with thrusting spears to infantry whose primary killing weapon was the sword. Other powers, wedded to traditional ways of making war, were simply unable to adjust to the complexity of the Roman system.

FROM HOPLITES TO LEGIONARIES

Although there is little that we can really know about Rome in the fifth century B.C., it is significant that the Roman historical tradition, when it started to be written down in the late third century, portrayed Rome as a small place, barely able to defend itself from its neighbors. This is somewhat misleading, since a conservative estimate, based on the territory occupied by the Roman state, suggests that the population was around 30,000, of whom roughly 9,000 would have been free males of military age.[2] According to the most likely reconstruction, the organization of this army paralleled that of the *comitia centuriata*, the principle voting assembly of the fifth century, which was divided into five classes, the first three providing men armed as hoplites, the next two providing men armed as light infantry.[3] This reconstruction explains certain anomalies in the structure of the fifth-century army, in which there were three divisions of "heavy infantry" with similar tactical functions.

An army of 9,000 men was not small by the standards of the fifth century B.C. Athens, at the end of the century, could field an army of roughly 10,000 hoplites; Sparta mustered perhaps 8,000 men, when Spartiates were combined with their Laconian allies, the *perioikoi*.[4] Both Athens and Sparta, of course, depended on their alliance systems to provide troops that would supplement their own contributions to a campaign. Rome likewise required the assistance of allies to muster a potentially overwhelming force on the battlefield. To gather such a force, Rome needed to deal with the Latin League to augment its power. What little we know about the relationship between Rome and Latium suggests that Rome's ability to compel adherence to its desires was considerably less than that of Sparta in the Peloponnesian League or Athens in the Delian.[5] It might even be prudent to read the record of border wars with the peoples occupying the hills to the East of the

Latin plain – the Aequi, the Sabines, the Volsci – as representing the sort of action that the members of the Latin League would support. If it is correct to see the fetial procedure as governing the relationship between states on the Latin plain, then this too may indicate that war was held to be an essentially defensive action.[6] The point of fetial embassies and requests for restitution was to ensure that the gods sided with Rome in righting a wrong – if there was no prior wrong, then there could be no war.

Dependence on an army made up of hoplites may also have restricted Rome's ability to fight. It is notorious that few hoplite battles in Greece ended in a decisive victory for one side or the other, and so too the inability of the peoples of the Latin plain to dominate their rivals to the West may stem from the difficulty of winning a decisive battle. Rome had no equivalent of the special Spartan training system for young citizens, the *agōgē*, that would enable its forces to gain a qualitative superiority over other hoplites, and it may have lacked the social unity necessary to mobilize its full resources for war. This is not the place to review the evidence for the "Conflict of the Orders," but it is of great interest that a Roman historian as well versed in the tradition of his own national history as Sallust could write that divisions between the *patres* and the *plebs* kept Rome weak.[7] Although there are obvious difficulties with Sallust's view in point of detail (he dates the end of the Conflict of the Orders to the years just prior to the outbreak of the First Punic War), it is not, a priori, an improbable understanding of the situation. The significance of Sallust's view may be underscored by the fact that the *comitia centuriata* comprised the essence of the army and that one of the major features of the legislative record of the fifth century suggests that inequitable social divisions remained a serious issue throughout the first century of the Republic. The fact that laws creating the tribunes of the plebs and other new magistracies and laws on marriage between plebeians and patricians and so forth were all passed through the *comitia centuriata* suggests that there were fundamental divisions between the group that provided the commanders of the army and those who served in it.[8] Amongst these laws, the two that are most interesting relate to (1) the creation of tribunes with consular powers to command the army and (2) the division of land captured from peoples defeated in war.[9] The creation of the consular tribunes appears to have been an act to ensure civic harmony rather than one to ensure that the commanders of the army were better at their job. The failure of repeated tribunician bills aimed at dividing amongst the plebs the land captured from defeated peoples may suggest not only that there was serious division on this point but that the magisterial class resisted pressure to reward soldiers with land.

The picture that emerges, albeit dimly, of Rome in the fifth century is of a state lacking any coherent imperial strategy. Military action was largely limited to self-defense. The reason for this was not so much that Rome did not have the strength for a more aggressive policy but rather that it did not then possess the social cohesion that would make such a stance possible. The hoplite army, which may have been politically viable, scarcely permitted the efficient exploitation of manpower resources, and it was tactically limited. It may be fair to say that this army was primarily a political institution that performed various tasks of self-defense with reasonable, but not spectacular, efficiency.

How and why did the Roman army become more efficient? It would perhaps be wrong to try to pin down any one cause or point in time; rather, as befits the circumstances of a military revolution, one must look for a series of events that could have served as catalysts for change. One of these events must surely have been the catastrophic defeat suffered by a Roman army at the battle of the Allia in 386 B.C.[10] Thirty years later Rome appears to be pursuing a far more aggressive policy towards its neighbors and to be doing so with vastly greater effectiveness. The other significant event in the interim was not military but political: the passage of the so-called Licinio-Sextian reforms in the early 360s.[11] The issues at stake – including the unequal distribution of land, eligibility for office, and debt – appear to have divided Roman society for several generations. The limitations imposed by the laws on land holding and debt payments appear to reveal concerns about the land-holding peasantry. The new requirements that one consul a year be a plebeian and that plebeians be added to an expanded college of decemviri sacris faciundis appear to have satisfied an emergent class of nobiles. A third process, one that began earlier than the sack of Rome but picked up speed in the immediate aftermath of the Gallic sack, was the annexation of new land to the ager Romanus and the foundation of new colonies. Colonies were seen, at least in part, as defensive settlements that would enable Rome to gain advance intelligence of movements amongst potentially hostile peoples, while the confiscation of land from conquered states would restrict their ability to fight again.

Although the practices of colonial foundation and confiscation appear to have been defensive, they would also have provided a way in which the Roman peasantry could profit from victory in war. Perhaps the most important feature of the developments of the late fifth to mid-fourth centuries was that they gave tangible rewards for fighting to the classes that would make up the bulk of the Roman army, both as officers and men, rewards that took the form either of enhanced status or of access to new lands. The new aggressiveness of the Roman state plainly upset its traditional allies, the Latins, who rose in revolt against Rome in the year 341.[12] But now the balance of power had shifted decisively in Rome's favor; the Latins were defeated by 338 and were brought into a new relationship with Rome.

The settlement of 338 was dictated by Rome and involved the complete restructuring of Rome's relationship with its allies. Rome would no longer deal with the Latin League as a military institution. Instead, each city would have an individual treaty with Rome specifying the contribution that it would henceforth make to the Roman army as well as the relationship of its inhabitants to the Roman state – some were given citizenship, others were given a semi-citizen status (*civitas sine suffragio*), others remained allies.[13] The alliance system was as important as the transition away from hoplite warfare, for it gave Rome the ability to mobilize the manpower of its allies with unprecedented efficiency.

It is to the second half of the fourth century that the adaptation of a new style of fighting should be dated. According to a tradition that was current in the early first century B.C.:

> In ancient times, when they used rectangular shields, the Etruscans, fighting in phalanxes with bronze shields, compelled them to adopt similar weapons, and were defeated. Then again, when other people were using shields such as they [the Romans] now use, and fighting in small units, imitating both, they defeated those who had introduced the excellent models. Learning siege craft from the Greeks, and how to destroy walls with machines, they compelled the cities of their teachers to do their bidding. (Diod. 23 2.1 tr. Walton adapted)

In two other versions of this tradition, it is specifically stated that the Romans learned how to use oblong shields from the Samnites.[14] That this change should be dated to the fourth century is confirmed by an invaluable picture of the army in action during the 280s from a highly unusual perspective: that of an enemy. Hieronymus of Cardia, who served with Alexander and a variety of his successors, used Pyrrhus' own memoirs when he wrote the description of the battle of Asculum in 283 B.C. that is the basis for a passage in Plutarch's *Life of Pyrrhus*:

> The Romans, not having the opportunity for sideways shifts and counter movements as before, fought, of necessity on level ground, face to face; and, hoping to defeat the hoplites before the elephants came forward, fought fiercely with their swords against the pikes, heedless of their own lives they looked to wound and to kill, holding their own suffering as nothing. (Plut. *Pyrrh.* 21.6)

In the sentence immediately preceding the passage quoted here, Plutarch has said that Pyrrhus had drawn up his own formation to deprive the Romans of their favored tactics. This Roman army is plainly capable of a degree of mobility impossible for dense lines of hoplites and also capable of using the sword in close combat.

It is this point that permits the interpretation of a passage from Dionysius of Halicarnassus, which must also derive from an account that is roughly contemporary with the Pyrrhic War: "Those whom the Romans call *principes*, fighting with cavalry spears held in the middle with both hands and aligned in close order accomplished many things" (20.11.2). The use of the present tense to describe a category of soldier that no longer existed in his own time suggests that Dionysius, who wrote this in the first century B.C., is following the wording of his source very closely. He thus provides the earliest evidence for the tripartite division of the legion into three groups, the *hastati*, the *principes*, and the *triarii*.[15] The most important question raised by this passage, when it is compared with the passage from the *Life of Pyrrhus*, is how to reconcile the description of the *principes* fighting with spears and the description of the army as a whole fighting with swords. The answer to this question is perhaps quite simple: Dionysius' source is identifying the *principes* by a weapon that immediately sets them apart from the other troops in the Roman line. What he is saying is that you can tell the *principes* because they are the ones with the long spears and because they initiate combat with their spears.[16] If they did not do this, there would be no point in arming them with thrusting spears in the first place. The *hastati*, who engaged the enemy first, were armed with throwing spears (from which their name derived), while the *principes*, or "most important" men, would engage the enemy if the *hastati* failed to achieve a breakthough, beginning their attack with a different weapon.[17] The use of a thrusting spear makes sense if they were expected to engage after an initial phase of combat where missile weapons would play a significant part; they may be the "most important" because their intervention would be expected to prove decisive. If they failed, the battle would fall to the *triarii*, who are described by Plautus as men who come to the aid of others in an emergency.[18]

While the passages in the *Life of Pyrrhus* and Dionysius of Halicarnassus are invaluable as descriptions of the Roman army in action in the 280s and 270s, the value of the tradition represented by Diodorus is less clear. The ultimate source for this tradition clearly intended to establish a pattern, identifying changes in Roman armament with each major adversary in Rome's past, but the assumptions that the author makes are plainly problematic. Why should we think that the Romans required contact with the Etruscans to learn about hoplite armor when they had their own contacts with the Greek world? And when we know that the Roman army captured numerous cities in Italy in the course of the fourth century, why should we think that the development of effective siege technologies postdated the development of the legion organized into maniples? There is really no good reason to believe any of this. Archaeological evidence shows that hoplite armor was common in the fifth century, but there is no direct evidence other than the passage in Plutarch that enables us to date the adoption of the new legionary tactics. It is possible that it should be dated as late as the Samnite war, but the enhanced efficiency of the Roman army in the 340s might well suggest that the development took place in the middle rather than at the end of the century. One passage that is sometimes adduced to support a late date for the new system – Livy's statement that the people passed a law in 311 requiring that the tribunes commanding the four legions of the Roman army be elected rather than appointed by the consuls – simply means what it says.[19] The problem with using this passage to establish the date for the introduction of the manipular legion is that it presupposes an earlier reform that was more substantial (the doubling of the size of the army). If the doubling of the number of legions can be associated with the introduction of the new tactics, this passage is in fact evidence for the earlier introduction of the new organizational scheme, placing it before the turning point of the Third Samnite War. As the Roman army appears in the account of the war with Pyrrhus to be well versed in its tactical scheme, there is no good reason to follow some scholars who would associate the references to the manipular legion to the time of that war. What is important is not the fact that our first reference to these tactics dates to the 280s but rather that the description of Roman behavior suggests a well-practiced force.[20]

Although the lack of evidence prevents us from dating the introduction of the manipular legion with precision, it is nonetheless clear
that the conditions of a military revolution had been satisfied by the end
of the fourth century. The Roman state had been reorganized to permit
the more efficient use of its resources, it had developed a new tactical
doctrine, and it had developed a political culture in which aggressive war
was seen as bringing benefits to the population at large. This last point
will continue to be of extreme importance for the history of the army in
the Republic. To return again to Sallust, it was his view that Rome was
able to conquer the Mediterranean world because the governing class
was united in its aims with the broad mass of the Roman people. The
crisis of the Republic stemmed from the alienation of the lower classes
from the governing class, which sought its own enrichment without
regard for the interests of other elements of the body politic.[21] This
interpretation of Roman society was not his alone; it is implicit in the
Augustan settlement as the *principes* sought to define roles for different
constituencies within the state after the civil wars of the first century,
and it is implicit in Polybius' analysis of the Roman constitution in the
second.[22] It was Polybius who stressed the point that the Roman army
was more effective than others because it was made up of citizens who
saw themselves as the defenders of their homeland. When the organs of
civil government failed to provide for the interests of the peasantry and
the poor, it would be the members of those groups under arms who
would bring down the Republic.

IMPERIALISM AND THE NATURE OF BATTLE

By the beginning of the third century B.C., the Roman state was capable
of mobilizing extraordinary manpower reserves, and of employing those
troops with great flexibility on the battlefield. The Roman people, who
decided on matters of war and peace through the votes that they took in
the *comitia centuriata*, were evidently predisposed to vote for war. Their
response to an incident off the port of Tarentum in 282 was to vote to
send an embassy to Tarentum demanding the surrender of the city.[23] In
264, when even the senate demurred at the prospect of sending an army
to support the people of Messina in Sicily, the Roman people voted to
send the consul Appius Claudius with an army to their aid, allegedly
because they were convinced that the war would be profitable.[24] In 218,
the Roman people voted to send ambassadors to Carthage to demand
the withdrawal of Hannibal's army from the city of Saguntum in Spain,

and they did so on the understanding that the ambassadors would declare war if their demands were not met.[25] In 229, the Roman people had voted to send a large expedition to Illyria to avenge the murder of some ambassadors who had been sent to order the Illyrian queen to restrict the piratical activities of her people,[26] and they would send another expedition there in 219. Much earlier, in 238, they had also voted for the seizure of Sardinia and Corsica.[27]

This series of decisions raises the question of whether or not the Roman state was preternaturally belligerent.[28] The answer to this question is probably no. In the third century B.C., war was seen as a basic element of the relations between major states. Minor states in the Greek world would normally resort to arbitration to solve disputes in this period, but the rulers of the post-Alexandrine successor states in the East appear to have regarded the demonstration of their military might as a feature of their claim to royalty.[29] Well after the death of Alexander the desire to rule "the whole" of the world that he had ruled was a respectable one.[30] What is striking about the events outside Messina in the summer of 264 is not simply that the consul Appius Claudius would attack both his potential allies, the Carthaginians, and his ostensible foes, the Syracusans. Perhaps even more significant is that both Hiero of Syracuse and the Carthaginian generals were ready to fight him. Romans did have reason to fear aggression from other states and were not necessarily more apt to fight than others.[31]

What set Rome apart from either Carthage or a Hellenistic kingdom is that the people who would do the fighting decided to do so.[32] In a monarchy, people did as the king decided, and he had a professional army with which to fight his wars. At Carthage, the bulk of the fighting was done by mercenaries. Why then were the Roman people willing to declare war and bear the consequences with their own persons? We cannot answer this question for certain; arguably one factor was that the Roman people shared with their leaders the vision that a war would consist of a battle or two, at which point the enemy would sue for peace. It appears that the armies of the Italian wars fought, at best, about one major battle per campaigning season, and even in a conflict like the Third Samnite War, the bulk of the summer was spent besieging towns in the hinterland.

When the Roman army entered battle, it did so with the intention of annihilating its foes. Hoplite warfare tended to be deadly only if one side broke and ran, and a battle involving phalanxes would be decisive only if the auxiliary troops – be they cavalry, light infantry, or exotica like elephants – could achieve clear superiority in another part of the field so that one of the phalanxes would be outflanked. Roman tactics, however, were designed to attain victory in the main battle line.[33] After an initial barrage of spears, the *hastati* would advance with their swords, seeking gaps in the enemy ranks (as implied by Plutarch's reference to the mobility of Roman formations).[34] If they could not break through, they would fall back and the missile barrage would continue until another opportunity for close combat presented itself.[35] Pyrrhus, who was plainly a very able soldier, recognized the tactical prowess of the legion very rapidly and so varied his own formations after his first encounter with the Romans. According to Polybius, he "used not only Italian weapons, but even Italian soldiers, placing units of these and units from the phalanx in alternate order in his battles with the Romans" (18.28.10).[36]

With an army whose strength lay in the attack, Roman generals were notoriously aggressive. There may be no more telling observation on this point than Polybius' discussion of the difficulties that Roman admirals had in dealing with storms at sea:

> In general terms the Romans rely on force in all matters, thinking that it is necessary for them to carry on, and that nothing is impossible once they have decided upon it; they succeed in many cases because of this, in some, however, they fail spectacularly, most of all at sea. On land, attacking men and the works of men they usually succeed because they are matching force against equal force, although they do sometimes fail; but when they encounter the sea and the weather and fight them with force, they suffer great disasters. (1.37.7–8)

This tendency was readily observed by their adversaries, though there was not always much that they could do about it. In the First Punic War, the Carthaginians rapidly abandoned set battles, unless, as was the case with Regulus' invasion of Africa, they had no choice. Instead they forced the Romans to engage in a series of long sieges against powerfully fortified positions. In the Second Punic War, Hannibal's great early successes stemmed from his ability to take advantage of Roman tendencies, using his cavalry to outflank Roman armies after extended periods of conflict and so to demoralize them.[37] The campaign that ended in the battle of Cannae is in many ways a perfect example of the way that the inherent aggressiveness of the Romans' approach to war played into the hands of their enemy. Although the historiographic tradition blamed the catastrophe on the folly of Varro, he is hardly to be criticized for seeking a decisive battle – despite the fact that Fabius had shown how to frustrate Hannibal in the previous year.[38] The Roman people did not vote to give the consuls an especially large army only to have them hide in the hills: they expected them to bring Hannibal to battle and end the war.

The rather simplistic approach to war as an instrument of policy revealed by the actions of the Roman people made it impossible to construct any sort of plan for the conquest of the Mediterranean. They viewed war as an event that should end with a decisive battle, to be followed by the defeated state placing itself at the mercy of the Roman people, and this may help explain the halting steps towards empire that were taken in the course of the third century: Sicily, Sardinia, Corsica, and Spain appear to have been occupied so that the Carthaginians would be deprived of bases. Evidence from Greece in the wake of the Illyrian wars reveals that land was taken from cities as *ager publicus* without there ever being a garrison. The policies used in Italy were simply applied to a new region.[39]

THE ROMAN NAVY

The First Punic War saw a radical change in the structure of the Roman fleet. In the fourth and early third centuries, we hear of officials known as the *duumviri navales* who commanded a fleet of twenty ships.[40] Although we know of only two actions undertaken by this fleet – one in 311, when an effort was made to implant a colony on Corsica, and one in 282, when a squadron was destroyed by the Tarentines – it is likely that the main purpose of these ships was to control piracy.[41] This fleet appears to have been replaced in 278, when the Roman state decided to depend entirely on the naval forces of allied states.[42] The existence of a large seafaring population would prove decisive in the years of the first war with Carthage, for, while Rome assumed responsibility for building the necessary ships, it required the preexisting skills of naval architects throughout Italy to help in the actual construction of the ships. Livy's detailed account of the distribution of responsibilities amongst various Italian communities for the construction of the fleet that Scipio would use to sail to Africa in 205 gives a good sense of the system, though in this case he specifically says that the *socii navales* bore the expense of building the ships since the treasury at Rome could no longer do so.[43]

The main line of battleship in the third century B.C. was the quinquireme, a ship that was well suited to a rapid military build up. Unlike the trireme, which required 150 skilled rowers to operate, the quinquireme, which had fifty to sixty oars, each manned by five men, would have required only one skilled man per bench.[44] This made it possible for Rome to recruit rowers from inland allied states, which it would need to do on more than one occasion, as the losses incurred through storms and the rare Carthaginian victory were horrendous. Another advantage of the quinquireme was that it was a less nimble vessel than the trireme, which made the development of Roman boarding tactics using the *corvus* a possibility. There is a very real sense in which the Carthaginian dependence on this sort of warship made it possible for Rome to catch up. It is perhaps significant that, with the exception of the fleet that Antony brought to Actium, which included the fleet of Ptolemaic Egypt and was very much on the old-style Hellenistic model, the fleets used in the civil wars at the end of the Republic consisted of lighter, more nimble craft.[45]

Although we have little direct evidence on this point, it appears that the command of individual ships was left to navarchs who were experienced sailors. If it is correct to generalize from the evidence of the later imperial fleets, where rowers and sailors were regarded as *milites*, the navarch was held to be equivalent in rank to a centurion, and the commander of the marines was a decurion, then we may surmise that Roman soldiers on the ships of the First Punic War were commanded by allies.[46] This may help explain why, when there were no extraordinary demands upon regular military manpower, the regular complement of forty marines was drawn from the *proletarii*, who were otherwise not recruited into the army.[47] Overall command of the fleet, of course, devolved upon the shoulders of a Roman magistrate, and many magistrates, as the passage from Polybius quoted above suggests, were novices.

Perhaps as a result of the fact that the fleet was dominated in its day-to-day operations by non-Romans, naval activity was always regarded as somehow other than Roman. It was not considered necessary to maintain a major fleet between wars, and when fleets were raised in the late Republic, the burden was largely borne by the allies – Caesar's description of the enormous fleet gathered by Pompey in the winter of 49–48 B.C. gives some impression of the capacity of the allies in this regard and of the way that the fleet was assembled. In his list, he divides units of the fleet according to the provinces in which they were raised, suggesting that Rome had simply transferred the style used in Italy to its new lands.[48] The speed with which Pompey was able to raise this fleet gives us some perspective on his other great ship-raising endeavor, the campaign against the pirates in 67. Given the speed with which the Republic could raise fleets like this when the need was felt to be great enough, the fact that the "pirate crisis" should have occurred at all (assuming that the crisis was real) raises questions about the capacity of late republican government to govern.

Despite the immense importance of fleet actions at various points in the history of the Republic, and the decisive nature of fleet actions in the civil wars after Caesar's murder in 44 B.C., the Roman navy would always remain a second-class institution as compared with Rome's land forces. Rome's dependence on its subjects to supply the fleet made it something of an "un-Roman" activity, and the un-Roman nature of the fleet was finally confirmed in the Augustan age when command of ships in the standing fleets at Misenum and Ravenna was given over to freedmen.

NEW TASKS

With the defeat of Carthage in 241, the Roman state was confronted with a new problem: how to govern a region outside of Italy. On a conceptual level, the word *provincia*, which appears to have originally meant "an area where the Roman state sent its army," had come to mean a "task assigned a person," "territory where a magistrate was sent on a mission," or "territory subject to Rome."[49] Polybius refers to *provinciae* in Italy prior to the First Punic War, and in his translation of the treaty between Rome and Carthage in 241, he uses the plural to refer to lands ruled by Rome, both in Sicily and, by implication, in Italy as well.[50] Shortly thereafter, Sardinia and Corsica were seized from the Carthaginians, though it appears that they were not placed under the control of magistrates until 227. So too in the wake of the First Illyrian War, Rome acquired *ager publicus* from the lands of Pharos and very probably other places as well, but in this case no magistrate with *imperium* was appointed to oversee the administration of these lands, which may simply have been leased by the censors.[51] In none of these areas was there a permanent garrison. This style of administration changed dramatically in the wake of the Second Punic War with the acquisition of the former Carthaginian lands in Spain. In the first few years of Roman rule, it appears that area was ruled *pro consule* and that Roman troops were sent home in 199.[52] In 198, the election of six praetors instead of four, as had been the practice since 227, indicates a shift in policy. Livy says that the first praetors were ordered to fix the boundaries of their *provinciae*.[53] The result of this decision by the senate was to spark a series of conflicts with local tribes that would continue, with few interruptions, until the reign of Augustus. It would also lead to the transformation of the conditions of service in the Roman army, for, after the first couple of years, new magistrates tended to bring new drafts of troops to reinforce the existing garrison.[54] The senate appears to have recognized that this was a problematic situation at first – especially as military service in the wake of the Second Punic War had lost much of its appeal for the Italian peasantry – but there was little that could be done about it. Since troops were hard to raise, those who had been conscripted had to be retained, and this made service in Spain ever more unpopular.[55]

While we learn of the dispatch of new drafts to Spain from the narrative of Livy, we are not told anything of the impact that long-term service had on the soldiers themselves. At some point regular winter camps had to be established and regular systems of supply had to be set up. Some system was evidently in place by 171, when ambassadors from Spanish towns showed up in Rome to complain that they were being robbed, leading to the first recorded case *de repetundis*.[56] Soldiers stationed abroad for long periods of time would have formed relationships with the local inhabitants, and new communities would have begun to form around the legions. Men who left the service may have decided that they no longer wished to return home, and deserters would have found ways to live with the local population. By the middle of the century, it appears that the army had developed a reputation for luxurious living and poor discipline. Mancinus blamed his failure before Numantia on the poor quality of the army that he had inherited from Pompeius, who had been defeated by the Numantines the year before.[57] Scipio Aemilianus, by implication, agreed with him when he ordered all the prostitutes and camp followers away from the army so that he could restore appropriate discipline before setting out for Numantia in 133.[58] As he did so, Tiberius Gracchus was claiming that the peasant stock that had made the army great had been ruined by the growth of large estates, necessitating his proposals for land reform.

Gracchus' claims about the depopulation of Italy have long since been shown to be false, and while Scipio's actions in reforming the army made edifying reading in later handbooks, both men – and it is safe to take them as representative of the ruling class at Rome – had missed the point. Despite the fact that trouble had been brewing over conditions of service in Spain for twenty years before the tribunate of Tiberius

Gracchus, the senate had failed to address the real issues.[59] Soldiers who were sent to Spain had to make lives for themselves there because they did not know when, or if, they would come home. The regular rotation of magistrates through the Spanish commands made it impossible for the soldiers to form close relationships with their generals, or to feel that their generals would become their advocates before the governing body of a state that may have seemed to have forgotten them. The soldier who lacked an advocate would become an advocate for himself, either through mutiny, desertion, or simply by refusing to buy into the system of military discipline. The problem would become worse in the course of the next twenty years.

MARIUS

It is regrettable that we have no coherent narrative other than the summaries of Livy's history for the last quarter of the second century B.C., for if we did, we might better be able to appreciate the problems that beset the Roman army. What we do know, however, is highly suggestive. The decade and a half inaugurated by the construction of the *via Domitia* – a significant event, as it is connected with the establishment of a permanent Roman presence north of the Alps – witnessed an unprecedented string of defeats at the hands of a variety of enemies. In 119 a Balkan tribe, the Scordisci, defeated Sextus Pompeius, the governor of Macedonia.[60] In 113 Germanic tribesmen who had entered Gaul in the previous year defeated a consular army under the command of Papirius Carbo.[61] In 110 the army sent to deal with Jugurtha of Numidia surrendered, and in 109 the same tribesmen who had defeated Carbo defeated a second consular army, this time commanded by Junius Silanus.[62] The consul Lucius Cassius was defeated by the Tigurini in 107, and in 105 the Cimbri destroyed a pair of armies at the battle of Arausio.[63]

Whatever the reasons for these disasters – and they should not, by any means, be attributed to a single cause – the overall impact was to predispose both the Roman people and, as the lack of recorded opposition may indicate, the nobility to allow one man to make the army better. Gaius Marius, who had gained credit by defeating Jugurtha, was elected to five successive consulships from 104 to 100 so that he could repel the threatened invasion of the Cimbri and the Teutones.

Marius, one of whose claims to office had been that he was well versed in the military arts, appears to have been a genuinely competent officer who had a genuine understanding of both military technology and organization, beginning, it seems, with the way that the army was recruited. Up until 107 the fiction existed that Roman soldiers were men of property. In fact the definition of an *adsiduus*, or a citizen with the necessary property to become a legionary, had been reduced to such a low level prior to 107 that the elimination of the requirement altogether had little practical effect in the short term.[64] In the long term, however, it had significant impact, strengthening the soldier's identification with his unit and his general.

None of this would have mattered so much, perhaps, if Marius had not proven an able field commander, and it may have been the authority that accrued to his reputation as a general that caused his other reforms to be adopted by other armies of the Republic (there was no central command that could mandate their adoption). The chief reforms of Marius on the operational level were as follows:

- enhanced training of individual soldiers by using the techniques employed in gladiatorial *ludi*;
- a new *pilum* designed so that its shaft would break off on contact with an enemy shield, making it harder to withdraw;
- the requirement that soldiers carry two weeks of supplies in their packs while on campaign;
- institutionalization of the cohort instead of the maniple as the basic tactical unit within the legion;
- the use of the eagle standard for all legions.

Not all of these reforms were completely original. The grouping of maniples into larger formations called "cohorts" dates at least as far back as the end of the third century (the word is used by Polybius).[65] The order concerning packs appears to have been a return to an earlier practice that had been generally abandoned during the previous thirty years as armies based in the provinces acquired civilian followings.[66] The new design for the *pilum*, which is specifically attributed to Marius, may not be particularly significant; the nature of the reform, however, suggests that the tactical use of the *pilum* was already well established. If that is the case, then the basic style of battle that its use implies was also established.[67] Caesar makes it plain that a Roman army would approach to within a certain distance of the enemy (he does not specify what this distance was) and halt to throw volley after volley of *pila* at the enemy with the intention of breaking up the front ranks; these enemy soldiers would become vulnerable after they dropped shields encumbered by the *pila*.[68] It is precisely this phase of the battle that he ordered his men to cut short at Pharsalus so that they could come to blows with Pompey's front rank more quickly.[69] Training by gladiatorial instructors is likewise a sign that the use of the sword had remained preeminent in the army. That said, the author of the pseudo-Caesarian *African War* gives a fascinating insight into what exactly this training entailed when he says that Caesar rallied his frightened troops by calling off the paces at which the weapons of their enemy would be effective – acting like a "*lanista*."[70]

Although some of the Marian reforms are less dramatic than they may seem at first glance, the overall impact of his regime appears to have been significant. The eagle clearly became the focus of a soldier's emotions, and people remembered individual eagles. Thus Catiline displayed an eagle that was specifically said to have been Marian when he was attempting to draw supporters to his cause in 63.[71] The formalization of the role of the cohort led to a significant improvement in the tactical flexibility of the legion, since a legion of ten cohorts is in fact a more complex organization than a legion of thirty maniples. In the manipular legion, a general had to deal with thirty unit commanders, something that limited his ability to issue complex orders. When the general could deal with ten unit commanders who would be responsible for making sure the men under their command followed orders, he could expect more of them.[72]

The sum of the Marian reforms was greater than its constituent parts. By giving units permanent standards, Marius created a sense of unit loyalty that appears to have been far greater than before. Caesar's account of the Gallic and Civil Wars reveals that men felt a very strong attachment to their units, took pride in the history of their collective accomplishments, and felt a positive sense of rivalry with other units in the same army. By stressing greater training and discipline, Marius reversed the trend of the previous decades, during which the army appears to have become less and less efficient. In so doing he laid the foundations for the professional army of the principate. What was lacking, however, was support from the state for what had become, de facto, an army of long-serving professional soldiers as opposed to the highly trained and motivated militia described by Polybius.

The critical issue with the professional army was its demobilization. Soldiers who had been away from home for a long period of time were harder to reintegrate into civilian society. They had formed close bonds with colleagues, and they needed the wherewithal to make new lives for themselves. Because the state had no formal way of providing for those needs, the terms under which an army would be disbanded were determined by the general.

Land ownership was often the key to enabling a man to leave the legions successfully. Although grants of public land, *ager publicus*, had been made to soldiers in the early part of the second century, the practice appears to have ceased by about 150, quite possibly because the absorption of *ager publicus* by members of the upper class, together with the complaints of allies who might otherwise have been making use of the land, created a sufficiently strong interest group to make an end to it.[73] Marius reintroduced the notion that soldiers should be given land on a very large scale at the end of a campaign, and in so doing he altered the relationship of the army to the state.[74] Since the state could never bring itself to institute a regular retirement package for soldiers, it was left to individual generals to negotiate for their men as best they could. The result was that the more powerful the general, the better the chances of substantial rewards for his men and the greater the personal loyalty they would feel for their leader.

THE ROLE OF THE ARMY IN THE DESTRUCTION OF THE REPUBLIC

The first century B.C. was an exceptionally violent period in the history of the Mediterranean world, and the Roman state was required to raise armies on a scale unmatched since the Second Punic War (especially large armies were assembled during the periods of civil war). A society as highly militarized as first-century Italy was a society in which there could be – and would be – extreme pressure for change.[75] The conservative policies favored by the bulk of the governing oligarchy only made these pressures worse, and the disloyalty of the army to the state was only one feature, albeit the most significant one in the long run, of the unrest generated by the conservative tendency in Roman politics.

It is something of a paradox that, while Marius made the Roman army a better fighting force, he also made it less loyal. The person who was ultimately responsible for the loyalty of an army to the state was the general, and although it was indeed a rare general who would wish to jeopardize his future standing in the aristocracy by siding with his men, such generals did exist. It is a striking illustration of the difference between the members of the senior officer class and those who served as centurions and soldiers that when Sulla decided to march on Rome in 88, only one of his senatorial officers would initially follow him, whereas the army did. Sulla's message to his men had been simple: crooked politicians at Rome were cheating them of rewards that were justifiably theirs. Sulla's sense of the soldiers' feelings towards the government of the *res publica* is all the more striking because he had not been in command of this army for more than a year. As a result of the levy that Marius and his supporters were able to raise in 87, the troops assembled to attack the state vastly outnumbered those left to defend it, and this is further testimony to the frustration of the peasant class in the early 80s B.C. When Sulla returned in the late 80s, the men who had followed him through Greece and Asia Minor probably cared little, if at all, for constitutional issues – or, by this time, for issues of class. Sulla's soldiers saw their self-interest linked with the success of their general and were willing to massacre thousands of prisoners after the battle of the Colline Gate.

The willingness to slaughter fellow peasants and to settle on land seized from Italian communities makes it plain that Sulla's veterans cannot be seen as representatives of the interests of a class other than that constituted by the soldiers of Sulla. Military discipline and unit loyalty became the most powerful forces in determining the way that soldiers would act in the course of the first century. Of this point there may be no better illustration than an incident that occurred in Caesar's campaign against Pompey's generals Afranius and Petreius in Spain during the latter part of 49. After having thoroughly outmaneuvered his rivals, Caesar had held his men back from an attack that, so he says, would have resulted in a bloody but complete victory. On the day after this act of mercy, the men from the two armies began to fraternize. As Caesar presents it, the soldiers looked first for men whom they knew or who had come from their home territory. Afranius' soldiers then thanked Caesar's men for not having attacked on the previous day and asked whether they could trust Caesar if they surrendered to him.[76] Assured on these points, the troops of Afranius and Petreius asked whether Caesar would spare the lives of their generals, and they then sent senior centurions to negotiate the surrender of the army, which would be signified by their bringing their standards into Caesar's camp. Not for these men were the great issues of the day, the state of the *res publica*, the safety of tribunes, and such like; they were interested in themselves. What is perhaps even more striking is that, although they had been on the verge of surrender, the soldiers of Afranius and Petreius remained loyal to their generals when Afranius armed his guards and servants to restore discipline. Petreius then summoned the army to a meeting before the generals' tent and asked that each man swear an oath that he would "not desert or betray the army and its generals, and would not take council for himself, separately from the others." Petreius swore the oath first, followed by Afranius, the tribunes and centurions, and finally, the soldiers who were called forward century by century. Once the swearing of the oath was complete, the generals ordered that any person harboring one of Caesar's men in the camp should bring him forth so that he could be executed.[77] Caesar admits that these actions restored the army to its former willingness to fight.

By the beginning of the first century B.C., the Roman state had acquired what was essentially a professional army that was fast on its way to becoming the "total institution" of the imperial period – that is, an institution dominated by its own interests against those of "outside groups."[78] What the Roman state had not acquired by the beginning of the first century was the bureaucracy needed to handle such an army. The army of Rome had always been an instrument of politics, representative of the political system of its time. In the early centuries of the Republic, its structure mirrored the highly stratified society of the preceding regal and patrician periods. In the fourth to third centuries B.C., the emergent community of interest between the men who served and the aristocrats who commanded the army contributed mightily to the acquisition of empire. In the later second century, the army evolved from a highly skilled militia, composed of soldiers whose service was defined on a campaign-by-campaign basis, into a long-serving professional army, and there are signs that it lost its sense of direction. The reforms of Marius reinforced the growth of professionalism while at the same time creating a sense of class identity, divorced from civilian life, that made the army the tool that would permit Sulla and then Caesar to dismantle the government of the Republic.

NOTES

1   See the classic essay, Roberts 1967, 195–225 (reprinted in Rogers 1995, 13–36). The essays collected in Rogers (1995) offer an excellent introduction to the debate as to whether a military revolution actually occurred as Roberts suggests. For a somewhat more wide-ranging discussion of military revolutions, drawing on the work both of historians and modern defense analysts, see M. Knox and W. Murray 2001, 1–14, esp. p. 7 for the definition accepted here.

2   Cornell 1995, 207, for 500 B.C. On the principle he accepts, there would be no substantial increase in the next century, as the territory of Rome increased only slightly.

3   Cornell 1995, 181–94.

4   Both these numbers are the object of controversy. I have adopted here the high figure for Spartans favored by A. Andrewes, in Gomme, Andrewes, and Dover (1970, 110–17); for Athenian numbers, see Hansen (1981, 19–32).

5   Cornell 1995, 299–301.
6   Watson (1993, 62) pointed out that the procedure was intended to preserve peace. See also Oakley (1993, 13–14), who likewise observes the defensive mentality of the fifth century.
7   Sall. *Hist.* fr. 11 (Reynolds). See discussion in McGushin 1992, 76, on the text, 76–81, on the thought.
8   Millar 2002, 105 (= Millar 1989, 148).
9   For the creation of consular tribunes, see Livy 4.6.8; Cornell 1995, 335–8; Drummond 1989, 192–5. For attempts at agrarian legislation, see Livy 4.36.2–4 (424); 43.6 (421); 44.7 (420); 47.8 (416); 49.11 (414); 51.5 (413); 52.2 (412); 53.2 (410).
10 For this date, see Polyb. 1.6.2; 18.2; cf. Walbank 1957–1979, 1:185–7.
11 Livy 6.34.1–42.14; cf. Oakley 1997, 1:645–61.
12 Livy 8.3.8–12.3; Oakley 1997–2004, 2:407–51, 477–538 (considering other accounts as well); Cornell 1995, 347–52.
13 Livy 8.14.1–12; cf. Oakley 1997–2004, 2:538–59.
14 Von Arnim (1892) for the text of the "*vaticanum ineditum*," which is reproduced as *FGrH* 839 fr. 1; see also Ath. *Diep.* 6.273, a section that contains fragments of Posidonius. The phrase *kata speiras* can indicate either maniples or cohorts (LSJ s.v. *speirê* is inadequate on this point, while Mason, 1974, ignores Polybian usage on which see Walbank 1957–1979, 2:302), but in an author of first century B.C. date must mean cohorts – or less tendentiously, as suggested above, small units. The phrase *kata speiras* is also used in the *vaticanum ineditum* with reference to Roman formations prior to the introduction of the Etruscan phalanx!
15 For Hieronymus, see Hornblower 1981, 141–2; for details of the passage, see Rawson 1991, 48–50.
16 See Rawson (1991, 49–50) on the nature of the spear.
17 See Rawson (1991, 50) for the meaning of *principes* and the role of the *hastati*, on which see also Ennius fr. 266 and the discussion in Skutsch (1985, 446), who shows that this cannot be an accurate picture of the *hastati* at the time that Ennius wrote or in the battle that would have been described in Book 8, the source of the fragment. Book 8 of the *Annales* dealt with the Second Punic War.
18 Varro, *L.L.* 5.89, for Plautus; cf. Rawson 1991, 56; Oakley, vol. 1, 1997, 464.
19 Livy 9.30.3. Cornell (1995, 354) takes this as evidence for the date of the manipular reform. Livy himself appears to have thought that it coincided with the introduction of the *stipendium* in 406, on which see Livy 4.59.11; Diod. 14.16.5; Oakley 1997, 1:630–32.
20 See Keppie (1984, 19) on a mid fourth century date for the reform; Oakley (1997–2004, 2:456) places the change in tactics at the end of the fourth century.
21 Sall. *Jug.* 41–2.
22 For the Augustan reform, see Rowe 2002, 21; for the link between the description of the constitution and the description of the army, see Walbank 1972, 132.
23 App. *Sam.* 7.1–8; Dion. Hal. 19.5–6; Dio Cass. fr. 39; cf. Franke 1989, 456–8.
24 Polyb. 1.11.2–3.
25 Polyb. 3.15.4–13; 20; cf. Rich 1976, 38; Harris 1979, 200–5; Briscoe 1989, 44–7.
26 Polyb. 2.8.1–13; App. *Ill.* 7.17–19; Dio Cass. 12 fr. 49; cf. Derow 1973, 118–34; see Errington (1989, 86–90) on problems in the narrative.
27 Polyb. 3.16 (Illyria); cf. Errington 1989, 91–4. Polyb. 1.88; 3.10.3; Plin. *NH* 22.5; cf. Harris 1979, 168 (Sardinia and Corsica).

28 See Harris (1979, 1–53) for the classic statement that Rome was preternaturally belligerent; see, though, the balanced response in Rich (1993, 38–68) and Oakley (1993, 28) to the notion that Roman society was shaped by war, which is not the same thing as saying that it was exceptionally prone to war. See too Dyson (1985, 271–9), who looks at the "frontier" mentality of the Roman people and their tendency to believe that they were at risk.

29 Ager 1996, 20–2.

30 Hornblower 1981, 166–71.

31 Rich 1993, 63.

32 Polyb. 6.52.4, 6–7.

33 Keppie 1984, 19.

34 See esp. Polyb. 18.30.5–11.

35 On the alternation between missile and sword combat, see Sabin 2000, 14–16.

36 This passage surely derives from the same source as that used by Plutarch in his *Life of Pyrrhus*, as the formation that Polybius is describing appears to be the same as that described at Plut. *Pyrrh.* 21; see also Polyb. 2.66.5; cf. Walbank 1957–1979, 1:280.

37 Sabin 1996, 73–7.

38 Polyb. 3.106.7, 108.1, on the senatorial support for the aggressive approach to Hannibal in 216; for the problem with the tradition concerning Varro, see now the lucid summary in Briscoe 1989, 51–2.

39 Derow 1991, 261–70.

40 Theil 1954, 32.

41 For Corsica, see Theophr. *Hist. plant.* 5.8.2 (the authenticity of the account is shown by Theil 1954, 19). The main sources for the debacle at Tarentum are App. *Sam.* 7; Livy *Per.* 12; Dio Cass. fr. 39, 4; Flor. 1.18.4–5; Oros. *Hist. contra paganos* 4.1.1.

42 Polyb. 1.20.13–14 on the absence of a Roman fleet in 264; for the date of the change to 278, see Theil 1954, 29; for reorganization of the system in 267, see Theil (1954, 333), which points to the creation of the *quaestores classici* in that year.

43 Livy 28.45.14–21.

44 Theil 1954, 100.

45 Kienast 1966, 15–16.

46 Kienast 1966, 23–4, 39–40; on marine officers, see n. 44, which adduces Livy 28.45.17 for continuity from the mid Republic.

47 Polyb. 6.19; cf. Theil 1954, 77.

48 Caes. *B Civ.* 5.3. The anomalies are a separate division for Rhodian ships (Rhodes retained an independent navy of some capacity even into this period) and a *classis liburnicae atque Achaicae*, a combined squadron of ships drawn from the Dalmatian coast, identified by distinctive type and a standard provincial fleet. As neither place was as big as, e.g., Asia or Syria, the two units may have been combined so that they would be of roughly the same strength as the others.

49 Betrand (1989, 214–15), though not admitting the final version offered in the text, which seems to me to be necessitated by what appears to be the case, that magistrates were not regularly dispatched to Sardinia/Corsica or Sicily until 227, on which point see Ferrary 1988, 18–19.

50 For Italy prior to the First Punic War, see Polyb. 2.19.2; cf. Ferrary 1988, 15 n. 33. For the treaty of 241, see Polyb. 3.27.4; cf. Ferrary (1988, 13–18), though his

suggestion that the word *eparchia* could translate *imperium* (which is true) does not
seem to hold here in light of the plural *eparchiais* in the text.

51   Derow 1991, 261–79.
52   Richardson 1986, 75; Harris 1989, 122–3.
53   Livy 32.28.11.
54   Livy 32.28.11; contrast Livy 33.43.7–8 with Richardson 1986, 83, 86.
55   Richardson 1986, 95–100.
56   Richardson 1986, 114–15.
57   App. *Hisp.* 83; cf. Rosenstein 1990, 100.
58   The sources are collected and discussed in Phang 2001, 246–7.
59   Taylor 1962, 19–27.
60   *SIG*³ 700.
61   Livy *Per.* 63; App. *Celt.* 13; Vell. Pat. 2.12; Obsequens, 98.
62   Livy *Per.* 64; Sall. *Jug.* 37–8; Oros. *Hist. contra paganos* 5.15; Eutr. *Brev.* 4.26; Flor.
     1.36 (Jugurtha); Livy *Per.* 65; Flor. 1.38; Vell. Pat. 2.12 (Silanus).
63   Livy *Per.* 65; Caes. *B Gall.* 1.7; Oros. *Hist. contra paganos* 5.15; [Cic.] *Ad Herenn.*
     1.15.25 (Cassius); Livy *Per.* 67; Granius Licinianus 33.1–17; Dio Cass. fr. 91; Plut.
     Luc. 27, *Mar.* 11, *Sert.* 3; Vell. Pat. 2.12; Diod. Sic. 36.1; Oros. *Hist. contra paganos*
     5.16; Eutr. *Brev.* 5.1.
64   Gabba 1976, 9–15.
65   Polyb. 11.23.1; cf. Walbank 1957–1979, 2:302.
66   Roth 1999, 71–2.
67   Plut. *Mar.* 25; cf. Keppie 1984, 66.
68   Caes. *B Gall.* 1.25.3–4; 52.3; 2.27.4; see also Sabin 2000, 12.
69   Caes. *B Civ.* 3.93.1. Caes *B Civ.* 1.46.1 suggests that a large supply of missile
     weapons was available. Although the action described outside Ilerda in 49 was
     not a set battle, it does suggest that regular legionaries were trained to engage in
     extended missile combat if necessary.
70   [Caes.] *B Afr.* 71.1.
71   Sall. *Cat.* 59.3; Keppie 1984, 67.
72   Goldsworthy 1996, 33–4.
73   For grants in the first half of the second century, see Brunt 1988, 241, n. 4.
74   Brunt 1988, 278–80.
75   Patterson 1993, 92–112.
76   Caes. *B Civ.* 1.74.1–4.
77   Caes. *B Civ.* 1.76.
78   Pollard 1996, 212–27.

4: THE CRISIS OF THE REPUBLIC

Jürgen von Ungern-Sternberg
(Translated by Harriet I. Flower)

⨍⨯

TIBERIUS GRACCHUS AND THE CONFLICT
OVER LAND REFORM

When Tiberius Sempronius Gracchus took office as tribune of the plebs on 10 December 134 B.C., everything in the Roman Republic seemed to be in fine working order. Rome's dangerous rival Carthage had been destroyed; the kingdom of Macedonia had become a province; the whole world of the Hellenistic states was now under Roman control. Rome faced the annoyance of a slave revolt in Sicily and a guerilla war around the town of Numantia in Spain, but neither conflict posed a serious threat, and both were already in the process of being brought to a successful conclusion. In the city of Rome itself, the leading men of the most prominent political families, the nobility of office (*nobilitas*), dominated political life from their seats in the senate. They knew how to bring one or the other recalcitrant magistrate to heel, and the same applied to the occasional tribune of the plebs who might prove too independent.[1] They were flexible enough to integrate talented and ambitious social climbers into their ranks[2] and clever enough to include all the citizens in the making of political decisions in the various types of assemblies – and particularly to entrust to them the choice between the rival candidates in the competition for political office.[3]

Less than a year later, everything had fundamentally changed, according to Appian of Alexandria, writing in the preface to his history of the Roman civil wars. A political clash had ended in assassination and death; further fighting would follow, first in the city and then for the city, eventually culminating in the short-lived domination of Caesar and finally in the establishment of the principate by Augustus. These events provided a grand and bloody spectacle, with its share of terrifying scenes and famous names. In its fall, the Roman Republic demonstrated once again the very energy that had made it so successful. Consequently, it comes as no surprise that historical thinking since Montesquieu has been challenged and shaped by the task of analysing the causes of the Republic's fall.[4]

Tiberius Gracchus' initial plan gave no indication of what was to come. His concern was with a land reform that was designed to increase the number of Roman citizens who owned land and consequently the number who would qualify as soldiers according to their census rating. An earlier agrarian law, probably dating to the beginning of the second century B.C., had limited portions of public land for individual use (*ager publicus*) to a maximum holding of 500 *iugera* (125 hectares). This was actually no small amount, and yet it seems that much more had often been appropriated.[5] Now this surplus land was to be doled out in small amounts to poor settlers, while previous occupants were to receive a clear title of ownership to the public land still in their possession as well as an additional 250 *iugera* for each of their sons.

Gracchus' proposal for reform was moderate, and yet it met with bitter opposition from the propertied classes. It was with good reason that Gaius Laelius had given up a similar project shortly before (Plut. *Ti. Gracch.* 8.4). However, Tiberius Gracchus could not retreat. As quaestor he had played a role in a catastrophic Roman defeat at Numantia (137 B.C.). A further failure would have been a disaster for the image (*dignitas*) of the young *nobilis* and for his future political career. As a result, he decided to implement his agrarian reform with the help of the assembly of the people but against the will of the majority in the senate.[6]

According to the letter of the law (in particular, the *lex Hortensia* of 287 B.C.), his actions were justified since any legislation passed by the plebs in their assembly was considered legally binding for the whole of the Roman people. However, it was not customary to introduce laws without the endorsement or against the will of the senate. In this context it is understandable that the senate arranged for another tribune of the plebs, Marcus Octavius, to veto the whole proceeding. Even so, it was certainly unusual for Octavius to persist in his veto when a vast majority of the people wanted to pass the law.[7] His actions contributed to an escalation of the crisis. Tiberius Gracchus was responsible for the assembly's decision to remove his obstructive colleague from office, despite the sacrosanctity of Octavius' position as tribune, and thus to eliminate this obstacle to his agrarian reform. The senate, in turn, refused to give the newly formed agrarian commission, which was to redistribute the land, the necessary financial resources to do its job. Tiberius Gracchus tried to obtain money by transferring from the senate, which traditionally had responsibility for foreign affairs, to the people the power to dispose freely of the royal treasury that Attalus III of Pergamum had recently left to Rome. His highhanded actions allowed his opponents in the senate to accuse him of seeking one-man rule (*regnum*) – a deadly accusation in Roman politics.

The unintended result of all of this was a crisis with no way out, despite the fact that neither side had yet taken any action that was technically against the law. In fact, that was the real reason for the crisis. Rome had not a written constitution, but a traditional one that had developed over time, according to which all the participants worked towards a consensus through mutual cooperation rather than making use of their full legal powers.[8] In the year 133 this consensus was destroyed when the senate continued to block a sensible reform and a tribune of the plebs sought to overcome the senate's opposition by deposing a colleague from office. The masters of the Mediterranean world thought they could afford this conflict, since they were not subject to the disciplines imposed by an outside threat.

"For the nobility began to abuse their prestige and the people their liberty. Each man was taking, seizing and stealing for himself. And so everything was divided into two factions, and the state, which was in the middle, was torn apart" (Sall. *Jug.* 41.5).[9]

In face of the threats of his political opponents, Tiberius Gracchus saw his only way out in the completely unprecedented move of seeking reelection to the tribunate for the following year. Such a decision certainly appeared to be an act of decisive and permanent rebellion to these same rivals in the senate. A disturbance in the electoral assembly and the hesitation of the consul presiding in the senate, which was meeting nearby, caused Scipio Nasica, the *pontifex maximus*, to seize the initiative. Gracchus and his supporters fell without resistance before the unexpected attack of the senators. Further prosecutions in the following year claimed numerous additional victims.

Ancient commentators already grasped the meaning of these events:

This was the beginning of civil bloodshed and of the free reign of swords in the city of Rome. From then on justice was overthrown by force and the strongest was preeminent.

Disagreements between citizens that in an earlier time had usually been settled through mediation were now decided by the sword. Wars were not started over the issues but according to the rewards. This state of affairs was hardly surprising. For precedents are not limited to their origins. However narrow their first path, a broad road is then created with great latitude. Once the path of justice has been abandoned, men rush headlong into wrongdoing. No man considers a way too low for himself which has brought rewards to others. (Vell. Pat. 2.3.3–4)

In this passage, Velleius states clearly that the shedding of citizen blood brought about a fundamental change in the rules of politics at Rome. What had happened once could happen again at any time and could even be surpassed by an escalation of violence. However, a schism in political methods had preceded the use of force as a last resort in political conflict. In his use of the popular assembly to oppose the political will of the senate, Tiberius Gracchus had invented a new style of popular politics (*popularis via* or *ratio*). The defenders of the traditional leading role of the senate now began to define themselves in opposition to the new politics as "the best men" (*optimates*).[10]

The contrast between these political approaches never led to the formation of two political parties in the modern sense, since each Roman politician's primary interest remained his individual career (*cursus honorum*).[11] However, the political split remained latent and threatening, like the memory of the violent end of Tiberius Gracchus. It was Tiberius' assassination that made the year 133 a turning point in Roman history and the beginning of the crisis of the Roman Republic.

GAIUS GRACCHUS

Initially, of course, a settlement still seemed possible. A commission of three men began its work of measuring and reapportioning the land on the basis of the new agrarian law: many boundary stones attest to this activity.[12] But opposition arose from a new quarter when the commission started to confiscate public land (*ager publicus*) that was being used by Rome's allies. In this way the question of the status of the allies grew out of the agrarian problem, since Rome had continued to gain the upper hand in its relationship with its Italian allies. The decision of the optimates to put a widespread stop to agrarian reform (in 129 B.C.)

while being unwilling to meet any of the demands of the allies proved disastrous. Gaius Gracchus staged strong opposition to an attempt, through a tribunician law (126 B.C.), to forbid allies even to enter the city.

The younger of the two brothers had started his political activities as a member of the agrarian commission. As tribune of the plebs in 123 and 122, he now undertook a comprehensive attempt to solve Rome's existing problems.[13] At the same time, he applied the lesson learned from his brother's death: the supporters of a single reform project had not been sufficiently powerful to protect Tiberius from the counterattack of the optimates. Consequently, his various laws were designed to appeal to a variety of interest groups. Gaius himself represented them with a rousing style of public speaking that made him the greatest orator in Rome between Cato the censor and Cicero.[14]

His initial concern was for the people of the city (*plebs urbana*), who were dependent for their survival on a regular supply of grain, their staple food, at a reasonable price. His grain law (*lex frumentaria*) was designed to meet their need. It was a practical solution, but it met with heavy opposition from the optimates, who pointed to the new burdens that would be imposed on the public treasury. In reality the optimates feared for their own personal influence, which they could exercise through private distributions of grain. Gaius' wooing of the propertied classes, who were just beginning to define themselves as the equestrian order (*ordo equester*) in contrast to the senators, was more problematic. In social terms, the boundary between the two orders was fluid, but they were politically divided by their participation or nonparticipation in the running of the state. Gaius blurred this very distinction by appointing equestrians as jurymen in Rome's first permanent court to control extortion by provincial governors (*quaestio de repetundis*).[15] In the past, juries composed of senators, the peers of the accused, had indeed proved to be ineffectual (App. *B. Civ.* 1.22.92). Yet the equestrians, many of whom had financial interests in the provinces, especially as tax collectors (*publicani*) or as businessmen, could scarcely be considered neutral adjudicators. At the same time, Gaius increased their involvement by transferring to Rome the tax contracts for the wealthy province of Asia, the former kingdom of Pergamum, which in effect handed them over to the large corporations of tax farmers (*publicani*). In revisiting the land problem, he also took the landowning classes into consideration in his planning of colonies in Italy and especially in his refoundation of the destroyed city of Carthage, where bigger initial investments for settlers were needed than elsewhere.[16]

In a third initiative, Gaius Gracchus took up the question of the allies. It seems likely that he proposed Roman citizenship for the Latin allies and improved legal rights for the other Italians. If he in fact did this, he clearly ventured into territory that was particularly dangerous for him. His opponents in the senate soon showed that in the meantime they had learned to use popular tactics (and even demagoguery) to advance the cause of their optimate political agenda. Gaius Fannius, the consul for 122, whom they had won over to their cause, together with the tribune Marcus Livius Drusus, succeeded in convincing the people that any extension of the citizenship would mean that they would have to share their privileges with others. In addition, Drusus proposed his own programme of new colonies under favourable conditions, although the programme later came to nothing.[17] However, in the short term Gaius Gracchus' popularity was seriously undermined. He was unable to achieve reelection to the tribunate for the year 121 B.C.

These developments already revealed that it was impossible to use the yearly office of tribune as the basis for a long-term political agenda. At the same time, it soon became equally clear that the diverse interest groups Gaius had appealed to could not be brought together to form a solid coalition. In a situation of conflict, the equestrians were inclined to support the existing political status quo (Sall. *Jug.* 42.1). It was not difficult for the consul Lucius Opimius, Gaius' enemy, to engineer a suitable crisis.

Gaius had reacted to the violent death of his brother Tiberius and to the persecution of his followers by giving new meaning to the old right of appeal called *provocatio* (*lex Sempronia de capite civis*). According to this principle, only the assembly of the people or a court authorized by that assembly could impose the death penalty in a political case. However, in a moment of crisis, this legal right of appeal was of little practical use. When the followers of Gaius killed a man under uncertain circumstances, Opimius induced the senate to declare a state of emergency by implementing the first suspension of the constitution (*senatus consultum ultimum*).[18] By occupying the Aventine, the supporters of Gracchus made a vain appeal to the tradition of the secession of the plebs during the "Conflict of the Orders." The consul mobilized both senators and equestrians against them, as well as regular units of soldiers. He went on to celebrate his bloody victory by building a temple specifically to the goddess of Concord (*Concordia*).

The optimates had won another victory – and this time a more decisive one. After Opimius' acquittal in the following year on charges of having put Roman citizens to death without trial, all tribunician activity ceased for a period of almost ten years.[19] By the year 111, agrarian reform was brought to a conclusion in three well-crafted, overlapping laws.[20]

It is evident that at this point the senate had overplayed its hand. Putting off problems was not the same as solving them; this was especially true for the agrarian and the allied questions. These issues, combined with the defence of the rights of the people, continued to provide material for popular politics, not in the form of a coherent "movement" but nevertheless with some degree of continuity.[21] In addition, the popular agenda was guaranteed by the constant possibility of recalling the memory of the Gracchi, the protagonists and first martyrs of the cause.[22] Their memory was enhanced by the reverence accorded their mother Cornelia, who was highlighted in Roman historiography with a prominence unparalleled for a woman in the Republic.[23]

MARIUS AND THE JUGURTHAN WAR

The impetus for a renewed clash came from outside Rome, initially from a colonial war in Africa. In reality the intriguer Jugurtha, king of Numidia, was never able to pose a serious threat to Rome. Yet it was for this precise reason that the war dragged on and provided material ready to hand for tribunician attacks on the generals of the traditional office-holding caste (the *nobiles*).[24] The war also provided the long-desired opportunity for the new man (*novus homo*) Gaius Marius to reach the consulship (in 107 B.C.).[25] With the help of his quaestor, Lucius Cornelius Sulla, he managed to arrange for the handing over of Jugurtha to the Romans, which resulted in a final victory in the war.

Marius' return to Rome proved to be just in time for a new and more important task. Beginning in 113 B.C., the Germanic tribes of the Cimbri and Teutones had destroyed several Roman armies, most recently at Arausio, where two generals were defeated in succession (105 B.C.). In reaction to the crisis, Marius was elected for 104 B.C. to the first of five consecutive consulships: extraordinary times demanded extraordinary measures. He used his special mandate for a reform of the army that introduced both tactical and technical innovations (fighting in cohorts) but above all widened the basis for military recruitment. For the war against Jugurtha, Marius enrolled not only the regular levies but also volunteers who did not own any land (Sall. *Jug.* 86.2–3). These men were now called *capite censi* rather than by the older, less flattering name of *proletarii*. In this way, Marius made a decisive break in the connection between military service and land ownership that had been taken for granted up to his time. His army reform drew the logical consequences from the failure of the Gracchan agrarian reform program while reintroducing the same issues in a different guise into day-to-day politics in Rome. Soldiers who did not own land needed a position in civilian society after the end of their military service. Their backgrounds in the Italian countryside suggested that they needed settlement back on the land.[26] And there had been occasional precedents for rewarding veterans with long records of service by giving them grants of land.

From as early as 103 B.C., Marius, in cooperation with the tribune Lucius Appuleius Saturninus, sought just such an arrangement for the veterans of the African war.[27] After Marius' victories over the Teutones at Aquae Sextiae (102 B.C.) and the Cimbri at Vercellae (101 B.C.), he and Saturninus together planned to found a number of veterans' colonies outside Italy in the year 100. The optimates were extremely displeased, since they were in principle opposed to the settlement of Roman citizens in the provinces.[28] At the same time, they did not wish to admit to themselves that such obstructive tactics actually forced the general and his soldiers to undertake shared political action. In 100 B.C. the majority in the senate were admittedly also helped by the clumsy and excessively self-assured agitation of the populares in support of Saturninus. Violent incidents once again gave the senate the opportunity to declare a state of emergency (*senatus consultum ultimum*) against their opponents. In the event, Marius himself took the lead. At the decisive moment, he did not dare, after all, to break with the establishment.

FURTHER ATTEMPTS AT REFORM

Once again the optimates had managed to rid themselves of an inconvenient tribune of the plebs, albeit at the high price of an ever growing stalemate over reform. This became evident in the year 95 B.C., when the consuls Lucius Licinius Crassus and Quintus Mucius Scaevola passed a law to send all Italians living in Rome back to their own home cities. Asconius (67–8 C) rightly identified this law as a fundamental cause of the war with the allies, just as the Stamp Act of 1765 helped to precipitate the revolt of the North American colonies against England.[29]

Meanwhile, a surprising turn of events produced a new reforming tribune in the person of Marcus Livius Drusus, who in 91 B.C. once again attempted a broad programme of reform that even had the support of leading senators. Just as Gaius Gracchus had done, he combined a whole package of reforms aimed at all the various groups who were politically important. His programme included a grain law as well as agrarian legislation and, most importantly, provided for the transfer of the jury courts to the senators. To facilitate this change, 300 equestrians were to be co-opted into the senate.[30] The outcome, however, was more opposition to the programme than support, especially because the tribune had passed his law in an illegal single vote (*lex satura*). He had also acted contrary to religious omens (*contra auspicia*), as the leader of the opposition, the consul Lucius Marcius Philippus, was quick to point out. Even though the circumstances were favourable, a reform of the state (*res publica*) proved to be impossible. The interests of different groups, even within the ruling classes, were too sharply divided. Rome was not subject to any external threat that could have imposed compromises, although these were the years when Mithradates VI of Pontus and the Parthians first came to the attention of the Romans.

From the start, the odds were against Livius Drusus' last great project, the extension of citizen rights to all the inhabitants of Italy. He launched his initiative in the summer of 91 B.C. in cooperation with allied leaders, such as the Marsian Quintus Pompaedius Silo, who was to become one of the two (hostile) consuls of the Italians once the revolt had started. By the time Drusus was murdered in the autumn, under circumstances that remain unclear, he had already failed and war had become inevitable.[31] Yet by no means all the allies joined in the fight against Rome. Etruria and Umbria stayed essentially quiet, and the same can be said for the Greek cities in the south and most of Campania. The revolt was staged by the Oscan and Sabellian tribes from the Marsi to the Samnites and Lucanians, joined by cities in southern Campania (Nola and Pompeii). Even so, the conflict was dangerous and costly for Rome, especially since both sides were relying on the same training and were fighting according to the same military strategies. In essence this was an Italian civil war, and Rome was able to secure victory as soon as she made the political concession of extending her citizenship (in several laws) to all the inhabitants of Italy south of the Po valley (90/89 B.C.). A completely unanticipated result was the creation of a unified Italy that soon became Romanised through the rapid and general spreading of Roman municipal institutions to the local towns.

In the short term, however, serious consequences resulted from the prolonged fighting on Italian soil, notably in the form of a significant blurring of the boundary between military and civilian life, a boundary that had always been strictly observed by the Romans. Several generals now began to pursue their own political agendas in a prelude to the clash between Marius and Sulla in the year 88 B.C. Through a bill proposed by the tribune of the plebs P. Sulpicius, Marius had the command against Mithradates VI transferred to himself. The consul Sulla refused to accept this, since the senate had designated the command for him. Sulla went to his army, which was encamped at Nola, and convinced the soldiers that a change of general would mean that the new commander would take different soldiers with him to the lucrative battlegrounds of Asia. Against the will of the senate, Sulla marched on Rome at the head of his army and once again secured for himself the command in Asia.[32] At the same time, he banished and proscribed his enemies and provided the first example of a formal declaration of Roman citizens as public enemies (*hostes*).[33]

Sulla's march on Rome represented an immense escalation in the level of violence compared with the deaths of the Gracchi and of Saturninus in internal armed conflicts. Sulla started the first formal civil war. Ancient observers expressed this clearly, especially Appian (*B Civ.* 1.269–70):

> And thus sedition developed from conflict and ambition to murders, and from murderous deeds to open war. This citizen army was the first to storm its native city as if it were enemy territory. And from then onwards internal discords were only settled with weapons. The city of Rome was frequently attacked and there was fighting around the walls and all the other effects of war. The perpetrators of violence were not inhibited by any respect for the laws or the constitution or their own country.[34]

SULLA

Starting in 90 B.C., Mithradates VI of Pontus had been able to use the universal dissatisfaction with Roman rule to achieve a rapid advance, first in Asia Minor and then also into Greece. In 88 B.C. 80,000 Romans and Italians were said to have become the victims of his bloody reprisals in Ephesus. Rome's power, however, remained overwhelming. Rome could even afford to conduct the war against Mithradates with two armies that were hostile to each other. Sulla was on the one side, and on the other the army sent out by his rivals, the leader of whom was the consul Lucius Cornelius Cinna in Rome, who had seized power in Italy in 87 B.C. and had outlawed Sulla. Nevertheless, Sulla was able to prevail on both fronts. At the peace of Dardanos (85 B.C.), Mithradates had to content himself with being allowed to retain his own kingdom of Pontus.[35]

Sulla was now free to prepare his forces for an invasion of Italy and for a new "march on Rome" with quite different dimensions from the first one. Initially his opponents were far stronger than he, but they did not include any individual who understood the rules of civil war in the way that Sulla did. Consequently, he gained ground rapidly after landing at Brundisium in 83 B.C., especially through the support of the young Gnaeus Pompeius. Pompeius had raised an army at his own expense – completely illegally – and had been recognized by Sulla without hesitation as a "private general" (*privatus cum imperio*). By the end of 82 B.C., Sulla had achieved victory, accompanied by a bloody settling of scores with the Samnites, who had maintained their armed resistance to the end, and with his opponents in Rome. Many senators and equestrians were designated as public enemies and robbed of their possessions when their names were put on proscription lists.[36]

In the meantime, however, it soon became clear that Sulla had fought not just for himself but for a cause. In 82 B.C. he was named dictator with supreme power to reorganize the state (*dictator legibus scribundis et reipublicae constituendae*) by means of a law introduced in the assembly by the interrex Lucius Valerius Flaccus. His reforms were designed to draw a lesson from the developments of the decades since the tribunate of Tiberius Gracchus. He cut back the tribunate of the plebs while at the same time putting the senate at the center of Roman political life again and giving order to the magistracies and to the administration of the laws.[37]

Many of his measures remained in effect in the long term, including the reorganization of the permanent courts, the expansion of the priestly colleges, the enlargement of the senate to 600 members, and the senate's automatic acceptance of the annually elected quaestors, of whom there were now to be twenty every year. However, Sulla was not able to achieve his real goal. The tribunate of the plebs was too deeply rooted in Roman tradition to be closely controlled by the will of the senate. Nor could it be made unattractive by his ban on former tribunes' holding further political office.[38] But, above all, the senate had lost most of its leading members in the civil wars and proved to be incapable of playing the central role that Sulla had conceived for it. This was especially the case because new challenges were constantly arising in Rome's large empire, challenges that could not be met by the average magistrate with limited means. Furthermore, Sulla the dictator could not erase from people's memories his own example of high-handed pursuit of personal and political goals.

POMPEIUS

Sulla himself had promoted the man of the hour, Pompeius, who was already self-consciously claiming the cognomen Magnus and who had, through sheer obstinacy, obtained a triumph for his victory in Africa.[39] After Sulla's retirement and early death (78 B.C.), Pompeius served as legate to Quintus Lutatius Catulus and helped him to put down the revolt of M. Aemilius Lepidus (77 B.C.).[40] He then managed to obtain a command in Spain against Quintus Sertorius.[41] After some mixed successes, he returned home victorious from Spain (71 B.C.) and managed to crush the last remnants of a slave revolt. As a result, he shared in the victory over Spartacus, which had actually been won by Marcus Licinius Crassus.[42] Despite their rivalry, they joined forces for the consular elections for 70 B.C. Pompeius reached the highest office without ever having been a member of the senate.

The shared reform programme of Pompeius and Crassus eliminated important elements of Sulla's system but was by no means revolutionary. The rights of the tribunes were restored in full, censors were then elected who managed to expel sixty-four unsuitable members from the senate, and finally the long-standing battle over who should serve as jurymen in the courts was settled in a compromise.[43] It was against the background of these reforms that Marcus Tullius Cicero achieved one of his greatest rhetorical successes in his prosecution of Gaius Verres. He forced the repressive governor of Sicily to go into exile. Amongst Verres' defenders was Quintus Hortensius, who had been the most prominent orator of the day, but from now on Cicero established himself as the lawyer most in demand.[44]

In characteristic fashion, Pompeius had refused to become governor of a province after his consulship, as was the usual custom (Vell. Pat. 2.31.1). He was still in search of extraordinary tasks, and he did not have to wait long for one to appear. For some time the Mediterranean had been made unsafe by pirates, whose broad operations and mobility could not be successfully tackled by individual provincial governors.[45] Consequently, it made perfect sense to enact a special law (*lex Gabinia*) in 67 B.C. granting Pompeius a command (*imperium*) over all the coastal regions, with many legates and almost unlimited financial resources. In this way the unity of the empire became visible, at least for a moment.[46]

Pompeius had never before made such a brilliant display of his organizational talent or of his diplomatic skill. Within a few weeks, he forced the pirates to capitulate and made the Mediterranean into a truly Roman sea (*mare nostrum*).

And yet a greater task already awaited him, in the form of the war against Mithradates VI that was still going on despite the major victories of Lucius Licinius Lucullus. Armed with extraordinary powers through a special *lex Manilia*, Pompeius defeated the king and advanced over the Caucasus until he almost reached the Caspian Sea. His exploits recalled those of Alexander the Great. Afterwards he concentrated on reorganising the East into a system of client kingdoms, of which Judaea was now also one. In 63 B.C. he had captured Jerusalem and demonstrated his victory to law-abiding Jews by entering the holy of holies in the Temple. He also annexed Syria, thus bringing a final end to the kingdom of the Seleucids.[47]

Meanwhile, in Italy, people awaited the return of the victorious general and feared that it would resemble Sulla's. Preparations were made on all sides, by Crassus and by Caesar, who had just won his first great success with his promotion to high priest (*pontifex maximus*) in 63 B.C., and also by the senate, where the young Marcus Porcius Cato had just emerged for the first time in the debate over the punishment of the Catilinarian conspirators on 5 December 63 B.C.[48] Cicero made the defeat of the Catilinarian conspiracy his main claim to fame as consul, and Sallust also helped to immortalize it with his monograph on the topic. However, its causes and its context were obscure, even for contemporaries, especially since Lucius Sergius Catilina died bravely in battle early in 62 B.C.[49] The rapid end to the conflict deprived Pompeius of the chance for a new military mission in Italy, and it also strengthened the self-confidence of the senate and especially of Cicero himself, who now based his politics on the ephemeral political alliance between senators and equestrians, the illusion of a "harmony of the orders" (*concordia ordinum*).[50]

In the short term, the optimates could feel that they had been justified when Pompeius landed at Brundisium at the end of 62 B.C. and dismissed his troops. A "march on Rome" would have been possible, but it would only have led to a totalitarian régime, which, in the absence of any real justification, would not have lasted. Pompeius did want to be the leading man in Rome, but within the framework of the existing constitution. Meanwhile, the senate proved foolish in its chicanery, since it wanted neither to ratify Pompeius' settlement of the East nor to allow reasonable provision for his veterans.

CAESAR

The results became clear in 60 B.C., when Caesar was elected consul for the next year and made a political alliance with Pompeius and Crassus (the so-called first triumvirate). Their friendship (*amicitia*) could have been a traditional alliance within the framework of what was usual in Roman political life. Yet their agreement that nothing should be done in Rome that was displeasing to any of the three (*ne quid ageretur in re publica quod displicuisset ulli e tribus*. Suet. *Iul.* 19) changed the rules of the game. There had never been a time when three men had conceived of the notion that their private arrangements should regulate what would happen in Rome. For there had never before been three men with the necessary resources and power to impose their vision on the state. Hence, it was appropriate that the historian Asinius Pollio later decided to begin his work about the civil wars with the year 60 B.C. (and that the twentieth-century historian Sir Ronald Syme should imitate him). Cato had already repeatedly insisted that the downfall of the Republic started with the initial friendship between Pompeius and Caesar, not with the subsequent war between them.[51] As it turned out, Cicero refused to join the pact, thus taking perhaps the most principled stance of his political life.[52]

From the start, the year of Caesar's consulate was marked by the optimates' profound distrust of a man who had always regarded popular methods (*popularis via*) as his political creed. With the help of Caesar's fellow consul, Marcus Calpurnius Bibulus, the optimates pursued a policy of blind obstructionism to Caesar's agrarian legislation and to his subsequent measures. They could not, however, prevail against the might of Pompeius' veterans, whose opposition to the optimates helped Caesar finally gain the means to greater power.[53] Since his legislation was being challenged by the optimates on legal grounds, he needed the political clout to defend it, even after 59 B.C.[54] Caesar was given the provinces of Cisalpine Gaul and Illyricum for five years (through a *lex Vatinia*). Acting on a proposal of Pompeius, the senate then added Transalpine Gaul and thereby set the stage on which Caesar would make world history.

At the time, no one could foresee the wide geographic sweep of the military successes that Caesar would achieve in Gaul in the following years. He started with the war against the Helvetians, against the Suebian leader Ariovistus, and against the Belgi and moved on to two expeditions to Britain and two crossings of the river Rhine, which was to become the border between Gaul and Germania. Finally he captured Vercingetorix at Alesia.[55] The Gallic war was a gigantic plundering raid designed to provide Caesar with a powerful army and with the financial means he needed to fulfill his political ambitions in Rome. He destroyed Celtic civilization and deprived hundreds of thousands of their lives or their freedom. The cool elegance of his writings (*commentarii*), which were designed to inform the Roman public about his deeds, cannot disguise these facts.[56] At the same time, of course, the conquest of Gaul marked Rome's decisive step over the Alps that led to the Romanisation of the West and consequently shaped the future of Europe for all time. In this case, a single individual, Julius Caesar, embodies the ambivalence that characterizes the Roman empire in general. The history of the Roman empire, like that of most empires built through "blood and iron," has created a positive image, more positive than for the emergence of most other empires.

Meanwhile, political life in Rome went on, with the attention and agreement of Caesar.[57] Rome teetered between normality and crises[58] that were caused by the fiat of the three leading men but also by the actions of Publius Clodius Pulcher. In the year of his tribunate (58 B.C.), Clodius made the ordinary people of the city of Rome (*plebs urbana*) a significant power in politics for the first time.[59] By comparison, the exile and return of Cicero (58/57 B.C.) was a second-rate phenomenon that was of primary concern only to Cicero himself, who had a great deal to say about it in various writings. Cicero's loss of political influence ushered in the first period of his activity as a writer and produced a number of important works (notably *De republica*, *De legibus*, and *De oratore*).[60]

The conference at Luca in April 56 B.C. once again revealed the true relationships of power. Pompeius and Crassus received second consulships and Caesar secured an extension of his command in Gaul. These arrangements can be accurately described as "a conspiracy to divide power amongst themselves and to destroy the previous form of government" (Plut. *Cat. Min.* 41.2). Despite a long period of interim government (*interregnum*), which pushed the elections into the year 55 B.C., the three achieved their objectives. Pompeius secured a five-year command in Spain, in addition to the control over the grain supply (*cura annonae*) that he already had. Crassus was given Syria as his province, where he was to die in 53 B.C. at Carrhae in a war against the Parthians.

The year 52 B.C. opened to scenes of chaos: again no consuls had been elected (resulting in a further interregnum), and the riots after the murder of Clodius on 18 January made a reconciliation between Pompeius and the optimates easier. Pompeius was elected as sole consul

(*consul sine collega*) and married Cornelia, the daughter of Metellus Scipio. He then made his new father-in-law his fellow consul. Once again a dynastic marriage put the seal on a new political alliance, just as Pompeius had previously been connected with Caesar until the death in 54 B.C. of his former wife Julia, the daughter of Caesar.[61] In reality the new marriage was only a precarious bond between two partners who distrusted each other. Yet it was enough to cause the break between Pompeius and Caesar, a break that in turn led to the civil war.

The famous question ("*Rechtsfrage*") concerning the limits of Caesar's command in Gaul and the conditions under which he immediately sought a new consulship in 49 or 48 B.C. (as well as the repeated attempts of the optimates to thwart his plans in 51 and 50) is only one element, albeit an important one, in the confusion of intrigue on both sides.[62] On the one hand, hatred of Caesar was too great, on the other, his determination to get his own way at any price was too strong, to allow for a peaceful solution.[63] As Cicero saw at the time, the Roman Republic (*res publica*) would in any case be the victim.[64]

DICTATOR PERPETUUS

After Caesar crossed the Rubicon with his veteran army in January 49 B.C., Pompeius was forced to abandon Italy in a hurry. Pompeius' hope lay in his strength at sea and in a victorious return, with the armies in Spain and in the East, in imitation of Sulla.[65] But his war of attrition proved useless against an opponent who conquered Spain in short order and then himself brought the war across the Adriatic. Pompeius was decisively defeated at Pharsalus in August 48 B.C. and met a violent end as he fled to Egypt. Caesar made himself sole ruler of the whole Roman empire by 45 B.C., after further victories in Egypt (at the side of Cleopatra), Asia Minor,[66] Africa, and Spain.

Caesar waged his wars not only with military skill but also with political acumen. He took every opportunity to spare his defeated opponents (*clementia Caesaris*).[67] However, the task of consolidating the power he had won proved beyond him. In his capacity as dictator, first for ten years (46 B.C.) and then for life (*dictator perpetuus*, from February 44 B.C.), he passed many reforms in the short time remaining to him. His reforms included the new calendar based on the solar year, laws to reorganize the courts and the administration of the provinces, and above all far-sighted policies regarding colonization and the extension of Roman citizenship.[68] But his rule was based on the advice of his cabinet and of his close friends, not on consultation with the senate, which had no choice but to heap him with ever new honours, resulting even in virtual deification – so unprecedented that these same honours hint at subversion.[69]

Yet, even as things were, Rome wanted not an efficient monarch and the peace he had created but rather the Republic, despite all its weaknesses. Caesar may have shown more foresight in turning down the repeated demands for a restoration of the Republic made by Cicero and others. Yet he was setting himself up against a tradition that went back for centuries and was still vital.[70] It is unclear whether he really wanted to be a king at the end of his life and what plans he had for the Parthian war or for the future. But "the question of ultimate intentions becomes irrelevant. Caesar was slain for what he was, not for what he might become."[71] It is significant enough that on the Ides of March 44 B.C., republicans and disappointed Caesarians acted together under the leadership of Brutus and Cassius.[72]

INTERPRETATIONS OF THE CRISIS

The crisis of the late Republic proved thought provoking both for contemporaries and for later historians throughout antiquity.[73] At first, its causes were principally sought in the ethical sphere, especially in the decay of morals. And subsequent events made the crisis appear as a teleological process that led to monarchy. Montesquieu made the rise and fall of the Roman Republic a paradigm for modern historical thought,[74] comparable only to Gibbon's account of the Roman Empire,[75] which he wrote some fifty years later. According to Montesquieu, it was the problems associated with the size of the empire and with its administration that made the republican constitution unable to function properly. This interpretation is surely correct, especially if one adds the observation made by Posidonius and Sallust, namely, that Rome's new role on the world stage led to the disappearance of the readiness to compromise in internal political affairs.[76]

Since the nineteenth century, reliance on the testimony of Cicero and Sallust, as well as consideration of more modern problems, has tended to produce a characterization of the crisis in terms of the struggle between two parties, the optimates and the populares.[77] Their conflict seemed to mirror the clash between aristocrats and democrats (or conservatives and liberals). The violence of the crisis also recalled modern revolutions, such as the great French Revolution and later ones.[78] The subsequent debates have done much to illuminate the structure of Roman politics. They have revealed that optimates and populares were choosing between different political strategies rather than simply representing closed groups.[79] Roman concepts of citizenship and the fabric of social relationships and obligations have been put into sharper focus.[80] It has also become clear that the revolutions of the modern age cannot serve as models to elucidate the conflicts of the last century of the Republic.[81]

At the moment there is a tendency to stress the normality of political life during the late Republic.[82] This seems justified insofar as none of the main participants was proposing a different constitution, with the result that what happened was not part of a teleological process but constituted a "crisis without an alternative."[83] Yet it was a genuine crisis whose problems should not be minimized, notably the challenges facing the poor in the city (*plebs urbana*)[84] and even more importantly the agrarian issues, including the need to make provision for veterans of the army. Through its refusal to produce a solution to these problems, the senate created serious doubts about its own legitimacy as the ultimate governing body, which in turn caused the soldiers to stage repeated "marches on Rome."[85] In this context, it was logical that Augustus finally put an end to the crisis through a military dictatorship, even though he disguised his régime as the restoration of the traditional republican political order (*res publica*).[86]

NOTES

1   Taylor 1962; Eder 1969; Lintott 1992.
2   Gelzer 1969; Hopkins 1983; Burckhardt 1990.
3   Cf. the discussion between Jehne 1995; Millar 1998; Yakobson 1999; Hölkeskamp 2000; Ryan 2001.
4   Montesquieu, *Considérations sur les causes de la grandeur des Romains et de leur décadence* (Amsterdam, 1734).
5   Plut. *Ti. Gracch.* 8; App. *B Civ.* 1.7.26–9.37; contra Bringmann 1985, but see von Ungern-Sternberg 1988. For the *lex agraria*, see now de Ligt 2001.
6   Bernstein 1978, 160–97; Stockton 1979, 61–86.
7   Badian 1972, 706–16.
8   Meier 1997, 45–63. In fact, Polybius (6.11–18) already says this in his description of the Roman constitution.
9   See von Ungern-Sternberg 1982, 263–8.
10 Cic. *Rep.* 1.31: "For as you see the death of Tiberius Gracchus, and before it the whole political style of his tribunate, divided the one people into two factions." Cicero presents a partisan view in this passage by ascribing all the blame to Gracchus, yet his judgement is much more to the point here than in his famous definition of *optimates* and *populares* at *Sest.* 96–101.

11   Meier 1965; Burckhardt 1988.

12   Degrassi 1957, Nr. 467–75; Bracco 1979; Grelle 1994.

13   Both the chronology and the content of the individual laws raise many problems.
     For the sources, see the fundamental treatment by Münzer 1923; cf. Stockton
     1979.

14   Malcovati 1976, 174–98.

15   See Lintott (1992) for the edition of the extortion law, of which larger fragments
     survive. He leaves open an identification with the *lex Sempronia* or with the *lex
     Acilia* (166–9).

16   The law had been introduced by the tribune Rubrius, an ally of Gaius Gracchus.

17   Burckhardt 1988, 54–70; for the optimates' use of *concordia*, see 70–85.

18   von Ungern-Sternberg 1970, 55–67; Nippel 1995, 57–69.

19   Broughton (1951–1986) has only two tribunes in his list of magistrates from 119
     to 112 B.C., of whom one was Gaius Marius, in 119 B.C.

20   App. *B Civ.* 1.27.121–4. Lintott (1992, 282–6) identifies the fragments of the *lex
     agraria* of 111 B.C. with Appian's third law (and more tentatively with Cicero's *lex
     Thoria* (*Brut.* 136). But see de Ligt (2001, 123–44) who rightly identifies Appian's
     second law with the *lex Thoria*.

21   Perelli 1982; Mackie 1992.

22   Early examples are the agitation of the tribune Gaius Memmius, probably accu-
     rately portrayed, at least in outline, in the accounts of Sallust *Jug.* 31 and *Ad Her.*
     4.22.31, 36.48.

23   Plut. *C. Gracch.* 19 in the style of Greek philosophy; Barnard 1990; Bauman 1992,
     42–5; Burckhardt and von Ungern-Sternberg 1994, 126–32.

24   Sall. *Jug.* 5.1; Timpe 1962.

25   Carney 1970; Evans 1994; for the self-image of the *homo novus*, see Vogt 1955;
     Wiseman 1971.

26   Gabba 1976, 20–69; Brunt 1988, 240–80.

27   Von der Mühll 1906; Cavaggioni 1998, 101–15.

28   Bleicken 1998b, 722–77; but see Lintott 1994b, 99.

29   Mommsen 1874–1875, vol. 2, p. 222: "And what made things worse was the fact
     that the proposers of the law were by no means amongst the most hardened and
     unyielding Optimates. Rather they were clever men, who were otherwise held in
     high esteem. Quintus [Mucius] Scaevola, like George Grenville, was a lawyer by
     nature and a statesman as a result of political circumstances. More than any other
     individual Scaevola first kindled war between the senators and the equestrians and
     then between Romans and Italians, as a result of his honourable but damaging
     insistence on legal correctness. Similarly, the orator Lucius Licinius Crassus was
     a friend and ally of Drusus and one of the most moderate and insightful of the
     Optimates."

30   Gabba 1976, 131–41; Burckhardt 1988, 256–67.

31   Sherwin-White 1973, 134–49; Keaveney 1987; David 1994; Mouritsen 1998.

32   Levick 1982a, 503–8; de Blois 1987; Dahlheim 1992, 197–220; von Ungern-
     Sternberg 1998, 607–24.

33   von Ungern-Sternberg 1970, 74–80, 119–20.

34   Characteristically, Cicero never recognized the significance of the chain of events.
     See Diehl 1988, 125–32, and especially Bernett 1995.

35   Kallet-Marx 1995, 153–60, 250–90; Mastrocinque 1999, 41–90.

36 Seager 1994a, 187–97.
37 Badian 1970; Gabba 1976, 131–50; Hantos 1988; Hurlet 1993; Meier 1997, 246–60.
38 Thommen 1988, 1989.
39 See the impressive account of his early career at Cic. *Leg. Man.* 61–63; cf. Gelzer 1959; Seager 1979; Greenhalgh 1980–1981.
40 Hillman 1998.
41 Plut. *Pomp.* 17; Konrad 1995; König 2000.
42 Guarino 1979; Rubinsohn 1993; Christ 2000, 243–8. On Crassus, see Marshall 1976; Ward 1977.
43 A third each was made up of senators, equestrians, and *tribuni aerarii*, whose census rating was close to that of the equestrians (Bruhns 1980). Pompeius seems not to have been involved (Seager 1994b, 225–7).
44 Gelzer 1969b, 36–50; Mitchell 1979, 133–49; Habicht 1990, 25–7; on patronage in the law courts, see David 1992.
45 A drastic account is given by Cic. *Leg. Man.* 31–33; Plut. *Pomp.* 24; cf. Dahlheim 1977, 145–52; Pohl 1993; Schulz 2000.
46 Dahlheim 1977, 153–60.
47 Sherwin-White 1984, 186–234; 1994; Kallet-Marx 1995, 320–34; on Lucullus, see Keaveney 1992.
48 von Ungern-Sternberg 1970, 86–122; Drummond 1995.
49 Syme 1964, 60–102; Wiseman 1994a, 346–58; Giovannini 1995.
50 Strasburger 1982a; Meier 1997, 270–80, 314–15.
51 Hor. 2.1; Plut. *Pomp.* 67; Syme 1939.
52 Cic. *Att.* 2.3.4; Rawson 1975, 106–7.
53 In a prophecy with hindsight, Sall. *Cat.* 54.4: "He wanted a great command, an army, and a new war, in which his personal talents could shine."
54 Caesar turned down a belated offer of a compromise from the senate (Meier 1975).
55 Gelzer 1960, 92–156; Meier 1982, 277–421; Dahlheim 1987, 56–67; Wiseman 1994b, 381–91, 408–17; Canfora 1999, 110–39.
56 Collins 1972.
57 Maier 1978.
58 Gruen 1974; Meier 1997, 7–23.
59 Nippel 1995, 70–8; Tatum 1999, 114–75; Mouritsen 2001, 47–61.
60 Griffin 1994, 715–28.
61 Gelzer 1960, 133–8.
62 Most recently, Girardet 2000, 679–710.
63 Raaflaub 1974, 13–105; Meier 1982, 11–25, 422–37; Canfora 1999, 140–51.
64 Cic. *Att.* 9.5.2–3; cf. Livy's preface.
65 That is the usual interpretation. Canfora (1999, 183–9) follows Napoleon's verdict in judging the surrender of the city without a fight as a serious strategic mistake.
66 The source of the famous announcement of victory: *veni, vidi, vici* ("I came, I saw, I conquered"; Suet. *Caes.* 37.2; Plut. *Caes.* 50.3).
67 Alföldi 1985, 173–386; but Cato Uticensis was not the only one to refuse Caesar's offer.
68 Gelzer 1960, 266–70, 288–90; Yavetz 1979, 61–185; Jehne 1987; Rawson 1994, 438–58.
69 Weinstock 1971.
70 Strasburger 1982b, 343–421.

71 Syme 1939, 56.

72 Bruhns 1978, 167–83; Yavetz 1979, 186–214.

73 Bringmann 1977; Hampl 1979; Levick 1982b; Lintott 1994a; Sion-Jenkis 2000.

74 Montesquieu, *Considérations sur les causes de la grandeur des Romains et de leur décadence* (Amsterdam, 1734).

75 Gibbon, *The history of the decline and fall of the Roman Empire* (London, 1776–1788).

76 Posidonius quoted at Diod. Sic. 34/35.33 = *FGrHist* 87 Fr. 112; Sall. *Jug.* 41.1–5; von Ungern-Sternberg 1982; Bleicken 1998c; reservations by Eder 1996.

77 Cic. *Sest.* 96f.; Sall. *Jug.* 41–42; for the history of the term, see Strasburger 1942, 775, 782; cf. Brunt 1988, 32–45.

78 Mommsen 1874–1975; Syme 1939.

79 Meier 1965; Martin 1965; Burckhardt 1988; Ferrary 1997; a step back to an earlier argument in Perelli 1982; on the meaning of democracy in Rome, see Nicolet 1983.

80 On the Roman citizenship, see Nicolet 1976; Bleicken 1998a. On Roman social relations, see Gelzer 1969a; Nicolet 1976; Brunt 1988, 351–502, 524–6; David 1992, 1997.

81 Hackl 1979; Heuss 1995a, 1995b; Christ 2000, 1–15, 482–4.

82 Strongly argued by Gruen 1974; cf. Girardet 1996; Welwei 1996; Millar 1998; Yakobson 1999; contra now Jehne 1995; Deininger 1998; Hölkeskamp 2000.

83 Meier 1997.

84 Brunt 1966; Mouritsen 2001.

85 Brunt 1988, 240–275; von Ungern-Sternberg 1998.

86 Meier 1990.

PART 2

ROMAN SOCIETY

5: Under Roman Roofs: Family, House, and Household

Karl-J. Hölkeskamp

❦

Introduction: The Paradigm of Patriarchy

I t is a truism that the family forms the basic unit of any society and, at the same time, reflects its ruling principles, values, and views, and this is certainly true of Rome. As in all societies, the structure of the basic family unit was made up of a complex compound of criteria and factors that, in their relative importance to the whole as well as individually, could and did differ considerably at any given period and were subject to change over time. Legal status, age and gender, wealth, social standing and rank, traditions and ideologies, attitudes and patterns of behaviour based on them determined the position of a Roman, male or female, in society as well as in his or her family. Republican society at large was characterized by the omnipresence of hierarchies and of overlapping power relations. Distinctions of status and rank abounded, not only between Roman citizens or provincials and the mass of slaves with no rights, but also between magistrates and ordinary citizens, between generals and soldiers, patrons and clients, senators and the plebs in the Roman street, and even within the privileged classes.

The image and idea of the Roman family was deeply influenced by a combination of hierarchy and power. At least in law and in ideology, all relations within the household centred on authority, obligation, and coercion.[1] The aristocratic value system was defined by a number of traditional factors: superiority, rank, authority, talent, and achievement in the service to the state (*res publica*), on the one hand, balanced by subordination, acceptance, and deference, on the other. Similarly, the ideal of the well-ordered Roman household depended on patriarchy, that is, on the power of the male head of the household. This ideology of the family was deeply entrenched and never called into question, let alone seriously challenged. The ideal household also served as the paradigm of authority and of social order in society and in the state as a whole. In this respect, if not in others, the notion of the patriarchal household was more than a mere 'figment of the Roman jurist's imagination or fossilized imprint of archaic customs'.[2]

In the everyday life of a member of the political class, 'public' and 'private' roles and responsibilities overlapped and were indeed inextricably interlocked. For an aristocrat (*nobilis*), being the head of a large house was as much a characteristic of his powerful position in the uppermost eschelon of society as belonging to the senate. Consequently, the prominent senator had to be publicly visible in the Forum, in the Curia, and in the lawcourts but also – in other functions – in his representative house, which, as a physical and social space, provided an equally important stage for the permanent assertion of his status and influence.

STEREOTYPES AND STATISTICS: SOURCES AND APPROACHES

A central aspect of the ideological system mentioned above was the stereotype of the 'extended' or 'joint' family of three generations under a single roof, dominated by an aged patriarch, the 'father of the family' (*paterfamilias*) – the towering and forbidding figure at the head of the household, severe and authoritarian, sometimes arbitrary and downright tyrannical, but also righteous and just. He ruled supreme over his wife – the chaste and industrious mistress of the house, spending even her spare time on spinning and weaving. He lorded it over his adult sons – brave and dedicated to service to the state (*res publica*) in war and peace but obediently returning under their father's roof and unquestioningly submitting to his authority. Similarly, his daughters obediently awaited their father's choice of husbands, even as his daughters-in-law were bringing forth and rearing the youngest generation of the family. The father held sway over the slaves and freedmen – hardworking, loyal, and devoted to their master – and over the family property, house, land, and cattle. Autocrats of the old school were held up as examples (*exempla*) against indulgence, indolence, and weakness. The famous censor Ap. Claudius Caecus, old and blind though he was, ruled over one large 'house' (*domus*), including four sturdy sons, several of whom went on to become consuls, five daughters, and many clients – and rule he did, as later tradition emphasised. Not only did he maintain 'authority' (*auctoritas*) but 'command' in the strict sense (*imperium*) over his whole household, in accordance with the customs and 'discipline' of the forefathers.[3]

This stereotype was inseparably linked to the (late) republican Romans' particular picture of their past. They nurtured the ideal of an original state of uncorrupted innocence, when blissful simplicity, self-sufficiency, and austere frugality were the hallmark of life on the small peasant farms in old Latium. Another paradigmatic figure, the legendary L. Quinctius Cincinnatus, did not own large estates (*magna latifundia*) but had only a few acres beyond the Tiber, which he himself was ploughing when, as the "only hope of the Roman people's dominion" (*spes unica imperii populi Romani*), he was summoned by the senate to assume the dictatorship and save the commonwealth. His 'honourable standing' as head of his house (*dignitas patris familiae*) was never affected by his reduced circumstances.[4] This stereotype in turn served as a foil and, implicitly and often explicitly, as a sharp contrast to the Romans' own present, of which they invariably painted a gloomy picture of moral corruption, decline, and decadence due to extravagant luxury, the opulent *dolce vita* of the *jeunesse dorée*, frivolity and adultery on the part of the womenfolk, and all sorts of vices.[5]

The stereotype of the patriarchical family in the good old days is a cultural construct that served propagandistic and other ideological ends. At the same time, it does tell us something about moral values, attitudes, and ambitions and perhaps about collective fears and nostalgic hopes – at least those of the middle-aged male members of the urban élite in the second and first centuries B.C., like the elder Cato and Cicero, who themselves produced the extant literary texts or who patronized their authors.[6] None of these texts, however, can be taken as evidence of social reality, that is to say, as evidence of the basic structure or the everyday functioning of early or even mid-republican families. By the period of the earliest surviving literary records – that is the first decades of the second century B.C. – the old Republic of Cincinnatus and Claudius Caecus was a thing of the past, and the new 'imperial Republic' had already become the most powerful and by far the richest state of the whole Mediterranean. The discourse of decline, represented by Cato among others, was omnipresent, and the stereotypes were well established.

Yet, there is some literary evidence that allows us a few intimate glimpses into family life and the wheeling and dealing of an upper-class male as head of a family. Cicero's correspondence touches on all aspects of his own everyday life, including the notoriously elusive intimate aspects of marital emotions and parental affection, of chagrin and sorrow.[7] There is also other material that provides us with some information on attitudes, conventions, and values – for example, the extant comedies by Plautus and Terence. But we are faced with a problem: most of the evidence is later, sometimes much later, than the Republic.[8] The main legal sources date from the high Empire or even from late antiquity. That means that the family in republican law, and especially the early development of the interlocking legal systems of marriage and divorce, dowry and other property, guardianship, adoption and inheritance, can only be reconstructed in outline. The same is true for another important genre of evidence for family life and life cycles. The bulk of the relevant epigraphic evidence – above all dedicatory inscriptions on tombstones – dates from the centuries after the fall of the Republic. Once again, this material is less than representative in more than one respect: its geographical distribution is uneven, the vast majority of extant funerary inscriptions come from urban rather than from rural contexts, and the epitaphs were put up by certain social groups and classes with their own particular epigraphic habits.

Although this group of documentary evidence does lend itself to numerical analysis, the problem of the statistical representativity of samples and of the generalizability of conclusions based on them remains a matter of discussion.[9] Due to the almost total absence of data in a reliable chronological series, we cannot ever hope to be able to analyse long-term trends of fertility and mortality or patterns of marriage, divorce, and remarriage. Nevertheless, under the influence of studies of later, better documented periods of European history and of the innovative methodological approaches and conceptual perspectives developed in these studies,[10] our understanding of the Roman family has made some progress during the last three decades.[11] We have been confronted with systematic criticism of apparently self-evident dogmas with respect to, for example, the power and the reciprocity of obligation in the Roman family, power and filial duty (*potestas* and *pietas*), ideology and reality.[12] We have seen a vivid discussion about concepts and categories such as the 'extended' versus the 'nuclear' family and their applicability to the Roman family and its variants. Last but not least, the available statistical data, combined with general models and parameters in computer simulation, have given rise to new ideas about, and insights into, structures and patterns of fertility and mortality, the average age of men and women at marriage, median life expectancy, and, above all, the impact of these patterns on the structure of the family. These new approaches, their concrete results, and the conclusions to be drawn from them have been, and will certainly remain, controversial. The discussion is still under way.[13]

However, a broad consensus seems to have emerged on a few general patterns. First, the nuclear family – parents and children, as opposed to the extended family of the stereotype – seems to have been predominant, at least in the urban upper classes of the late Republic. Second, although there is no empirical evidence to assess fertility, the birth rate was certainly considerably higher than in modern times – perhaps as high as 35 or even 40 births per 1,000 people per year. This is no more than an informed guess based on general probabilities, comparisons, and the assumption that the Roman population did not dramatically decrease. In other words, fertility must have balanced a mortality rate that was very high, as is to be expected in any preindustrial society. This is the third point of the general consensus: it is more or less accepted that for Romans the average life expectancy at birth was well under thirty years of age, possibly not more than twenty-five years. However, given the particularly high infant mortality rate (only about half of newborn children reached the age of ten), this stark figure by itself is somewhat misleading. Romans who were lucky enough to survive until the age of twenty had an increased life expectancy. At this age, on average, they had another thirty-five years or so to live. Fourth, the average age of marriage of men and women differed noticeably. Girls usually married rather early by modern standards, that is, in their late teens, and girls from senatorial families even earlier, at about fifteen years. Men tended to marry about ten years later – (future) senators in their mid twenties[14] and other men at just under thirty years. On the basis of these trends and ideas, ambivalent and inconclusive though they may be, an attempt to give a rough outline of what the Roman family and its household seems to have looked like in the (late) Republic may not be an altogether futile exercise.

FAMILIA, GENS, DOMUS: CONCEPTS, CONTENTS, CONTEXTS

The Crux of Clear-cut Categories

We should take the Romans' own linguistic categories as a starting point, and not only for the sake of convenience and convention. This approach produces results that are as apparently paradoxical as they are telling.[15] First, the Latin term *familia*, on which the English word 'family' and its equivalents in other modern languages are based, does not have the same semantic range and meaning as the word we normally use today. It seems self-evident that the notional, that is nuclear family is made up of the individuals of the father-mother-children triad; in today's parlance, moreover, 'the whole family' may also include paternal as well as maternal siblings, cousins, and aunts and uncles. By contrast, in his treatment of *familia* and of the predominantly legal meanings associated with the concept, the great imperial jurist Ulpian (*Dig.* 50.16.195) began by distinguishing between *familia* as *res* in the sense of 'property' or 'estate', on the one hand, and *familia* as people, on the other. This is not the only notion totally alien to modern ideas of the family. Another is certainly the other definition of *familia*, namely, a group of slaves under their 'master' (*dominus*) and belonging to his household. This definition excludes the free members of the household.

When used for free persons, however, the term *familia* could refer to, in the first place, all those 'naturally or legally subjected to the power' of its head, including wife, children, and grandchildren. It could also encompass the wider circle of the 'agnates' – that is, the kin related by blood through males up to the sixth degree. This means that a man's sons and daughters were in the same *familia* as his brothers, his brothers' children, and his sisters. His married sisters' children, however, and his wife's siblings were not in his *familia* but were members of their husbands' *familiae* or their fathers' *familiae* respectively. The agnatic principle also underlies the third meaning of *familia*: according to Ulpian, the concept could also be used for all persons descended from a common ancestor through the male line – 'as we talk of the Julian family (*familia Iulia*)' (*Dig.* 50.16.195.4).

In this last passage, however, as indeed in many other contexts, nonlegal as well as legal, the concept of *familia* is used in a rather loose sense. The legal and social phenomena that Ulpian chose to subsume under this category here would actually have been called *gens* in strict, traditional republican terminology. In this sense, the *gens* – the anthropological term 'lineage' is a better translation than the misleading 'clan' – was a much wider community than the *familia*. The *gens* comprised not only the agnates and more distant relatives but all freeborn descendants of a (mostly distant and sometimes fictive) ancestor, such as the *gens Iulia* that claimed to have descended from Aeneas. Some patrician *gentes*, such as the *gentes Fabia* and *Cornelia*, were known to have common cults, rituals, and burial places and to share distinctive customs. However, these characteristics do not seem to have been universal, and there is no evidence that, in the mid and late Republic, aristocratic lineages retained a strong sense of cohesion or even embarked on concerted action in politics as collective groups.

What every *gens* did have in common was the name. The republican system of three names (*tria nomina*) for men was arranged around the gentilitial name (*nomen gentile*).[16] The first name (*praenomen*) was not distinctive. Apart from a few *praenomina* used exclusively in certain families (like *Appius* in the *gens Claudia*), there were only some seventeen praenominal names available for all Roman males, and women did not even have *praenomina*. It was the middle name, or *nomen gentile*, that constituted the identity of a Roman. For example, *Iulius*, *Fabius*, *Claudius*, and *Cornelius* were names borne by all descendants of these patrician *gentes*, and *Caecilius*, *Sempronius*, *Tullius*, and many others were borne by those of plebeian status. Since the mid-Republic, a third element came into use, especially among the élite: the surname (*cognomen*). Some surnames were derived from nicknames referring to personal qualities, others were just straightforward adjectives, but most had etymologies that were rather obscure. The legendary censor of the late fourth century, for example, became known as *Ap.* (for *Appius*) *Claudius Caecus* ('the Blind'), and the full name of the famous orator and consul in 63 B.C. was *M.* (for *Marcus*) *Tullius Cicero* ('Chickpea'). Such *cognomina* often served to distinguish individual branches (*familiae*) within extended *gentes*. The Cornelii Scipiones (Fig. 1) were just one branch of their *gens*; other branches included the Cossi, Lentuli, and Sullae.

A similar definitional messiness characterizes the shades of meaning attached to another concept closely related to *familia* and *gens*. The semantic range of 'house' (*domus*) partly overlaps with their spectrum of contents and connotations.[17] The word was regularly used to denote not only the physical house but also the entire household actually living in the house, including wife and children as well as slaves, freedmen, and occasionally even clients. It was only at the end of the Republic and in the early Empire that yet another meaning of *domus* began to emerge. The concept increasingly was used for a broader group than that for which *familia* would have been appropriate – a group that included not only the agnatic kin (ancestors and descendants in the male line) but also cognates. Terminology mirrors a fundamental social and cultural process of change in which relations by blood through females became ever more important for 'family' identity and prestige.

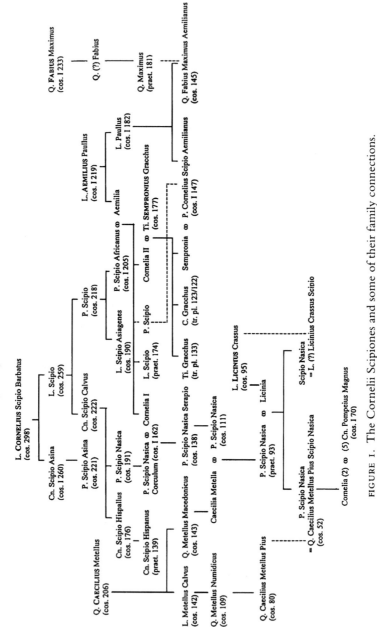

--------- adoptions, *gentes* in BOLDFACE SMALL CAPITALS

FIGURE 1. The Cornelii Scipiones and some of their family connections.

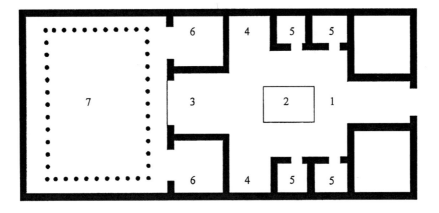

1 *atrium*   2 *impluvium*   3 *tablinum*

4 *ala*   5 *cubiculum*   6 *triclinium*   7 *peristylium*

FIGURE 2. Ground plan of a typical *atrium* house with peristyle.

In contrast to the concepts of *familia* and *gens*, *domus* always em-phasized the spatial anchorage of the familial group. The physical *do-mus* – especially the aristocratic urban residence of impressive size and elegance – was central to the Roman construction and conceptualiza-tion of social status.[18] A typical upper-class *domus* (Fig. 2) was organised around a spacious reception hall (*atrium*) that was partly open to the sky and had a basin in the floor to collect the rain (*impluvium*). The *atrium* was the most communal area of the *domus*. Together with the entrance area and the adjoining rooms (*alae* and *tablinum*), it formed the social façade of the *domus*. It was here that many family ceremonies, social as well as religious, took place. For example, the funeral procession would start from here. It was also in this area that the symbolic marriage bed (*lectus genialis*) and the shrines of the household gods (*lares familiares*) were kept. Above all, the *atrium* was where the aristocratic head of a house-hold (*dominus*) would perform many of his public roles. As a patron, he would meet his clients in the *atrium*, and as a senator or magistrate, he could hold informal political meetings here.

In the *tablinum* – ideally the next room on the main axis of the entranceway and *atrium* – family accounts and, if the *dominus* and his ancestors had held high magistracies, official records were stored. It also served as the room where the *dominus* looked after family business, often together with his wife, the mistress of the house. Neither here nor anywhere else in the *domus* was there anything like the strict gender segregation so typical of Greek houses. Roman women were visible, and they moved about in the middle of male life in terms of domestic space as well as social occasion.[19]

A *dominus* of aristocratic rank (and his wife) needed a great deal of space – not only private (sleeping) rooms (*cubicula*) but also public and semipublic space, for receiving and entertaining specially invited guests, for example. The space of a *domus* would include dining rooms (*triclinia*) and interior courtyards with open and covered walkways (peristyles). A 'busy' house (*domus frequentata*) was literally crowded with clients, friends, and all sorts of people calling on the master (*dominus*), and such crowdedness was the visible and tangible indicator of his rank, prestige, and influence.[20]

For the Roman aristocrat, however, the *domus* was more than just the representative centre of his marital, familial, and social life; it was inseparably associated with lineage and family tradition. It literally housed the visible and tangible assets of his accumulated symbolic capital. On the *atrium* walls, there were family trees, and the wax masks representing his prominent ancestors (*imagines*) were kept there. The accompanying inscriptions (*tituli*) recorded not just his and his family's genealogy but especially the achievements of his ancestors as senior magistrates and triumphant generals.[21] The trophies of their (and his own) victories in battle were often quite ostentatiously fastened to the façade of the *domus*. Even if a great family had died out and its *domus* housed new inhabitants, the spoils were not to be removed: such houses had a lasting *genius loci*, and, according to Pliny, they 'eternally celebrated triumphs even though their *domini* had changed'.[22] More than anything else, it is this idea that highlights the ideological and conceptual coalescence of *domus*, *gens*, and *familia*, 'house' and 'family', lineage and tradition.

The Letter of the Law

As in most cultures, the Romans formed a certain ideal type of the family that was regarded as the norm, legally as well as ideologically. The notional republican *familia* was a predominantly legal construct that consisted of a precisely defined membership and a universal and unchanging structure of power relations.[23] The *familia*, in the strict sense of the concept, was centred on and literally headed by the oldest living male (the legal definition of *paterfamilias*). It comprised all those under his 'paternal power' (*patria potestas*), not only his descendants, male and female (*filii* and *filiaefamilias*), born to him and his legitimate wife (or successive wives), and his adopted sons, but also the children of his sons and so on in the male line, through as many generations as might be simultaneously alive. His wife, the *materfamilias*, was also considered a member of the *familia*, but only if she had come under her husband's control – literally 'entered his hand' (*convenire in manum*) – and that depended on the legal form of their marriage.[24] When passing into the legal control (*manus*) of her husband, the future wife had not only to give up her previous status of daughter (*filiafamilias*) in the paternal power of her father (*pater*), but she also had to leave the agnatic family of her birth altogether in order to enter into her husband's *familia* – or into that of his father (*pater*). After all, in principle *patria potestas* was not subject to any limitation by age but continued so long as the parties involved were alive. Consequently, it was only on the death of the *pater* that the members of his *familia* became legally independent (*sui iuris*). Anything like a statutory age of majority was totally unknown. Indeed, it was only on the death of their legal father that the adult married sons (*filiifamilias*) themselves became *patresfamilias* in their own right, even if they had already 'fathered' children. In other words, it was only on the death of their grandfather that these children passed under the legal power (*potestas*) of their natural fathers. In turn, this very same principle entailed that any Roman without a living male ascendant, even if he was a bachelor or still an immature boy (*pupillus*), necessarily and automatically was technically a *paterfamilias* – according to the letter of the law so precisely explained by Ulpian.

The legal power (*potestas*) of the father (*paterfamilias*) – a unique and specifically Roman institution, as another imperial jurist observed (Gai. *Inst.* 1.55) – was virtually unrestricted, extensive, and, in the strict terms of traditional law, even 'total'.[25] The father's concrete rights and powers make up an impressive list. His legal authority was established at birth: a child born in wedlock (*iustum matrimonium*) immediately came under the *potestas* of the *paterfamilias*. Once again, only the father had the right to recognize the newborn infant as legitimate and, as it were, worth rearing. It was he who raised the baby from the ground, where it had to be placed after birth, and by this gesture (*filium* or *filiam tollere*) he accepted the child as a new member of his *familia*. However, he could also refuse to raise it up; in that case, the child was to be exposed and left to die or to be enslaved.

This latter option was considered part of the notorious right of the *paterfamilias* to put his own children to death with impunity, even his adult sons and daughters (*vitae necisque potestas*). This was, and still is, considered the central or at least the most remarkable element of the rights of *patria potestas*.[26] The father could inflict punishment on all members of his *familia*, including his wife (if *in manu*), for offences that threatened the reputation of his *familia*. This sort of household jurisdiction included the right to have them put to death for serious crimes – without trial in a court and without the approval of magistrates or judges but only after taking the advice of a family council. Moreover, the father had the right to sell his children into slavery or deliver them into bondage (*nexum*).[27]

Other powers were less terrifying but could be of considerable practical importance. A father was also in control over his children's marriages. Not only did he have the decisive say when it came to arranging them, but the approval of the *patresfamilias* of both spouses (if both were still *in potestate*) was also formally required for a legitimate marriage, and either father could even compel a divorce. The *paterfamilias* alone could embark on legal action in court, and he alone held full ownership of absolutely everything that any member of his *familia* might possess or acquire. Once again, even his wife and his adult sons (not being *sui iuris*) had no independent proprietary or other legal capacity. His *patria potestas* thus included not only the full power of alienation, such as in the sale of property, but also the right to dispose of the estate by will and at will. Only the *paterfamilias* had any right to make a valid will (there were archaic solemn procedures for this legal act), and he was free even to transfer most of the patrimony outside his *familia* by disinheriting his own descendants and instituting unrelated heirs.[28]

Rules and Realities

Such a stark catalogue of powers is, however, far from being the whole story. The law and its underlying ideology – as conceptualized in the stereotype of the traditional family outlined above – presuppose and affirm the primeval character of the role of the *paterfamilias* in terms of powers and prerogatives. This construct is part and parcel of the ideology of a culture based on the asymmetry of all social relations in terms of power, influence, and rank and of a political culture in which power and obedience always and everywhere take precedence over individual liberties and each person's freedom of choice.

In reality, however, the *paterfamilias* was hedged about by certain legal limitations and, even more so, by social conventions and moral norms. Blatant violation of these norms could result not only in a serious loss of public standing and reputation (*dignitas*) but also in formal sanctions, such as a reprimand by the censors (*nota censoria*). The actual use of virtually all his powers was thus subject to qualifications and limitations, some of which, according to Roman tradition, were even enshrined in time-honoured statutes.

Once again, the notorious *vitae necisque potestas* is the obvious case in point: killing a son was certainly not a widespread practice of Roman fathers, let alone a daily reality. The *paterfamilias* was expected not to take any serious action without having consulted a council of male relatives and friends. Condemnation of sons to death was also restricted in many other ways, as the (rather few) notorious accounts of such extreme paternal severity, authentic or invented, regularly emphasise.[29] What these stories actually show is that killing a son was almost always a sacrilege, except in extremely rare circumstances – namely, when a father as consul embodied the state (*res publica*) and when this *res publica* had been badly represented or even betrayed by the son involved. The true character of this power was, once again, mainly ideological and at the same time, in a way, symbolic and formal.

Moreover, there seem to have been at least some rules regulating the gruesome practice of infanticide and child exposure. The extent of exposure and (therefore) its function as a method of birth control remain a matter of controversy.[30] The Twelve Tables, Rome's earliest law code, required that newborns who were sickly or severely deformed be exposed. But according to a law attributed to the founding hero Romulus, this could only happen after five neighbours as witnesses had approved, and according to the same law, exposure of sons and first daughters was forbidden. The law was probably invented, but this very fact in itself indicates that the practice, though taken for granted and widespread, was not altogether uncontroversial.[31]

The sale of children, or especially of adult sons, into slavery was certainly never practised in the middle and late Republic (if ever before). Even in early laws, there were limits to this paternal prerogative: daughters were not to be sold at all. And even if the sale of a son had ever been a real option, by the time of the Twelve Tables in the fifth century B.C., it was developing into a ritualized procedure through which a son could achieve freedom from paternal power (*emancipatio*). The father had to sell his son to a third party, who then formally freed (manumitted) him, and the son reverted into his father's legal power (*potestas*). This process of sale and manumission was repeated a second and a third time, at which point the father's legal claim was terminated.[32]

The legal principle requiring paternal consent to children's marriages was not, at least in the world of the upper class in Cicero's day, the most important part of the complex process of arranging marriages. Legally, there was no specific form of consent. 'Informed acquiescence' on the part of the *pater* would suffice, and certainly his active participation in the negotiations of terms with regard to dowry and other arrangements would count as such. Regularly, however, relatives – male as well as female – and the mothers of the prospective spouses in particular were involved in the process of matchmaking, not only as advisers and mediators but also in more active roles.[33] We know of a well-documented and particularly telling example of such a process and its niceties. While the *paterfamilias* Cicero was absent from Rome as governor of Cilicia, he left the arrangement of his beloved daughter Tullia's third marriage to his wife Terentia and to Tullia herself and even gave them permission to make decisions. Eventually he went along with their choice, although he was less than enthusiastic about the specific candidate and would have preferred somebody else as son-in-law.[34]

There were other spheres in which paternal powers in traditional law constituted a mere potential that a father would use only in extraordinary circumstances. It is very doubtful that the *paterfamilias* could enforce marriage against the will of a son or a daughter. And it was certainly unacceptable, at least socially, to bring about the dissolution of a marriage by the sheer exercise of *patria potestas*.[35]

Similarly, although a father had a very wide flexibility in the transmission of property upon his death, there were legal and above all conventional limits. The alienation of vital family property and especially the disinheritance (*exheredatio*) of children was also subject to restrictions and was rather uncommon. For example, sons in their father's legal power (*in potestate*) had to be instituted heirs or they had to to be explicitly disinherited by name. If a father failed to observe these and other formal rules, his will was null and void.[36] Moreover, disinheritance of this kind was regarded as appropriate only in extreme cases. To be cut out of inheritance in this way was a disgrace, a punishment for bad behaviour.[37] The normal expectation was that the *paterfamilias* instituted all his descendants as heirs – above all, those who under the law of intestacy, the substance of which was already laid down in the Twelve Tables, would come first in the order of succession. 'His own heirs' (*sui heredes*) included those who became independent of paternal authority on his death: his sons and daughters, his grandchildren by predeceased sons, and his wife, if she had been under his legal control (*in manu*).[38] All these family members, male or female, were to take equal shares.

Intestacy, it is true, was avoided among the propertied classes, and wealthy *patresfamilias* left wills in order to distribute their estates unequally (e.g., among sons and daughters), to take account of other kin than just the nearest blood relatives, and to specify all sorts of other legacies. In fact, the legal instrument of disposing of the patrimony by will was vital for the particularly flexible Roman patterns of transmitting property to the next generation. Testation as a legal system, as well as the underlying culturally conditioned 'strategies of heirship', became even more varied through the social recognition of kinship bonds through women as wives and mothers, which resulted in a gradual broadening of potential heirs to include in-laws (*cognati*) and in other changes with respect to women's position in the law of succession.[39] However, even if actual practices and, as a consequence, the law of succession had become very complex by the end of the Republic, the circle of 'his own heirs' (*sui heredes*) and their share in a patrimony remained at the centre of legal and moral notions about succession and about the general standards of equitable division of estates.[40]

Patriarchal control and power relations within marriages were also less straightforward than the traditional law would have us believe. By the end of the Republic, the old form of marriage (*cum manu*) had almost completely been replaced by another type of marriage in which the wife did not transfer to her husband's control.[41] This practice involved far-reaching legal as well as practical consequences. The wife – according to Cicero (*Top.* 14), a 'mere *uxor*', not a *materfamilias* in the strict sense – did not become a member of her husband's *familia* but retained her place in her natal kin group, as a daughter (*filiafamilias*) under the legal control (*potestas*) of her own father, or else remained legally independent (*sui iuris*) if he had died or had emancipated her. In the former case, she continued to participate in the property regime of her original *familia*, in particular, as a potential heiress. It was also a consequence of this legal situation that children born to this type of marriage did not become members of the woman's *familia* but automatically, by coming into the *potestas* of their *pater* on birth, belonged to the husband's kin group. In other words, these mothers and their children, though the children were born in legal wedlock, could never legally belong to the same *familia*.

There were other consequences with respect to property and inheritance. It was a well-established convention that a legal marriage (*matrimonium iustum*), in whatever form it was contracted, was accompanied by the transfer of a dowry (*dos*) from the bride or her *paterfamilias* to the husband.[42] The scale of the dowry naturally depended on the wealth of the parties involved. In any case, the dowry was not just a kind of wedding present but could be considerable and could include, for example, substantial sums of cash and landed property. In the non-*manus* form of marriage, however, the dowry did not pass into the full ownership of the husband (or, again, of his *paterfamilias*) – he remained in control of the dowry only for the duration of the marriage. The whole amount, except for a fraction for the children, had to be returned to the woman (if the marriage was dissolved either by divorce or by the death of the husband) or to her family (in case of her own death). Any other, nondotal property that the wife received – for example, through inheritance from her father – remained in her ownership. And if she was *sui iuris*, she then had a completely independent right to dispose of such property, which could be enormous among the upper classes.

In real life, the legal status of dowries and of other property in marriage only became relevant when a separation was pending.[43] In the first century, B.C. a divorce was a straightforward business and easy to bring about, either by mutual agreement or by unilateral repudiaton. In neither case did it involve recourse to the law, unless there was a dispute about the restitution of the dowry. It could be initiated by either party, husband or wife, by an action as simple as giving notice by 'sending a messenger' (*nuntium mittere*).

It is generally accepted, however, that this apparently rather extraordinary state of things was the result of a long and complicated historical process. According to tradition, in earlier times only the husband (or, again, his *paterfamilias*) had the right to divorce his wife, especially for adultery and other transgressions. If a transgression was involved, the husband was entitled to keep the dowry. If, however, a wife was divorced for no valid reason, her husband would be subject to sanctions, and he had to restore her dowry. From the mid-Republic onwards, as non-*manus* marriages became customary, the return of the dowry became the rule in any case. The widespread use of the new open marriage allowed the possibility of a divorce intiated by the wife or by her *paterfamilias*. This development, in turn, eventually made it possible for a wife (who was neither *in manu* nor *in potestate* but completely *sui iuris*) actually to divorce her husband on her own initiative and unilaterally.

There was yet another paternal right, the exclusive hold on any family property, which would seem particularly awkward and oppressive, especially in the everyday life of adult sons if they were members of the social and political élite. The great historian of Roman law, David

Daube, described the situation as follows:

> Suppose the head of a family was ninety, his two sons seventy-five and seventy, their sons between sixty and fifty-five, the sons of these in their forties and thirties, and the great-great-grandsons in their twenties, none of them except the ninety-year-old Head owned a penny. If the seventy-five-year-old senator or the forty-year-old General or the twenty-year-old student wanted to buy a bar of chocolate, he had to ask the *senex* for the money.[44]

Apart from the fact that such a succession of generations appears a bit too quick even by Roman standards, this scenario is patently at variance with all we know about social realities and the everyday life of the upper classes in the late Republic. Sons in Cicero's letters do not appear as suppliants asking for a little pocket money to cover trivial expenses. To a large extent, the fact that they did not have to beg for money was due to social pressures. A senatorial father was simply expected to provide for his son and prospective heir in a style appropriate to his son's and his own status. Upper-class education included some traveling to Greece, and embarking on the usual political career involved substantial spending. In Cicero's day a sufficient allowance could be as much as a knight's minimum annual income. After all, quite a few ambitious young men would put themselves up in temporary lodgings at exorbitant rents. But living on the Palatine or elsewhere near the Forum, the hub of political and social life, was definitely worth it.[45]

There was yet another, more formal means of mitigating the legal proprietary incapacity of an adult son (*filiusfamilias*) – the peculiar institution called the *peculium*. The *peculium* was a fund or even a piece of landed property that was granted by a *paterfamilias* to his adult son and that the latter managed on his own to generate income for use in business and in public affairs. Although the *peculium*, as well as any annual allowance, was revocable at the discretion of the *paterfamilias*, the upper-class son de facto enjoyed some financial independence that enabled him, for example, to establish a separate household and have a residence of his own, especially when he got married.[46]

Last but not least, there were certainly many fathers and sons who were on good terms, and the emotional bond between them would preclude rows over money. The ideologically inspired archetype of the old-style 'severe father' was counterbalanced by the concept of the benevolent and caring 'indulgent father'. This ideal and its complement, the virtue of filial respect enshrined in the typically Roman concept of *pietas*, play a prominent part in the Roman system of social values and code of behaviour.[47] This is also true for the general sentimental ideal of family life, which included not only parental love but also the expectation of conjugal affection and of a companionate (not necessarily equal) marriage.[48] Even upper-class arranged matches could lead to such a relationship. Strangely enough, in spite of an age difference of about thirty years, Pompey and Caesar's daughter Iulia were known to be an extraordinarily happy couple. However, this particular case (and the way it became the talk of the town) also shows that this degree of marital accord was extraordinary. It is certainly true that the reality of family life was characterised by a 'complex mixture of love and frustration, discipline and leniency, devotion and independence', as it was in other times.[49] In Roman society, as we shall see, these ideals were rather difficult to live up to.

Lifestyles and Life Cycles

We certainly have to allow for a broad range of variants with respect to familial and residential arrangements. Many aged parents could and probably had to live with their married children (or vice versa) – especially if they did not belong to the affluent élite and could therefore not afford separate accommodation or full-scale households with slaves and attendants. Even some upper-class families, it is true, continued to live in old-style patriarchal households in the late Republic. There was not only the example of the autocratic Ap. Claudius Caecus. There was also young M. Crassus (later famous for his wealth, if not for his political and military aptitude), brought up in the 'modest house' of his father, who had been consul in 97 B.C. and was a general honoured with a triumph and a censorship. The father's two older sons also continued to live there, even after they had married – and they all used 'to dine at the same table' (Plut. *Crass.* 1.1). Caesar's mother Aurelia, a widow who did not remarry, seems to have lived with her son and his second wife Pompeia.[50] And equally famous was the case of the brothers Aelii, no less than sixteen of them at one time, who all lived in a very 'little house' (*domuncula* is Valerius Maximus' word), together with their wives and a great many children, and jointly owned another property in the *ager Veiens* – one that needed 'fewer labourers than it had owners'.[51]

However, the pure type of the multigenerational extended and co-resident family was certainly not representative of lifestyles and

domiciliary habits in the late Republic. At least in the urbanized populations of the Western part of the empire, the residential family will usually
have consisted of the basic nuclear unit – husband/father, wife/mother,
young children, and possibly nubile daughters until they married.

This statement, in turn, needs some explanation and qualification.[52] On the one hand, we should remind ourselves that under any
circumstances, traditional or modern, the nuclear family is never static,
because it necessarily moves through various stages, from the founding
couple, to the couple with children growing up, to the couple whose
adult sons and daughters have married and left their parents' household.
On the other hand, the demographic factors mentioned above – fertility, average age at marriage, and life expectancy – deeply influenced
the life cycles and indeed lifestyles of individuals as well as families.

Plausible calculations on the basis of the assumptions described
above lead to some fairly clear, if general, results. As men married
relatively late and their life expectancy was limited, the proportion of
fatherless children at each age must have been rather high by modern standards. Probably up to one-third of young Romans had already
lost their fathers at the age of fifteen, when upper-class girls usually
entered marriage, and about half at age twenty, when all women typically married. Roughly two-thirds of Romans had no living father
at age twenty-five, when upper-class young men customarily married
and were generally considered to be fully competent to manage property. More than two-thirds were fatherless at thirty, when all men were
married and the privileged few among them usually embarked on a
senatorial career. When senators in their early forties competed for the
highest magistracies, possibly not more than one in fifteen had a father
alive.[53]

Conversely, however, infant and child mortality, as well as the
many other vicissitudes of life, could also lead to middle-aged or older
men being left without living issue. Consequently, adoption of promis-
ing youths with a good family background and sometimes even of adult
men of proven standing was not uncommon among the political class.
Adoptio, the transfer of a (young) man still *in potestate* to another family
with the consent of his natural father, and *adrogatio*, the act by which
a man who was legally independent (*sui iuris*) placed himself under the
potestas of another man by his own will, were elaborate legal procedures.
They served to secure the continuity of the *familia*, the transmission of
a great name, its cults, and its wealth.[54] A well-known familial tragedy
illustrates both sides of the coin. After one son of L. Aemilius Paullus,
the famous victor of Pydna, had been adopted by the Cornelii

Scipiones and another by the Fabii Maximi (cf. Fig. 1), their natural father, Aemilius, lost his remaining sons, and his own line became extinct.[55]

There are several conclusions to be drawn from these considerations: First, beyond the legal and social constraints mentioned above, the practical relevance of *patria potestas* must have been rather limited for objective reasons. Many Romans were already orphaned before adulthood, and quite a few women and most men were legally independent (*sui iuris*) when they married for the first time. Second, Daube's image of the consul holding *imperium* and commanding armies but still legally subject to his father did not, therefore, have much to do with social realities. This is obviously also true for the model of the patriarchal three-generation household: most Romans simply cannot have experienced living together under an aged autocrat.

The demographic realities mentioned above had further ramifications, especially as they were inextricably linked with other cultural practices. Although juridical texts and ideological constructs suggest the stability of the ideal-type *familia* over time and with respect to its composition, the actual situation must again have been very different. In reality, the core unit of the nuclear family was rather fragile, as it was subject to disruption and recomposition.[56] On the one hand, the combination of low life expectancy and the practice of late male and early female marriage necessarily led to many women being widowed when still young and in their childbearing years; on the other, many men were widowed as a result of a notorious risk of premodern societies: the death of young women in childbirth.

There was yet another common cause of the dissolution of marriages, namely, divorce, which was easy to obtain under the law and in practice. Evidence abounds for dozens of divorces in the relatively well-documented decades in the middle of the first century B.C., with an abundance of interesting details about possible motivations and actual moves, more or less public scandals, and omnipresent gossip whenever particularly prominent people like Sulla, Pompey, Lucullus, and Caesar were involved. It is, however, far from clear whether divorce was really extraordinarily frequent, at least among the urban élite of the late Republic and in comparison with the practices of other societies. Even a comprehensive compilation of all examples does not allow us to draw conclusions in terms of statistics, and we are still left with the problem of how to define 'frequency'.[57]

At any rate, we do know that remarriage – of widowers and widows as well as divorcees of both sexes – and even 'serial marriage' were

(div. = divorced; dec. = deceased; $\overset{86}{\infty}$ = date of marriage)

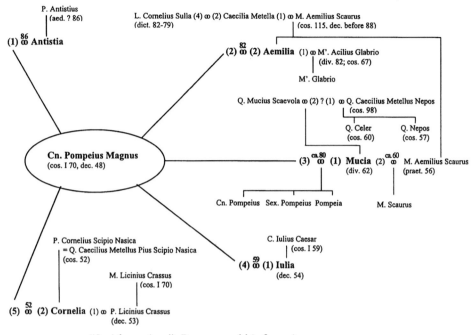

FIGURE 3. "Serial marriage": Pompey and his five wives.

usual by any standard, in spite of the cultural ideal of the woman who only had one husband during her life (*univira*).[58] Pompey's five marriages are a well-known case in point (Fig. 3). After divorcing his first wife Antistia in 82, Pompey married Aemilia in a match arranged by the dictator Sulla, who was keen to cement the alliance with the young man (Pompey was about 24 at the time). Aemilia was Sulla's stepdaughter by his fourth wife, Caecilia Metella, who had been the widow of M' Aemilius Scaurus, consul in 115 and influential *princeps senatus*. Before the marriage could take place, however, Aemilia also had to divorce her spouse, M'. Acilius Glabrio (the future consul of 67), although she was pregnant by Glabrio. Soon after her new marriage and her move into the new household, Aemilia gave birth to a son and died. A year or two later, Pompey married Mucia, another lady with an aristocratic background, who was well connected in more than one direction. Descended from a line of consuls, this daughter of the consul of 95 was also closely related to the famous Caecilii Metelli. In due course, probably in the early 70s, Mucia bore Pompey two sons – Gnaeus and Sextus – and a daughter. After his return from his Eastern campaigns in 62, however, Pompey divorced her (for her alleged adultery during his absence). About three years later and after abortive attempts to strike a marriage deal with the younger Cato, Pompey married Iulia, Caesar's only daughter. It was her first marriage, and she was probably still in her teens. Her engagement to another man had to be cancelled to make possible a match that was to seal the alliance between her father and her husband, who was by now in his late forties (and six years older than his new father-in-law). This union lasted only five years, until Iulia died in childbirth in 54. Finally, two years later, Pompey married Cornelia, daughter of his colleague in the consulship of 52, just widowed through the death of her first husband P. Licinius Crassus, who was the younger son of Crassus the triumvir and had been killed in his father's ill-fated Parthian campaign. Cornelia must have been about thirty years Pompey's junior. This marriage ended when Pompey was killed in 48.[59]

Even if Pompey showed more 'conjugal mobility' than other men of his class and standing, the pattern of remarriage was certainly not altogether unusual among the social and political élite.[60] Sulla and Mark Antony were also married five times each, Caesar three times, and a less prominent figure, a certain Statius Abbius Oppianicus, a knight from Larinum, had no fewer than six wives.[61] Mark Antony's third wife Fulvia had previously been married (and widowed) twice. Her first husband had been the famous tribune P. Clodius Pulcher, and her second the equally famous C. Scribonius Curio, tribune in 50 and Caesarian commander in the Civil War. Matches like these often served rather immediate political ends. They were obviously meant to seal alliances between prominent figures and their families – alliances that were sometimes as fragile and ephemeral as the marriages themselves.[62]

Results and Ramifications

Roman concepts and categories, with their emphasis on the law and on power relations, seem to be somehow at variance with the complex reality in which personal relations, bonds of family duty (*pietas*) and mutual obligation, ideals and norms, lifestyles, cultural habits, and social pressures are inextricably intertwined. Above all, the various meanings of *familia* and *domus* never fully coincided with the modern idea of the nuclear family. In many cases, concrete meanings were only clarified by particular contexts or were left ambiguous (often deliberately). Even if there was no precise Latin word for the nuclear family, the Romans could and did distinguish the core group of a household by describing it as constituted through its individual members, once again typically in relation to its male head: a man with his wife and children (*uxor* or *coniunx liberique*).[63]

Much epigraphical and literary evidence as well as general considerations indeed suggest that the type of family in which most Romans lived for most of their lives consisted of this triad. However, such a statement needs to be qualified in several respects. First, this household nucleus was surrounded by a spectrum of other relations under the roof of a single *domus*, including other blood relatives and slaves of both sexes. Second and more importantly, even if the life of any individual Roman, male or female, was characterized by the basic experience of the 'nuclear' constellation, that 'nuclear' group was not only subject to change due to the natural life cycles of its constituent members, but also to a change of these members that could be quite rapid, at least by modern standards. As premature death and divorce, remarriage, and relocation were common, many Romans successively formed, and lived in, several nuclear families.[64]

A middle-aged upper-class man might have had children by several wives and have raised all of them in his household. Their mothers – if still alive – might also have remarried and borne further children with their new husbands (who in turn might have children from previous unions). Many young Romans, therefore, grew up with a stepmother, sometimes not much older than themselves. When young Iulia married Pompey in 59, she became the stepmother of Sextus and Gnaeus, who were in their late teens by then (and whose mother Mucia had indeed married again and had another child; see Fig. 3). If Iulia had had children herself, they would have grown up with their half-siblings in one household. At the same time, serial marriage created networks of familial relationships that extended well beyond the immediate household, as many individuals had blood relationships with people outside the nuclear group that they were actually living in at any given point of time. These included not only uncles, aunts, and cousins of their own age but also half-siblings. That is why the Romans eventually came to conceptualize the structure of the family, both agnatic and cognatic, as stretching up, down, and also sideways from each individual.

In the end, then, it is less surprising that the Romans did not themselves develop a clear-cut concept for the ideal nuclear triad, which indeed does not appear to define the basic feature of their complicated familial worlds. These worlds were characterized by an extreme fluidity and by a variety of possible combinations of elements of nuclearity and other, more extensive associations. The Romans knew many different types of the 'complex' family created by remarriage and of the 'cognate' family (in the general sense of the concept),[65] which was centred on the individual and included kin in the male as well as the female line and also other persons linked to these relatives.

NOTES

1 Saller 1994, 72, 102; cf. Lacey 1986, 123–37; Thomas 1996, 228–40.
2 Dupont 1992, 105.
3 Cic. Sen. 37; cf. Pro Cael. 33–4; Val. Max. 8.13.5.
4 Val. Max. 4.4.7; cf. Cic. Sen. 56; Livy 3.26.8–12; Plin. NH 18.20.
5 Dixon 1992, 3–4, 21–4, 44–5; Saller 1994, 102–5.
6 Dixon 1992, 34; Saller 1994, 5. Cf. Gardner (1997) on what can be known about lower-class families.
7 Cf. Bradley 1991, 177–204; Dixon 1988; 1997.
8 Cf. the collection of source material (in English translation, with short commentary) in Gardner and Wiedemann 1991; cf. also Hanson 1999, 43–58.
9 Saller and Shaw (1984) and Shaw (1984, 1987) remain fundamental; cf. also Clauss 1973; Hopkins and Burton 1983, 69–107; Saller 1986, 11–17; Parkin 1992, 5–19 and passim; Saller 1994, 1–69; Martin 1996, 42–9, 53–7, and passim; Parkin 1999.
10 Cf. especially the contributions by P. Laslett in Laslett and Wall 1972. Cf. also Wall, Robin, and Laslett 1983; Dixon 1992, 12–19; 1997.
11 The best general introductions into the whole field are Rawson (1986) and Dixon (1988, 13–40; 1992, 1–35). For more detailed discussions of particular problems, see the contributions in Rawson 1986, 1991; Andreau and Bruhns 1990; Kertzer and Saller 1991; Burguière et al., 1996; Rawson and Weaver 1997; see also Bradley 1991, 1993.
12 Saller 1984; 1986; 1994, 71–153; see also 1997 and 1999.
13 Cf. especially Saller 1994, 9–69; Martin 1996; Parkin 1999 (contains further references).
14 Cf. also Syme 1987.
15 Saller 1984; 1994, 74–88; Garnsey and Saller 1987, 127–9; Dixon 1992, 1–3; Gardner 1998, 1–5.
16 Salway 1994, 124–8; Hanson 1999, 21–6.
17 Saller 1994, 74, 80–4; 1984, 336–7, 342–9.
18 Saller 1984, 349–55; 1994, 88–95; cf. Wiseman 1987; Clarke 1991, 1–29; Dupont 1992, 90–102; Wallace-Hadrill 1994, 3–16 and passim; Flower 1996, 185–209; Nevett 1997; George 1997; Hanson 1999, 60–6; Patterson 2000, 259–67; Hales 2000.
19 Wallace-Hadrill 1994, 8–10.
20 Vitr. De arch. 6.5.1–3; Cic. Off. 1.138–39; Att. 1.18.1, 2.22.3; Sen. Ep. 21.6; Tac. Dial. 6.2. Cf. Wallace-Hadrill 1994, 4–5; Saller 1994, 91–2; George 1997, 301–11 and passim.
21 Flower 1996, 16–59, 159–184, 185–222.
22 Plin. NH 35.7; cf. 35.6–8 passim. Cf. Wiseman 1987, 394–6.

23 The following definitions and descriptions are based on Crook 1967a, 98–113; Kaser 1971, 44–57; Lacey 1986; Rawson 1986, 7–9; Garnsey and Saller 1987, 126–9; Dixon 1992, 2–3, 40–5; Gardner 1998, 1–2; Saller 1994, 74–7; 1999, 184–93 and passim.

24 Cf. for details: Watson 1967, 19–25, 29–31; 1975, 9–19; Treggiari 1991a, 16–28.

25 Kaser 1938; 1971, 505; Watson 1967, 76–101; 1975, 40–51; Saller 1986; 1994, 114–32.

26 Cf. for details: Thomas 1984; Harris 1986; Saller 1994, 115–17.

27 Cf. Watson 1975, 117–19.

28 Cf. for details: Crook 1967b; Watson 1968; 1971; 1975, 52–70.

29 These accounts are fully discussed in Thomas 1984; Harris 1986, 82–9; Saller 1994, 115–17.

30 Cf. Eyben 1980–1981, 14–19 and passim; Harris 1982; 1994 (contains further references); and now see Shaw (2001 31–56) on the ritual of "raising the newborn."

31 Cic. *Leg.* 3.19; Dion. Hal. *Ant.* 2.15.2. Cf. Harris 1986, 94; 1994, 15–7.

32 XII Tab. 4.2 at Gai. *Inst.* 1.132–4; cf. Dion. Hal. *Ant.* 2.27.1–4 (another law of Romulus). Cf. for details and possible motives for this peculiar procedure: Gardner 1998, 10–13, 104–13;

33 Cf. Saller 1994, 119, 127–8; Dixon 1985; Treggiari 1991a, 125–45; 1991c.

34 Cic. *Fam.* 3.12.2; *Att.* 5.4.1, 6.1.19, etc. Cf. for the details: Treggiari 1991a, 127–34 (contains discussion of the evidence).

35 Treggiari 1991a, 146–7, 459–61; 1991b, 33–4.

36 Cf. for details: Watson 1971, 41–5; Kaser 1971, 586–9.

37 Cf. Crook 1967b, 120–2; Champlin 1991, 107–11; Saller 1994, 122–3, 164.

38 XII Tab. 5.4–5. Cf. on *sui heredes* and intestate succession: Kaser 1971, 85–90, 580–5; Watson 1971, 41–2, 175–87.

39 Crook 1986; Moreau 1986; Dixon 1988, 41–70; Champlin 1991, 111–30; Garnsey and Saller 1987, 141–7; Saller 1994, 163–80; Gardner 1998, 209–52.

40 Cf. Crook 1967a, 118–25; 1986; Champlin 1991, 111–17, 126–30; Saller 1994, 119, 163–8. Cf. also Thomas 1996, 240–5; Gardner 1998, 15–34, 276–8.

41 Cf. Crook 1967a, 103–5; Treggiari 1991a, 32–6; Dixon 1992, 71–83.

42 Cf. for legal details and concrete practices: Watson 1967, 57–76; Treggiari 1991a, 323–64; Saller 1994, 204–24.

43 Cf. for different formal procedures of divorce: Watson 1967, 48–56. Treggiari (1991a, 435–73) provides the best treatment and full documentation.

44 Daube 1969, 75–6.

45 Saller 1994, 124–5, on Cic. *Att.* 12.32.2, 14.7.2, etc. Cf. also Bradley 1991, 163–4; Dupont 1992, 106.

46 Crook 1967b, 119–20; Saller 1986, 16–17; 1994, 119, 123–5; Treggiari 1991a, 410.

47 Eyben 1991; Saller 1994, 102–114.

48 Dixon 1991, 1997.

49 Saller 1994, 7; cf. 5–8 passim; Dixon 1991, 111, 113.

50 Plut. *Caes.* 7.3, 9.3, 10.2; Suet. *Iul.* 13 (Caesar); cf. Dixon 1988, 200; Bradley 1991, 163.

51 Val. Max. 4.4.8; Plut. *Aem. Paullus* 5, 6–7.

52 Cf. for example, Treggiari 1991a, 410–13; Champlin 1991, 104–7.

53 Saller 1994 120–1.
54 Dixon 1992, 111–13; Gardner 1998, 114–208; Corbier 1991a, 63–76 and 1991b, 135; 142–3.
55 Polyb. 31.28.1–3; Liv. 45.41.8–12; Plut. *Aem.* 5.5, 35.1–3, 39.10, etc.
56 Saller 1986, 15; 1994, 228–30; Rawson 1986; Bradley 1991, 125–49; 1993, 242, 249; Dixon 1992, 7–9, 10–11; Martin 1996, 45–59 (contains a detailed critique of the straightforward 'extended'/'nuclear' family dichotomy).
57 See Treggiari (1991, 473–82; 1991a) for details and documentation; Dixon 1992, 9–10, 66–9.
58 Humbert 1972; Moreau 1986; Bradley 1991, 156–76; Treggiari 1991a, 235, 500–2, and passim; Corbier 1991a, 49–63; 1991b, 128, 134–7; Thomas 1996, 254–8.
59 Haley 1985; Bradley 1991, 166–8.
60 Saller 1984, 342–9; 1994, 74, 95–6, etc.; cf. also Thomas 1996, 228–30, 235.
61 Moreau 1986; Bradley 1991, 136–8.
62 Dixon 1985; Dupont 1992, 111–12; Corbier 1991b, 136–42.
63 Saller 1984, 342–9; 1994, 74, 95–6, etc.; Treggiari 1991a, 411; Thomas 1996, 228–30, 235.
64 Treggiari 1991a, 411–12; Saller 1994, 81–3. Cicero (*Off.* 1.54, 1.58) and the famous jurist Q. Mucius Scaevola (Gell. *NA* 4.1.17) presuppose a distinction between parents and married couple: *pater, materfamilias*, and children on the one hand and (*tota*) *domus* (and the *familia* of slaves) on the other. Cf. also Dixon 1991, 9–11 and passim.
65 Shaw 1991, 71–2; cf. also Moreau 1986, 187; Bradley 1991, 169–72; Martin 1996, 58 and passim.

6: WOMEN IN THE ROMAN REPUBLIC

Phyllis Culham

⟨⟩

IMAGES OF WOMEN IN THE EARLY REPUBLIC

Romans of the imperial period believed that many women in the archaic era inspired others by their practice of Roman virtues whereas other early women's actions illustrated the consequences of vice. Lucretia, for example, committed suicide after she was raped by an Etruscan prince of Rome while her father and her husband were away. He had threatened to kill her and a male slave in her bed as evidence that he had surprised her in base adultery. That threat to her modesty (*pudicitia*) compelled her to comply with his demands. After he left, she summoned her husband and father. They arrived with friends, and she swore them all to revenge against the rapist. Then she killed herself to prove her innocence and to keep her example from justifying a lack of chastity (*castitas*) in other women. The vengeance she had inspired supposedly brought down the Etruscan dynasty that controlled Rome and thereby led to the founding of the Roman Republic (Livy 1.58–60; Dion. Hal. 5.32.4–35.2).

The myth of Lucretia exemplifies many Roman virtues: it stresses the supreme womanly virtues of *pudicitia* and *castitas*; its heroine is a woman who held lineage and family to be more important than her personal interests; it allows a woman to exhibit the Roman virtues of bravery and determination; it demonstrates that her role in preserving the family from shame was a vital one; it ties her moral qualities to the establishment of the Roman state. Another famous example of death in defense of *pudicitia* was Verginia, killed by her father to preserve her from rape (Livy 3.44–48, Dion. Hal. 11.28–38).[1] One recent book argues that *pudicitia* was not so much a sexual virtue as the feminine equivalent of male loyalty (*fides*), a measure of fidelity to male kin and to household.[2]

Nearly five hundred years after its creation, the Roman Republic was destroyed in a series of civil wars. During the period of "restoration" under Augustus, whom we count as the first emperor, Livy and Dionysius of Halicarnassus wrote highly colored literary versions of this legendary material about the dawn of the Republic. Neither was the modern sort of historian who aims at getting as close as possible to a sound understanding of what people actually experienced in the past. The Roman Livy wanted to inspire his contemporaries, whom he found degenerate, with moral examples (*exempla*) they could follow (or avoid, as appropriate). Dionysius, a Greek rhetorician, endeavored to find intellectually and morally attractive aspects of Roman culture that he could ascribe to Greek origins. Valerius Maximus and Plutarch also told stories about women in the early Republic. Valerius, writing in the mid first century A.D., offered a compilation of moral *exempla* under thematic headings rather than a historical narrative that purported to explain events. Plutarch, a Greek with a superb philosophical education, wrote even later (c. 100 A.D.). Although he had a serious scholar's fascination with Roman antiquarian material, he too usually pursued a moral purpose.

Little material from the pre–Punic War Republic, let alone the regal period, can be taken seriously as history; the dramatic tales of women are even less historically reliable than the rest, with the possible exception of a few stories connected with events that might have been noted in priestly annals or preserved (with distortion) in the lore of great families. Romans of the late Republic and the imperial era, who thought that the early Republic valued chastity and modesty in a woman above all other virtues, believed that personal and familial morality was good for the state and immorality bad. They attributed to elite women the ability to enhance or to degrade the moral order and thereby the security of the state. Consequently, they also believed that the early Republic had enforced morality among women through the unquestioned authority accorded the male heads of lineages.

Some later sources purported to offer citations to legal material from the dawn of the Republic, but none of the early codes survived into the late Republic (if the material had indeed been collected into "codes"). Later writers were working, at best, with what historical compilers and legal scholars of the mid Republic believed those laws had been. Dionysius and Plutarch believed they had material from the "Laws of Romulus," although Romulus himself is transparently mythical. Dionysius thought the laws provided that a husband could kill a wife for adultery or for drinking wine. Men were required by that same code to raise all sons born to them but were required to raise only the first-born daughter. Plutarch apparently believed that the Laws of Romulus forbade wives to divorce husbands but allowed a husband to divorce a wife for poisoning his children, adultery, or counterfeiting his keys.[3] If a man were to put his wife aside for any other reason, he would lose half of his property to his wife and the other half would be offered to Ceres (Plut. *Rom.* 22). Although these provisions appear to be extremely restrictive for women, they would also have protected women from expulsion from their households for frivolous reasons.

Most modern scholars assume that these later narratives made memories of archaic customs into "law codes," but the ancient material also preserved implicit contradictions. The extreme reaction to women's drinking caught the later imagination;[4] however, the archaic Roman elite had long been culturally entwined with their Etruscan counterparts, who shocked Greek contemporaries with integrated dinner parties and women who enjoyed wine with enthusiasm.[5] Many writers have noted contradictions embedded in the Roman tradition on divorce. Even the Laws of Romulus supposedly allowed for it, and Cicero believed that the famous Twelve Tables did too (*Phil.* 2.28.69). Dionysius, although obviously mistaken, asserted that the first divorce did not occur until the mid Republic in 231 B.C. (2.25.7); later Romans apparently believed that their earliest law codes provided for divorce, even though those provisions were used rarely, if at all.

Finally, Roman legend allowed one potent public role to women of the archaic era, namely, intercession. The prototypical instance was the articulate intercession of Hersilia and other captured Sabine women. They dashed onto a battlefield in a rain of spears and interposed themselves between their husband-captors and the fathers and brothers who were assaulting Rome to reclaim them. It is significant that the myth made Hersilia the only married woman to be abducted (by accident, of course) and that some versions have her (re)married to Romulus himself (Livy 1.13; Dion. Hal. 2.45–6; Plut. *Rom.* 14–16). The Sabine women supposedly won over their male kin by showing them how their Roman husbands treated them with "goodwill and honor."[6] Another famous instance was Veturia, the mother of Coriolanus, who together with his wife Volumnia interceded successfully to stop her son's treacherous attack on Rome (Livy, 2.40). Clearly, the ancient sources assume that Roman women were always citizens of the state as well as members of families, which cannot be said of their Greek contemporaries.

WOMEN IN RELIGION IN THE
ROMAN REPUBLIC

Richlin commented that "the study of Roman women's religion is still in its infancy,"[7] and the same can fairly be said of attempts to assign meaning to women's participation in the Republic's religious observances. Roman women were not confined to women's quarters within households, nor excluded from public space, nor relegated to women's observances. Women had apparently been necessary to the performance of certain vital Roman rituals even before there was a Republic. One problem confronting the modern scholar is that Romans themselves did not often remember the original significance of the older aspects of their religion.

The most obvious example of the antiquity and centrality of women in state cult was the college of Vestal Virgins, who are surely the most famous Roman religious figures today. Later authors believed that the college of Vestals was so ancient as to antedate Rome itself; witness the legend that Romulus was born to a Vestal who had been raped. Girls who were to be Vestals had to be between six and ten years old, free of any physical imperfections, in possession of two living parents, and in the authority of the male head of the family (*patria potestas*). They were selected by the chief priest (*pontifex maximus*) from eminent families and were committed to serve for a minimum of thirty years. Many chose to remain Vestals for life. They served Vesta, the goddess of the hearth, a very old deity who was rarely personified as a woman. There were no anthropomorphic images of her in her own dwelling (*aedes*) in the Forum; she was simply and directly represented by the fire on her altar, which served as the great hearth for Rome. The Vestals lived together near the *aedes* in the Atrium Vestae and had to maintain the fire on Vesta's altar.

Vestals have attracted much scholarly as well as popular attention because of their utterly anomalous appearance and status. They wore a distinctive hair style otherwise used only by brides on their wedding day. As soon as a Vestal entered the Atrium Vestae as a child, she was removed from the *patria potestas* of her father or grandfather. In a state that always claimed that the family was vital, Vestals were supposedly the only Romans without family. If a Vestal became ill, she would not be sent to her own birth family but to the home of a selected matron.[8] Although women who were *sui juris* (i.e., not under the authority of any man) and male minors not in *patria potestas* could make wills and dispose of property only with the consent of a tutor, a Vestal needed no tutor.

When a Vestal went out in public, she was accompanied by a *lictor*, a man bearing symbols of authority. *Lictores* otherwise accompanied senior magistrates, not priests (with the sole exception of holders of the very ancient position of *flamen Dialis*). Rome had no full-time male priests, but the Vestals were supported by the state and were full-time professional clergy, along with the priestess of Ceres and Proserpina. Although most women were apparently segregated into women's seating in theaters, Vestals were assigned particularly good reserved seats. They perhaps wore the *stola*, usually reserved for married women. In short, Vestals lived outside the categories of gender, legal status, and even age.

Of course, the Vestals were central to the celebration of the festival of the Vestalia in June when the *aedes* was open to other women for eight days. They made the *mola salsa*, the holy spelt cake, for that occasion. This nasty-sounding salted cake was used at observances for Jupiter Optimus Maximus and at the Lupercalia. The Vestals used ashes from the festival of the Fordicitia in April and blood from the October Horse in a concoction for the Parilia festival. The Vestals need not actually all have been present for the collection of their ritual materials or for the use of their products at the festivals, but they were certainly deeply integral to and well informed about the Roman festival year. In August they attended the Consualia, a particularly riotous festival with chariot racing. In times of crisis they made special appearances, for example, in the procession at the Amburbium when Caesar was marching against Rome in 49 B.C. The Vestals must have worked with many male priests and magistrates. They also participated in the quasi-private observances for the Bona Dea, the Good Goddess, whose worship was otherwise reserved for matrons in distinguished households, and they made offerings of their hair at the temple of Juno Lucina, who eased childbirth.

Both ancient and modern authors have paid more attention to Vestals' derelictions than to their duties.[9] Vestals were beaten (in the dark and through a curtain to preserve their modesty) if they let the sacred fire go out, but loss of virginity was a more serious offence. Vestals who were thought unchaste were buried alive. Vestals were sometimes accused of unchastity when something had gone wrong militarily or when political tensions were rising. However, the religious mechanisms of investigation – interpretation of prodigies and consultation of oracular books – often allowed elite men to claim to resolve a pressing problem without inquiring into such irresolvable questions as whether a Vestal was actually a virgin.[10]

Other female religious functionaries also demonstrated that women's religious involvement was not limited to women's observances.

The wife of the *flamen Dialis* was called the *flaminica Dialis*. The couple had to observe onerous religious prohibitions of great antiquity. The *flaminica* had a role in purificatory ceremonies in February and made a public appearance in the procession of the Argei (straw figures) in May. The two served as a pair; the death of either partner led to the appointment of another couple. Thus, one of Rome's most prestigious and ancient priesthoods required the constant participation of the priest's wife. Women were ordinary participants in the Roman crowds at major festivals, but there were some rituals that assigned roles to one gender or the other. Many women's observances featured respectable married women (*matronae*). The point of these rituals was usually to secure fertility and health.

Slaves and freedwomen had their own observances. The Nonae Caprotinae in July commemorated a legendary event during the sack of Rome by the Gauls in roughly 390 B.C., when maids (*ancillae*) supposedly gave themselves up to be raped by the invading barbarians in order to save their mistresses. The festival must have been fun for both slave women and citizen men. Men erected shacks of fig-tree branches just out of town and offered the women a feast. Slaves wearing their best clothes joked with the men and fought a mock battle among themselves.

Even prostitutes had a role in religious observances. They were apparently included in the little understood festivities on 1 April. That was the date of the Veneralia, supposedly a festival of Venus, when women also honored Fortuna Virilis (Masculine Luck). Ovid thought that prostitutes might even join married women in cleansing and redecorating the cult statue of Fortuna Virilis (*Fast.* 4.133–4). The month of April offered many opportunities for prostitutes to engage in religious activity. On 23 April 181 B.C., a second temple to Venus Erucina (Venus of Eryx, known for her temple prostitutes) was dedicated outside the city. Roman prostitutes began to make offerings there on the anniversary date, which happened to be that of the Vinalia, when wine casked the previous fall was opened. The Floralia in honor of Flora was on 27 April. It was known for licentious games and performances. In the early second century A.D., Juvenal implied that prostitutes performed naked and fought in gladiatorial contests at the Floralia (6.250–1).

Women's participation in major observances on the Roman festival calendar reveals some noteworthy patterns. Women tended to be associated with the worship of deities conceived of as female, yet most of those same deities had male priests. Few of the temples or observances that featured one gender actually excluded the other. Women's participation in the ritual calendar of the Republic carefully and visibly marked status differences among women, just as political rank awarded to men was displayed in the stripes on their togas. The assembly of women for public observances meant that women met outside their own households and had a chance to share news. It also gave them experience at organizing themselves to undertake religious functions like the adornment of statues.[11]

Cults of Greek origin introduced new and foreign elements. The celebration of the Bona Dea in early December, for example, muddled the categories of public and private, male and female, and Greek and Roman. We do not even know if the goddess was originally Roman or Greek. Her festival was held in the home of a current magistrate, and the elite women selected to attend were there because of their husbands' electoral standing. The husband of the household was, nonetheless, expelled from the *domus* for the duration of the rite. The goddess's real name, the rites, and the ritual implements had to be kept hidden, reminiscent of the secrecy observed in the famous cult devoted to Demeter and Kore at Eleusis and of the Athenian exclusion of men from the festival of the Thesmophoria. In spite of the private performance of the ritual, Cicero described it as performed *pro populo Romano*, on behalf of the Roman people (*Att.* 1.12–3), and the Vestal Virgins attended with the distinguished matrons. The celebration apparently amounted to quite a party, with musicians and wine.[12] A notorious scandal erupted in 63 B.C. when P. Clodius, disguised as a hired female musician, attempted to sneak into the home of Julius Caesar while the rites were being held there. The Vestals assumed authority on the scene and made the very Roman decision that the rite had to be repeated. The consequences of that evening rippled through Roman politics for years.

WOMEN IN THE MID-REPUBLIC

It is a truism of Roman history that the Punic wars in the third century B.C. were a political, military, diplomatic, and economic watershed for the Roman Republic. Changes in these spheres of activity inevitably had a great impact on women, eventually giving them more wealth and autonomy. In the crisis of the Second Punic War, much of which was fought in Italy, Roman leaders were desperate for explanations and solutions. Traditionalists among them claimed to find religious causes and cures, and much of the associated religious activity involved women.

Some of the ceremonies to placate the gods required women to assume visible public roles. In 218 and 217, as the war began, and again in

207, prodigies required matrons to make offerings to Juno Regina.[13] In 207, matrons had to select treasurers from among themselves to handle their contributions. Some of them conducted a public sacrifice. Selected maidens joined the matrons in performing a hymn in procession, which undoubtedly required practicing together. The events of 207 introduced "a new chapter in women's affairs,"[14] presumably because prosperous farmwomen were knit into social networks in Rome. Another important occasion was the arrival of a deity new to Roman cult, the Great Mother (Cybele), from Phrygia in Asia Minor. A group of elite matrons met her at Rome's port at Ostia in 204 and conducted her to Rome.[15] Since women's participation in state cult was vital, conduct that seemed to preclude their participation drew attempts at regulation. After the disastrous battle of Cannae in 216, Fabius Maximus and then the rest of the senate were supposedly uneasy at the public lamentations by women all over the city. The senate regulated the public conduct of matrons by limiting mourning to thirty days so that they would be available for rites in honor of Ceres and Proserpina.

The year 215 saw the passage of the *lex Oppia*, which regulated the public appearance of women by keeping them from wearing more than a small amount of gold or purple garments[16] and riding in a carriage within a mile of the city of Rome except when performing public rites. This purely sumptuary law was meant to enhance social cohesion in a time of extreme hardship. There are two possible additional contexts for the prohibition on the use of carriages. The first is the "excessive" mourning of the previous year; taking away carriages might well have cut down on public appearances by elite women. A second problem might have been the engagement of a few elite women in extraordinary politicking.[17] Although women were still able to carry out all their functions in official observances, the prohibition on appearance with a large amount of gold would have affected some elite women who participated in those rites.

Of course, when the state was faring so badly and women were already under scrutiny, Vestals were in danger. Two Vestals were found wanting in chastity after Cannae. One committed suicide before she could be buried alive. The unchastity of two Vestals was so extraordinary and so dangerous a prodigy that it required a rare expedition to consult the Delphic oracle. In 206 a Vestal who let the flame go out was scourged. Livy's highly colored account of the war years often featured women behaving badly. In 213 many Romans were supposedly turning away from Roman rites to practice newer cults, but Livy claimed that women in particular were neglecting the traditional religion. The cult of Venus Verticordia, Changer of Hearts (toward chastity) was introduced in 215, supposedly because many women left alone by the war had entered less than respectable relationships. Those dedication rites too required the election of women to participate, although it is not clear who the electors were (Val. Max. 8.15.12; Plin. NH 7.120).

Women were much more visible in public during the war years. The absence of most able-bodied men would have left women less subject to male authority. The intrinsic dangers of the situation would have driven many women to seek the most current news or to supplicate the gods. Anyone inclined to view women censoriously would have had more opportunities to do so as they appeared at public shrines and other well-frequented sites. Although immanent danger to the Roman home front ended with the Second Punic War, constant deployment of manpower throughout the Mediterranean world in the second century B.C. kept Roman gender relationships from reverting to what they had been before the war.

The culture wars of the second century B.C. illustrate elite male disapproval of some social changes. Cato the Elder and others reacted to a group of concerns that they probably perceived as interrelated: a rapid increase in elite wealth from wars in the cash-rich eastern Mediterranean; decline of other families into poverty with the loss of male labor; an increase in cultural and social influence from wealthy, sophisticated Greek-speaking states in the eastern Mediterranean; elite women's acquisition and even control of financial resources; and, probably, a decrease in women's tendency to defer to men in various contexts. During the Second Punic War, women had been viewed as cultural symbols and moral bellwethers. Cato and others of his persuasion saw women in the postwar era as harbingers of a new materialism that threatened old values and social cohesion.

Plutarch's life of Cato was written nearly two and half centuries later, and Cato's devotion to the ideal of a respectfully affectionate nuclear family resonated with Plutarch's own sentimental inclinations. Nonetheless, Cato's ostentatious insistence that his family came before private (not public!) business was part and parcel of the cultural program he was always ready to urge on others. We can now recognize that enthusiastic defense of traditional configurations of the family is probably evidence that these configurations are in the midst of change. In spite of some conventional jokes, Cato never expressed resentment of women in general. He insisted that men should not strike their wives or indulge immoderately in commercial sex (Plut. Cat. Ma. 20.2, 9.6; for old jokes, see 9.6, 17.7, 20.2).

Cato's own marital choices devolved from the same fears that led him to oppose the repeal of the *lex Oppia*. After the death of his first wife, who had been "more noble than wealthy," he consorted with one of his slaves. She did not behave in an obsequious fashion and thereby annoyed the rest of the household, so he married the young daughter of one of his clerical assistants (Plut. *Cat. Ma.* 20.1, 24.2–4). Cato's fear of upheaval over relative status in his household, his desire to maintain the affections of his family, and his avoidance of wealthy wives closely match the concerns of Plautus' contemporary comedies.

The movement to repeal the *lex Oppia* came in 195 B.C. Livy's version of the debate in the senate was his own creation, but the reaction from elite women themselves was much more important. Women arrived from the countryside and surrounding towns to form a crowd that blocked streets into the Forum and besieged the houses of tribunes supporting the law (Livy 34.8.1–3). Livy had Cato claim that the two tribunes proposing repeal inspired the riot, but Roman matrons had practiced organizing themselves in the religious observances of the Second Punic War. Most of those women could not have been there if male kin had objected very strongly, and all voters were male. Men who supported the repeal were probably moved less by arguments for equity like those Livy provides than by the desire to have their female relatives display their economic success as well as by the desire to live amicably with them. Cato, who feared rising social disparities, wanted to shut down most avenues of elite and competitive display. He suffered a rare loss on the issue of regulating women's appearances; the *lex Oppia* was repealed.

Just a decade after the repeal of the *lex Oppia*, another incident revealed male uneasiness with women's preeminence and with new cultural and social developments. The alleged Bacchanalian conspiracy of 186 B.C. is surely the most discussed event of the second century among modern students of Rome. Noted above was the Republic's concern to maintain the worship of Ceres and Proserpina in 216 after Cannae; clearly the senate was not intrinsically hostile to Greek rites, women's rites, or meetings for rites other than those of the old state cults. A bronze copy of orders issued by the senate in 186 suggests the kinds of restrictions that were imposed on the Bacchic cult centers (*CIL* I^2.581 = *ILLRP* 511 = *ILS* 18). Men were not to be priests in the Bacchic cult; no member of the cult could hold an official-like position or be appointed an official or act as one; there were to be no secret rituals. What survived the suppression and destruction of Bacchic cult centers in 186 were small informal groups composed mainly of women and with exclusively female leadership.[18]

The restrictions on the popular Bacchic cult were intended to prevent the corruption of Roman manhood implied by initiation into a woman's cult suspected of engaging in moral degradation and even crime. Roman men, men with Latin status, and men from peoples allied to Rome could not enter a meeting of Bacchic women without specific authorization by the senate (lines 7–8; allegations of effeminacy at Livy 39.15.9, 13–14). At the same time, the senate wanted to ensure that the traditionally female leadership of the cult could not be confused with authoritative Roman priests and magistrates.[19] Women malfeasants might be executed by their male guardians. Otherwise the state saw to executions. Informers collected rewards big enough to make them wealthy, so the freedwoman prostitute who had come forward with the initial accusations certainly profited from the episode.

The decade of the 180s saw repeated outbreaks of senatorial hysteria. Livy believed that women poisoners had operated earlier in the Republic. In 331 B.C., 170 women were convicted in what he considered the first poisoning trials in Rome. Two women, singled out before the roundup of the 170, had evoked suspicion by making concoctions that they claimed were medicinal – and that probably were. It could simply be that an outbreak of illness was blamed on human agents and that women healers were targeted.[20] The affair was a precedent for the belief that conspiratorial networks of Roman women were out to murder their husbands and magistrates of the state. According to Livy, Bacchic worshipers had been murdering people everywhere too (39.8–19). Fear of gender and ethnic corruption in the Bacchic rites was clearly part of the atmosphere of the 180s, during which decade Roman magistrates saw cabals everywhere. Two thousand people (presumably including women) from rural areas were condemned for poisoning in 184. In 180 the senate reacted to the death of a consul and other eminent men by setting up two special investigations, one for poisoning in Rome and one for poisoning in rural areas; the rural commission condemned over three thousand alleged poisoners, presumably of both genders. A generation of relative calm intervened until the levelling of accusations in 151 against the wife of a serving consul and another woman married to a former consul. Both women were condemned and handed over to relatives for execution.

Elite women attained new levels of affluence and public visibility in the mid Republic, and that was just one element in a bundle of social changes evoking unease in many senators. Newly extreme class differentiation created very wealthy women and desperately poor women. Male mortality in the century's wars left women of all classes unsupervised.

Wealthy women might aspire to influence or even power and attempt to attain their goals by violence, some thought. The justly resentful poor of both genders were caught up in mass condemnations.

Women in the Economy of the Roman Republic

Since elite families competed at displaying prestige, and since there was simply more wealth available to distribute in the second century, the disposition of dowries became an ever more important issue. Increasingly elaborate contracts governed large dowries under various unpleasant contingencies: "It is not clear whether the Romans were more materialistic than moderns or simply more realistic and efficient about their materialism."[21] Whatever the legal arrangements, people began to think of dowries as wives' property, although husbands administered them. Upon the simple dissolution of a *sine manu* marriage, the dowry was restored to the wife's family, either intact or in timed payments. Since dowries could include slaves, household goods, land, or cash for investment, repayment might be very disruptive for the husband and even for his family.

Plautine comedies of the era depicted the well-dowered wife whose husband feared her anger. This was a Roman stereotype, not borrowed along with plots from Greek originals. Underlying that stereotype was male uneasiness toward women who held the power conferred by significant assets. Even a woman's slave might fail to show adequate respect for his mistress's husband. Mere residence didn't mean that one obeyed the man of the house. *Aulularia* in particular illustrates the tensions of the time. It has long been recognized that lines 498–502, in which extravagant wives want purple clothing, gold, carriages, maids, and carriage attendants, show that the play was closely contemporary to debate over the repeal of the *lex Oppia*. Plautus assumed that women who brought significant assets to a marriage would expect that more of the income of the household would be expended on them. Conversely, women without dowries were not in a good bargaining position. Given the dearth of formal markers for *sine manu* marriage, gossips apparently assumed that a woman who entered a relationship with a man without bringing assets with her was really entering concubinage. That supposition could prove to be a great inconvenience to their children.

Losses in war from the time of the Second Punic War to the end of the next century left more women legally independent, whether it was husbands or fathers who had been killed. Unless wills dictated other arrangements, women inherited equally with all others legally subject to a man. The *lex Voconia* of 169 B.C. was an odd attempt to deal with the resulting issues. Since its limits were expressed not in absolute amounts but as a percentage of the estate, the law cannot have been intended primarily to keep women from amassing wealth, as Cicero realized (*Rep.* 3.17). Nonetheless, it kept any woman, even an only daughter, from inheriting more than half of an estate in the highest property class, given that she could not be named heir nor take more than the heir in a legacy. The general tenor of the law encouraged the naming of male heirs in the top financial strata, and it probably represented an effort to keep funds immediately available to men to support senatorial careers, a point of interest only to the most elite families.[22] The interests of multiple daughters in these elite families received a blow in the *lex Falcidia* of 40 B.C. at the end of the Republic. It limited to 75 percent the total portion of the estate that could be withheld from the heir and given in legacies. Doting fathers tried to evade all these provisions with significant success, and the distribution of wealth in dowries helped.

In legal theory, women never fully controlled their own assets until the Empire opened the prospect of freedom from the institution of *tutela*, the necessity of having some of one's financial activities approved by a tutor. Most scholars have recognized that *tutela* cannot have been very onerous. First, *tutela* simply did not cover most financial transactions. Women could spend income on whatever frivolities they wished or invest it to make themselves more money, and they could alienate personal property. The only items that could not be transferred were the old *res mancipi*, the items the landholder needed for farming. Indeed, *tutela* was later assumed to be onerous for the tutor, who might often be disinclined to pay much attention to a task whose supposed beneficiary was unlikely to thank him for his interference.

This understanding of the original purpose of tutors for women sheds light on another issue: the comparatively late development, under Greek influence, of the theory that women should have tutors because they were feather-brained (*propter animi levitatem*). The famous legal scholar Gaius in the late second century A.D. referred to this as a common but false legal theory of his own day, and he ascribed its origins to the *veteres*, the jurists of the late Republic and early Empire (Gai. *Inst.* 1.144.190–1). Gaius pointed out that the theory of mental incapacity as the origin of *tutela* was incompatible with the fact that women's tutors were not liable for financial losses (as were tutors of minors) and that tutors in his day were compelled to consent to just about anything. Perhaps men retained a pointless legal institution to preserve the appearance of male authority over property.[23]

Other women were commodities to be managed. Roman household slaves had immeasurably better lives than did those who labored in the fields, and the great majority of female slaves would have been in the home. In the late Republic, a literate elite among female slaves served in comparatively cushy clerical positions in the great households. Still, household slaves were routinely beaten and sexually exploited. Female slaves as young as seven were given to older male slaves as rewards. Plautus is often thought to have been comparatively sympathetic to slaves for a Roman writer, but the modern reader is shocked by casual orders to hang up and beat two older female slaves in a scene that we are apparently supposed to find rollicking (*Truc.* 775–82). Nor were female owners any more moderate, judging from Sassia's calling in of contract torturers to deal with her household.[24] Commodification meant that slave women were routinely separated from their children by the sale of children, the exposure of children as surplus (much more likely for girls), and the sending of a child or mother to another house owned by the same elite family. Slave women as well as men in household service frequently obtained freedom, but they had continuing financial and social obligations to their former owners.

Women at the upper and lower ends of the free economic spectrum had economic motives for limiting births. Although it was up to a free father to decide whether to expose a child, women could use birth control. Abortion was widely attempted but was considered a preemption of the father's right to decide. Except for an exclusive, educated elite, most Romans were confused about the distinction between contraception and abortion. Many readily available herbals were abortifacients and might act contraceptively or abortively when consumed orally or introduced into the vagina; popular confusion was therefore understandable. Women also attempted abortion by means of inserting implements into the uterus. These might perforate the uterus and cause uncontrollable bleeding or a fatal infection; however, this method must have produced more reliable abortifacient results than did herbal concoctions (especially at later stages) or no one would have risked it. Ancient intuitive reactions and modern attempts to generate statistics both suggest that the reproductive rate at the end of the Roman Republic was remarkably low for a premodern society; witness Augustus' attempts to encourage the birth of children by legislation rewarding marriage and reproduction. The question is whether the reproductive rate fell to low levels – levels that would persist throughout most of the

Empire – primarily because of the exposure of infants or because of contraception. The modern literature leans toward contraception.

Since many households in the late Republic were sites of economic production, the location of women primarily in households did not separate them from business concerns. The country villas of the elite were supposed to be economically productive as well as pleasant seasonal residences, but even the slave corps on a farm needed women's labor. The agricultural manuals, which offer a highly idealized picture of life on the well-managed farm, assume that a farm manager (*vilicus*), who might be a slave, a freedman, or even of free birth, needed a wife (*vilica*) for good management and his own happiness. The *vilica* herself was either a slave or a freedwoman. She supervised other female slaves in such traditional women's tasks as making clothing for the field slaves and cooking. Columella conceived of her household duties as encompassing work in all the buildings of the complex, including pens and stalls as well as kitchens (*Rust.* 12.3). Cato made her a sort of matron stand-in who was supposed to see to the ritual well-being of the household (*Agr.* 143). Other rural women slaves were much less fortunate. When they were not assisting the *vilica*, they were sometimes made available to male slaves as rewards. Some were even sent out with male shepherds to help tend herds, cook and carry firewood, and serve as sexual rewards (Varro, *Rust.* 2.10.6–8).

Many houses in town during the Republic leased out shop space along the street, and small retailers sold and often slept in such shops or in small freestanding structures. By the end of the Republic, there were already shops to appeal to elite men and women. We know much less about the artisanal workforce of the Republic than we do about that of the Empire, but we can assume that women who worked in operations like goldsmithing establishments and perfumeries were of freed status at best and had probably been given or sold to a skilled male worker who had originally been a slave himself. In any case, neither Roman housing nor commercial activities were strongly segregated by socioeconomic stratum, and women of all classes and legal statuses passed through the crowded streets together. That is probably one of the factors behind wealthy women's desire for a carriage or at least a protective phalanx of maids.

Even in elite households women were supposed to work wool. The belief that good women worked wool was the equivalent of the equally romanticized and rhetorical conviction that Roman men should be farmers of simple tastes living in the countryside. Even the *vilica* was supposed to work wool whenever she had no immediate duty

(Columella, *Rust.* 12.3). Lucretia was working wool when she was seized by the evil Etruscan prince. "She worked wool" (*lanum fecit*) and similar expressions were shorthand on tombstones for "she was a conventional wife who maintained respectability." When Augustus tried to lead a return to what he believed were simpler, better values, he boasted that his wife and daughter made clothes for him (Suet. *Aug.* 73). Spinning and weaving equipment could be set up in the light of the atrium, so they also served as a visible symbol of the enterprise and respectability of the *materfamilias* to anyone who walked through the door. In short, the making of wool thread, cloth, and garments was invested with so much symbolism and even emotion in the late Republic that it is difficult for us to determine how it all actually happened. In affluent households, the wife might supervise a crew of slaves (usually women) who produced garments for the whole household, while the surplus could be sold.

Some unlucky women worked in the hospitality and entertainment sectors of the economy. The vast majority were slaves, although a fortunate few attained freed status and even some affluence. Rome and other Italian cities were full of inns and brothels, which might not have been easily distinguished. Most of the female musicians who were ubiquitous by the late Republic were more like musical prostitutes than performers who might be offered respect. Their training started in early childhood. Some belonged to the great households, and others with talent might have performed mainly in those households. Of course, purely commercial establishments varied, and more luxurious brothels attempted to attract a more elite clientele. The inhabitants of such houses would have had greater material comfort than those relegated to curtained cubicles in shacks or to streetwalking.

A few especially clever women from this milieu sometimes acquired elite male friends who introduced them to new circles and, probably, to affluence. Aulus Gellius (4.14) preserved a delightful vignette of the independence exercised at the highest economic ranges reached by women in the hospitality profession. In 151 B.C., a drunken magistrate went to the house of Manilia and tried to force his way in. She threw a rock at him; he charged her with assault. In a rare show of unanimity, all ten tribunes vetoed her prosecution on the grounds that his conduct had been outrageous. In the late Republic, women from the highest political elite, enslaved female attendants, and musicians intermingled in privately organized parties that served as occasions for public travel and consumption. Elite women with their servants – but sometimes without their husbands – attended dinner parties, musical evenings, beach parties, boating trips, and spas. Among the political elite, men often called on women in the absence of their husbands to conduct business or simply to offer social greetings. They incurred no disapproval, not even from the absent spouse.

WOMEN IN THE LATE REPUBLIC

Modern authors have sometimes used the term "emancipation" to describe the status and activities of women by the end of the Republic. They were not referring to legal processes that formally changed the status of women so much as inferring from the sources that women were more visible in public, more involved in political activity, and less encumbered in both public and private realms than they were to be again for the better part of two millennia.[25] Women and men were both subjected to extreme class differentiation in a republic in which political power and even the ability to exercise rights of citizenship rested on economic status. The power of the Republic was monopolized by an elite among males in the senate, and it is not surprising that the spectacular examples of emancipation were women from those very influential households.

We can only guess at the significance of some developments within the public religious sphere, in which women had long been active. Vestals were not simply trapped in political controversy; they provoked it. As early as 143 B.C., a Vestal intervened in the rancorous, polarized politics characteristic of the late second century and first century B.C. Appius Claudius Pulcher scheduled a triumphal parade that the senate had refused to authorize. A tribune tried to exercise his veto to stop the procession and to pull Claudius from his chariot. His daughter Claudia, a Vestal, clung to her father, staying in the chariot during the parade (Val. Max. 5.4.6; Cic. *Cael.* 34). In a remarkable constitutional anomaly, the personal sanctity of a Vestal had trumped the veto power of a tribune.[26]

Another Vestal paid a price for her public activity. In 121 B.C., the year in which Gaius Gracchus and his adherents were murdered, the Vestal Licinia dedicated an altar and other items at the temple of the Bona Dea. The political significance of her act has been debated, but it would be foolish to think it unrelated to her trial for unchastity in 114–113. Although she and one of her colleagues were acquitted, a senatorial faction had them retried in a special court. They were condemned along with all their alleged lovers and accomplices (Dio Cass. 26.87; Asc. 39–40).[27]

In spite of the dangers, some Vestals continued to take political sides openly. Vestals interceded with Sulla on behalf of Julius Caesar's life and property. Intercession was a respectable activity for women, but Caesar had no relatives among the Vestals, and Sulla was a very dangerous man who was already responsible for the death of thousands. This politicization led to more accusations of Vestals in 73 B.C. The charges were heard before special courts rather than before the closed circle of the *pontifices*, and all involved were acquitted. In the mid 60s, the *pontifex maximus* lost his ability to choose Vestals; he was required instead to pick twenty candidates from whom one girl would be chosen by lot. Perhaps that was an effort to depoliticize the position.

Funeral orations for aristocratic women also rendered women politically visible. Julius Caesar seized the occasion of his aunt Julia's funeral in 69 B.C. to make a programmatic statement by the display of images of her husband, the notorious Marius, for the first time in twenty years (Plut. *Caes.* 5.2). Eulogies for women did not have to be taken up with lists of offices and could be devoted to political manifestos of principle. When Porcia, sister of Cato the Younger, died in 45, her devotion to her brother's politics gave some an opening for anti-Caesar ranting and presented a problem for those trying to stay neutral (Cic. *Att.* 13.37.3, 13.48.2).

On rare occasions, elite women entered forensic arenas themselves, an event so striking that Valerius Maximus (8.3) could collect the anecdotes of women who engaged in public argumentation. Cicero (*Ver.* 2.1.94) expressed horror at dragging respectable women into court to be stared at, but a woman who maintained a noble bearing in the unfamiliar legal arena could emerge with her reputation enhanced. Sempronia, daughter of the great Cornelia, was summoned to an irregular popular meeting by a hostile tribune. She faced down his browbeating and a hostile mob and thereby became the protagonist of an anecdote on aristocratic unflappability (Val. Max. 3.8.6).

A small group of women within the senatorial elite, namely, the daughters of rhetoricians and legal experts, had access to rhetorical and legal education and even religious lore. The most spectacular instance of this phenomenon in the Republic was that of Hortensia, daughter of Cicero's great legal and rhetorical rival Hortensius. In the chaos that followed Caesar's assassination, a triumviral edict of 42 B.C. required 1,400 of the richest women on the census list to submit to a special levy on their property. Some of them supposedly tried to approach the triumvirs through the women of their families. When that failed, they marched up to the triumvirs' stand in the forum. It was Hortensia who articulated their position, and bystanders agreed that she had her father's flair (App. *B Civ.* 4.32–4; Val. Max. 8.3.3; Quint. *Inst.* 1.1.6).

Much of the argument concerning the role of women in the late Republic has focused on a small set of women to whom ancient sources attribute great influence. On the one hand, it must be said that the allegation of influence by women was a conventional political insult, that women were respected only as representatives of legitimate family interests, and that women who stepped outside narrowly bounded legitimate interests were subject to hostile vituperation. On the other hand, one must concede that women were integral parts of their powerful families, that evidence points clearly to their involvement with state affairs, and that men, too, usually acted on behalf of family and lineage and found that compatible with their own interests. One must in any case discard any evidence heavily infected with the exaggeration or stock insults of comedy and rhetoric.

The epitaph *CIL* 6.1527 (31670) = *ILS* 8393, which dates from the period of the civil wars, has been much studied by scholars interested in the social history of the senatorial class, since it preserves a husband's idealized portrait of his wife and their marriage. The text, which might have served as her eulogy, speaks of her deference to her husband, care of her home, and duty (*pietas*) to her natal family in terms that might have been used centuries earlier.[28] It has been less often noted that the wife was apparently sophisticated in her understanding of the law and not reluctant to use it in defending family interests. As a young, just married woman whose husband and brother-in-law were overseas, she drove the prosecution of the murderers of her father and his wife, who would otherwise have avoided punishment in the chaos of civil war. The family of her father's wife then tried to overturn her father's will. After she faced them down, they gave up without a suit.[29] Her husband thought it highly laudable that she took particular care to protect the interests of her sister, who had entered a *cum manu* marriage and was legally in a different family. He could have added that she was extremely brave; many were murdered for less at the time. She also worked wool.

This eulogy is a reminder that women's lives were as disrupted as were men's by social, legal, and political chaos during the Republic's death throes, which went on for two decades. Scholars usually counsel students not to project the public actions and interventions of women in the highest stratum of power onto women in the lower strata. Perhaps the reverse would be more valid, and one should assume ubiquitous heroism by women in the preservation of family interests.[30] Perhaps the degree of women's emancipation or independence of action at the end of the Republic can best be measured by the degree of Augustus' determination in the imperial era to restore the ideology of what conventionally worded tombstones call the *domiseda*, the woman who confined her interests to her household.

NOTES

1   The tales of Lucretia and Verginia illustrate the common theme of rape. Romulus, the founder and first king of Rome and his twin Remus were born from the god Mars' rape of the Vestal Virgin Rhea Silvia (Livy 1.3.11–4.3). Romulus and his band of freebooters were able to turn their rude settlement into a city only by seizing the daughters of their Sabine neighbors. Lucretia's reaction to her rape set rolling the cascade of events that would establish the Republic. Beard noted that the rape motif in many Roman foundation legends embarrassed Livy, who carefully politicized the stories to take the focus off the violence and stress the policy implications. See Beard 1999, 1–10.
2   Fantham et al., 1994, 225.
3   There are difficulties in understanding the crucial lines of Plutarch's text. Many modern scholars have taken the "poisoning of children" to mean abortion, but that is not the only possible interpretation.
4   Dionysius was echoed by Pliny (*NH* 14.14), Valerius Maximus (6.3.9), and Cato as quoted in Aulus Gellius (10.23), where other examples of disapproval of female drinking are cited.
5   Ath. *Deip.* 12.517d–e; Hodos 1998, 202–3.
6   Plut. *Rom.* 19; Mustakallio 1999, 57.
7   Richlin 1997, 331.
8   Staples 1998, 143.
9   Beard 1995, 172.
10 Staples 1998, 136.
11 See Richlin (1997, 344) on "women's localities" at religious sites.
12 If the participants consumed any of the wine, as their usually more repressed Athenian counterparts were wont to do at the Thesmophoria, that is an interesting anomaly in view of the supposed disapproval of women drinking. Juvenal (2.82–7, 6.314–17) maintained that the participants drank the wine all too enthusiastically in the Empire.
13 Affluent freedwomen made a contribution to Feronia, an old deity of the central Italian woodlands who came to be associated with Libertas, perhaps as a result of this occasion (Livy 21.62.6–9, 22.1.8–18). Note the sequestering by status in publicly assigned religious roles.
14 Bauman 1992, 27.
15 At that point, we leave history and enter the realm of creative historiography. Supposedly one of the matrons, Claudia Quinta, was of suspect *pudicitia*. She called on the ship, which had run aground, to follow her if she were chaste, and then she tugged it free. Later versions of the story made Claudia a Vestal. The name Quinta looks like a birth-order nickname. If so, that would indicate that the highest ranking families like the Claudii might rear five daughters, at least according to the assumptions of later authors.

16 Probably at least some restriction on the color of clothing is involved (Culham, 1986, 236–7).

17 Supposedly, Pomponia, the mother of Scipio Africanus, had been campaigning for his brother to be elected *aedile*. The anecdote will not work chronologically as it stands, but since it is from the more sober Polybius (10.3.4), it is possible that women might have used the highly respectable cover of religious activities to engage in contacts for other purposes.

18 Flower 2002.

19 Flower 2002.

20 One would simply dismiss the whole episode as a historiographic invention directed at the families of certain named women if it were not that the conviction of so many women was seen as a prodigy and led to the appointment of a dictator to drive in a ceremonial nail to dissolve the situation as though it were a plague. That should have led to entries in priestly annals.

21 Dixon 1992, 67.

22 Gardiner 1986, 175.

23 Gardiner 1986, 22.

24 Cicero (*Clu.* 177), on the basis of which Saller (1991, 160) makes the argument that there were beating and torture specialists available for hire by the end of the Republic.

25 For contrasting views on the "emancipation" of women, see Dixon (1983) and Hillard (1989, 1992).

26 The story is caught up in the historiographical motif of the hauteur of the Claudii, so caution is necessary.

27 Licinia's dedication at the temple of the Bona Dea was presumably taken as (and was probably meant to be) a recognition that the killers of Gaius were not patriots but murderers whose act ought to be expiated and as criticism of the intransigent attitude of the majority of the senate. The *pontifex maximus*, the great jurist P. Mucius Scaevola, ruled that the dedication had been defective (Cic. *Dom.* 136–7). The astonishing accusations that Licinia and her colleague Aemilia had taken multiple lovers simultaneously as well as had affairs with each other's brothers is the surest sign that senatorial factional politics was involved.

28 Contemporary inscriptions even referred to a standard catalogue of women's virtues that rendered it difficult to praise an individual and win belief; cf. *CIL* 6.10230 = *ILS* 8394 = *FIRA* 3.70. Probably the complaint about formulaic expression was itself formulaic.

29 Hemelrijk 1999, 113.

30 The question of competing imperatives of human nature in time of crisis was of great interest in antiquity and led to Appian's collection of anecdotes on how women acted during the civil wars (*B Civ.* 4.23.93–5).

7: THE REPUBLICAN ECONOMY AND ROMAN LAW: REGULATION, PROMOTION, OR REFLECTION?

Jean-Jacques Aubert

⌀

T he half millennium that runs from the revolution of 509 to the beginning of the principate saw the transformation of the Roman state from a regional power into a world empire. Thus, to speak of the Roman economy in the singular is misleading, as there is little justification, other than the common denominator of the political institutions referred to as "republican," to consider in one and the same chapter an economic system that underwent the most drastic changes, while showing endless diversity with regard to times and places, structures and scales, or actors and goods. Clearly, however, a family of small farmers settled in the vicinity of Rome throughout the period would have seen much less change than their counterparts in the more rapidly developing area surrounding Paris from the Renaissance until our time. Although a substantial part of the population in Antiquity remained involved in agricultural production at all times, the Roman people of the republican period went through a series of social and economic revolutions of global historical significance. Roman imperialism in Italy and around the Mediterranean Sea was accompanied or followed by economic and fiscal exploitation of newly formed overseas provinces. It resulted in uneven demographic growth, the enrichment of the upper classes, some degree of urbanization linked with colonization, and the development of municipal institutions. There was an increase in long-distance trade in both imports (food, slaves, metals and other kinds of raw material, and luxury goods) and exports (finished goods such as pottery and gold and silver coins), made possible by monetization and the development of a reliable communication network of roads, rivers,

Note: All dates are B.C. unless specified otherwise.

and harbors. Massive transfers of people (slaves, traders, soldiers, and to some extent colonists), the adoption of Latin or Greek as linguae francae, and the gradual, though fragile, pacification of conquered territories and seas brought in the most advanced level of globalisation the world was to know before the twentieth century.

Ancient literary sources had little to say about economic history but recorded nevertheless a few striking facts and events. The annalistic tradition, chiefly represented by Livy and Dionysius of Halicarnassus for the earlier period, mentions recurring tension between patricians and plebeians about debts and land use. The authors' perception is blurred by the long period separating the events and the earliest available records. For the second and first centuries, we dispose of contemporary sources, such as the treatment – normative rather than descriptive – of the villa phenomenon in the agricultural treatises of Cato the Elder and Varro. Retrospective accounts of dubious completeness and accuracy, such as Tacitus' history of moneylending (*Ann.* 6.16) or Pliny the Elder's history of the Roman coinage (*NH* 33.42–47), provided ancient historians with a basis that they either had to build upon or try to ignore. Ancient economic history, however, still relies to a large extent on those countless, though cryptic, allusions spicing the works of republican and imperial writers: the record of the discovery of the monsoon at some point during the Hellenistic period by an anonymous merchant bound from India to the Red Sea on a voyage allegedly motivated by greed is adduced rather casually by the same Pliny (*NH* 6.100–101, 106), even though it may have been one of the most significant changes in the organization of seaborne trade, from which the Roman aristocracy was to derive so much pleasure in the form of imported luxury goods. How many events of such importance failed to be recorded in Antiquity or were forgotten in the process of transmission is impossible to establish.

Archaeological remains can supplement the literary sources in significant ways:

• Periods of greater or lesser activity in public building, such as the so-called mid fifth century crisis,[1] are documented by the relative dating of excavated architectural structures.
• Regional surveys show large-scale villas coexisting with or replacing more modest dwellings in the countryside, such as the Valle d'Oro near Cosa in Southern Etruria,[2] and they point to changing patterns of agricultural settlement.
• The typology of discarded amphorae may reveal far-reaching dietary revolutions, such as the extension of wine drinking, combined

with bread eating (instead of the eating of porridge [*puls*]), among the Roman population in the second and first centuries.[3]

The study of the number of identified dies on coins from hoards or individual finds, in connection with what is known about metal supply (from mining, war compensation, taxes, confiscations and fines, and demonetization of previously existing foreign or domestic currencies), allows some attempt at quantifying the size of monetary issues.[4]

Greek and Latin inscriptions from the republican period, though less numerous and diverse than for the imperial period, shed a different light on both public and private affairs. Like papyri from Hellenistic Egypt, they keep cropping up at a steady pace, thus providing us with new material that will most likely change or qualify our views on the ancient economy, too often shaped until recently by biased or naive representations offered by literary writers of the Augustan and imperial periods.

Modern perceptions of economic structures and phenomena can be informed by common historical sense and sometimes by models borrowed from other preindustrial societies.[5] They will never amount, however, to more than the sum of a collection of individual facts anchored in specific times and places, from which historians are free to extrapolate or not, in order to construct their own representation of a phenomenon too complex to be grasped, even though the sources available to them are more explicit, diverse, and abundant.

Aware of these limitations, I have decided to present some aspects of the economic history of the Roman Republic from a legal perspective. Methodologically, it can be observed that practically all types of sources can be put to use to illustrate how Roman treaties, statutes, edicts, and jurisprudence both affected and/or reflected economic and social life. Roman law, public and private, developed as a product of Roman society, adjusting to existing though changing circumstances while aiming at shaping the context in which the next generations would operate. Treaties and statutes were regarded as precisely datable in the ancient written sources; on the other hand, edictal law elaborated by mostly anonymous magistrates (praetors, aediles, and provincial governors) and jurists' law are admittedly more loosely or less clearly connected with specific historical circumstances, while offering better evidence for understanding the theoretical background of legal institutions bearing on economic life. The examples discussed below have been selected for the importance of their subject matter, for their antecedents and aftermath, for their function as turning points in a series of events that illustrates a larger phenomenon, and for the many different ways they have come down to us. They all have great relevance for students of economic history, even though some may appear rather marginal. This short chapter does not claim to be a comprehensive treatment of the subject.

THE FIRST TREATY WITH CARTHAGE (509/7)

According to the annalistic tradition, reported by Polybius (3.22–23), the economic history of the Roman Republic begins with a treaty between Rome and Carthage concerning seafaring and the definition of zones of economic and military influence. All commercial transactions concluded in Sardinia and Africa were strictly regulated, limited to purchases or sales pertaining to the maintenance of (commercial?) ships, and controlled by appointed civil servants (the Carthaginian equivalent of later Roman *apparitores*). By contrast, in Sicily, then partly a Carthaginian territory, Roman traders enjoyed the same rights as anybody else, such as Greeks and natives. It is remarkable that the earliest reported agreement of the republican period would deal with sea trade and include special provisions about commercial preserves and zones of free trade, where international commercial law would apply. Whatever the historicity of the deed, it shows that some second-century historians were ready to accept early republican Rome as a would-be maritime commercial power in the western Mediterranean Sea.[6] It also reminds us that early Rome was surrounded by more powerful and possibly more advanced neighbors (Etruscans, Greeks, and Italic peoples) with whom an economic relationship had to be established and regulated.

THE *FOEDUS CASSIANUM* (493)

That Rome would conclude treaties with Latin peoples at an early date comes as no surprise. Military victories were a source of enrichment, public and private, and allies, like partners, were to share in the profits of war (*praeda, manubiae*),[7] in the form of movable goods, slaves, livestock, and land. Treaties were also a likely way to sanction private ownership outside the city limits. The *foedus Cassianum*, which was to define public and private relations between the Roman state and Latin communities down to the first century, acknowledged private contracts (*idiotika symbolaia*) as enforceable in a court of law (Dion. Hal. *Ant. Rom.*

163

6.95.2). The extension of the *ius commercii* to noncitizens was a first step towards economic imperialism and suggests that production in agriculture and/or manufacture yielded regular surpluses to be exchanged through barter or sale for other desirable items.[8]

THE TWELVE TABLES (451–449)

The economy of the mid fifth century is best reflected in the first and only "codification" of the law during the republican period. The work of a committee of ten, the majority patricians, the Twelve Tables had supposedly benefited from the influence of the Greek cities (more likely in southern Italy than in Attica), which then formed a monetized society. The text is partly lost but can be reconstructed on the basis of numerous quotations and paraphrases in later writings.[9] Various provisions attest to the concept of civil liability with (pre?)monetary compensation (*poena;* cf. I.14–15), acknowledge private property (denied through theft or *furtum;* cf. I.17), allude to periodic market days (*nundinae;* cf. III.6),[10] and take for granted slavery and manumission of slaves (*servus,* I.14 and *passim; libertus,* V.8; and *mancipium,* VI.1), which is distinct from the special status of debt-bondage (*nexum,* VI.1). Interestingly, we find here an early trace of a master's civil liability (*noxa*) for his slave's wrongdoing, the seed of a major development centuries later in Roman commercial law. The overall picture is that of a predominantly rural community, busy with preventing, punishing, or compensating damages caused to crops (*fruges, seges, acervum frumenti;* cf. VIII.4–6) and working on estates (*fundus,* VI.3, or *hortus herediumve,* cf. VII.2–5) organized along the lines of a managerial unit with its staff (*familia,* V.3–10) and capital (*pecunia,* V.3–10), its exact nature a mystery, though probably not cash. Wine and vineyards are attested to (VI.6/8 and perhaps X.6), but reference to olive cultivation is notoriously missing. Pastoralism is sporadically mentioned (VIII.3), but draft animals are more visible (*iumenta,* cf. I.3 and VII.6–7; *quadrupes?* cf. VIII.2). Local roads exist, to be maintained and repaired by private owners (VII.6–7). Most remarkable in terms of commercial law is the fact that deceit (*fraus*) and malice aforethought (*dolus malus*) are explicitly called unacceptable in certain kinds of relationships (between *patronus* and *cliens,* cf. VIII.10/21, or between *tutor* and [*pupillus*], cf. VIII.9/20). Last but not least, real contracts (*nexum, mancipium*) formally performed *per aes et libram* ("by means of bronze and scale") can be further specified by additional oral statements regarded as legally binding. The door is wide open for the introduction (in the late third or early second century) of consensual contracts, a major step in the history of trade.

The picture put together here contrasts with that derived from the above-mentioned treaties in that the community lurking behind these provisions seems to form a rather closed society, showing no sign of commercial contacts with more distant overseas markets. The monetary system rests on weighed bronze ingots, certainly not the most practical instrument for trading.[11] But one should not infer too much from such a lacunary text, whose primary purpose was not to provide later historians with a complete and accurate description of the society that elaborated and interacted with this law.

One disputed question raised in connection with the Twelve Tables concerns loans and rates of interest. In a famous and problematic text, Tacitus (*Ann.* 6.16) mentions as part of the Twelve Tables (VIII.7) a provision restricting the rate of interest to eight and a third percent (monthly?), a provision reenacted in 357 by a plebiscite sponsored by two plebeian tribunes, M. Duilius and L. Menenius (Livy, 7.16). Historians of the Roman Republic have debated the reasons why the same provision would have been reenacted less than a century after its first introduction. Whether it had been ignored or reversed in times of crisis (the Gallic sack of 386) or wrongly attributed by Tacitus to the decemviral legislation is irrelevant. Whatever the right solution, it is obviously part of a historical trend in which loans in kind or in money were seen as a threat to the social order and had to be controlled through legislation. The sources record no fewer than twenty-seven bills aimed at limiting the rate of interest (either by prohibiting loans altogether or permitting them only in special circumstances) or protecting debtors against unduly harsh treatment inflicted on them by their creditors.[12] The proto-history of Roman banking was a period of strict regulation, though the laws were difficult to enforce.

THE *LEX POETELIA PAPIRIA DE NEXIS* (326/313)

Even the prohibition of loans at interest introduced by the *lex Genucia de feneratione* of 342 (Livy, 7.42.1)[13] did not succeed in freeing debtors from the fear of sustaining drastic physical consequences to their persons. Defaulting on loans entailed capital punishment (Twelve Tables III.6) or enslavement, either as *servi* or as *nexi*. The former were sold abroad (Gell., *NA* 20.1.47: "*trans Tiberim peregre*"), while the latter were expected to pay off their debts in bondage (Varro, *Ling.* 7.105), that is, within the community. The condition of *nexus* upset the social order more visibly, since the demotion attached to personal liability was, theoretically speaking, reversible, but brought dishonor upon the debtor unlikely to be compensated for by an eventual turn of fortune. A tale told by Livy (8.28), of a young debtor who was sexually harassed by his creditor and cruelly abused and who then appealed to popular sympathy and protection, provided the context for passing a law whereby debtors would no longer be held physically liable for their debts. The abolition of *nexum* in the late fourth century was regarded in later historiography as a new beginning of freedom and a major step in the "Conflict of the Orders" pitting patricians against plebeians. It was probably a turning point in the economic history of republican Rome as well, in that credit could be extended with a new kind of security: landed property or personal belongings. It also underlines the marked distinction between contracts and delicts as sources of obligations. Until then, failure to repay a debt was considered a breach of trust (*vinculum fidei*) and was dealt with like a fault (*noxa*) deserving punishment (*poena*); from then on, loans became a purely economic matter, guaranteed by family assets.[14]

It is probably no coincidence that our sources reveal the simultaneous appearance of the first professional bankers (*argentarii*) in Rome (310 B.C.; Livy, 9.40.16)[15] and the decision of the Roman state to issue its own coinage instead of relying on foreign (i.e., Greek) coins. The question of rates of interest would come up again later on, but it would no longer be possible to control it solely by legislation.[16] The availability of cash, of whatever denomination or metal, was henceforth a factor to be reckoned with. The level of indebtment of the upper classes would also bear on the deterioration of the political climate at the end of the republican period.

THE *PLEBISCITUM CLAUDIANUM* (218)

While most of the legislation passed during the third century pertains to political matters, this should not obscure the fact that this period saw crucial economic developments, including those associated with the expansion of the empire to Sicily and Sardinia at the end of the First Punic War (264–241). The military victories of the Roman fleet resulted in the creation of overseas provinces and the opening of new markets. The conditions were ripe for the development of seaborne trade, with all the associated risks and opportunities for profit. Commercial ships were expensive to build and maintain, and only a substantial investment in capital could enable a mariner to embark on the potentially profitable business of long-distance shipping. Members of the upper classes were prime candidates to risk their wealth in such tricky ventures. Shortly before the beginning of the Second Punic War (218), the plebeian tribune Q. Claudius proposed a bill barring senators and senators' sons from owning and operating commercial ships able to carry more than 300 amphorae, a size deemed more than sufficient to transport products from their agricultural estates to the market. While Livy (21.63) described the plebiscite as a measure devised by politicians close to the people to weaken the economic interest of the elite, it is clear that the main beneficiaries of the prohibition were those who were rich enough to invest in large ships without being senators, namely, the increasingly visible and ambitious members of the equestrian order.

The sheer fact that the prohibition was enforced over a long period – long enough for Cicero to invoke it against Verres in the early 60s (2 Verr. 5.17.44–18.45), in spite of an apparent rhetorical admission to the contrary – and was reenacted by a lex Iulia repetundarum (possibly in 59)[17] shows that a strictly political explanation, intended as an illustration of the Conflict of the Orders, is not acceptable. The law was taking aim at the natural tendency of the upper classes to engage in lucrative activities likely to distract them from the life of leisure that was necessary to the conduct of public affairs. It was not profit itself that was regarded with suspicion, but big profit attached to big risk-taking (despite Cic. Off. 1.42.150–1). Incidentally, Livy's phrasing suggests that senatorial landowners were expected to produce agricultural (and other) surpluses to be transported on smaller boats (i.e., riverboats) and sold at nearby markets. The measure, like the ban of senators from public contracts,[18] was also meant as a check on corruption and designed to prevent potential conflicts of interest for provincial governors. Consequently, large-scale seaborne trade was left in the care of those who chose not to pursue a political career, as illustrated by one branch of the gens Sestia from Cosa, whose name appears on large quantities of amphora stamps found widely, in particular in a late second or early first-century shipwreck off Marseilles. Although the evidence of the stamps is directly connected not with wine production or distribution, but with the making of the containers, it is remarkable that Cicero (Att. 16.4.4) records that some Sestii owned large ships in the year 44, while other members of the same family had embarked on a full-scale political career.[19]

As of the late third century, the Roman state appears to have become careful to restrict the economic activities of its ruling class in order to ensure its survival by preventing its possible economic and hence social and political demotion as a result of entrepreneurship gone awry. This concern fell short of keeping the senatorial order from getting involved in commercial ventures, but it did force the senate to devise new schemes that would prove beneficial to the further development of commercial law. At the same time, the *plebiscitum Claudianum* turned out to be the first of a series of measures intended to define the dignity and economic role of the ruling order.

THE *LEX METILIA FULLONIBUS DICTA* (220/217?)

Pliny the Elder provides, again, the only ancient reference to a rather bizarre *plebiscitum*, in the context of his treatment of earth and chalk (*cretae Cimoliae*). Several varieties were known to have different properties, and *Sarda* (from Sardinia), *Umbrica* (from Umbria), and *saxum* were used by fullers in the laundering of garments. Both *Sarda* ("*inutilis versicoloribus*") and *saxum* ("*inimicum coloribus*") were used exclusively on white cloths, while *Umbrica* was mainly in demand for the shiny look it gave to garments. Colors were admittedly more difficult to handle: *Sarda* combined with sulfur fumigations was supposed to do the job, as long as the dye was of good quality. Otherwise, the dye was blackened and blurred. It is not altogether clear why Pliny (*NH* 35.57.197–198) refers here to the *lex Metilia* in connection with the censors of 220, C. Flaminius and L. Aemilius. Still enforced in the mid first century A.D., the statute was meant to regulate the work of launderers with regard to the use of detergents, perhaps imposing the preliminary use of the cheaper variety (*Sarda*) and reserving the use of the more expensive ones (*Umbrica* and *saxum*) for the finishing touch. If so, the law was interfering with the way private customers wanted to spend their own money and should be seen as the first of a long series of *leges sumptuariae* limiting extravagance among members of the elite.[20] On the other hand, it has been suggested that the *lex Metilia* was more in tune with the *plebiscitum Claudianum*, in that the regulations of laundering shielded the senators who wore a *toga praetexta* (white with a purple stripe on the edge) from the shame attached to the publicity of vastly unequal garb.[21] Whatever the correct interpretation, it is certainly an early instance of the intrusion of the state into the private sphere of business at the level of minute details.

THE *LEX OPPIA SUMPTUARIA* (215–195)

Shortly after the introduction of the *lex Metilia*, women became the target of additional and more drastic legislation introduced by the tribune C. Oppius in the darkest period of the Hannibalic War. Taking advantage of the military crisis caused by the defeat at Cannae (216), the law called for restriction pertaining to the possession of gold (hence of gold jewelry), the wearing of colored clothing, and the use of private transportation (horse-drawn vehicles) in town. The law, apparently accepted without protest at the time, was attacked as soon as the military threat had receded. Thus, in 195, a famous (fictitious) debate pitted the consul M. Porcius Cato against the tribune L. Valerius, one of the two advocates for the abrogation of the law (Livy, 34.1–8). To the former's plea to check female taste for luxury – a landmark in the history of misogynist rhetoric – the latter responded by pointing out that emergency measures ought to be lifted once circumstances allowed it. Although the law was then repealed, the many *leges sumptuariae* that followed during the next two centuries bear witness to the phenomenon of general enrichment of the Roman aristocracy and to the many ways this aristocracy chose to squander or to invest its wealth. Sumptuary legislation is good evidence not only for elite consumerism but also for innovative measures to curb socially challenging behaviors: Sulla's law of 81 imposed (lower than market) maximum prices on luxury food served at banquets in order to discourage this kind of competition among aristocrats.[22]

THE VILLA PHENOMENON AND THE LAW OF AGENCY

Faced with the restriction on seaborne trade imposed by the *plebiscitum Claudianum* of 218, aristocrats were expected to invest their increasing wealth in agricultural land. Many did so by channeling their propensity to show off into the acquisition of large estates in desirable locations not too far from the capital city (the Bay of Naples and southern Etruria). They built mansions combining the amenities of city life with the charms of the country. The availability of large amounts of cash and the lack of other commercial opportunities promoted the villa phenomenon from the early second century onwards.[23] Besides the architectural diversity produced by anonymous planners and craftsmen, luxury villas showed three distinctive features (Vitr. *De arch.* 6.6):

- As temporary places of residence for their owners, they were comfortable, equipped (*pars urbana*) with state-of-the-art facilities (e.g., baths), and highly decorated with mosaics, wall paintings, colonnades.
- As agricultural concerns oriented towards both self-sufficiency and the production of marketable surpluses, they included a *pars rustica* with food-processing tools (a mill and wine and oil presses), storage space (granaries and cellars), stables for livestock, cells for the staff, and workshops and sheds for industrial activities. Nearby roads and waterways made it easy for the owner and his guests to travel to the estate, for tools, goods, and extra hands to be brought in, and, conversely, for saleable items to be exported.
- The relative proximity of individual dwellings, hamlets, villages, or towns provided a source of labor and a local market for perishable products.

Despite its natural attraction, country life was seen by aristocratic landowners as at best a temporary retreat from their hectic city life or their extensive travelling on business, whether public or private. Regular absences from the estate compelled landowners to delegate the exploitation of the land to tenants (*coloni, conductores*) or managers (*vilici*), according to how much control they wanted to retain over the organization of production. Cato the Elder, in his treatise *De agricultura* (c. 160), and M. Terentius Varro, in his three books on *Res rusticae* (c. 37), spell out the duties and prerogatives of farm managers employed in villas staffed with slaves.[24] Because of the need for product diversification linked with the villa economy and imposed by the goal of self-sufficiency and because of the pressure to keep the permanent staff busy in spite of the seasonal aspect of agricultural work, it became clear that, in order to be efficient, estate managers – who were predominantly slaves, according to the extant, largely epigraphic sources – had to be empowered with the capacity to make contracts with suppliers, contractors, workers, customers, and other outsiders.

Until the second century, people could obligate themselves in Roman law through their own contracts and their delicts but could not make another person liable. The only exception to this principle was that slave owners were held responsible for the misconduct and crimes of their slaves (noxal liability in the Twelve Tables). It is likely that at some point during the second century, if not before, an unknown Roman praetor issued an edict providing for an extension of the master's (or principal's) liability for his dependents' delicts to the contracts concluded by them (slaves and sons-in-power).[25] Then the creation of various legal remedies (called *actiones adiecticiae qualitatis* by legal historians) allowed principals to choose how much control they wanted to retain over the transactions performed by their agents. The alternatives were to give them special permission (*iussum*) on a case-by-case basis, a general mandate (*praepositio*) in connection with the management of a business, or a free hand in the organization of their economic activities (*libera administratio peculii*). These initial choices determined in turn the extent (total or limited) of the contractual responsibility they were ready to shoulder.

Thus empowered, farm managers who were in charge of villas and their staff could become efficient economic actors, as employers, producers, and traders. The system devised by the Roman praetor was most practical in the context of the villa economy but could be adapted to other economic sectors. This is possibly what Cato the Elder resorted to in order to circumvent the ban of the *plebiscitum Claudianum*. According to Plutarch, Cato would lend money to a large group of people brought together into a legal partnership (*societas*) for the purpose of shipping, would then join the partnership as one among equal members, and would be represented on the ship by a freedman. Because the company was large enough, it could invest in several ships at the same time and thus minimize the risk while securing huge profits. In this way, Cato made good use of the openness of the money market and of the high rate of interest attached to bottomry loans.[26]

It is unclear how much seaborne trade increased during the second century or in years previous. Even though senators were theoretically barred from participating in shipping ventures, there was certainly no lack of candidates to invest in this sector of the economy. The development of the law of indirect agency, which was probably created to satisfy the needs of land-based business enterprises, whether agricultural or not (*Dig.* 14.3, *actio institoria*), was readily adjustable to the operation of a ship (*Dig.* 14.1, *actio exercitoria*). The latter, however, had specific features and requirements: the ban attached to the *plebiscitum Claudianum* excluded the dependents of senators from both the position of shipper (*exercitor*) and captain (*magister navis*); both principals and agents could be elusive characters; the maintenance of a ship called for constant input of money to pay for equipment and repairs; and long-distance seaborne trade was an incontrollable and therefore risky business (making the credit of any agent difficult to check). Thus, the extension of the law of indirect agency to the shipping business may be seen as a later development made possible by its tested success in a more confined context, such as agriculture, industry, land-based trade, services, and professional associations (*collegia*).[27]

THE *LEX AGRARIA* OF 111 B.C.

The second century saw two trends of major economic significance: the extension of the empire over the whole of Italy, North Africa, and the Greek East and the development of seaborne trade. The villa phenomenon described above was only one aspect of the former trend. New territories were annexed and then redistributed to individuals (*viritim*) or to newly created Roman or Latin colonial communities. What could not be turned into private land remained public land, to be rented or used by cultivators and cattle breeders. The conquest was the result of military operations carried out by citizen soldiers dragged away from their farms for increasingly long periods of time. Upon their return, they usually lacked the interest, incentive, or opportunity to resume farming, and they sold or relinquished their estates to larger landowners who were better equipped, both financially and organizationally, to ensure their continuous cultivation and their profitability. A massive influx of slaves – 150,000 Epirotes in 167, according to Livy (45.34.6) – provided cheap manpower for agriculture, thus creating conditions, at least temporarily, of unfair competition with small landholders.

A natural concentration of landed property among the richest members of the aristocracy was no new phenomenon. Legislation introduced and eventually passed in the fifth and fourth centuries,[28] from the *rogatio Cassia agraria* of 486 (Livy, 2.41.3) to the *lex Licinia Sextia de modo agrorum* of 367 (Livy, 6.35.5),[29] shows how lawmakers, usually plebeian tribunes, tried to dispose of public land and to limit access to grazing grounds for fair sharing while sparing the interest of the elite. Even though the chronology of the history of *ager publicus* before the Punic wars is rather shaky, it seems that the problem became more acute in the late third century. Distributions to individual citizens, such as those carried out after the conquest of Picenum and Cisalpine Gaul (*lex Flaminia de agro piceno et gallico viritim dividendo*, Cic. *Brut.* 14.57), went to naught because owners were eager to sell their plots to large landowners before moving to the city. However, the existence of a middle class of farmers was instrumental for the survival of republican political institutions. Major agrarian reforms, reenacting the limits imposed on the use of public land, were attempted by Tiberius and Caius Gracchus between 133 and 123, to be bloodily crushed by the aristocracy.[30] These reforms, as part of a larger package, aimed at giving individuals possession – but not ownership – of public land for cultivation in exchange for a rent. The individuals had no right to sell the land, and thus the historical trend towards concentration of land in the hands of the aristocracy was effectively blocked. In addition, some land was explicitly excluded from distribution by C. Gracchus and was to remain public.

In 111, this scheme was partly reversed by an agrarian law preserved in a much damaged inscription:[31] it provided that Gracchan *possessores* could acquire titles of ownership for holdings up to 30 *iugera*. The issue of landownership and cultivation by then extended outside the Italian territory, since parts of the law refer to plots located in North Africa or Achaea.[32] Although this statute confirmed Gracchan allocations, it also opened the door to further concentration of land and had the effect of attracting small landholders to the city while provoking a steady rise in the price of land.

The agrarian policy of the Roman state throughout the republican period promoted private ownership by allocating land on an individual basis or with the creation of colonies. Some marginal land could not easily be assigned because of the lack of adequate access roads and for various other reasons. The agrarian reforms of the second century make evident the willingness of reformers to include non-Roman citizens (allies and Latins) in the distribution of land, which had obvious political and demographic implications. They also remind us of the reformers' conscious effort to devise a credible alternative to large-scale landownership dependent on tenants or direct management with servile staff while at the same time boosting Italian urbanization through the creation of colonies. The overall phenomenon heightened the need for the development of an improved road system (*lex Sempronia viaria;* App. *B Civ.* 1.23; Plut. *C. Gracch.* 6.2).

It is perhaps ironic that such a complex and constructive program was also advertised by Tiberius Gracchus' archenemy, P. Popilius Laenas (consul 132), who, just after quelling a slave revolt in Sicily, boasted that he was the first to favor cultivators over grazers for the use of public land (not necessarily a sign of receding pastoralism in the face of expanding intensive farming). His achievements include the construction of a road leading from Rhegio to Capua, with bridges, milestones, and relay stations, as well as the forum and public temples in Polla, a town in Lucania (*ILS* 23).

The road system had started out as a necessity for military campaigns (in the late fourth century) and was by the late second century undoubtedly geared towards economic development and political unification. It was to become one of the most enduring creations of Roman civilization.

THE *LEX PUTEOLANA PARIETI FACIUNDO*

Historians are not sure how major public projects were actually completed. While military personnel, private and public slaves, and forced labor may have been involved in building roads,[33] harbors, and public buildings, there is also direct evidence (from the Roman colony of Puteoli, founded in 194) of public contracting with private entrepreneurs for this purpose. The *lex parieti faciundo*, dated to the year 105 and preserved in an inscription engraved somewhat later (*FIRA* III² 153), is a very detailed document drafted by local magistrates (*duumviri*) that describes the job of building a wall across from the temple of Serapis. Would-be contractors (*redemptores*) were required to provide sureties in the form of people (*praedes*) and landed property (*praedia*), respect set dimensions and quality standards (in terms of construction materials employed), and finish the work to the satisfaction not only of the magistrates letting out the contract but also of a council of former magistrates attended by at least twenty members. Payment was to be made in two installments, half at the time of contracting and the balance upon completion and approval of the work.

THE *LEX PUTEOLANA DE MUNERE PUBLICO LIBITINARIO*

Not much more than a generation later, the same colony is found contracting out, possibly with other tasks, the sensitive mission of clearing the town – and presumably its territory – of human corpses and of carrying out capital punishment of convicted criminals and delinquent slaves.[34] In order to be able to hold the entrepreneur and his partners liable for dereliction of duty, punishable by heavy fines, the colony granted the company a monopoly with fixed rates. The contract imposed precise conditions concerning the staff: it excluded the labor of children, the elderly, and physically impaired persons and prescribed a minimum of 32 workers to guarantee the efficiency needed to ensure public health. While moonlighting was not prohibited, services were strictly regulated, and penalties were threatened in case of imperfect compliance with the provisions of the contract. Most interesting is the fact that a striking lack of coherence in the terminology used in the document – the entrepreneur being referred to as either *manceps* or *redemptor* – suggests that the job description may be the result of a collage of provisions related to separate jobs, presumably let out to different people at different points. If this hypothesis is correct, the Puteolan *lex libitinaria* may illustrate the phenomenon of the concentration of work in the hands of one company in the late republican period. Besides performing the task of undertakers and executioners, the entrepreneur and his partners may have been entrusted with other public tasks that would have been described in the lost part of the inscription (first column[s]?).[35] How far back the original draft of the respective parts of this *lex contractus* goes we will never know. But the need for efficient sanitation must have antedated the foundation of the colony.

THE *LEX RHODIA DE IACTU*

It is quite likely that Roman law drew heavily from local practices long in use.[36] A puzzling illustration of the longevity of local customs brings us back to navigation. In a collection of texts excerpted in Justinian's *Digest* (14.2), some classical jurists discuss a mysterious *lex Rhodia*. Otherwise unattested in our sources, this law deals with compensation (*contributio*) in case of partial jettison of cargo as well as other topics connected with sea transportation. It is likely that the so-called Rhodian law was not a statute but a job description for ship captains (*magistri navium*) and shippers (*exercitores, navicularii*) based on practices developed in the eastern Mediterranean during the Hellenistic period.[37]

The literary sources and the archaeological material (imported and exported goods, shipwrecks, and harbors) show that seaborne trade greatly benefited from the expansion of the Empire and the contact with and demise of powerful competitors (Rhodes in 167, Carthage and Corinth in 146). Maritime roads were far from safe. Aware of this problem, the Roman senate addressed it, at least in the eastern part of the Empire, through a series of measures that stretch from the *lex de provinciis praetoriis* of 101/100 B.C.[38] to Pompey's major campaign against piracy in 67 (*lex Gabinia de bello piratico*).[39] Although piracy and robbery had to be fought with military means, seaborne trade was highly vulnerable to other dangers, above all of a climatic nature. Storms were acts of God (*vis maior*) that classical jurists regarded as bearing on the law of both property and contracts. If a captain saw fit to throw overboard part of the merchandise in order to save both the remnant and the ship, the financial loss was to be supported equally among freighters (*vectores*) in a gesture of solidarity with those whose sacrifice was instrumental in limiting or preventing a disaster. Cicero, in a rhetorical context (*Off.* 3.23.89), suggested that slaves may have been occasionally killed in that way and for that reason, a behavior that a classical jurist like Paulus tried to discourage by excluding slaves reported missing at sea from the global estimation of the loss for which contribution was to be paid by other freighters (*Dig.* 14.2.2.5). While it is possible that the original law provided only for cases of jettison, it is remarkable to find that late republican jurists extended the provision to cases involving ships being ransomed by pirates.[40]

Problems occurred everywhere, but some places were at higher risk than others. Shallow waters and river mouths, where merchandise had to be transferred from one kind of boat to another (*scapha* and *navis oneraria*), were particularly dangerous. It is then no surprise to find the Augustan jurist Sabinus referring to the mission of *urinatores*,[41] divers who specialized in underwater rescue operations. Their intervention may be attested in the shipwreck called Madrague de Giens (off Massilia in Gallia Narbonensis), where noticeable voids among carefully loaded containers can be explained either as the work of *urinatores* or as a result of earlier, unsuccessful jettison.[42]

CONCLUSION

The metaphor of voids and salvage operations leads us to our conclusion. No history of the ancient economy can claim to recover much of what has sunk into oblivion. Any account will be of necessity biased and partial. The ancient sources that survived are often ambiguous. As an example from Roman law and economic history, consider the notorious statute prohibiting the cultivation of olives and wine directed *c.* 129 at Transalpine Gaul. Was it a matter of protectionism against anticipated export to Italy and Rome of cheaper provincial products (cheaper because of the high price of land in Italy) or should we understand it as a way to maintain a high demand for Italian products in the Gallic market?[43] Likewise, a single late source refers to air pollution caused by a smoked-cheese factory in Minturnae and to the owner's liability and obligations related to it. Are we to consider pollution a second- or third-century A.D. economic development, despite the fact that Ovid, in the Augustan period, knows of bad sanitary conditions at Minturnae?[44] While the answers to these questions do matter, it is clear that all legal sources tend to illustrate the complexity of ancient economic life and to show how much interest politicians, magistrates, and jurists had in it.

International treaties, bills, statutes, regulations, legal writings, job descriptions, and legal instruments were the documents most likely to survive in large enough quantities to make possible the reconstruction of social and economic phenomena (e.g., *leges sumptuariae, feneraticiae, agrariae,* etc.). In the absence of models built in a more fully documented context, we cannot expect to achieve quantification. The account presented in this chapter is no more than one perception of a manifold and changing reality.

One purpose of this chapter is to show that, on the basis of legal enactments or documents, historians of antiquity can reconstruct some salient features of economic history. More space and more time would have called for more instances and more details and nuances. In the end, however, the picture would have remained sketchy at best.

NOTES

1 Colonna 1990.
2 Greene 1986, 107.
3 Tchernia 1986, 58–60.
4 Crawford 1974; Howgego 1992; Harl 1996.
5 For demographic studies, see Lo Cascio 1994; Harris 1999; Scheidel 1999, 2001; Morley 2001.
6 Scardigli 1991, 47–87. For the authenticity of Polybius' date (507 B.C.), cf. Cornell 1995, 210–14.
7 Aberson 1994; Rouveret 2000; Tarpin 2000.
8 See Cornell (1995, 295, 299–301) with reference to Dionysius of Halicarnassus (*Ant. Rom.* 7.53.5) for an allusion to the grant of equal rights (*isopoliteia*) to Latin communities.
9 I use here Crawford's (1996) edition (2:555–721, mostly 578–82); cf. Cornell 1995, 272–92.
10 De Ligt 1993.
11 Zehnacker 1990.
12 List in Rotondi 1912, 99–100.
13 Poma 1989.
14 Peppe 1981; Savunen 1993; Waelkens 1998.

15 Andreau 1987, 337–44.

16 Barlow 1978; Andreau 1999, 90–9, with bibliography.

17 Confirmed by the new Leiden Fragment of Paulus' *Sententiae* (ed. G.G. Archi et al., 1956) 3 (p. 5): "Senatores parentesve eorum, in quorum potestate sunt, vectigalia publica conducere, navem in quaestum habere, equosve curules praebendos suscipere prohibentur: idque factum repetundarum lege vindicatur." Nicolet 1980; D'Arms 1981, 5, 31–9.

18 Cass. Dio 55.10.5, 69.16.2 (Xiphilinus); Asconius 93 C.; Nicolet 1980, 390, n. 15.

19 D'Arms 1981, 55–61.

20 List in Rotondi [1912] 1966, 98–9; cf. Wyetzner 1995, 2002. XII Tables X.2–8 (regulating funeral expenses) shows that the propensity undoubtedly existed much earlier.

21 Wallinga 1996. For the date, cf. Livy 22.25 M. (Metilius was tribune of the plebs in 217).

22 Wyetzner 2002; cf. Gell. *NA* 2.24.11; Macrob. *Sat.* 3.17.11.

23 D'Arms 1970; Percival 1976; Greene 1986, 88–94; Dyson 1992, 74, 77–88; Smith 1997; Lafon 2001.

24 Aubert 1994, 117–200; Carlsen 1995.

25 Aubert 1994, 71–5.

26 Plut., *Cat. Mai.* 21.6; D'Arms 1981, 39–45.

27 Aubert 1994, 90–1, chapter 4 (clay artifacts), chapter 5 (services); 1999a (professional associations); 1999b (seaborne trade); 2001 (nonagricultural sectors, mostly in Roman Egypt); cf. De Ligt (1999), who favors an earlier date.

28 List in Rotondi [1912] 1966, 94–5.

29 Rathbone (forthcoming) suggests a later date (in the 290s) for the Licinian law.

30 The history is told by Appian, in the first book of his *Civil Wars*, and by Plutarch in the *Lives of Ti. and C. Gracchus*.

31 Crawford 1996, no. 2; Lintott 1992; Gargola 1995; De Ligt 2001.

32 A dispute about the cultivation of both private and public land opposed two communities in Liguria in 117 (*ILS* 5946) and required the decision of Roman arbitrators.

33 Roth 1999, 214–17.

34 Aubert (forthcoming).

35 *AE* 1971, no. 88, to be compared with *AE* 1971, no. 89 (a similar law from nearby Cumae that applies to the territory of Baiae); Aubert (forthcoming).

36 Cf. *lex Hieronica* for the collection of *vectigalia* in Sicily before and after the Roman conquest.

37 Rougé 1966, 397–413; De Martino 1982.

38 An inscription partly preserved in two copies, from Delphi and Cnidos; cf. *Roman Statutes*, no. 12 (Crawford 1996, 231–70).

39 Rotondi [1912] 1966, 371–2, with references (mostly to Cic. *Pro lege Manilia*).

40 Paulus (34 *ad ed.*) *Dig.* 14.2.2.3, citing Servius, Ofilius, and Labeo.

41 Callistratus, citing Sabinus (2 *quaest.*) *Dig.* 14.2.4.1.

42 Greene 1986, 25–6, citing Tchernia et al., 1978, 29–31.

43 Cic. *Rep.* 3.9.16; Tchernia 1986, 93–4.

44 Ulpianus (32 *ad ed.*) *Dig.* 8.5.8.5, quoting Aristo's *responsum* (early second century A.D.) to one Cerellius Vitalis, with Ovid *Met.* 15.716.

8: ROMAN RELIGION

Jörg Rüpke

∞

R oman religion neither existed as a discrete cultural practice in its
own right nor could it be found hidden beneath other cultural
practices. It was only in the very late Republic that there were
attempts to coin cumulative descriptions like *sacra et auspicia* (Cic. *Nat.
D.* 3.5), meaning 'cults and divination', yet it is only Cicero who uses
religio as a generic term encompassing a group's duty towards, and care
of, the gods. Cicero's *religio*, however, encompasses neither the organizational infrastructure and degree of coherence of these activities, nor
their shared symbolic language, nor any related metaphysical reflection.
To talk about Roman religion, therefore, is to talk about a range of cultural practices conforming to *our* notion of religion; this notion has, to
be sure, grown out of Roman thought and terminology, but it has been
strongly influenced by Christian discourse and the eighteenth-century
Enlightenment.

It is no improvement to substitute the plural 'religions' for the
singular 'religion'.[1] This use of 'religions', which is fashionable at the
moment, goes even further in suggesting the existence of a plurality of
self-contained and neatly separated religious traditions or systems, on
the model of early modern Christian denominations.[2] By contrast, this
chapter aims to demonstrate both the internal pluralism and the characteristic lack of clear external borders in Roman religious practices
within their ancient Mediterranean context. The coexistence of private or family religious loyalties to special groups like the Bacchanalian
cults is part of a religious 'division of labour' and represents a range of
religious options and activities on different social levels. Only the political élite identified such activities as an alternative to a 'religion of the
Roman people' (Livy 39.13: *alterum iam prope populum esse*). The conflict
of the Bacchanalian affair in 186 B.C. neatly illustrates how ancient religion could have a history of its own. The nature of our extant sources

makes any study of Roman religion before the third century B.C. a study of religious aspects of the social and political history of Rome. The discussion that follows will concentrate on important aspects of 'Roman religion' (as defined above) from the late third century until the time of Caesar, with special emphasis on the last century B.C.

THE RANGE OF RELIGIOUS PRACTICES AT ROME

When Cicero mentions both *sacra* and *auspicia* in the definition of 'religion' quoted above, he juxtaposes a vast range of diverse cultic practices with a fairly clear-cut ritual, a special set of *divinatory* practices, known as 'the auspices'. However, Cicero's combination of these two Latin terms can hardly be considered an ethnographic inventory, especially since it comes from a member of the augural college, the priesthood entrusted with the supervision of auspices. If, on the other hand, one concentrates on the interrelationship between religious and political practices or on the prominence of religion in the textual remains of late republican literature, Cicero's description is entirely accurate. 'Augural law' was the most spectacular field for the interlacing of religious and political strategies and for the religious foundations of the Roman élite's rules governing political decisions.[3] Practices that frequently seem to us to involve manipulation of religion in fact constitute the ingrained religious traditions of a society that simultaneously produced radically sceptical accounts of religion.

Divinatory practices are a universal phenomenon. Techniques to learn about the future, conceptualized as something predefined by the gods or by fate, are widespread and ease the burden of making decisions by indicating their outcome in advance. Divination could appear in a variety of forms and was usually an attempt to overcome uncertainty in situations where a difficult decision was to be made. At the same time, risks could also be reduced in other ways. Sometimes it seemed important to relate one's own actions to the cosmic order. Geomancy or astrology, with their purported knowledge about this cosmic order, offered techniques to determine places or times for inoffensive 'intrusion' into the natural order of things. Finally, divination could be a means of seeking the approval of the gods. At Rome, the politically dominant cult practices conform to this latter type. A Roman would ask for Jupiter's consent for an action on the very morning of the proposed action. The answer would be sought mostly in the behaviour of birds, known as 'translators' (*interpretes*) of Jupiter's will. Lightning bolts could also demonstrate Jupiter's assent. There are certainly elements of Etruscan traditions present here, but the rich and complicated Etruscan system of lightning types and direction, interpreted by the professional priesthood of the *haruspices*, was reduced by the Romans to the mere appearance of lightning in the sky.

Roman divination was not restricted to augury performed by magistrates and priests (augurs), and the area of signs, as well as the range of persons taking the auspices (*auspicium privatum*), was said to have been larger in earlier times.[4] The analysis of entrails continued to be practiced as part of sacrifices. It constituted, however, not a technique to learn about the future but rather a system that expressed the risk of communication between men and gods – and at the same time overcame such risk through the same process. A visible interest in astrology started in the late second century B.C., and by the end of the first century B.C., the basic astrological tenets of the planetary week seem to have become common knowledge.[5] The interpretation of dreams is already presupposed in Plautus (*Rud.*, *Mil.*). An important and rather underrated phenomenon must have been the *vates* or prophets, whose memory has been reduced to some derogatory remarks in the surviving texts of the mainstream tradition.[6] But the concept of *vates* in Augustan poetry and especially in the early works of Horace cannot be understood without a reconstruction of its institutional background, which consisted of figures who addressed the Roman public, although not in any official capacity, on topics concerning both the future and ethics.

By contrast, the auspices were fully integrated into the constitutional framework of the Republic. Their legal basis (namely, the *leges Aelia et Fufia*) had been elaborated during the latter half of the second century B.C., when written 'constitutional guidelines' were first envisaged at Rome. Politically relevant roles were restricted to the highest echelon of magistrates (with *imperium* and *auspicium*) and, in certain functions, to the augurs as a body (to give judgement and advice) or as individuals (for the observation of special signs and advice). In practice, the technique of the interpretation of signs itself seems to have been fairly easy, despite a rather large body of rules that were apparently no longer applied. When he observed the flight and the cries of birds before sunrise, the observing magistrate used a formula (*legum dictio*) to specify in advance what the relevant signs would be. Even this exercise was frequently replaced by the so-called *tripudium*. A person in charge of caged hens observed whether the animals were greedy or reserved when they picked at the fodder offered to them. The reaction of the birds was open to effective manipulation, as contemporary Romans were well aware. Likewise the observation of a lightning flash was no matter of empirical 'scientific validation': the very announcement that such a sign was anticipated constituted the factor relevant for religion and politics. Hence a political opponent's declaration that he was looking for hindering signs was taken already as the effective realization of the celestial veto of the proceedings at hand.

The obligatory "taking of auspices" by the presiding magistrate before important actions (popular assemblies, voting, elections, departing for warfare) gave divine approval to these actions while at the same time laying them open to auspical critique and obstruction. Given the range of legitimate participants and of actions involved, augural law complicated the processes of political decision-making.[7] Thus, augural practice enabled the formalization of opposition and dissent in a way that overrode majority votes in a consent-oriented élite. However, the effectiveness of the veto should not be overrated. Even augural dissent was usually ignored in legislative decisions. Here, the auspices were just one of the ways to opt out of the procedures for making a political decision. The augural delegitimization of a newly elected magistrate was, however, decisive. Divine consent for the leading figures of the community and for their most important actions was no less important than were majorities of human votes. Augury constituted a system for enforcing societal consent and for temporalizing dissent. Furthermore, prodigies (i.e., supernatural events observed as spontaneous signs of divine anger) enlarged this 'system' by further variants, which were open to interpretation by every Roman citizen but were also filtered by priesthoods and magistrates and had to be dealt with by means of special ritual procedures.[8]

It is the methodological option of any nontheological approach towards religion to 'explain' religious practices as social practices without any reference to the existence of superhuman beings (gods) and without any judgement on their existence. Hence, the reconstruction of social functions is not a surprising disclosure but rather the consequence of this methodological option. Such a determination of functions is open to criticism on account of its lack of a basis in the sources and its consequently limited explanatory value.

It seems useful, before turning to other types of religious practices, to put divination into a broader context by describing other types of public ritual. From the Middle Republic onwards, religion – first the building of new temples,[9] then the financing of games[10] – developed into an area of primary importance for the public display of wealth and its use to benefit the community as a whole. Obviously, the resulting prestige for the individual and for his descendants reflected and enlarged the prestige of the offices that regulated the access to these opportunities. The ritual of the triumph was the most important. The triumph originated in the rendering of honour to Jupiter and corresponded to the ceremonies of departing for war. In time, the triumphal procession turned more and more into a magnificent presentation of booty and feats of war, ending with donations and spectacles for the populace.[11] The right to wear triumphal dress, to erect triumphal arches and statues, and to be buried within the city wall perpetuated this prestigious moment. I suspect that the list of the triumphators, the *fasti triumphales Barberiniani*, was the first of the lists of officeholders to be publicly displayed on stone.[12]

Despite the fact that a small number of ritual forms dominated the literary record, and probably also the public's perception, it is important to note the varied forms of religious ritual in the areas considered so far. The *supplicationes* ('supplications'), for instance, were used as a crisis ritual in the Middle Republic. As a reaction to a military catastrophe or as preparation for a difficult war, a day could be declared when the whole adult population was encouraged to approach and pray in the temples (all opened up for the event) in order to implore the goddesses and gods of Rome to restore their harmonious relationship with the people of Rome.[13] The same ritual of processions to all the temples could be employed to offer thanks. This variant came to be used as an instrument to honour generals, especially in the Late Republic. In reaction to a written report about a major victory or about the end of a war, supplications to the immortal gods were declared 'in the name of the general'.[14] The length of the supplications corresponded to the appreciation felt for the victory and for the victor himself: in the third and second centuries B.C., supplications lasted from a maximum of three days to an exceptional five days, while in the years from 45 to 43 B.C. no less than three supplications of fifty days each were held.[15]

The major games developed out of a few ancient horse races (*Equirria, October equus*), and they were influenced by the dramatic spectacles of Greek origin staged in southern Italy. The number of games and their length multiplied during the decades surrounding the beginning of the second century B.C. All these games were staged in rather provisional settings in the valley of the Circus Maximus as well as on the Campus Martius. By contrast, the first stone theaters, built in the middle of the first century B.C., were not intended as permanent structures for specific games but as parts of vast building projects with a significance of their own (e.g., the theatre of Pompeius).

Fortunately, the archaeological record has not only preserved traces of these massive projects but can also supplement the élite-oriented literary discourse on matters of private religion. Thousands of votive objects made of clay illustrate areas of religious activity that have barely left any literary traces and frequently not even any epigraphic record. For the fourth to first centuries B.C., several votive deposits have been found in central Italy (with a remarkable decline or shift towards specifically local types at the end of the period).[16] Typically, a wide range of objects, often miniatures, has been found. The distribution of similiar or identical types points to the role of artisanal mass production, but it also indicates the wide range of individual needs cared for by every single cult. Specialties notwithstanding, it is nearly always impossible to determine which god was being invoked merely on the basis of the votive objects found. In imitation of practices in mainland Greece, which influenced Italian production even before republican times, central Italy especially favoured the use of reproductions of parts of the human body. Legs and feet are most common, followed by arms, eyes, breasts, and genitals. Representations of inner organs (e.g., intestines or the uterus) might even include abnormalities and ulcers, but we must realize that all these objects do not document individual anatomical findings but are instead the results of mass production that have been chosen as interpretations of a person's own health problems.[17]

The special areas of individual rather than collective risks and anxieties include illness, economic success or failure, childlessness, the risks of childbirth, and occasionally long-distance travel. Vows (vota) thus form an important thread in the religious practices of all parts of Roman society, finding archaeological expression both in small-scale objects of everyday use and in temple buildings worth hundreds of thousands of sesterces, promised at the turning point of a battle. Even close to the very centre of Roman religion, around the Via Sacra and the Forum Romanum (at the place later occupied by the Meta Sudans), deposits of votives used right into the second century B.C. have been found (Fig. 4).

Despite the term 'crisis ritual', the rituals under discussion formed part of a sequence rather than being isolated events. Biographies of individual Romans reveal sequences of actions, typically starting with familiarity with the deity concerned (as a result of individual or family tradition), prayers and consultations, the fulfilling of the vow and its documentation, the resulting publicity, and the propensity for a new engagement with the divine. Such sequences, while not restricted to

FIGURE 4. Excavation of the Neronian Meta Sudans between the Palatine, the Flavian amphitheater, and the arch of Constantine has brought to light remnants of republican cult deposits that demonstrate the presence of individual votive religion in the center of the city. (Photo J. Rüpke)

any individual god, would normally be enacted within the circle of gods available in the person's familiar surroundings. However, special traditions, publicity, success, and an inviting local environment (baths, for instance) did favour the growth of certain cults of regional or even supraregional importance. Lavinium and the sanctuary at Ponte di Nona attracted thousands of worshippers on a regional scale. At Rome, on an island in the Tiber, a sanctuary of the healing god Aesculapius (Greek Asklepios) was established; the date of the transfer of this cult from Epidaurus in Greece is 293 B.C.[18] Together with famous oracular cults (again Lavinium, later on Praeneste with its great centre of Fortuna), such healing cults formed a religious infrastructure that transcended political boundaries.

Other areas of individual worship are less accessible to us. When Cato the Censor wrote *De agricultura* (*On Agriculture*) shortly before the middle of the second century B.C. he produced a normative text on the investment in and managing of an Italian farm. Religion was part of the enterprise, a technical and social necessity for the farmer. Cato and some antiquarian writers offer us a glimpse of the minimal daily routine of burning scraps of food in the hearth and praying to the tutelary spirits of the house (*lares*) or to the head of the family (*genius*). Rituals surrounding childbirth, name giving, coming of age, marriage, death, and burial are hardly ever described, and then only in texts written several hundred years after the supposed practice was current. Archaeology, for example in Ostia, does not encourage the view that any architectural structures like house altars, let alone sumptuous ones, were common in middle- and lower-class homes.[19] It is always reasonable to expect a broad range of attitudes towards religious traditions and their traditional obligations, even in a premodern society, and it is difficult to determine exactly what these attitudes were during the Republic.

It is even more difficult to determine the level of participation of the populace in public ritual. Judging by occasional literary references and institutional features, the New Year's festivities on the 1 January (*kalendae Ianuariae*), the festival of the *Saturnalia* in December, and other celebrations that encouraged local festive activities in families and neighbourhoods must have had a high level of participation. The splendor and the material rewards of watching a triumph must also have produced a huge number of spectators. But for simple reasons of space, nearly all other centrally staged rituals could not accommodate more than a tiny percentage of the Roman populace as witnesses. When the calendars of religious groups from imperial times can be reconstructed, we find that hardly more than one or two dates from the 'official' calendar have been integrated.

Without any doubt, religious groups already existed during the Republic; indeed, the literary and archaeological evidence of the Bacchanalia proves the existence of group formation based primarily on religion as early as the third century B.C. (Fig. 5).[20] The formation of comparable Orphic circles in Greece happened parallel to the formation of the Greek city states (*poleis*). Evidence for professional associations, usually united by and often named from a common cult, also comes from republican times. The historiographical tradition attributes their original foundation to Numa. Later tradition tended to see all these groups as delegates of central religious organization,[21] but their actual structures seem to follow the contingencies of local coherence and of individual initiatives and interests. Although only a few names are known from the second and third quarters of the first century B.C.,[22] they show the range of religious diversity outside the cults cared for directly by the Roman élite. For example, Favonia M. f. and Casponia

FIGURE 5. Fresco with Dionysiac scenes, from the Villa of the Mysteries, Pompeii. The Dionysiac scene recalls the presence of Greek and Hellenistic cults in Italian cities, including Rome. (Photo J. Rüpke)

P. f. Maxima were public priestesses of Ceres, and C. Vergilius C. l. Gentius and A. Calvius Q. l. served as functionaries in the funerary centre of Libentina.

Apart from the extremely scanty epigraphic and very partial archaeological record, the bulk of our knowledge about popular religion during the Republic stems from literary sources that (a) date from imperial or even late imperial times and (b) intend to entertain (Gellius, Macrobius), to interpret canonical works (Servius), or to utter polemics against paganism (Arnobius, Augustine). Most of the basic data involved go back to late republican and Augustan antiquarian sources, but the authors are not impartial observers and are in fact themselves a very special part of the religious history of the Late Republic.

Rome, as a growing commercial and political centre in central Italy, had never been isolated. This circumstance is attested, in different ways, by the presence of Greek artisans and myths, by oriental motifs, and by the fifth-century treaties with Carthage. However, the three Punic wars dramatically increased the intensity and the scope of external contacts. In addition to commercial, military, and political aspects, these encounters also had a cultural dimension. While absorbing (and pillaging) an attractive and in many ways superior culture, the Roman élite had to define and assert its place in an enlarged Mediterranean world (*oikumene*). One way was to find a place within the large and complex mythological framework offered by Hellenistic Greeks, who themselves worked towards the ideological integration of an 'empire' of independent cities and states. The legendary groups that were said to have dispersed in the aftermath of the Trojan War, that of Aeneas foremost among them, offered numerous genealogical lines and were part of the Greeks' own thinking, transferred to Rome by means of Greek-educated marginal men like Livius Andronicus, Naevius, and Ennius, who produced Latin epics (for the *symposia* of the rich) and Latin drama (for the religious festivals of the citizens).[23]

Yet the transfer of the Greek form of interstate communication based on the establishment of common mythological links was not successful in the long run.[24] Mythological epic did not flourish before Virgil, nor did drama after the end of the second century B.C. (even in the form of the *fabula praetexta*, which dealt with subjects of Roman history). Likewise, the traditional Roman mechanism of establishing foreign cults, through peaceful transfer or *evocatio deorum* from captured towns, came to a definite halt during the latter part of the second century. Instead, Roman senators – many of whom were also priests – started to elaborate local Roman traditions, both by writing narrative histories and by organising and systematising political and ritual practices. The legislation on augury and its uses (*obnuntiatio*) and on the election of priests (*rogatio Licinia* and *lex Domitia*) formed one side of the coin,[25] while antiquarian literature dealing with religious traditions formed the other.[26]

Beginning with Varro, the intellectual pressure of Greek philosophy and theology led to the apologetic creation of 'three types of theology'.[27] The idea of a civic theology (*theologia civilis*) was used to provide a systematic theoretical framework for the actual and contingent practices of Roman cult. Hence, the 'documentation' of Roman cult, as given in Varro's *Antiquitates rerum diuinarum*, aimed to bring it into line with the requirements of a proper system. Rome's multifaceted polytheism had to be organized according to the principle of functional clarity. The *di selecti* and *di certi*, the 'selected' and 'certain' deities, were those to whom an explicit function could be attributed and who could be invoked in prayer and cult. Without any doubt, the Romans' conception of gods tended to multiply deities and their specific attributes instead of integrating different aspects into more and more complex personalities for individual gods. Yet the characteristic dryness of the seemingly limitless Roman 'pantheon', as noted by generations of scholars, is due to the specific literary and rhetorical intentions felt by the authors of our most important sources, who were writing Roman religion in the face of Greek philosophy and rationality.[28]

MECHANISMS OF INTEGRATION

The picture of Roman religion during the Republic offered so far has concentrated on diverging lines of development, although the intellectual efforts of contemporaries who elaborated unifying schemes, such as Cicero and Varro, have also been mentioned. These were not the earliest attempts to make religion manageable. The forcible reduction of religious options implemented by the persecutions of groups such as the Bacchanalians, philosophers, Jews, astrologers, and devotees of Isis are but the extreme end of the spectrum.[29] In the discussion that follows, three areas of internal religious organization will be highlighted: priesthoods, the calendar, and the sacral topography of the city of Rome.

There were many priests and priestly groups (*sacerdotes, collegia, sodalitates*) that engaged in some annual rituals. With the exception of the female *Vestales* and perhaps the *flamen Dialis*, for whom religious duties constituted a full-time job,[30] these priests performed their religious duties as a merely part-time or even spare-time activity. Prosopography serves as a good indicator of the public importance of the various priesthoods. No members of the republican Arval brethren or Sodales Titii are known by name. Of the approximately twelve minor *flamines*, each of whom cared for the cult of special deities, only two can be tentatively identified for the whole time of the Republic, a *flamen Carmentalis* in the fourth century and a *flamen Floralis* in the third (Fig. 6).[31] Of all the Salii, only six are known, and those only due to exceptional events or to numismatic self-advertisement. The first known Lupercus (a priesthood restricted to equestrians under the Empire) would have entered the college in about 60 B.C. By contrast, for most years after the beginning of the Second Punic War, between one-third and two-thirds (sometimes more) of the members of the augural college are known; the rate for the *pontifices* never drops below one-third.

From the second half of the third century onwards, the pontiffs assumed a central position in the organization of Roman public cult.[32] Their duties included supervision of the full-time priesthoods of the Vestal Virgins and the priests of Jupiter (*flamen Dialis*), Mars, and Quirinus, and perhaps they even had some authority in relation to the augurs.[33] The growing importance of their traditional knowledge

FIGURE 6. *Denarius* of C. Servilius, Rome mint, 57 B.C. The reverse probably alludes to the first *flamen Floralis*. (Kestner Museum, Hanover, Inv. 3050: *RRC* 423 / 1; photo Christian Tepper, courtesy of Kestner Museum)

of processional law, their judgement in matters of the sacred or profane status of land, which affected property rights, and their right to regulate the calendar by intercalation formed the basis of their duties and of their increasing prestige.[34] In fact, their prestige paralleled that of the augurs; monthly meetings on the Nones (augurs) and the Ides (pontiffs) completed the parallel. Even the scribes of the pontiffs were accorded, as *pontifices minores*, the prestige of a priesthood. In 196 B.C. the task of performing ritual meals at the temple of Jupiter (*epula*) was excluded from the agenda list of the pontiffs and given to the newly founded priesthood of the 'three men for the meals' (*tresviri epulonum*). Enlarged to seven and even ten members during the last years of Caesar, this was the fourth college to be counted among the 'major colleges' by the imperial period. Yet such an equality between the priestly colleges – reflected in the careers, ritual roles, and political powerlessness of the priests – was in no way prefigured during the Republic. The partially hierarchical position of the pontiffs contrasted with the sphere of operation of the augurs and with the very special task of the *decemviri sacris faciundis* ('ten [later fifteen] men for the performance of rites'), whose only function was to inspect the Greek hexameters of the Sibylline books at the request of the senate. On the basis of the answers found in these books, the ten men proposed ritual remedies against fearful prodigies. The Roman calendar, probably dating originally from the fifth century B.C., was characterised

by weak astronomy and strong practical usefulness. By the beginning of
the third century, it had been developed into an instrument (*fasti*) that
effectively controlled the time slots for political and juridical activities
outside the senate's meetings. It took account of the sacral allotment of
time to certain deities (the *feriae*), in the same way that land was allotted as divine property, but the Roman *fasti* never served as a liturgical
timetable. The drive to fix Roman traditions in writing led, however,
to the employment of a written scheme for the annual pattern of religious festivals and the associated juridical designation of each day. In
addition to explanations of the *feriae*, the annual commemorative and
festival days of temple foundations were inserted. This initiative took the
form of a private calendar painted on a wall, created in connection with
the building programme of a censor, Marcus Fulvius Nobilior. Nobilior's calendar was copied and used as a complex historical document.
However, a conscious calendar policy and calendar religiosity, using the
calendar and calendrical dates as a means of propaganda and reflection,
did not arise before the last decade of the Republic, with Caesar's introduction of the 'Julian calendar' and the subsequent proliferation under
Augustus of decorative calendars carved on marble.[35]

Finally, attention is due to the role of religion in the categories
and implementation of property rights with regard to land. Roman
law distinguished public and private property. Public property could
be allotted to deities and could thus become 'sacred' (*sacer*), private
property could at most attain some of the character and protection of
'religious' property by being used for tombs, and walls could attain the
special protection of being *sanctus* ('hedged', Gai. *Inst.* 2.3–9). Thus,
property law required the senate's involvement every time a new cult
was instituted, insofar as the cult intended to build or dedicate a temple
or any sacred spot (e.g., an altar or a grove). Nobody was allowed to
give public property to the gods without the permission of the Roman
people or the senate. Generals were free to designate parts of their booty
for the building of a temple for a god of their own choice, but in order
to find a spot in Rome (and to be assigned the job of formally dedicating
the building and its precinct), the general had to obtain the consent of
the senate.[36]

No master plan of Rome's sacral topography existed; the proliferation of temples followed the pattern of public building in general (Fig.
7). In the Late Republic, the focus (and the possibilities) shifted from the
Forum, the Palatine, and Capitol Hill to the Campus Martius. Location
had no ethnic implications. Aesculapius was placed outside the sacral
boundary proper (the *pomerium*), but Mater Magna (the goddess of the

FIGURE 7. Temple B at the Largo Argentina has been identified as the temple of "Today's Luck" (*Fortuna Huiusce Diei*) vowed by Q. Lutatius Catulus at the battle of Vercellae in 101 B.C. The image of the goddess was about 8 m high (i.e., about half the diameter of the temple). Rivalry between competing generals led to variations in choice of deity and type of cult. (Photo J. Rüpke)

orgiastic cults of Cybele) received a temple on the Palatine. As in a few other cases, the sanctuary of Dea Dia, the agricultural goddess of the Arval brethren, was located far outside the city, but these shrines did not connect to form a sacral ring around the city. The processional route of the *Amburbium* ('around the city') is simply not known. What we do know about other 'border rituals', such as the *Terminalia* ('festival of the boundary markers') and the *Compitalia* ('festival of the crossroads'), is that they were connected with a specific place on the border, but there is no evidence that any 'perfect circles' existed.

Public law, as far as divine property was concerned, was shaped by the dynamics of social differentiation and by its architectural consequences. Private building and garden projects encroached upon sacred groves, many of which had already become obscured by the time Varro was writing.[37] On the other hand, private architecture imitated sacral buildings. In general, the élite were those most often present at religious rites, and public priesthoods were at the same time private banqueting circles offering a context for leading Romans to meet, to discuss, and to sacrifice on private grounds.[38]

THE PLACE OF RELIGION IN ROMAN SOCIETY

The Romans claimed – in the persona of Cicero – to be 'the most pious of all peoples'. The most obvious correlate is the large number of cults – cults that had been imported from everywhere. Yet there was nothing like an organized Roman pantheon, no parallel to the Homeric circle of gods, who unified the religions of Greek cities by means of literary communication. Here and there a list or a grouping of gods might reflect social structures, but there is no methodological basis for the reconstruction of ancient society from a Roman pantheon.[39] Roman religion served the ruling class and enabled the communication of the élite and the people at games, in supplications, and during crisis rituals. Religious rituals sometimes helped to express social divisions as well as to differentiate Romans along lines of gender, age, and juridical status. They sometimes served the (never totally) internal procedures of the Roman nobility in the distribution and the use of power. If there are orders, they are partial. If there was a religion of the city (*'polis religion'*),[40] it was not one organizing superstructure but a sectorial analytical tool.

Given the extraordinary expansion of Roman power in Italy and throughout the Mediterranean, combined with the extension of

Roman citizenship in Italy, Roman religion appears as a medium of communication rather than a medium of separation in politics. The ritual of appropriating foreign gods (*evocatio deorum*) established links with political entities that had been defeated or destroyed.[41] In the area of divination, foreign specialists (*haruspices*) who came from the leading families of Etruscan cities were used as advisers. The one official oracular collection consulted by the senate, the Sibylline books, was written in a foreign language (Greek) and was of foreign origin. By acknowledging and expiating prodigies beyond the borders of Rome and Latium, religion established links and claimed control over independent Italian communities.[42] At the same time, Roman citizens were not as free as citizens of Greek *poleis* to take part in 'secret cults'. Religion did not have to be indigenous, but it had to be practiced in public. No unified Roman religion existed, but there were no independent religions either. To talk about 'Roman religion' is to talk about cultural practices that fit our notion of religion. Yet a study of these practices still seems a worthwhile exercise, for understanding Rome better and also Praeneste, Lavinium, Pompeii, and Brundisium.

NOTES

1 Mary Beard, John North, and Simon Price (1998) used the title *Religions of Rome* for their masterly two-volume history.
2 For a history of the term 'religion', see Smith (1998).
3 Jerzy Linderski's (1986) brilliant, though surprisingly nineteenth-century *Staatsrecht*-oriented, synthesis on augury is titled *The augural law*.
4 See Cic. *Div.* 1.28; Livy 4.2.5; Festus *Gloss. Lat.* 316.18–20L; Auson. *Opusc.* 16.12.12 Prete.
5 Barton 1994, 32–7; Stuckrad 2000.
6 Wiseman 1992.
7 Cf. Liebeschuetz 1979, 15.
8 Rosenberger 1998.
9 See Ziolkowski 1992.
10 Bernstein 1998.
11 Rüpke 1990, 217–34.
12 See Rüpke 1995b.
13 For the *pax deorum*, see, e.g., Livy 31.8–9.
14 Livy 41.17.3; Cic. *Phil.* 14.22.
15 Rüpke 1990, 216.
16 They are published in a series of their own: *Corpus delle stipi votive in Italia* (Rome: Bretschneider). An overview of the material is given by Comella 1981; for the urban sanctuary of Minerva Medica (?), see Gatti Lo Guzzo 1975; for Lavinium, see Fenelli 1975; even at the sanctuary of Iuppiter Latiaris on Monte Cavo, the usual range of objects (statuettes, parts of the body) have been found: see Cecamore 1995.

17 See Forsén (1996) for Greece.
18 See Livy 10.47.6–7; Ov. *Met.* 15.622–744.
19 See Bakker 1994.
20 Pailler 1988.
21 Livy 2.27.5: *collegium mercatorum*; 5.50.4: *collegium Capitolinorum*.
22 See Rüpke, forthcoming *Fasti sacerdotum*. Clesipus Geganius, L. Septumius, and P. Cornelius P. l. Surus are known as *magistri Capitolinorum*, a Pupius A. f. as *magister* of the *pagus Ianicolensis*, L. Tullius and T. Quinctius Q. f. of other *pagi*, and Caltilius Caltilae l. as *magister* of the *vicus Sulpicius*. *CIL* VI 32455 attests people leading the care of a sanctuary, perhaps of Jupiter Fagutalis on the Mons Oppius.
23 Wiseman 2000.
24 See Scheer 1993; Erskine 2001.
25 Beard et al., 1998, 109–10.
26 Overview: Rawson 1985.
27 Summarily, Mansfeld 1999.
28 See Moatti (1997) for an attempt to write a history of the process of implementing Greek rationality at Rome during the last century of the Republic.
29 For the Chaldaeans, see Cramer 1954; for Isis, see Malaise 1972.
30 Rüpke 1996.
31 Cic. *Brut.* 36; *RRC* 423/1.
32 Taylor (1942, 291), followed by Szemler (1972, 78), dates the popular election of the *pontifex maximus* already to the first half of the third century, but a date in the last third, before 212, is more plausible.
33 Gladigow 1970.
34 *Lex Acilia* of 191 B.C.; see Rüpke 1995a, 289–330.
35 This hypothetical historical reconstruction and deconstruction of the supposedly 'Numaic calendar' is fully argued in Rüpke 1995a.
36 Aberson 1994; Orlin 1997.
37 Cancik 1986.
38 Rüpke 2002.
39 This is valid even for such general structures as are assumed by the Dumézilian scheme of three functions (e.g., Dumézil 1970, 141).
40 For a general criticism of the concept applied to Rome and a historical account of its genesis, see Bendlin 2000; for its difficulties in Greek contexts, see Cole 1995.
41 Gustaffson 1999.
42 MacBain 1982.

PART 3

ॐ

ROME'S EMPIRE

9: ITALY DURING THE ROMAN REPUBLIC, 338–31 B.C.

Kathryn Lomas

൬

T he history of republican Italy is one of conquest and Roman expansion but also one of many different peoples and communities and the strategies they used both to integrate with and to resist the influence of Rome. What it is emphatically not is a linear process of Roman expansion and the disappearance of local cultures and identities.[1] Ancient Italy was not an ethnic or political unit but a region of extreme diversity. It contained many different ethnic groups, each with its own language, culture, economy, and forms of social and political organisation (Fig. 8), and as Roman power began to expand, complex systems for controlling conquered areas and mediating relations with other states evolved piecemeal. As a result, Roman Italy, even after it became a politically unified entity in 90 B.C., had a high level of cultural diversity and strong regional identities that coexisted with central control and Roman influence.

One of the most central – but also one of the most problematic – concepts with which the historian of Roman Italy has to grapple is that of Romanisation. The process of cultural, as opposed to political, integration with Rome is notoriously difficult to define in theory and to identify in action. Roman culture itself was neither unified nor static but rather disparate and constantly changing. It also operated in different ways at different levels of society.[2] Roman cultural influence may have meant something very different to different social groups. Also, the process of cultural exchange is not a passive one. Italian communities were not simply passive recipients of Romanisation but were active participants in the process of cultural change, selecting some aspects of Roman culture while rejecting others or adapting them to their own local cultural agenda. Even in instances in which a Roman framework was imposed on a non-Roman community – the foundation of a colony

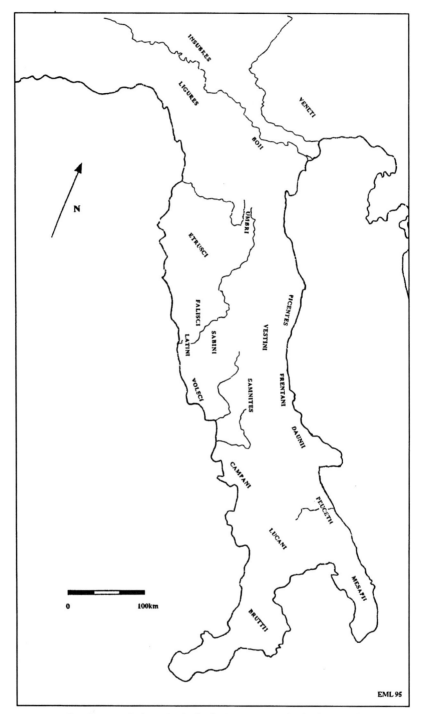

FIGURE 8. Pre-Roman Italy: principal ethnic groups. (Elizabeth Lazenby)

is perhaps the most obvious example – the population did not blindly accept a blanket imposition of Roman culture. The history of republican Italy, after the Social War and political unification, as well as before, is not one of linear Romanisation but of an ongoing process of interaction between Roman and non-Roman cultures.

The archaeological evidence for the history of republican Italy is copious and still growing. It is not, however, without its problems. The literary source material includes a number of detailed and extensive accounts of the various wars by which Italy was conquered and of the subsequent Punic and civil wars of the second and first centuries B.C., but these are by later authors such as Livy, Diodorus, and Appian and are almost exclusively written from a Roman point of view. For the Italian side of the equation, we have ever increasing archaeological evidence and a substantial body of inscriptions and coins but no surviving narrative giving the non-Roman point of view. As a result, we must constantly adjust our interpretation of the literary source material in light of its Roman viewpoint and seek to integrate it with the nonliterary evidence in an attempt to produce a fuller understanding of Roman Italy and its development.

PRE-ROMAN ITALY AND THE ROMAN CONQUEST

Roman Italy was characterised until well into the Principate by a high degree of regionalisation and the continuing importance of regional cultures and traditions. The roots of this regionalisation lie in the ethnic diversity of pre-Roman Italy and its variations in culture and organisation. From the seventh century B.C. onwards, some regions of Italy became populated with urban societies that were similar (although not identical) in organisation to the Greek city-state (Fig. 9). Indeed, many Latin communities, including Rome, started to develop a distinctive urban identity, as did settlements in Etruria and Campania. By the sixth century B.C., all of these regions had flourishing urban centres that exhibited a high degree of social and economic complexity and had acquired monumental public buildings and a rich material culture.[3] Southeast Italy also started to develop towards an urbanised society in the sixth century. Settlements grew rapidly in size and complexity, and by the fourth century, many could be described as cities.

In Appenine Italy, by contrast, the indigenous form of state organisation was primarily nonurban. The Samnites, for instance, maintained

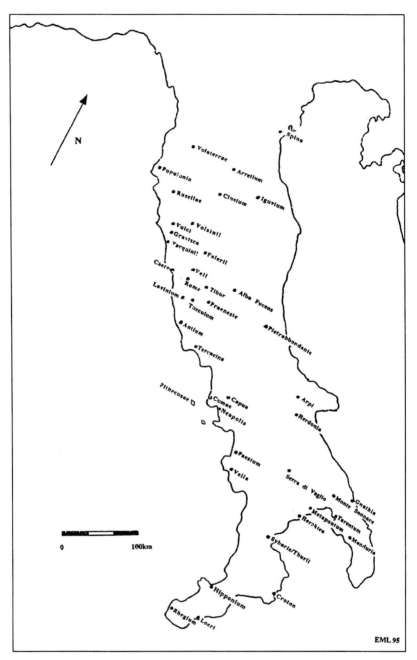

FIGURE 9. Roman Italy: major pre-Roman sites. (Elizabeth Lazenby)

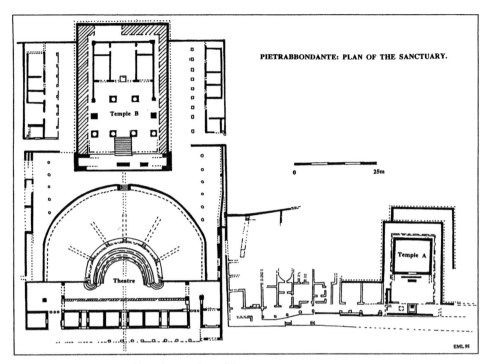

FIGURE 10. Pietrabbondante: plan of the sanctuary.

a separation between their settlements and the various forms of communal or state activity they engaged in. They lived in villages or on farms dispersed throughout their territory (Livy 9.13.7), but each locality (*pagus*) had a hill fort for defensive purposes and a religious sanctuary that acted as a focus not just for sacrifices and festivals but also for markets, legal hearings, and assemblies of the local people.[4] These assemblies seem to have chosen magistrates to govern them in much the same way as a city was governed and to have banded together into larger political units, each known as a *touto*. These in turn seem to have formed a federation, known to modern historians as the Samnite League, which had the power of declaring peace and war.[5] A number of larger and more elaborate sanctuaries probably served as the meeting points of the *touto*, and a particularly large and imposing example at Pietrabbondante (Fig. 10) has been identified as a possible headquarters of the Samnite League.[6] It would be untrue, however, to regard Appenine Italy as either entirely nonurbanised or as more backward in its culture and organisation than other regions. Recent research suggests that some sites, such as Larinum, started urbanising as early as the fourth century B.C., and certainly before the Roman conquest.[7] Even areas such as central Samnium, the Sabine territory, and Picenum, which in some cases did not urbanise until the first century B.C., should not be regarded as primitive. It is clear from the evidence of inscriptions, coin legends, and the physical remains of sanctuaries that communities in these regions had a strong state identity and effective forms of organisation well adapted to a highland area.

Roman interactions with other Italian states also played a part in the continuance of diversity. Rome began to expand at the expense of other Latin states as early as the sixth century B.C., and by the end of the Latin War, in 338 B.C., it dominated a significant part of Latium, southern Etruria, and northern Campania. However, Rome, possessing only the rudimentary administrative machinery of a city-state, had no means to control and govern such an extended territory by direct means. As a result, Rome exercised control over Italy, not by direct government, but by a complex network of alliances backed up by grants of Roman citizenship and by intermittent programmes of colonisation. This effectively meant that most Italian communities, even those with colonial status, enjoyed local autonomy and self-government, although under a greater or lesser degree of supervision by Rome, until 90 B.C.

The peace settlement of 338 B.C. included a number of innovative features. One was the imposition of Roman citizenship on some states, either full citizenship or the more limited *civitas sine suffragio*, which conferred civil rights but not the right to vote, thus disbarring holders from participation in the political process.[8] This extension of full or modified Roman citizenship to other Italian communities was, in the fourth and third centuries B.C., a means of Roman control and exploitation of Italian manpower and resources. Rome viewed these communities (*municipia*) as having obligations to it, especially the obligation to provide access to local Italian manpower and military support.[9] Roman citizenship became more sought after in the second century B.C., but in earlier times it was viewed as a punishment and was greatly resented. In 304 B.C., for instance, the Aequi were willing to go to war because they feared that Rome would try to force them to take Roman citizenship if they accepted peace.[10] Autonomy was highly valued, and Roman citizenship could be seen as a gross imposition and was fiercely opposed.

The settlement of 338 B.C. also introduced the concept of Latin status. This had nothing to do with Latinity as an ethnic origin but was a package of legal rights and obligations that could be granted to a community by Rome. The package included the rights of trade and intermarriage with Roman citizens and the right to restricted participation in the Roman political process, subject to a residence requirement (at Rome). However, Latin status also imposed obligations to assist Rome in times of war.[11] These military obligations forged close social and economic links between Rome and the Latins and also made the Latins the core of Rome's fighting strength. Particularly at the elite level of society, legal protection for trade and commercial contracts facilitated economic interaction, and the legitimacy of offspring from intermarriages between Romans and Latins maintained familial connections between Rome and the Latin communities.

The final element of the settlement was the dissolution of the Latin League, a federation of Latin cities, and its replacement with bilateral treaties, tying each individual state to Rome on a one-to-one basis and breaking up the decision-making bodies of the league, which had provided a forum for multilateral decisions. Each state now had a relationship only with Rome, not with other former members of the league, and this effectively destroyed the communal identity of the Latin states and allowed Roman domination.[12]

As Roman power expanded after 338 B.C., Rome separated the conquered Italians into the three categories: Roman citizens (with or without the vote), Latins, and allies. By doing this, Rome was able to extend control by building up a network of alliances, voluntary or imposed. It thereby sidestepped the need to make alternative administrative arrangements – the vast majority of communities continued to be self-governing – and avoided the highly contentious task of imposing change and limiting autonomy. This arms-length approach allowed Rome to gain kudos for its apparent magnanimity and to maintain the convenient fiction of being merely first amongst equals.

The majority of Italian states were independent allies (*socii*), whose relations with Rome were governed by treaties.[13] We know that these were bilateral agreements and that they created a web of alliances with Rome very firmly at the centre, but their terms are poorly documented. The *foedus Cassianum* of 495 B.C., which formed the basis of later treaties, is purportedly quoted verbatim by two sources (Dion. Hal. 6.95; Cic. *Balb.* 53), and inscriptions recording treaties have survived, but all of these are of a later date and relate to alliances outside Italy.[14] Furthermore, all of these examples are very general in their terms. All establish peace between Rome and the other signatory and stipulate that each shall assist the other with armed force if attacked. Some states undoubtedly obtained more favourable terms than others, depending on the circumstances in which the treaty was made, but the details are mostly not known. In most respects, all allies were, in theory, self-determining, independent states, although during the second century B.C. Rome began to interfere increasingly in their internal affairs and to consolidate the growing differences in status between Roman citizens and Italians. Needless to say, as Rome's power grew, the defensive nature of these alliances came to be honoured more in the breach than in the observance. The levying of troops from allies and Latin colonies became an annual event as Rome's wide-ranging interests and obligations made annual campaigns, and eventually a standing army, a necessity. The principle that if Rome or one of its allies was threatened, Rome could call on the whole alliance for support was also rapidly established. In 225 B.C., an invasion by the Gauls prompted Rome to institute an emergency levy and demand from its allies a record of their full fighting strength (Polyb. 2.24). From the fourth century onwards, the growing disparity between the power of Rome and that of any one of its allies ensured that each alliance rapidly evolved from an alliance between equals, as it was in theory, into a hegemonic structure dominated by Rome.

The strength of this system was tested and ultimately proved by Hannibal's invasion of Italy in 218 B.C. Although some of Rome's allies revolted and joined forces with Hannibal, the majority remained loyal, and his defeat secured Rome's position as the dominant power in Italy. The second century B.C. was a time of transition for both Rome and Italy, partly because the initial postwar period of reconstruction was followed by a great influx of wealth, along with exposure to new cultural influences, due to Rome's conquest of Spain and much of the Greek East. As a result, the imbalance between the status of Rome and that of her allies became increasingly obvious and increasingly resented.[15] Nevertheless, it was a period in which Italy flourished, despite the growing friction with Rome.

The immediate postwar period was inevitably one of recovery and reconstruction but also of continuing tension. Rome was heavily committed to war in Spain (from 197 B.C.) and Macedonia (from 200 B.C.), and its allies suffered a consequent drain on their economic and military resources. In Italy, there was considerable unrest, and the pacification following the departure of Hannibal was a long, slow business. Settlements with some of the allies who had revolted had already been reached, but some were still under military governorship. Apulia, for instance, continued to be a praetorian province as late as 186 B.C., and there was intermittent but widespread brigandage in this region throughout the 190s and 180s (Livy 31.29.9–10, 38.42.5–6,

39.39.8–10), which required a number of judicial interventions and the condemnation of several thousand people. The so-called Bacchanalian scandal of 186 B.C. is another example of senatorial willingness to suppress a perceived threat throughout Italy. The Bacchic cult, which became popular in the early second century, was widespread in Etruria and parts of southern Italy. When it spread to Rome, moral panic broke out, amid lurid allegations of orgies and murders carried out during the rites. The senate decreed that the cult should be suppressed, not only in Rome but elsewhere in Italy. An inscription recording the *senatus consultum* was to be published in all allied communities (Livy 39.8.1–14.8; *CIL* I².581), and a copy from the *Ager Teuranus* in Bruttium has survived. The anxiety about unrest in Italy was accompanied by an increasing heavy-handedness in dealing with Italians by individual senators, and an increasing willingness by the senate to discriminate against the interests of Italians, a willingness that ultimately led to the breakdown of relations with Italy and to the Social War.[16]

CITIES, SETTLEMENTS, AND COLONIES

One result of the piecemeal development of Rome's power was that, until 90 B.C., Italy was politically a complex mosaic of autonomous states loosely allied with Rome, although subject to an increasing level of interference and military imposition in the era after the Hannibalic war. In addition to alliances and grants of citizenship, Rome also engaged in a programme of colonisation (Fig. 11). In practical terms, colonisation was the principal means of assigning Roman citizenship or Latin status to a community, but it also had an enormous impact on the demography of Italy, on levels of urbanisation, and on the society and culture of the areas colonised.

Indeed, there can be no doubting the impact of a colonial foundation on a community. Colonies were typically founded on land confiscated from defeated enemies, but they differed widely in size, organisation, and status. Many communities designated as colonies of Roman citizens were not in fact new settlements but merely had a number of Roman colonists added to them. Their civic organisation, set out in a colonial charter, was changed to mirror that of Rome; it thus included a local senate and annually-elected magistrates headed by a board of two *duoviri*.[17] Typically, a citizen colony was small in size, often comprising no more than 300 settlers and their families, and the purpose of its establishment might well have been overtly strategic. Many colonies, in fact,

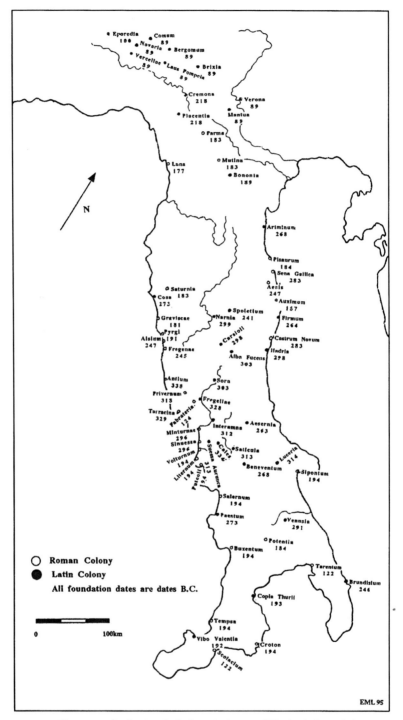

Eporedia
100

Comum
89

Novaria
89

Vercellae
89

Laus Pompeia
89

Bergomum

Brixia
89

Cremona
218

Verona
89

Placentia
218

Mantua
89

Parma
183

Mutina
183

Luna
177

Bononia
189

N

Ariminum
268

Pisaurum
184

Sena Gallica
283

Aesis
247

Saturnia
183

Cosa
273

Auximum
157

Graviscae
181

Spoletium

Narnia
241

Firmum
264

Pyrgi

Alsium
247

Caraioli
298

Castrum Novum
283

Fregenae
245

Alba Fucens
303

Hadria
298

Antium
338

Sora
303

Privernum
313

Fregellae
328

Tarracina
329

Fabrateria
124

Aesernia
263

Minturnae
296

Interamna
312

Sinuessa
296

Suessa Aurunca

Cales

Saticula
313

Luceria
314

Volturnum
194

Literrnum
194

Puteoli
94

Beneventum
268

Sipontum
194

Salernum
194

Paestum
273

Venusia
291

Potentia
184

Buxentum
194

Tarentum
122

Brundisium
246

Copia Thurii
193

Tempsa
194

Vibo Valentia
192

Croton
194

Scolacium
122

○ Roman Colony

● Latin Colony

All foundation dates are dates B.C.

0   100km

EML 95

FIGURE 11. Roman colonization in Italy, 338–80 B.C. (Elizabeth Lazenby)

were founded at vulnerable locations or on newly conquered territory to provide a core Roman presence and act as informal garrisons. This is most apparent in the foundation of *coloniae maritimae*, which were, as the name suggests, citizen colonies founded at strategic points along the coast to defend against pirates and to control formerly threatening coastal cities such as Antium, defeated by Rome in 338 B.C. after a fierce struggle.[18] There was an extensive programme of colonisation in 197 and 194 B.C. – involving settlements at Liternum, Volturnum, Puteoli, Buxentum, Croton, Tempsa, Sipontum, Thurii, and Vibo – that may have been prompted by the need to defend the coast of Campania, Lucania, and Apulia. This programme was backed up with an induction of new colonists in 186 B.C. to strengthen the colonies that had failed to flourish (Livy 32.29.3, 34.45.1–5, 39.45.5–9).

Latin colonies differed from this pattern in a number of important respects. Unlike citizen colonies, which were part of the Roman state, Latin colonies were self-governing. They each had a colonial charter establishing their administrative structures, which were usually based around a senate and a board of four annually-elected *quattuorviri*.[19] They also were much larger than citizen colonies and in many cases were entirely new communities, organised on Romanised lines. Latin colonies might consist of 2,000–5,000 settlers and their families, and even larger examples are known from northern Italy.[20] Many were founded in areas that had low levels of urbanisation or were suffering from depopulation. The primary purposes seem to have been to urbanise regions such as Samnium and the far north of Italy on suitably Romanised lines and to regenerate failing cities. In the 180s, a large-scale programme of colonisation in northern Italy urbanised at a stroke a region that was relatively newly conquered and at the same time provided a system of defence against possible Gallic incursions. Colonies at Bononia, Parma, Mutina, and Aquileia were of a more substantial size than the citizen colonies of southern Italy,[21] allowing them to fulfil an administrative role, not just to act as garrisons.

The impact of even a small colony could be significant. An archaeological survey of the Bussento valley in Lucania illustrates the extent to which a colony could undermine indigenous settlements and transform land use and economic activity. In the third century B.C., farms and villages were evenly distributed throughout the valley, between the small Greek city of Pyxus on the coast and the Lucanian city at Roccagloriosa in the hinterland. In 194 B.C., however, a Roman colony was founded at Pyxus (renamed Buxentum). During the following

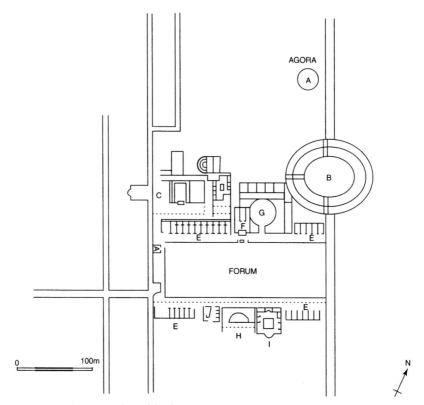

FIGURE 12. Paestum: plan of the forum and agora. A – ekklesiasterion/bouleuterion (*c.* 450 B.C.); B – amphitheatre (1st cent. B.C.); C – palaestra; D – lararium (2nd/3rd cent. A.D.); E – tabernae (3rd cent. B.C.); F – forum temple (*c.* 200 B.C.); G – comitium/curia (3rd cent. B.C.); H – imperial curia (2nd/3rd cent. A.D.); I – macellum (2nd-3rd cent. A.D.).

generation, Roccagloriosa declined and disappeared, and rural settlement became concentrated at the lower end of the valley, around the Roman colony.[22]

A little earlier, in 273 B.C., two Latin colonies were founded, at Paestum in Lucania and at Cosa in Etruria (Livy *Per.* 14; Vell. Pat. 1.14.7). These provide further examples of the impact of colonisation. Paestum, a Greek colony founded in the sixth century B.C., had been overrun by the Lucanians in 410 B.C. and fallen under Roman control during the Pyrrhic War of 281–70 B.C.[23] It was not in a state of serious decline, but it was situated in a strategically valuable region, and the colony may have been intended to dilute the Oscan and Greek population and pacify the

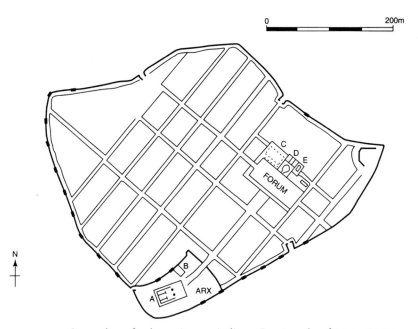

FIGURE 13. Cosa: plan of colony. A – capitolium; B – temple of Mater Matuta; C – basilica; D – comitium; E – forum temple.

area. Paestum already had a highly-developed urban infrastructure, but the Latin colony proceeded to reinvent this in a more Roman mould. The city's government was reorganised, Oscan and Greek disappeared from inscriptions in favour of Latin, and part of the centre of the city was rebuilt.[24] In particular, the Greek agora was replaced as the centre of public life by a new Roman forum constructed right next to it (Fig. 12). Cosa, on the other hand, was a new settlement, located on the coast of Etruria and dominating a harbour and fertile territory.[25] It was built at a small distance from the existing Etruscan village of Cusi and was a typical Roman colony. A regular street plan was imposed (Fig. 13), despite the steep terrain; a *capitolium* (a temple of Jupiter, Juno, and Minerva and an important symbol of Roman power) was built on the highest point in the colony; and an elaborate forum was constructed.[26] Urban cults and sanctuaries also had powerful symbolic connections with the identity of communities, and the building of a *capitolium* was an important part of founding a colony. It usually occupied a prominent position on the acropolis, as at Cosa, or in the forum, and it was closely modelled on the temple of Jupiter Capitolinus at Rome. The forum at

Cosa also took Rome as a model, adapting its Comitium – the meeting place of the city's government – from a Roman model.

In the era after the Social War, colonies were most frequently composed of discharged soldiers, and such colonists could alter the culture of a community even more drastically than nonmilitary immigrants. Sulla, for instance, settled colonies of his troops in communities that had opposed him, such as Pompeii, where a group of 2,000 to 3,000 colonists was added to a city with a population of only 10,000 to 12,000. This introduced a substantial new element into the citizen body, and inscriptions show that in little more than a generation the pre-Roman elite disappeared from positions of influence and were replaced by colonists.[27] In addition, Latin replaced Oscan as the language of the inhabitants, and fierce political strife broke out between the colonists and the indigenous population (Cic. *Sull.* 60–2).

In all of these examples, despite the substantial differences in the pre-Roman settlements and the circumstances of colonisation, the colonists imposed their own vision of Romanised existence, disseminating Romanised forms of urbanisation as well as settling large concentrations of Roman or Romanised people in already populated parts of Italy.

Despite the Romanising effects of colonisation in some areas, many areas of Italy already had a rich urban tradition of their own. Most of the communities were small, by modern standards, and few had a population in excess of 15,000 people. Nevertheless, they were communities with a complex social structure and their own distinct identities. Like Rome itself, most of these communities were dominated by a small number of influential elite families. We know, for instance, of the squabbles for power between the Pacuvii, Blossii, and Magii at Capua (Livy 23. 2–10) and between the Mopsii and Trebii at Compsa in 216 B.C. (Livy 23.1), and we know of the bid for domination by Dasius Altinius at Arpi in 213 B.C. (Livy 24.45–7). Many such elite families were as influential and eminent in their own regions as the grand senatorial families were at Rome. They also maintained networks of social contacts, symbolised by intermarriage and ritualised guest-friendships, with similar families within their region and beyond, including Rome itself.[28] Thus, the elite of Italy, including Rome, formed part of a complex network of family and social connections. Within a given community, life was highly competitive, for the leading men typically sought to demonstrate their wealth and status and to outdo their rivals.[29] Such competition was in many respects greatly to the benefit of the community as a whole. Ancient cities lacked any state provision for public services and amenities and relied on leading individuals to provide these at private expense, either as part of their magisterial duties or as a gratuitous act of generosity.[30] Private spending could fuel spectacular phases of urban development. The influx of wealth in the later second century, as Italians benefited from trade with the newly conquered eastern Mediterranean, funded a major period of urban development. Italian aristocrats ploughed their new wealth into public benefactions and lavish private houses. It was also a period of considerable cultural change, as greater contact with the eastern Mediterranean prompted an interest in Greek culture. At Pompeii, for instance, the forum was refurbished, with the addition of a new basilica and three smaller structures, and a new temple of Jove was under construction at the time of the Social War (Figs. 14 and 15).[31] The city also acquired two lavish sets of baths – the Forum baths and the Stabian baths – and a theatre, a type of building that was becoming popular in Campania and parts of Latium but was regarded in Rome as daringly, even dangerously, Greek.[32] This level of building and urban transformation was repeated across Italy, often funded by magistrates as a mark of their year of office or paid for through private benefactions by leading citizens. Even in the nonurbanised areas of Italy, we can see the same process at work. In Samnium, the new economic resources were used to monumentalise sanctuaries. At Pietrabbondante, for instance, a grand new temple, a theatre, a series of terraces, porticoes, and a water supply were built, and inscriptions attest to public works paid for both by magistrates and private individuals.[33] Sanctuaries in Latium also benefited; new theatres were added to the sanctuary of Diana Nemorensis at Nemi and the sanctuary of Fortuna at Praeneste.[34] Rome itself acquired its first marble temple, dedicated to Jupiter Stator, in 146 B.C. (Plin. *NH* 34.34, 34.40), and such a large amount of money was put into public works in Rome and Italy that the contracts are described as too numerous to count (Polyb. 6.17.3–4).

THE ECONOMY OF REPUBLICAN ITALY

Economically, the second century was a time of growth but also of intense change and destabilisation. Roman Italy was primarily an agrarian society, and many regions were rich in fertile land and natural resources. Campania and Etruria were especially noted for their wealth. Each state drew a considerable portion of its subsistence from its own territory, and a substantial proportion of the inhabitants of republican Italy maintained

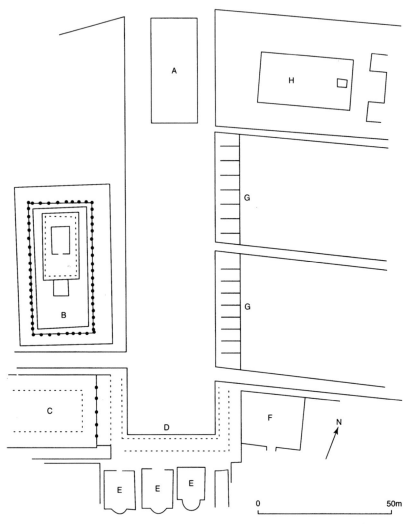

FIGURE 14. Pompeii: forum in the late second century B.C. A – temple of Jupiter; B – temple of Apollo; C – basilica; D – portico of Popidius; E – administrative offices; F – comitum; G – tabernae; H – macellum.

themselves by small-scale farming. There were, however, two key factors that introduced some fundamental and far-reaching changes into the economy of Italy in the middle and late Republic. One was the rapid growth of the city of Rome itself and the increasing concentration of elite interests there, which considerably distorted the economy of central Italy. Latium, southern Etruria, and northern Campania became a greatly enlarged *suburbium* for Rome – a hinterland whose economy

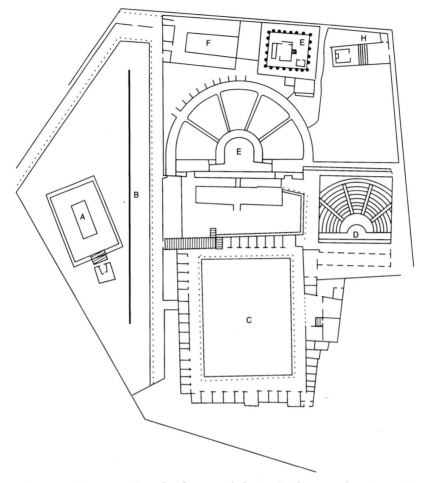

FIGURE 15. Pompeii: triangular forum and theatre in the second century B.C. A – Doric temple (6th cent. B.C., rebuilt in 2nd cent. B.C.); B – stadium; C – gymnasium?; D – odeion; E – theatre; F – palaestra; G – temple of Isis; H – temple of Zeus Meilichios.

was geared to supplying the markets of the city with luxury foods or perishable commodities that could not travel far.[35] The other was the impact of the Hannibalic war and Rome's subsequent conquest of a Mediterranean-wide empire. This opened up massive opportunities for trade and financial transactions in the newly acquired provinces, particularly in the wealthy eastern Mediterranean, and these opportunities were exploited by both Italians and Romans. It also brought an enormous amount of wealth into Italy and Rome and prompted a period of major change in the agrarian economy of Italy, from small-scale farm-ing to villa agriculture, causing considerable social and political strife in the process. However, this period of change was by no means the de-structive occurrence that is portrayed in the writings of some historians, both ancient and modern. The traditional view is that the devastation of the Hannibalic war and the changes caused by the conquest of an empire triggered an ever increasing demand for military manpower that depleted the Italian peasantry, taking farmers away from the land for long periods.[36] At the same time, the increased wealth from war booty and trading opportunities in the provinces, together with an increase in cheap slave labour, enabled the elite to buy up land and accumulate *ager publicus*, thus acquiring large estates run by slaves and dedicated to spe-cialised cash crops. Supposedly, the depopulation of the peasantry and the decline in military manpower were the inspiration for the Gracchan reforms of the second century B.C.

Archaeological evidence, however, indicates a more complex pic-ture. The development of villa agriculture was certainly not specifically a second-century phenomenon. Excavations and surveys in the territory of Metapontum and around Gravina in southeast Italy show develop-ment of substantial villas there in the third century B.C.[37] This shift from subsistence to estate-based agriculture undoubtedly gathered pace in the second century, but it did not become widespread until the first century in many regions. The size of the estates developed in this period is also a matter of contention. Although Pliny the Elder (*NH* 18.4) claimed that much of the land in Italy had been concentrated into huge estates (*latifundia*), which he considered to have been the ruination of the Ital-ian economy, there is a considerable body of evidence to the contrary. The picture that emerges from both archaeological and historical ev-idence is of an increasing concentration of land into the hands of the elite but in the form of medium-sized estates, not huge monolithic blocks of property. Cicero's accounts of his journeys around Italy and the provinces imply that he and his friends all had a substantial number of villas scattered throughout Italy, which could be used as staging posts on journeys or lent to friends, although only those situated in Latium or Campania were regularly used for longer stays.[38] Even within a par-ticular region, similar patterns of physically dispersed estates owned by a single person are found. The Etruscan Sextus Roscius owned a size-able estate near Ameria, but this comprised thirteen separate farms in the Tiber valley (Cic. *Rosc. Am.* 20). The archaeological evidence also supports the arguments against the development of large estates at an early date. Surveys of the Volturnus Valley, the *Falernus ager*, and other areas show that farms and villas of medium size were the norm until the end of the second century A.D.[39] Even in northern Campania, the region most closely associated with specialist wine production and therefore with the development of elite-owned and fairly specialised villas, the patterns of land ownership were not consolidated before the end of the second century A.D.[40] A similar pattern emerges in Samnium, where surveys around Ligures Baebiani indicate the existence of a flourishing Oscan elite whose wealth was based on medium-sized estates in the second century B.C. and a gradual concentration of resources into fewer hands during the early Empire.[41] Clearly, there is some measure of regional variation in this process, but overall the evidence does not point to a total collapse of rural populations or an agrarian crisis in the second century B.C. Excavations of villas at Francolise and Posta Crusta[42] indicate that, far from being *latifundia* of the type described by Pliny, they were estates that would have fitted comfortably within the Gracchan limit of 1,000 *iugera*.

The diversity of the republican villa is reflected in both literary and archaeological evidence. Roman writers such as Varro and Cato describe villas that grew grain, vines, olives, and fruit, raised livestock, and sometimes reared animals such as exotic fish and gamebirds for the luxury market. Excavations of villa sites reveal medium-sized, mixed-economy estates of the type described by Cato in his *De agricultura* rather than huge specialised estates (Plin. *NH* 18.4). The huge villa at Settefinestre in Etruria, for instance, had orchards, grain stores, and wine and oil presses, and there is evidence of stock raising.[43] The production of wine in republican Italy is particularly well documented in ancient literature, and the high survival rate of transport and storage amphorae allows study of the source of the wine and its trade. Southern Latium and Campania were particularly prominent wine-producing areas, and named vintages from these regions included Setian, Caecuban, and Falernian.[44] Even here, however, wine making was not an exclusive activity on many estates. The republican-period villas at Francolise in Campania have yielded signs of copious wine production but also of cultivation of grain, olives, and fruit.[45] The rearing of livestock is another phenomenon sometimes blamed for dispossessing the Italian peasantry. Tiberius Gracchus is said to have been inspired to introduce his land reforms by witnessing at first hand areas of Italy in which pasturage predominated (Plut. *Ti. Gracch.* 8). Pasturage was, however, a major part of the traditional economy of Apennine Italy. Much of Samnium and Apulia was crisscrossed by drove roads, enabling flocks to be moved between summer and winter pastures or driven from grazing grounds to the market. It was by no means a new introduction in the second century, although the scale of transhumance may have increased, and Cato (Cic. *Off.* 2.89) stressed the high rates of return on stock raising. Transhumance undoubtedly caused friction, as herdsmen were one of the least controllable groups of people in ancient society. However, there is no reason to suppose that large tracts of arable land were being turned over to pasturage.

Although agriculture was a major part of the republican economy, it was by no means the only element. Taxation, finance, trade, and manufacturing were all important, and the conquest of an overseas empire brought with it immense wealth and trading opportunities. The economic benefits can be judged by the fact that the booty collected enabled the senate to suspend direct taxation for Roman citizens in 187 B.C. and to abolish it permanently in 167 (Cic. *Off.* 2.76). Italian trading interests outside Italy were established by the third century, as demonstrated by the imprisonment of 500 Italians by Carthage for supplying its rebel mercenaries and also by the harassment of Italian merchants by Queen Teuta in Illyria in 230 (Polyb. 1.83.7–8, 2.8.1–3). However, the scale of wealth increased dramatically after the end of the Second Punic War, in particular with the grant in 167 of the status of a free port to Delos (Polyb. 30.20.7, 31.10), the centre of the slave trade. According to Cicero (*Off.* 1.150–51), trade and finance were not fit occupations for a gentleman unless conducted on an international scale, but trade with the Eastern Empire in the second and first centuries B.C. was conducted by both Italians and Romans, many of whom were not freedmen but came from leading Italian and Roman families. Senators were forced to operate through agents due to legal restrictions, but equestrians were prominent in trade and banking. Cicero's associate Cluvius was from an important Puteolan family and had a wide network of financial contacts and dealings in the provinces.[46] Other *negotiatores* (traders) known from inscriptions have names that link them with aristocratic Campanian families, such as the Heii, Statii, and Blossii.[47] Italians appear in inscriptions all over the Mediterranean, from the Dalmatian coast to Egypt and Asia Minor, with a particular concentration on Delos.[48] Their primary occupations were almost certainly trade, banking, and tax farming. The business dealings and social connections of entire families can be traced over several generations through inscriptions from Delos, and some individuals made considerable investments in the development of the island, notably the building of the Agora of the Italians and the Sanctuary of the Foreign Gods. Italian religious cults and associated *collegia*, such as those of the *Compitales* and *Mercuriales*, are documented, and many cities in the East had a *conventus civium Romano-rum* (an assembly of Roman citizens), which provided a focus for the activities of Romans and Italians.[49]

Italian and Roman *negotiatores* were involved both in the importing of commodities from the provinces and the exporting of Italian goods. The distribution of Campana A pottery, produced in large quantities in Campania, covers much of the western Mediterranean,[50] and the distribution of amphorae indicates that wine from Campania, Latium, and Etruria and Apulian olive oil were being exported in significant quantities.[51] Production of perishables such as textiles are less easy to document, but inscriptions from Pompeii show that the textile industry there was small scale, with artisans working in small groups. Some artisans (such as fullers) were housed in specialist workshops, others in more general *tabernae*. There was a high degree of craft organisation, with *collegia* of fullers, dyers, weavers, carders, and so on. Manufacture seems to have been a lower-status activity than either trade or agriculture, and no connections can be made between the textile industry and any elite families.[52]

THE SOCIAL WAR AND ITS AFTERMATH

The increased economic prosperity of the second century was accompanied by growing political friction between Rome and some of her Italian allies. An increasing tendency on the part of the senate to discriminate between Roman and allied troops, to exclude Italians and Latins from the city of Rome, and to discriminate against Italians during the Gracchan land distributions was accompanied by an increasingly heavy-handed and domineering attitude by many of the individual magistrates and senators in their dealings with Italians. In addition, whether to extend some or all of the rights of Roman citizens to Italians had become a major political issue in Rome from 125 B.C. onwards. Eventually, in 91/90 B.C., a significant number, although by no means all, of Rome's allies revolted and formed a breakaway state centred at the Apennine community of Corfinium, now renamed Italia (Diod. Sic. 37.2.4). The result of this short but bitter conflict was that Rome was forced to grant citizenship to all Italian communities south of the river Po, thus creating a politically unified Italy for the first time. This did not, however, imply cultural unity or the disappearance of the local cultures, and Italy continued to be a highly disparate region during the last century of the Republic.

The extension of citizenship clearly had a major impact on Italian communities and the way they conducted their public affairs. All Italian towns were expected to surrender their autonomy and take on the status of a community of Roman citizens (a *municipium* or a *colonia*), abandoning their own forms of government and taking on Romanised forms, as laid down in a Roman-style civic charter. However, this was a far more complex and less centralised process than it seems at first glance. The charter of Tarentum[53] shows a city administration modelled on that of Rome, with an annually-elected board of senior magistrates (*duoviri, quattuorviri*), a cursus of junior magistrates (*aediles*), and a senate composed of the leading men (decurions) of the community. It also lays down detailed regulations for the conduct of public life, with provisions for the management of public finances, fines for misdemeanors by magistrates (which could be channelled to a number of public ends), and regulations for controlling building and maintaining the fabric of the city. A more complete example, the *lex Genetiva Iulia* from Urso in Spain[54] is very similar in content. At one level, it seems to suggest that post–Social War Italy might have been a region of communities that were increasingly Romanised, at least at a structural level. However, other evidence suggests a more complicated picture. The *Tabula Bantina*, a bronze tablet from Bantia in Lucania, was reused, with a Latin inscription on one side and a law in Oscan, the indigenous language of the region, on the other.[55] Both inscriptions predate the Social War, but the Latin inscription, possibly dating to *c.* 120–100 B.C., is the earlier of the two, while the Oscan inscription probably belongs to the period just before the Social War. The Oscan inscription records a Romanised administrative structure for the town but does it in the local language – at a time when Latin appears to have been widely spoken by the ruling classes of Bantia and at a date before the Social War. In other words, Roman influence on civic government, even in an area that rebelled against Rome, was not just a postwar phenomenon. However, the converse is also true, and instead of imposing Roman forms of government, many charters may have adapted existing local forms and simply attached Roman titles to indigenous offices. For instance, Arpinum, Formiae, and Fundi were not administered by two *duoviri* but by boards of three *aediles* (*CIL* X.6105). In his letters, Cicero (*Fam.* 13.11) says that the region was particularly proud of retaining its local customs and saw this as an important symbol of local identity.

Other aspects of the aftermath of the Social War also had a drastic impact on Italian communities. One of these was Sulla's programme of colonisation, which targeted cities that had held out after 89 B.C. or had supported Marius. Each colony consisted of a substantial number of Sullan veterans who had settled on land confiscated from men killed in the proscriptions or known as opponents of the régime. Unlike some earlier colonies, most of these were not new settlements but were formed by adding colonists to existing cities. The example of Pompeii, discussed previously, indicates that this type of colonisation could be destabilising, leading to civic strife and displacement of population. Elsewhere, however, the first century B.C. was a period of social and economic continuity. At Volaterrae, for instance, surveys of the city's territory and examination of inscriptions show that there was a remarkable degree of continuity between the second century B.C. and the early Empire, with very little change in landholdings and a high level of social stability.[56] Boundaries between estates remained stable, and the same elite families, such as the Caecinae and Carinnae, are found in inscriptions ranging from the archaic period to the second century A.D.

After the Social War, local forms of statehood were supplanted by Roman-style cities, a process particularly prominent in Appenine Italy. Some religious sanctuaries with pre-Roman political significance began to fall into disuse, although this process was not complete until the early Empire. At Pietrabbondante, for instance, the sanctuary buildings fell into disuse following the loss of the city's political role, and the aristocratic munificence that had funded its second-century expansion was now targeted at the new Romanised cities, such as nearby Bovianum.[57] At Rossano di Vaglio in Lucania, the Lucanian sanctuary of Mefitis and Jove continued to be used but at a much reduced level, as the neighbouring Lucanian settlement of Serra di Vaglio was abandoned and political and social activity came to focus on the new Roman colony of Potentia, a short distance away.[58]

For the Italian elite, of course, the extension of citizenship brought with it great opportunities for social and political advancement. Italians who lived close enough to Rome or had the means to travel could exercise their right to vote, and the more moneyed and ambitious could stand for office and enter the senate. Relatively few, however, did so in the years between the Social War and the rise of Augustus, and the majority of Italian senators failed to rise high on the career ladder. Cicero, from a community that had gained citizenship in 188 B.C. and with a well-established network of family contacts with the noble families of Rome, is a spectacular exception, but many men of similar background failed to rise beyond the junior magistracies. Of the 192 *novi homines* known from the Late Republic, many of them Italian, only forty achieved the praetorship, and only one, Cicero himself, became consul.[59] It seems that it took approximately two generations for a newly-enfranchised Italian family to gain enough political influence and contacts at Rome to carve out a successful career there, and it is only in the Augustan period that men of Italian origin enter the senate or achieve high office in significant numbers. The network of social contacts between elite families throughout Italy, which is documented throughout the history of the Roman Republic, was no guarantee that the Roman senatorial class would be willing to share power, and Cicero's sensitivity on the subject indicates that an Italian background was a drawback.[60] However, not all Italian aristocrats aimed at a senatorial career. Some, such as the Roscii of Ameria (Cic. *Rosc. Am.* 15–16), seem to have been content to remain big fish in their localities instead of seeking office at Rome.

Despite these undoubted changes and other factors, such as the gradual disappearance of Oscan, Umbrian, Etruscan, and other local languages in favour of Latin during the course of the first century B.C., regional identities remained strong in the late Republic, and there is a perceptible tension between these identities and the newly acquired Roman citizenship. Cicero (*Leg.* 2.5) defined himself (and every Italian) as having two homelands: Rome, to which ultimate loyalty was owed, and his hometown, to which he retained an emotional commitment. Far from undermining local cultures, the need to renegotiate local identity imposed by the extension of Roman citizenship seems to have had the effect of reinforcing them. Although communities may have adopted Latin and adapted their public life to conform to Roman expectations, and although Italian nobles may have looked towards careers at Rome, local solidarity also increased. In Umbria, for instance, the notion of a collective identity as Umbrians appeared for the first time after the Social War.[61] Before this, the individual communities identified themselves as Iguvines, Camertes, or the people of Sentinum, but afterwards they began to develop a collective identity as Umbrians alongside their identity as Roman citizens.

The history of Italy during the Roman Republic is, therefore, closely bound up with the history of Rome, but it is also the history of numerous different states and regions, each with its own culture and modes of interaction with Rome. Although Rome provided some level of centralising influence, the conquest of Italy was in no sense an imposition of Romanisation at the expense of indigenous culture. The growing spread of Roman influence, as represented by the diffusion of the Latin language, Roman laws and forms of government, Roman cults, and Roman forms of architecture and urban development, is balanced by the continuation of local customs, cultures, and languages.

The crucial period of transition in Italy occurred between the Social War and the death of Augustus, a period during which Latin became the dominant language of Italy and many aspects of regional culture became subsumed under a general veneer of *Romanitas*, reflecting an increasing level of assimilation among the elites of Rome and Italy.

NOTES

1 Lomas 1996; Bradley 1997; Herring and Lomas 2000.
2 Terrenato 1997; 2001, 2–5.
3 Barker and Rassmussen 2000; Holloway 1994; Cornell 1995, 96–118.
4 Salmon 1965, 78–81; Oakley 1995; Dench 1995.
5 Salmon 1965, 78–81, 95–101.
6 Coarelli and La Regina 1984, 230–57.
7 Lloyd et al., 1997.
8 Sherwin-White 1973, 38–58; Humbert 1978.
9 Lomas 1996, 20–2.
10 Livy 9.45; Lomas 1996, 35, 48.
11 Sherwin-White 1973, 98–118.
12 Cornell 1995, 347–52.
13 Sherwin-White 1973; cf. Lomas (1993, 77–84) for an alternative view and Rich (forthcoming) for a more radical reappraisal.
14 Callatis: *ILLRP* II 516; Astypalaia: *IGRR* IV 1028; Mytilene: Sherk 1969, no. 26d.
15 Keaveney 1987, 21–44; Potter 1987, 50–4; Lomas 1996, 46–76.
16 Keaveney 1987, 21–44; Lomas 1996, 79–84.
17 Salmon 1969, 80–1; Sherwin-White 1973, 80–94.
18 Salmon 1969, 70–81.
19 Sherwin-White 1973, 108–16.
20 Brunt 1971, 85–7, 278–84.
21 Brunt 1971, 168–70.
22 De Polignac and Gualtieri 1991, 194–203.
23 Pedley 1990, 113–14.
24 Pedley 1990, 113–20.
25 Brown 1980.
26 Brown 1980, 32–45, 52–3.
27 Castrén 1975.
28 Wiseman 1971.
29 Lomas 1996, 217–23.
30 Veyne 1990, 5–13; Pobjoy 2000.
31 Laurence 1994, 20–7; Zanker 1998, 32–60.
32 Jouffroy 1986, 59–61; Lomas 2002; Holleran 2002, 46–9.
33 Coarelli and La Regina 1984, 230–57; Lomas 1996, 170–1, 179–80.
34 Holleran 2002, 46–7.
35 Morley 1996, 83–105.
36 Toynbee 1965; Brunt 1971; Hopkins 1978.
37 Carter 1998; Small 1991.
38 Rawson 1976.

39 Patterson 1987.
40 Arthur 1991, 81–7.
41 Patterson 1987.
42 Cotton 1979.
43 Potter 1987, 107–16; Carandini 1985.
44 Potter 1987, 110; Tchernia 1986.
45 Cotton 1979.
46 Andreau 1983, 9–20.
47 Hatzfeld 1919.
48 Hatzfeld 1912.
49 Wilson 1966, 13–18.
50 Morel 1981.
51 Tchernia 1986; Desy 1993.
52 Jongman 1988, 155–85.
53 *CIL* I² 590; Crawford 1996, 301–12.
54 *CIL* I² 594; Crawford 1996, 393–454.
55 Crawford 1996, 193–208, 271–92.
56 Terrenato 1998.
57 Patterson 1991.
58 Greco 1981, 171–2.
59 Wiseman 1971; Gruen 1974, 522–3.
60 D'Arms 1984.
61 Bradley 1997.

10: ROME AND CARTHAGE

John F. Lazenby

ᴄ℘ᴏ

The wars between Rome and Carthage, the Punic Wars, were arguably the most critical Rome ever fought. Before the first, Rome was a purely Italian power and its forces had never operated outside peninsular Italy; by the end of the last, its armies had fought in Sicily, Africa, Albania, France, Spain, Greece, and Turkey, and it had acquired its first provinces in Sicily, Sardinia, Spain, and Africa and now dominated the Mediterranean world. After Hannibal's brief appearance before Rome in 211 (all dates are B.C. unless otherwise noted), it was to be over 600 years before a foreign enemy next appeared at Rome's gates.[1]

The first war (264–241) was mainly fought in and around Sicily, apart from one or two Carthaginian raids on the Italian coast and a brief and disastrous Roman invasion of Africa in 256/5. It ended with the defeat of a Carthaginian fleet bringing supplies to the city's beleaguered army in Sicily. By the terms of the peace, Carthage was obliged to pay a huge indemnity and to withdraw its forces from Sicily and the islands between Sicily and Africa. Three years later, Rome used the opportunity of Carthage's involvement in a savage war with its mercenary army to increase the indemnity and seize Sardinia.

The second war (218–201) was very different (Fig. 16). Carthage had used the intervening years to build up its empire in Spain, and it was from this base that the Carthaginian general, Hannibal, launched his surprise invasion of Italy across the Alps. Within less than two years, he destroyed successive Roman armies at the Trebia (218), Lake Trasimene (217), and Cannae (216), the last battle seeing perhaps the worst losses ever suffered by a Western army on a single day. As a result, much of southern Italy defected to Carthage, including the two largest cities after Rome itself, Capua and Tarentum, and the greatest city in Sicily, Syracuse.

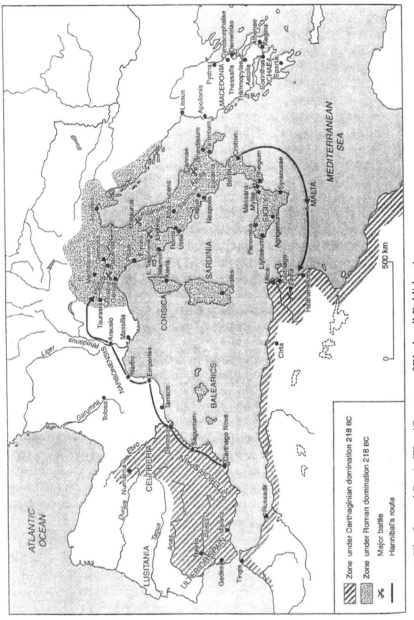

FIGURE 16. The Second Punic War. (Courtesy of Blackwell Publishers)

But Cannae finally taught Rome caution, and although Hannibal remained in Italy until the winter of 203/2, he was gradually confined to its toe and was never able to break Rome's hold on the centre and north. His last chance of victory in Italy evaporated with the defeat of his brother, Hasdrubal, and a relief army, at the Metaurus (207). Meanwhile, elsewhere, Syracuse was recaptured in 212 and Capua in 211, and though the Roman armies in Spain were destroyed that same year, a new and dynamic Roman general, Scipio, later 'Africanus', retrieved the situation and by 206 had driven the Carthaginians from the country. Scipio then invaded Africa in 204 and eventually defeated a recalled Hannibal at Zama in 202.

By the terms of the new peace, Carthage was confined to its original territory in Africa (roughly modern Tunisia), but it otherwise continued to prosper. It offered to repay its indemnity to Rome after ten years instead of the fifty stipulated in the treaty, though Rome refused. But Rome's ally, Masinissa, king of Numidia (roughly Algeria), continuously made trouble, and it was Carthaginian retaliation that in 150 provided Rome with the excuse it needed to intervene by force. The resulting third war dragged on until 146, but the outcome was never seriously in doubt. It ended with the destruction of Carthage.

The evidence for the three wars is of variable quality.[2] The first took place before Roman historiography began; the earliest Roman historian, Fabius Pictor, who wrote in Greek, was probably born towards its end. But we do have a sketch from the Greek historian Polybius (c. 200–c. 118); though not a contemporary himself, he was able to draw on at least one contemporary whose work is lost, Philinus of Acragas (Agrigento) in Sicily, and he also used Fabius Pictor. Philinus' pro-Carthaginian tradition is also partly preserved in the fragments of Diodorus (first century B.C.). The relevant books of Diodorus' younger contemporary Livy (T. Livius, 64? B.C.–A.D. 12?) have not survived, but his account is partly preserved in the surviving 'tables of contents' (*periochae*) and in the later works of Florus, Eutropius, and Orosius. What seems to be yet another tradition is reflected in the fragments of the much later Cassius Dio (c. A.D. 164–c. 230) and his Byzantine epitomator, Zonaras.

The second war benefits from the full text of Livy (Books 21–30) and that of Polybius up to and including his account of Cannae. For later events, unfortunately, only fragments of Polybius' work survive, though these luckily include accounts of the main battles and other significant episodes. For this war, Polybius was able to use the evidence of contemporaries, both men to whom he talked himself (see, e.g.,

3.48.12) and contemporary writers such as Fabius Pictor and Sosylus of Sparta, Hannibal's Greek teacher (Nep. *Hann.* 13.3), though he did not think much of the latter (see 3.20.5). There is also a great deal of evidence, much of it untrustworthy, from later sources such as Plutarch's lives of Fabius, Marcellus, and the elder Cato, Appian (second century A.D.), and Cassius Dio. Appian is, finally, the primary source for the third war; though he appears to have used Polybius' almost entirely lost account, which – at least in the war's final stages – was that of an eyewitness (see App. *Pun.* 132).

Substantial as this body of evidence may appear, it is almost wholly secondhand or worse. Thus, even where we probably know broadly what happened, there are uncertainties. For example, though thanks to Polybius we know something about the organization and equipment of Rome's armed forces, at least in his time (see 6.19–42), we know almost nothing about either the Carthaginian army or their navy. It is uncertain, for instance, what exactly a quinquereme was – the main battleship of both the Carthaginian and Roman navies – and apart from Polybius' description of the weapons and clothing of Hannibal's Spaniards and Celts at Cannae (3.114.2–4), there is little or no evidence about the Carthaginian army. Polybius tells us that, after Trasimene, Hannibal rearmed his Africans with captured Roman equipment (3.87.3), but does this mean he merely issued them with Roman armour or also with weapons? What weapons did the Africans carry at Cannae – Roman *pila* (javelins) and *gladii* (short swords) or pikes? Similarly, despite Polybius' attention to topography, we have only to think of the seemingly endless controversy about Hannibal's route through the Alps to realize that there are still problems.[3]

It is even more difficult to be certain why things happened. As far as we know, no minutes were taken of debates in the Roman senate or its Carthaginian equivalent, and very rarely do we have any evidence about the thinking of the commanders on either side, apart from what the later historians say. Polybius' account of the reasoning behind Scipio Africanus' attack on Cartagena in 209, based on a letter of Africanus himself (10.9.3), is unique. Indeed, apart, perhaps, from Scipio Africanus again, it is almost impossible to know anything of the personalities of the men involved. Polybius had access through his friend Scipio Aemilianus, the eventual destroyer of Carthage, to family traditions about Scipio Africanus (10.29.3), but of Hannibal's personality, for example, we really know nothing beyond what his deeds tell us.

It is also unfortunate that almost all the evidence we have is pro-Roman. If any Carthaginian wrote an account of the wars, it has not survived, and the nearest thing to a Carthaginian viewpoint we have are the few references to the lost work of Philinus, whose native city, Acragas, the Romans sacked in 261. Even Polybius, who might have been hostile to the people who had caused him to be exiled from his own country, became a member of the Scipionic circle, as we have seen. He could be critical of Roman policy, for example, Rome's seizure of Sardinia (3.28.1–2), but his absorbing interest in the reasons why Rome had come to be the dominant power in his world tended to lead him to see things through Roman eyes.

The main ongoing controversies about the Punic Wars reflect the limitations of the evidence. Good examples are the arguments about the origins of the three wars and about Hannibal's strategy and its viability.[4] The immediate cause of the first war is clear (Polyb. 1.7–11.12). A group of Campanian mercenaries, calling themselves the 'men of Mamers', their name for Mars, had seized Messina at the northeast tip of Sicily. When threatened by King Hieron of Syracuse, some of them appealed to Carthage, some to Rome. The nearest Carthaginian commander, based in the Lipari islands, sent troops to occupy the citadel, while the Romans, according to Polybius (10.3–11.3), debated whether to accede to the request. Finally agreeing, they appointed one of the consuls for 264, Appius Claudius Caudex, to cross to Messina, whereupon the Mamertines, by a mixture of threats and trickery, managed to get the Carthaginian garrison to leave. The Carthaginians promptly laid siege to the city and secured the help of Hieron of Syracuse, but Claudius was able to get men into the citadel. Though he opened negotiations, neither the Carthaginians nor Hieron would listen, thus effectively creating a state of war.

But why should the Romans go to war with two powerful states over a relatively minor overseas town when they had virtually no fleet and had been on friendly terms with one of the states, Carthage, for centuries? As recently as 279/8, they had concluded the last in a series of treaties with Carthage stretching back to the first year of the Republic, by which, among other things, Carthage undertook to provide naval aid if required against Pyrrhus of Epirus (Polyb. 3.22–6, esp. 25). Polybius' answer is that the Romans were apprehensive about the possibility of Carthage's securing control of Sicily and thus a bridge to Italy (1.10.9) but that popular greed for booty also played a part (1.11.2). Modern historians are only too willing to accept that greed was a factor in Roman thinking, though they would also add the greed of Rome's leaders for military glory.[5] But the strategic argument has been doubted on the grounds that Carthage was in fact no threat to Rome, and it has even been suggested that the Romans thought they would mainly, if not solely, have to fight Syracuse.

Although we may concede that 'greed' in some sense was partly behind Rome's attitude and that, as is the case with most wars, none of the belligerents was fully aware of what they were getting into, what matters is not what the truth was but what the Romans thought. There is some reason to believe that they had been suspicious of Carthage for a number of years, ever since a Carthaginian fleet had appeared off Tarentum in 272,[6] and they presumably knew that it had been Carthaginian troops who had occupied the citadel at Messina, however briefly. They could well have regarded Syracuse as the weaker enemy, but they can hardly have believed there was no risk of their having to fight Carthage.

The truth of the matter is probably that both sides miscalculated the reaction of the other. The Carthaginians and their Syracusan allies probably thought that Rome could not seriously interfere in Sicily in the face of Carthaginian naval power, and the Romans probably assumed, with their usual arrogance, that the Carthaginians and Syracusans would back down once they realized Rome was serious, as indeed the Syracusans soon did. The war also undoubtedly escalated beyond anyone's expectation with the Carthaginian decision to send considerable reinforcements to Sicily in 262 (Polyb. 1.17.4–6) and above all with the Roman decision to build a fleet late in 261 or early in 260. Thereafter, a war that had begun over one town in Sicily became a struggle for the whole island.

The immediate cause of the second war is similar to that of the first, and this is not a coincidence. The Carthaginians had been steadily expanding their empire in Spain, and the Romans can hardly have been unaware of what was going on. There is some evidence (Cass. Dio 12.48) that as early as 231 they sent a mission to find out what the then Carthaginian commander-in-chief in Spain, Hamilcar, was doing, and certainly, probably in 225, they sent envoys to his son-in-law and successor, Hasdrubal, securing his agreement not to cross the Ebro 'for warlike purposes' (Polyb. 2.13.7). But at some point, probably in the 200s, the town of Saguntum (Sagunto), further down the coast, appealed to Rome for protection, and towards the end of 220, another Roman embassy was sent to warn Hasdrubal's successor, Hannibal, not to attack the town. Hannibal, however, proceeded to do just that early in 219, and after the Carthaginian senate had rejected a Roman demand to repudiate his actions by handing him over, Rome declared war (Polyb. 3.15–33.1–4).

Polybius regarded the Saguntum incident as the 'beginning' of the war rather than its 'cause' (3.6.3) and instead identified three 'causes' (3.10). First was the 'wrath' of Hamilcar, Hannibal's father, who felt that he and the army he had led for many years in Sicily in the later stages of the first war had never themselves been defeated but had to make peace because of the defeat of the Carthaginian navy. The second and 'greatest' cause was Rome's unjustified seizure of Sardinia, which added the 'anger' of Hamilcar's fellow countrymen to his own. Finally, Carthaginian successes in Spain gave them the confidence to embark on another war. Polybius then justified his view that the wrath of Hamilcar was one of the causes of a war embarked upon by his son by telling the famous story of how, when about to leave for Spain, Hamilcar had asked Hannibal whether he wished to come. On Hannibal's gladly accepting 'and even somewhat unnecessarily demanding to go in a boyish way', his father made him swear a solemn oath 'never to show goodwill to the Romans' (3.11–12).

Polybius claims that this story came ultimately from Hannibal himself, and we should thus take seriously the notion that the second war was a war of revenge. But even if the story is true, it does not prove the revenge theory. A boy does not necessarily carry childish promises into adult life, and Hannibal's response to his own later defeat, when he insisted that Carthage had to make peace (Polyb. 15.19), hardly suggests the fanatic. Nor do his own actions in the year before his attack on Saguntum suggest that they were part of a plan to attack Rome. In 220 he was campaigning in the northwest, in the valleys of the Douro and Tagus (Polyb. 3.14), and although this could be represented as 'clearing the decks' in Spain before the invasion of Italy, it looks more like a continuation of the empire building begun by his father and brother-in-law.

Nevertheless, we can surely accept that there was a considerable hostility toward Rome both in Hannibal's family and among the Carthaginian people as a whole. Even if Hannibal was no Hitler, it is surely not just a coincidence that there was almost the same interval between the first and second Punic Wars as between the two world wars of the last century.

But although Polybius' three causes clearly form part of the background to the outbreak of war, they do not really explain either why Rome took such a stance over Saguntum or why Hannibal refused to back down. It is true that the Romans may have been apprehensive about the growing power of Carthage, but Polybius says that although they had received repeated warnings from Saguntum, they had hitherto paid little attention to them (3.15.1–2), and this presumably also goes for any warnings they may have received from their ally Massilia (Marseilles), which had long ago established colonies on the east coast of Spain, for example, at Ampurias and Rosas. Nor had Hannibal gone anywhere near the Ebro since he had succeeded Hasdrubal as commander-in-chief.

It is, however, possible that it was precisely Hannibal's appointment that induced Rome to send the crucial embassy. He seems to have succeeded Hasdrubal in the second half of 221, but it would not be surprising if there was some delay before Rome took notice of the fact. Unfortunately, we do not know exactly when Saguntum first established relations with Rome, but if, as is likely, it was after the Ebro agreement, the accession of a new, young general to the command of the Carthaginian forces in Spain might have seemed a good opportunity to add a reference to Saguntum to the Ebro agreement. Since the first war, the Carthaginians had repeatedly backed down when faced by Roman threats, and presumably the assumption was that Hannibal would be no different. Rome's lethargic reaction to his attack on Saguntum suggests they were simply not prepared for it.

But why did Hannibal not accept the Roman ultimatum? For those who believe in the 'war of revenge' theory, there is no problem, and Hannibal's intransigence and the speed with which he proceeded to attack Saguntum, early in 219, and then planned his invasion of Italy perhaps make up the best argument for believing the theory. But even if Hannibal was not bent on a war with Rome, we can still understand why he chose to ignore the Roman warning. He did, after all, have his reasons for attacking Saguntum. Polybius says that he accused the Romans of unjustly executing a number of Saguntum's leading citizens (3.15.7), and although he does not say who these were or when the incident occurred, it seems both likely that they were a pro-Carthaginian faction and possible that the latest Roman envoys had themselves been responsible. Furthermore, according to Polybius, when Hannibal sent to Carthage for instructions, he also accused the Saguntines, now led by a pro-Roman faction if the above hypothesis is correct, of wronging some of Carthage's own subjects (3.15.8).

These accusations may look like specious excuses, though there is no particular reason to believe them untrue; even if they were, we can still understand Hannibal's reaction without resorting to notions of revenge. If he backed down now, he may well have calculated, he would probably be subjected to increasing Roman interference in the affairs of Spain once word got out that the Carthaginians were afraid of Rome, and this was something neither he nor Carthage could tolerate.

In addition, he may have thought that Rome was bluffing, and even his plans for the invasion of Italy after the fall of Saguntum may not have been anything other than precautionary. Interestingly, Polybius says that they included instructions to his brother, Hasdrubal, 'if he himself happened to be elsewhere' (3.33.6), which suggests that he had still not finally made up his mind. Can we, then, be absolutely certain that he would have marched on Italy if Rome had chosen to turn a blind eye to the fate of Saguntum?

Polybius also goes into some detail about Hannibal's dispositions in the same chapter (3.33) and for once was able to use the best possible source, Hannibal himself. Polybius says (3.33.18) he found the details on a bronze tablet set up by Hannibal on the Lacinian cape, presumably in the temple of Hera, from the remains of which the cape derives its modern name (Capo Colonne). He nowhere describes Hannibal's strategic thinking, but it is just possible that we can get a glimpse of this from Livy, who says that Hannibal later advised Antiochus III of Syria to invade Italy on the grounds that 'Italy would provide both supplies and troops to an external enemy, but that if nothing was attempted there and the Roman people were allowed to wage war outside Italy with Italy's strength and forces, neither the king nor any nation was Rome's equal' (34.60.3). Before accepting that Hannibal ever actually gave such advice, one would very much like to know what Livy's source was. But it goes with the story of Hannibal's oath to his father, which Hannibal is alleged to have told Antiochus to convince him of his loyalty, and may similarly be true.

In any case, Hannibal's actions bear Livy out. Obviously he was determined to fight his war in Italy, and his release of Latin and Italian prisoners after his victories (Polyb. 3.77.4–7, 85.3–4; Livy 22.58.1–2) strongly suggests that he hoped to win Rome's allies to his cause. Fairly clearly, too, he did not intend the destruction of Rome itself. The terms of his treaty with Philip V of Macedonia, which Polybius quotes, clearly envisage Rome's being forced to accept conditions that would nonetheless allow for its continued existence (7.9.12–15), and the only time he ever approached the city, in 211, it was purely to draw the Roman armies away from Capua.

But did he foresee a short or a long war? His despatch of envoys to Rome after Cannae (Livy 22.58.2–7; cf. Polyb. 6.68.2–13) implies that he already hoped that Rome might be brought to the negotiating table, and the sources imply that he was bitterly disappointed at Roman intransigence. At first sight, too, time might appear to have been on Rome's side and a war of attrition not to Hannibal's advantage. But even if he had not learnt from his father's experiences in the first war, he presumably knew that it had lasted some twenty-three years, and his strategy for defeating Rome, as outlined in his advice to Antiochus, included using Rome's resources against the Romans. He may not then have expected Rome to collapse in the short term. Rather, victory would gradually incline its allies either to join what appeared to be the winning side or at least to remain neutral. Thus, Cannae may not have seemed as consequential for the outcome of the war as the refusal, as late as 209, of twelve of the thirty Latin states to supply their contingents to the Roman army. Livy says specifically that the Latins thought that 'if the Romans saw that all their allies felt alike in this, they would immediately think of concluding peace with the Carthagininans' (27.9.6).

In the end, of course, Hannibal's strategy was a failure, and it may well be that he was too sanguine about the attitude of Rome's allies. One wonders, indeed, how much he knew about the nature of Rome's relations with them. His knowledge of Carthage's relations with other states in Africa and Spain and of relations between allies in Greece may have led him to expect a much more volatile situation in Italy, whereas the strength of Rome's confederacy lay in its complexity. Was he aware, for example, of the differences between 'citizens', (many of whom were not originally Roman), the 'citizens with the vote' of Campania, the Latins, and the other Italians (some of whom had joined Rome more or less voluntarily, some only after long and bitter conflict)?

But one should not underestimate the extent of his success. When he took Tarentum early in 212, the two largest cities in Italy were in his hands and some 40 percent of Rome's allies on his side. For good measure, the largest city in Sicily had also defected from Rome, and the king of Macedonia had concluded an alliance. Though things almost immediately started to go wrong, with the Roman capture of the outer fortifications of Syracuse on the Epipolae plateau in April and the fall of the city towards the end of the year, even the fall of Capua in 211 was offset by the almost total destruction of the Roman armies in Spain that same year. As we have seen, the morale of Rome's Latin allies started to crack in 209, and there are hints of trouble in Etruria and Umbria from 212 onwards.[7] Though Livy may exaggerate the alarm felt at Rome when Hannibal's brother, Hasdrubal, reached Italy from Spain in 207, the fact that his conquerors were granted the first triumph awarded in the war is indicative of the relief felt at Rome, and who knows what might have happened had he been able to join Hannibal?

In any case, was there an alternative more likely to bring Carthage success? Standing on the defensive in Spain and Africa was the obvious one, but if there was one thing the first war should have taught the Carthaginians, it was that trying to fight Rome at a distance was a ruinous strategy. Rome's resources, particularly in manpower, were simply too great. The only chance was to cut it off from those resources and that meant fighting it in Italy. The best other alternative, if the truth be known, was not to fight it at all. Yet to allow Saguntum to get away with appealing to Rome was one thing. What if Cartagena followed, or Gades, or Utica? The logical outcome of a strategy of kowtowing to Rome's every demand was finally to have to abandon Carthage itself and resettle not less than ten miles from the sea, as Rome demanded in 150.

By the Third Punic War, the Carthaginians were clearly no match for Rome, but why had they lost the first two wars? The main reason is that Rome could in the end mobilize far more men. The total populations at the disposal of the two cities, at least in Hannibal's time, were probably not too disparate, but whereas military service was the duty of all Roman citizens from seventeen to forty-six and an essential feature of Rome's relations with her allies was their obligation to furnish it with troops, Carthaginian citizens apparently were not obliged to serve abroad, except possibly at sea. Carthage relied instead on mercenaries, hired more or less voluntarily from among its subjects. This may have meant that Carthaginian soldiers were initially more 'professional' than Roman soldiers, but the method of recruitment necessarily made them more difficult to mobilize, both for financial and other reasons. In a slogging match, Rome could simply outslog Carthage.

This was demonstrated in the first war most strikingly at sea. Rome may have won all but one of the battles, but it suffered a series of colossal natural disasters, in one of which, the storm off Camarina in 255, an estimated 15 percent of the adult manpower of Italy may have perished.[8] The curtailment of her naval efforts in the early 240s shows that even Rome was feeling the strain. But, in the end, Rome built a new fleet in 242, whereas after the defeat of the Carthaginian fleet off the Aegates islands early in 241, Carthage clearly could do no more, and its inability any longer to support its army in Sicily forced it to make peace.

Unlike the first, the second war was not a great naval war, yet sea power played a significant part even then. Roman manpower resources, however, were most amply demonstrated on land. As early as the end of the third year of the war, some 120,000 men had been killed or taken prisoner, and though losses were never to be as high thereafter, significant defeats in both Italy and Spain were still to come. Still, the number of legions continued to grow, reaching a peak of twenty-five in 212 and 211 and never falling below fifteen until after Zama.[9] Thus well over 100,000 Romans and Italians were under arms in the middle years, with perhaps an additional 50,000 serving at sea.

This meant that, while continuing to contain Hannibal and starting the reconquest of places that had defected to him as early as 214, Rome was also able to maintain forces in Spain from the beginning of the war and to send substantial reinforcements there after the disaster in 211. Elsewhere, it was able to counter Carthage's allies in Greece and Sicily and even to carry the war to Africa in a series of raids beginning in 217. Its strategic flexibility is vividly demonstrated by an anecdote in Livy, even if it is not true: when Hannibal was at the very gates of Rome in 211, a contingent of troops bound for Spain left the city (26.11.5).

A second reason for Rome's victory was undoubtedly sea power. This was obviously the case in the first war, which was largely fought out around the coasts of Sicily. Not only did Rome win all the major battles at sea save one (Drepana in 249), but it rapidly learnt how to exploit sea power, most notably by invading Africa in 256. Even though the venture ended in disaster, the survivors of the defeated army were rescued. In the end, it was Rome's newfound sea power that prevented the reinforcement and resupply of Carthage's army in Sicily and so compelled it to make peace.

The importance of sea power is not so obvious in the second war, but it is worth remembering that Hannibal was probably forced to go to Italy the long way round by land, in the first place, because he dared not risk being caught at sea by the numerically superior Roman fleet, and thereafter he only once received reinforcements by sea, in 215. Its meagre use of the sea was partly due to Carthage's almost complete failure to exploit the opportunities that the nature of ancient warships always gave a numerically inferior fleet,[10] but this very failure was a tribute to Rome's dominance at sea. When Carthage for once had a numerically superior fleet, off Cape Pachynon in 212, her admiral refused the challenge (Livy 25.27.12). In contrast, Rome again exploited sea power to the full, transporting its armies to Spain and reinforcing them, continuously raiding Africa from the beginning of the war and eventually transporting Scipio's army there in 204, as well as sending both naval and land forces to Greece and Sicily.

But though Rome had the advantage in both manpower and sea power, this advantage still had to be put to the best use, and a third reason for its success was undoubtedly the strength of its political system. We do not have to believe all Livy's patriotic rhetoric, but there appears never to have been a significant movement for peace amongst Rome's leaders, let alone the kind of treachery that disfigured the war efforts of so many ancient states. Throughout the wars, the normal processes of election and assignment to a sphere of duty went on, only once being suspended, and then only briefly and partially, when Fabius Maximus was appointed dictator after Trasimene. To some extent, indeed, this normality might seem to have worked to Rome's disadvantage, particularly in the first war, when commanders, however successful, were regularly replaced at the annual elections. In the second war, men like Fabius, Marcellus, and, above all, Scipio were frequently retained in command by proroguing their *imperium*.

But it was primarily the overriding control exercised by the senate that was so important. The composition of this body, whose members included everybody who was anybody in the Roman state, both made it a reservoir of 'all the talents' and gave it the overwhelming prestige – what the Romans called '*auctoritas*' – to ensure that its policies were implemented. Lacking Livy for the first war, we are not in a position to discern any opposition to the senate, and though tradition held that there had been some 'popular' opposition during the second war, exemplified by such men as Flaminius, Terentius Varro, and even Scipio, we should be wary of taking this tradition at face value. In any case, if we accept the tradition, these popular leaders were in favour of greater aggression, not peace. The overwhelming impression given by the sources is that it was the senate that was responsible for the overall strategy – deciding, for example, who was to command where and what forces each commander should have – and that the senate's decisions were accepted.

It is also arguable that the senate never really put a foot wrong. In the first war, it sent both consuls to Sicily after Claudius Caudex had established a foothold at Messina, and this immediate pressure led to Syracuse's suing for peace and the fall of Carthage's principal base in eastern Sicily, Acragas. In 261, the senate sanctioned the building of a fleet, realizing that Sicily could never be secured without one, and in 256/5 it carried the war to Africa. Despite the disasters at sea in 255 and 253, pressure was kept up in Sicily with the reduction of most of Carthage's bases in the west and the commencement of the siege of Lilybaeum. The further disasters at sea in 249 did not cause this siege to be relaxed, and in the end the building of a new fleet was sanctioned just in time to prevent the reinforcement of the remaining Carthaginian forces in western Sicily, thus bringing the war to a successful conclusion.

Even more striking is the senate's grasp of overall strategy in the second war. Although the decision to send his army to Spain de-spite Hannibal's approach to Italy was the decision of the consul in command, his judgement was evidently backed by his fellow senators, and thereafter a Roman military presence was maintained in Spain until his son, Scipio Africanus, destroyed the Carthaginian armies there in 206. Elsewhere, meanwhile, just enough was done (largely by sending naval forces) to keep Philip of Macedonia in check from 214 to 205, whereas the response to the greater threat posed by Syracuse's defection was more vigorous. Except in the years 214–211, pressure was kept up on the Carthaginian homeland in Africa by continuous raids, and when the time came to send an army there, despite some opposition, Scipio was adequately supported until he brought the war to a triumphant conclusion at Zama.

In contrast, there do seem to have been significant divisions amongst Carthage's leaders in the first war, particularly in the 240s, after Carthage's triumphs in 249 gave it perhaps its best chance of winning the war since its beginning.[11] In its account of the second war, the Livian tradition several times mentions opposition to Hannibal centered on the person of one Hanno, who may be the same Hanno who had advocated an 'African' policy in the 240s (Livy 21.9.4–10, 13, 23;12.6–13.8.4). This story of dissent may go back to the contemporary Fabius Pictor (though Polybius [3.8] poured scorn on some aspects of it), and opposition to Hannibal and his family could have contributed to his lack of support.

But whether Carthage's leaders, in contrast to those of Rome, were divided on strategy, their general ineptitude is striking. Whereas Rome's generals appear largely to have acted as the instruments of senatorial strategy, Carthage tended to appoint commanders to various tasks and then leave them to it, though retribution for failure could be savage (see, e.g., Polyb. 1.11.5; Zonar. 8.12). This meant that Carthaginian commanders tended to have more experience than their Roman counterparts, who, almost throughout the first war and at the start of the second, tended to be annually replaced. It also meant that Carthaginian commanders were often lacking in initiative and that their Roman counterparts were much more aggressive, knowing that weakness would lead to supersession when new officials were elected.

Thus, in the first war, Carthage seems largely to have simply responded to Roman initiatives, making little or no effort, for example, to carry the war to Italy, even when, as at the beginning, Rome had virtually no fleet. Even raids were infrequent, occurring only in 261 and in 248/7, and no attempt was made to land troops in southern Italy, where Roman rule was recent and resented. Well might the Carthaginian commander in Sicily from 247 to 241, Hannibal's father, Hamilcar, feel as many German soldiers did in A.D. 1918, that he had been 'stabbed in the back' (Polyb. 3.9.6–7).

In the second war, the Carthaginian navy, even granting that it was now numerically inferior, was never used to its full capacity, except perhaps in supporting the defection of Sicily in 213 and 212. A substantial Carthaginian naval presence in Greek waters, for example, might have made all the difference to Philip's operations, whereas it only appeared in 209 and did nothing before leaving the following year. The one successful attempt to reinforce Hannibal by sea, in 215, serves merely to point up how weakly he was supported. Indeed, a comparison of the forces sent to him with those sent elsewhere makes this especially obvious: Hannibal received 4,000 men, whereas at least 77,800 were sent to Spain, Sardinia, Sicily, and Liguria.[12]

Finally, it may be suggested, Rome won because, on the whole, it had the better commanders and in the end found in Scipio Africanus a better general even than Hannibal. It is true that Rome won virtually all the battles, both on land and sea, apart from those won by Hannibal. Thus at sea it lost only one battle in both wars, and on land, apart from Hannibal's victories, only three of any significance, Regulus' defeat in Africa in 255 and the destruction of the two Scipios' armies in Spain in 211. But it is not apparent that Rome's victories were due so much to the skill of her generals and admirals as to the fighting qualities of her soldiers and sailors, and in the case of most of her victories at sea in the first war, the device known as the 'corvus'.[13] The only generals who appear to have shown any special skill, apart from Scipio, are Regulus at Adys (Polyb. 1.30.4–14) and Metellus at Palermo (Polyb. 1.40) in the first war and Claudius Nero at the Metaurus in the second (Polyb. 11.1.2–12).

As for the question whether Scipio was Hannibal's superior, this may have been Polybius' opinion (see 15.16.6), and it is one held by some modern commentators.[14] It is not an opinion shared by the present author, and the mere fact that Scipio beat Hannibal at Zama is not conclusive, since by then Hannibal clearly had the inferior army and was weaker in cavalry. Polybius, indeed, praises the way he made the best of what he had (15.15.3–16.6). In strategy, Scipio's decision first to take the enemy's main base in Spain and then concentrate on destroying its armies rather than simply conquering territory was masterly, but his plan to invade Africa was nothing new and was sluggishly implemented. In contrast, Hannibal's invasion of Italy was a stroke of genius and was implemented with breathtaking speed. It took him just twenty-two months from his arrival in Italy to achieve a victory at Cannae that would have brought any other ancient state to its knees.

Tactically, Scipio was far superior to any of his fellow Roman generals, continually doing the unexpected and, at Zama at least, making no mistake that Hannibal could exploit. But here, too, his most sophisticated tactics – those employed at Ilipa (Polyb. 11.22–24) – seem pedestrian compared with Hannibal's at Cannae, which have been acknowledged from that day to this as one of the supreme tactical masterpieces in the history of warfare.

The consequences of the Punic Wars, though they are not as far-reaching as some have claimed, are not just to be seen in the extension of Roman power.[15] Basically, the institutions that had stood the Roman Republic in such good stead during the wars were stretched to the breaking point by the demands of empire. In the military sphere, for example, the prolonged commands of such men as Fabius Maximus, Marcellus, and Scipio Africanus and the anomaly of appointing the last as proconsul before he had held the consulship look forward to the era of 'professional' army commanders that began with C. Marius in 107. At the same time, prolonged warfare led inevitably to the replacement of armies of part-time soldiers by the full-time, professional army Marius inaugurated. It was inconceivable for a Scipio Africanus to use force in the political battles he was engaged in during the 180s, but less than a century went by before Sulla did just that.

Elsewhere, the disruption to Italian agriculture brought about by the campaigns in southern Italy from 216 to 203 and the continuing drain on Italian manpower caused by the warfare of the second century were clearly factors behind the period of revolution that began with the Gracchi in 133 and 123. By their time, too, Rome's relations with her allies had deteriorated, presumably at least partly because of the actual or suspected disloyalty of some during the Hannibalic war. Gaius Gracchus attempted to address allied grievances and was murdered for his pains, but the unrest continued and culminated in the so-called Social War of 91–89.

Above all, perhaps, as a result of the Punic Wars, the Roman governing class became too self-satisfied to grasp that the demands of empire might necessitate changes in the system under which victory over Rome's greatest enemy had been achieved. Time and again, in the second and first centuries B.C., members of this class resisted reform, often ultimately with violence, and, in the end, it was by violence that the Republic was destroyed.

Notes

1   Gibbon 1910, vol. iii, chapter xxxi, p. 217.
2   For more detailed discussions of the sources see Lazenby 1996a, 2–9; 1978, Appendix I, 257–64.
3   For a good exposition of the problems, see Proctor 1971; see also Lazenby 1978, 34–48, 275–7 (Appendix III).
4   On the former, see Hoyos 1998; Goldsworthy 2000, chap. 14; on the latter, Lazenby 1996b.
5   For this kind of view, see Harris 1979, 182 f.
6   On this incident, see Lazenby 1996a, 34–5, and references there.
7   Cf. Lazenby 1996b, 44.
8   Frank 1928, 685.
9   See the table on p. 418 of Brunt 1971.
10 See Rankov 1996.
11 Lazenby 1996a, 144.
12 Caven 1980, 258.
13 See Lazenby 1996a, 68–70.
14 See, e.g., Liddell Hart 1992.
15 See, e.g., Toynbee 1965; see now Cornell 1996.

11: ROME AND THE GREEK WORLD

Erich S. Gruen

⚓

By the middle of the second century BCE, the Roman colossus had cast a large shadow over the lands of the Greeks. The great historian Polybius, writing at that time, pronounced that Rome had subjected the whole world to its rule (Figs. 17 and 18). He added that the advance and increase of Roman dominion was now complete (3.3.9, 3.4.2). Polybius was wrong. Rome had much more expansion in its future. But not only that. The idea that the Hellenic peoples had been subjected to the rule of the western power oversimplifies a complex process and an ambiguous relationship. Polybius saw the outcome as fulfillment of a long-standing Roman goal (1.3.6, 1.6.2–8, 3.2.6, 3.32.7, 8.1.3, 9.10.11). From the vantage point of the mid second century, the extension of Rome's hegemony over the Hellenic East seemed inevitable and irresistible. Polybius, a Greek intellectual and statesman, composed most of his massive history while in exile as a hostage in Rome. It is not surprising that he conceived a relentless march of Roman arms gradually subjecting the Greek world to its will.

The subject of Roman imperialism lends itself too easily to the hazards of hindsight. Two generations after Polybius, the Roman Empire was a fact. And Roman writers were eager to put the best face on it. Cicero affirmed that Rome gained mastery over all lands simply by coming to the aid of its allies (Cic. Rep. 3.35). Neither avarice nor lust for power motivated the expansion, just the noble aim of defending the defenseless. Rome maintains its empire, so Cicero insisted, by serving as a bulwark for those who need protection. After all, nature herself ordains that the strong will govern the weak to the advantage of the latter (Cic. Off. 2.26–27; Rep. 3.37). It was but a short step from this to the celebrated lines of the poet Virgil in the Aeneid asserting that Rome's mandate is to govern, to spare the humbled and humble the haughty, and to supplement peace with law (6.851–3). In fact, the process was

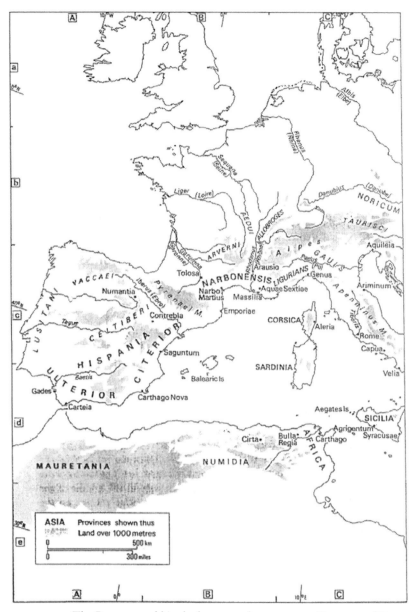

FIGURE 17a. The Roman world in the late second century B.C. (Courtesy of Cambridge University Press)

FIGURE 17b. (Continued)

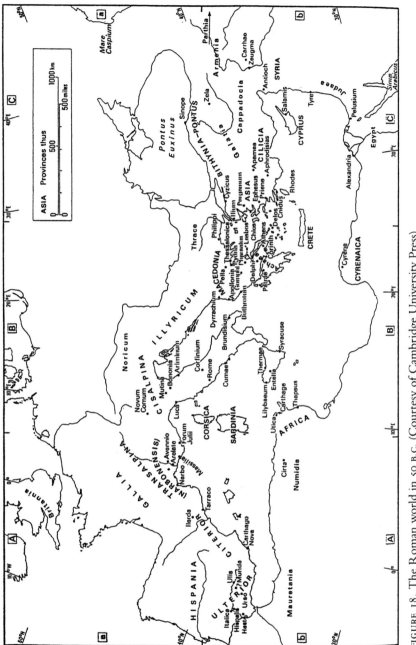

FIGURE 18. The Roman world in 50 B.C. (Courtesy of Cambridge University Press)

not so smooth, the motives not so pure or consistent, and the very idea of empire took a long time before reaching the level of conceptualization.

Even Polybius could not quite figure it out. He took Roman mastery of the world as fully accomplished by 167 B.C.E. Indeed, he decided to write his history with the objective of describing how, when, and to what ends Rome had achieved universal dominion (3.1.4). Yet he reached no clear conclusions on any of these matters. More than once he offered as explanation of Roman success the superiority of institutions, training, and experience (1.63.9–1.64.2, 3.2.6, 3.118.8–9, 6.10.13–14, 6.50.3–6). But elsewhere he resorted to the notion of *tyche* (chance or fate), not a matter of national qualities (8.2.3–6). A clear sense of motive eluded him as well. For the most part, Polybius regarded the acquisition of empire as a conscious Roman objective: the clashes with Carthage were part and parcel of a design for world dominion (1.3.6, 1.5.2–8, 8.1.3, 9.10.11). Yet he could also describe the steps of expansion as having their own dynamic, the First and Second Punic Wars and the contests with eastern kings following upon one another with irresistible momentum that outstripped human plans (3.32.7). Cicero was no less ambivalent. While he might take pride in Rome's protection of the endangered and patronage of the weak, he could also speak of power and dominion as ends in themselves. Ascendancy over the conquered could be its own justification (*Off.* 1.38, 2.26; *Phil.* 8.12). So, even in retrospect, Rome's imperial accomplishment proved difficult to define, explain, or account for.

"Empire" itself is a slippery concept. The Latin term "*imperium*" does not encapsulate it. The fundamental meaning relates to the issuance of commands; only later does the word take on the connotation of dominance or supremacy, and later still the sense of territorial holdings. When Roman expansion took place in the East, the concept was fluid and shifting and was never applied to geographical acquisitions.[1] Overseas empire as an articulated idea gained formulation only after Rome had achieved it in fact. Worldwide supremacy appears first not as a goal but as an accomplishment. Roman behavior in the East seems too erratic, unsystematic, and unpredictable to apply any neat labels. And the process was anything but linear. Romans threw their weight around in certain places and at certain times. On occasion they exercised firm authority, barked commands, or carried off the wealth of a state. On other occasions and in other circumstances, they shunned involvement or decision, showed little interest in tangible gain, and shrank from anything that could be characterized as "empire."

Rome had no presence in the Greek world of the East until the later third century B.C.E. Of course, Romans had encountered Greeks earlier and gained considerable familiarity with them. But the encounters were in Italy and Sicily. The invasion of Pyrrhus had been brief, without enduring consequences. The Greek colonies in the toe, instep, and heel of Italy and around the Bay of Naples had been settled centuries earlier, long before Rome emerged as a power. By the first half of the third century, they, like everyone else in the Italian peninsula, had come under Roman sway. And Sicily, including the numerous Greek cities on that island, fell to Rome's charge after the First Punic War. But this stirred no obvious interest by Rome in the lands of the Greek East.

Rome crossed the Adriatic in arms for the first time in 229. Polybius declared the event a milestone: no mere sidelight but central to comprehending the rise and march of Roman rule (2.2.1–2). But it may have been more central for Polybius' retrospective construct than for the policy of Rome. The military intervention came with sudden and potent force. Both consuls of 229 headed a naval armada and infantry troops of vast size against the Illyrian monarchy of the Ardiaei in Dalmatia, thus making short work of this "First Illyrian War" (Polyb. 2.11–12). The reasons for the move cannot be determined with certainty. Illyrian marauders in the Adriatic had for some time harassed and raided Italian merchants in those waters, but Rome had turned a deaf ear to their complaints. In the late 230s, however, the Illyrians moved into the southern Adriatic, dealt a surprising defeat to the Aetolian League, a major power in central Greece, turned Epirus and Acarnania into allies, and penetrated as far as the Straits of Otranto, directly across from the heel of Italy (Polyb. 2.2–5; App., *Ill.* 6–7). The Romans may have felt no imminent danger, but they could no longer afford to ignore the complaints of their allies in southern Italy, especially the Greek towns whose commercial activities depended on free access to that region and on the route from Corcyra to mainland Greece. Occasional piratical activities might be tolerable – but not when Illyria had become a political power poised on one side of the straits. Hence, the massive Roman invasion, delivering a swift and harsh lesson. The terms of the peace confirm the motivation for war: a prohibition on Illyrians sending any armed vessels south of Lissus (Polyb. 2.12.3). This reassured the Greeks of the Ionian Gulf and protected the traders of south Italy across the straits. Rome distributed some Illyrian territory to allies but withdrew its forces and relinquished its gains.

The Romans showed no further interest in Illyria for nearly a decade. And when they returned, the reasons were evidently much the same. Illyrian dynasts who had collaborated with Rome earlier developed ambitions of their own. One of them, Demetrius of Pharos, misjudging the neglect of Rome, expanded his power in the south, sailed beyond the line of Lissus, carried his assaults into the Peloponnese, and even moved into the Aegean in 220 (Polyb. 3.16, 4.16, 4.19; App., *Ill.* 8). Rome no longer looked away. Demetrius' activities revived memories among the Greeks of Illyrian depredations a decade before. Rome mobilized against Demetrius not because of what he had done but because of what he might become: a threat to the Adriatic. The Romans once again reacted with massive retaliation. In a major expedition by land and sea, Rome wiped out Demetrius' forces in a matter of months in 219, thus swiftly concluding the "Second Illyrian War" (Polyb. 3.16, 3.18–19, 4.66.4; App. *Ill.* 8). And what followed also duplicated the aftermath of the first war. The consuls brought their forces back home to celebrate triumphs. No troops remained, no governance was imposed. The Romans had made a demonstration of their awesome power. They need not and did not intend to do more. The Adriatic was safe (cf. Polyb. 29.4.2, 32.13.5). Rome took care to avoid any formal commitments in the East. These initial ventures betokened nothing resembling imperialism.

Rome's first clash with a major Hellenistic power came when its path was crossed by the energetic young king of Macedon, Philip V. In the early years of the war with Hannibal, Carthaginian victories stirred the ambitions of Philip, who seized the opportunity to conclude an alliance with Hannibal in 215 (Polyb. 7.9). Not that he intended a direct engagement with Rome (any more than Hannibal wanted him to). Philip entered into the alliance with the expectation that this would eliminate Roman influence in the Adriatric and in Illyria, the areas on which the Macedonian king and his new collaborator, Demetrius of Pharos, had trained their sights (cf. Livy 23.33.1–4; Zonar. 9.4; App. *Mac.* 1). The impetus for this contest, in short, lay not in Roman expansionism but in the ambitions of Macedon.

The so-called "First Macedonian War," in fact, engaged Roman interests or actions only marginally. Philip took the opportunity to advance Macedonian authority in Illyria, Epirus, and the cities on the Straits of Otranto. The Romans, heavily absorbed in the war against Carthage, could do little more than send a fleet to Oricum in order to maintain faith with their friends across the southern Adriatic. Insofar as they prosecuted a war against Philip, they did so largely by proxy. In 211 Rome concluded a military alliance with the Aetolian League, inveterate enemies of Macedon, and it was the Aetolians who would bear the brunt of the fighting. Roman ships took part in engagements in the next few years, and Roman commanders got a reputation for cruelty. But the Romans' principal objective was to keep their allies in the war while they concentrated on Hannibal.[2] That strategy proved ultimately delusive. The Aetolians eventually tired of being Roman cannon fodder, pulled out of the contest, and came to terms with Philip. Rome had little choice but to accept the fait accompli. The Peace of Phoenice in 205 concluded the First Macedonian War on terms that allowed Philip to retain most of his gains while abandoning any claims on the Greek cities of the Ionian Gulf (Livy 29.12.8–16). Rome established no beachhead there.

A far more serious move occurred five years later. After defeating Hannibal, Rome reentered the East in a major war against Philip, this time to be fought to a finish. The Second Macedonian War was no mere sideshow but a contest of significant proportions terminated only by a Macedonian surrender to the might of Rome. Its causes remain complex and disputed. A combination of motives may have prompted Roman intervention: anger with Philip, concern about a possible coalition of Hellenistic states, a desire to raise the esteem that had been damaged by questionable behavior in the previous war.[3] What needs to be stressed, however, is that, like its predecessor, this struggle, which occupied the years 200 to 197, by no means confined itself merely to Rome and Macedon. A whole range of intra-Hellenic rivalries played themselves out here. Diplomatic dealings between Rome, represented primarily by the general T. Quinctius Flamininus, and Macedon during these years had to take account of the demands and aspirations of various Greek states that had deep roots in Hellenistic history.[4]

Roman power, to be sure, smashed the Macedonian armies of Philip V,[5] putting Rome in a position to dictate the terms of any peace settlement. That makes the result all the more striking. The terms emerged only after elaborate discussions and a complex balancing of interests that took into account the territorial goals and ancestral claims of numerous Greek states. At the Isthmian Games of 196 in Corinth, Flamininus announced to an astonished Hellenic world that Rome would leave the Greeks free, ungarrisoned, relieved of tribute, and subject only to their own laws (Polyb. 18.46.5–15; Livy 33.32–3; Plut. *Flam.* 10.3–10). Flamininus did not here reach back into the Roman diplomatic arsenal to produce his expression of policy. The slogan had solid Greek credentials, long since employed by Hellenic kings and dynasts, a propaganda technique simply borrowed by the Romans. The familiar convention was surprising only in that the Greeks now heard it from the mouth of a Roman conqueror.[6] The slogan proved to be conveniently elastic and malleable – and had always been so in the Greek experience. "Freedom and autonomy" were entirely compatible with the hegemony of larger entities over smaller. Hence the peace arrangements reshuffled a host of alignments within the Greek mainland but imposed no Roman presence.[7] The Romans could posture as liberators without reordering the political geography of Hellas to suit any novel design of their own. In 194, in fact, Flamininus made yet another splashy pronouncement: the Romans would now evacuate the garrisons they had seized from Philip and would withdraw all their forces from Greece. He left to the Greeks the job of protecting the liberty that Rome had bequeathed them (Livy 34.48–9).

Was this hypocrisy and deceit? Did the Romans hide behind a screen of Greek sloganeering, only to institute a subtle protectorate that would assure their indirect control and provide a pretext for their return?

It might appear so. For the Romans did indeed return, and only three years later. This time they confronted the recalcitrant Aetolians, disgruntled former allies who sought a larger share of the territorial spoils than they had received, and, more importantly, the wealthy and extensive empire of the Seleucids, now ruled by Antiochus III ("the Great"). To interpret this, however, as another step in the inexorable Roman march to bend the Greek world to their will would be an example of drastic reductionism, as the situation was in fact highly complex. Internal Greek rivalries and traditional ambitions lay behind the developments. Aetolia's aggrandizement came not as resistance to Rome's growing hegemony but as an opportunistic move to benefit from Rome's departure. Appeals to Sparta and to Antiochus served to advance Aetolian territorial aims in Greece rather than to resist the western power that was now far away. Antiochus, for his part, expanded his holdings steadily at the end of the third and beginning of the second century, moving his forces all the way to western Asia Minor and the Hellespont. Rome had engaged in diplomatic sparring with Antiochus ever since the beginning of the decade of the 190s but had refrained from any direct interference with the king's advance. He was, in fact, an *amicus* (an acknowledged friend) of the Roman Republic. The Isthmian declaration of Flamininus in 196 had insisted on the liberty of Asian Greeks as well as those on the mainland (Polyb. 18.47.1–2; Livy 33.34.2–4). But despite remonstrances with Antiochus by Roman envoys, Rome left the king's acquisitions untouched. Neither party showed an inclination to come to blows. Far from it. Antiochus even pushed for an official treaty of alliance, which the Romans refused – as they did with other Greek powers. They preferred to avoid formal commitments in the East. Relations remained cordial nonetheless.

An Aetolian invitation to Antiochus in 192 set events in motion. The Syrian monarch welcomed the occasion to project himself as a champion of Greek liberty – a posture that had a long history in the house of the Seleucids. He had come to enhance his image, not to wage war. Rome and Antiochus competed to advance their reputations as benefactors of Greece. But report and rumor about aggressive aims rapidly circulated, doubtless spread by Antiochus' enemies in the East, notably Eumenes, the ruler of Pergamum. Tensions rose and Greek states hastened to take sides in the event of open conflict. That process, of course, only made conflict more likely. Rival propaganda drove the parties apart, and prodding by other ambitious states, Aetolia on the one side, Eumenes on the other, set the stage for war.

Here again Hellenic aspirations, not Roman expansionism, triggered conflict. The Aetolians hoped to recover territory lost in the settlement of 196, Eumenes intended to weaken Seleucid authority in Asia Minor, and Antiochus looked forward to acknowledgment as chief patron of Hellenic liberty. The outbreak of war stemmed from competing images projected by the principals rather than their eagerness for hostilities.[8] It signals no desire on Rome's part to extend a dominion into the East.

The solicitation of Roman arms, however, had devastating, even if unintended, effects. The military might of the Republic drove Antiochus out of Greece, subdued the army of Aetolia, and brought its troops to Asia for the first time, and delivered a decisive blow to the Seleucid forces. A Roman victory at Magnesia in 190 compelled surrender by the king.[9] The senate in Rome then imposed a humiliating treaty upon Aetolia (Polyb. 21.32.2–4; Livy 38.11.2–3). And the peace agreement of Apamea in 188 required Antiochus to abandon all his claims to territory west of the Taurus, to renounce any hope of advance into the Aegean or Europe, and to pay a huge indemnity (Polyb. 21.43; Livy 38.38). A new political geography in the Greek East would now indeed take hold.

But it was not the imposition of a Roman system. As with the Second Macedonian War, this "Syrian War" involved much more than a contest between Rome and Antiochus the Great. A host of other states engaged in the struggle, each for its own ends, some indeed instrumental in bringing it about in the first place, and all eager to benefit from its outcome. The map of the Greek world did indeed show some decided changes, and the powers that benefited most from these were

Macedon, Achaea, Pergamum, and Rhodes. Rome had once more put its military power on display, yet the aftermath of this war witnessed no Roman installation or annexation. If there was "hegemony" in any tangible sense, it would be difficult to discern. Antiochus retained his throne, as Philip had retained his. The Seleucid king was barred from westward expansion but retained full authority in the heartland of his empire, Syria, Palestine, and Mesopotamia. The inhabitants of Anatolia looked to more immediate hegemons like Eumenes and Rhodes. On the Greek mainland, Achaea held sway in the Peloponnese, Philip had made gains in Thessaly, and even the defeated Aetolians kept control of their confederacy. The familiar quarrels and resolutions of the Hellenistic world lay behind the new scenario, not the imperialism of Rome.

How far did Roman policy impinge upon the affairs of Greek states in the decade and a half after the peace of Apamea? The awesome power of the Republic lurked in the background, a prospective source of support to those who had been its allies in the Antiochene war and a hope for those who sought to better their fortunes in the aftermath of that war. Hellenic embassies regularly appeared in Rome importuning the senate and requesting assistance against their foes. But the Roman leadership in general held aloof from the quarrels and rivalries of Hellenic peoples. Diplomatic missions became formalities, and Roman pronouncements were little more than gestures. For the most part, the maneuverings by and contests among Hellenistic states operated along traditional lines and hardly seemed to reflect an awareness of any Roman "hegemony." These states maintained contact with Rome but pursued their own foreign policy, at times citing Roman encouragement but more frequently exploiting Roman indifference.

Macedon itself stayed free of Roman dictation. Philip V's ambitions had been curtailed but not shackled by military defeat. He had become an *amicus* of Rome and offered his services in the war on Aetolia and Antiochus. His gains from that conflict were considerable: not only territorial acquisitions but the cancellation of his indemnity payments to Rome. Release from that obligation sent a symbolic message that acknowledged Macedon's full autonomy. Philip's aggrandizement in Thrace and Thessaly called forth protests from his victims and appeals to Rome but led to no real restraint upon his actions.[10]

Little change ensued on that score when Philip's son Perseus succeeded to the throne in 179. He renewed *amicitia* with Rome and revived his father's policy of augmenting Macedonian influence abroad. But he did so through diplomatic connections, marriage alliances, and the bestowal of benefits rather than through aggressive expansionism. In 174

Perseus made an ostentatious trip to Delphi to consult the oracle and announce his good will to all Greeks, accompanied by an army that conspicuously refrained from any depredations while in Greece. The public relations move seems to have won Perseus considerable popularity. Those who hoped to curb his ambitions got no support from Rome.

The rise of Macedonian prestige and the increase in Macedonian influence was bound to cause misgivings among some Greeks, however. Eumenes, the king of Pergamum, in particular, felt anxiety, placing the worst construction upon every deed of Perseus and straining to rouse Roman action against him in 172. Rome might indeed be concerned about a dramatic rise in Macedonian authority in Greece, not because it menaced Roman interests or challenged any Roman hegemony but because it might upset the political balance and bring instability to the region. Even so, the senate was reluctant to intervene, preferring diplomacy to hostilities. Roman envoys dispersed around the Hellenistic world to ensure the continued benevolence of kings, leagues, and cities everywhere and, presumably, to deter Perseus from translating his popularity into belligerence. Complex diplomatic maneuverings followed, and these occupied more than a year. Neither side seemed eager to engage in open warfare. Rome may have hoped that intimidation would prevent it; Perseus preferred mediation but would not submit to humiliation. This left little room for maneuver. The Third Macedonian War broke out in 171. It came not as a consequence of long-simmering animosity or a clash of competing hegemonies but as an unanticipated breakdown in mutual trust.[11]

The war, however, like its predecessors, constituted much more than a clash between Rome and a major Hellenistic kingdom. A complex diversity of Greek feuds, animosities, and ambitions played themselves out, just as they had in the two previous Macedonian wars and the Syrian war. This was by no means a simple contest between superpowers.

One should note at the outset that Rome could not count on automatic loyalty or support from Hellenic states even in an effort ostensibly undertaken on their behalf. Roman embassies had to seek assistance for the cause rather than simply commandeer it. Guarded reactions came from various states. The Achaean League, which had an alliance with Rome, nevertheless wavered during the war, its counsels divided, and the support that it offered was decidedly lukewarm. The Romans even had to solicit the help of the Aetolian Confederacy, although it had signed a treaty in 189 to honor the majesty and power of Rome.

The Aetolians showed little enthusiasm for the war, maintained an independent posture, and made ad hoc decisions on grounds of security rather than commitment. Elsewhere, internal divisions racked states like Thessaly, Epirus, Acarnania, and Boeotia, none of whom automatically followed a Roman lead.[12] Perseus' initial success, in fact, generated jubilance in various parts of Greece (Polyb. 27.9–10; Livy 42.63.1–2; Diod. Sic. 30.8). Even the presence of Roman forces did not sweep Hellas unanimously into the fray. The Greeks did not consider themselves as compliant clients of the western power.

Rome crushed the Macedonian kingdom once and for all at the battle of Pydna in 168.[13] But Perseus had proved to be a far more formidable foe than the Romans had anticipated. The enthusiasm shown by many Greeks for Perseus must have rankled in Rome. Support for the western cause had been inadequate, and loyalty was suspect everywhere from Achaea to Pergamum. The Romans were determined to retaliate.

On the face of it, Pydna seems to be a decisive turning point. The measures taken in the wake of it indicate a much more forceful Roman posture and a determination to bend the Greek world to Roman will. The senate abolished the Macedonian monarchy, shut down the gold and silver mines, placed restrictions on economic activities, and instructed that half of the taxes previously paid would henceforth go to Rome (Livy 45.17–18, 45.29; Diod. Sic. 31.8). In Greek cities and states, ambitious politicians were swift to brand their rivals as secret sympathizers with Macedon, thus to stir Roman wrath and place themselves in authority. The Romans cooperated readily. They transported one thousand Achaean leaders to Italy, where they were held in a semi-hostage condition. They took similar actions against suspect political figures from Aetolia, Boeotia, Epirus, Acarnania, Thessaly, and Perrhaebia (Polyb. 30.7.5–7, 30.13, 32.5.6; Livy 45.31.4–11). The Roman commander L. Aemilius Paullus delivered an even more severe message to the Epirotes: he destroyed seventy Epirote towns and sold 150,000 men into slavery (Polyb. 30.15; Livy 45.34.1–6; Plut. *Aem.* 29.1–3). The island of Rhodes was victimized as well. Rhodian envoys had come to Rome to mediate between the major powers, only to discover the outcome at Pydna. An offer to mediate under those circumstances could only be interpreted as an act favoring Perseus' interests. The senate would make an example of Rhodes, as it had of allegedly perfidious Greeks on the mainland. Some senators even threatened war, and the body as a whole declared that the Rhodians were no longer friends of Rome. The pronouncement stirred rebellion among cities in the

Rhodian sphere of influence. And a further senatorial act made Delos into a free port, thereby drastically reducing the revenues that Rhodes had enjoyed from its harbor dues. The island's political prestige and economic well-being both sank precipitously (Polyb. 29.19, 30.4–10, 30.20–1, 30.31; Livy 45.3.3–8, 45.10, 45.20–5).

Even Pergamum, despite its substantial assistance in the war, suffered from Roman displeasure. Rumors of Eumenes' secret dealings with Perseus, however implausible, were exploited by his enemies or seized as a pretext by the Romans. The senate rejected Eumenes' claim on Thracian cities, offered no aid for his resistance to a Galatian invasion, and refused even to grant the king a hearing after he had made the long journey all the way to Italy (Polyb. 29.22, 30.1–3, 30.19; Livy 45.19–20, 45.34.10–14, Per. 46; Diod. Sic. 31.12–13). The Syrian ruler Antiochus IV had used the opportunity of the Third Macedonian War to conduct two invasions of Egypt, new additions to the long series of contests between the Seleucids and the Ptolemies. The aggressions, hitherto carried on with impunity, suddenly terminated in dramatic fashion. The Roman envoy C. Popillius Laenas received news of Pydna and instructions to halt the war in Egypt forthwith. The timing was perfect. Antiochus had already reached the outskirts of Alexandria when Laenas arrived with a brusque and unequivocal ultimatum. He demanded a withdrawal of Seleucid forces, and when the king hesitated, Laenas drew a circle in the sand around him, demanding a reply before he stepped out of it. Antiochus had no option but to comply (Polyb. 29.27.1–10; Livy 45.12.3–8; Diod. Sic. 31.2; App. Syr. 66). A Roman decision thus brought the Syrian-Egyptian war to an abrupt end. In view of all this, it is no surprise that Polybius identified the settlement after Pydna as the culmination of Roman control over the Mediterranean (3.4.2–3).

Did the year 168 mark the decisive turning point? Had the Hellenistic world now come under the direct suzerainty of Rome? The answer is not as simple as it might seem. The Republic had fought a long and exasperating war, largely unaided by those who should have rallied to its cause. The mood in the senate was one of fury and ardor for reprisal. Erstwhile friend and foe alike suffered from that Roman drive for retribution. But whether this amounted to an installation of Roman dominion over the East is another matter. The most surprising feature of the next two decades is not the contrast but the continuities with the past.

The Romans evacuated their forces from the East after the Third Macedonian War, as they had after each of the previous contests. There would be no Roman military occupation, nor indeed any Roman administrative structure. As the events of the war receded in time, Hellenic states gradually reverted to familiar patterns of political, military, and diplomatic behavior.

On mainland Greece, few changes of any consequence in the political geography occurred after the war. Greek hostages remained in Italy for the next two decades. But the leaders who ran affairs in the various states of Greece were certainly not doing Rome's bidding. The men in power after Pydna were, for the most part, replaced by political foes during that period.[14] The Republic showed little concern with the course of events in each state.

In Anatolia, the effects of Pydna seem barely discernible. Eumenes had been snubbed by the senate in Italy. He could therefore expect no support from Rome in his struggles with Prusias II of Bithynia and the Galatians. But he had had very little in the past, and he proved to need none in the present. Pergamene fortunes, in fact, flourished in the 160s, with no trace of any negative effects from Pydna. The successes continued under Attalus II, Eumenes' brother and successor, in the 150s. Protégés of Pergamum now held power in Bithynia, Cappadocia, and Syria.[15] If Rome ran affairs in Anatolia, no one seems to have noticed.

The Rhodians had reached a low point in the aftermath of Pydna. The senate had wished to make an example of their state. Once the demonstration had taken effect, however, the island proceeded to recovery. Rhodes resumed diplomatic activity and rebuilt a network of associations, including a link with Pergamum, a former enemy. There was economic improvement as well; commercial connections revived. By 164 Rhodes enjoyed a full-scale alliance with Rome.[16]

The humbling of Antiochus IV outside Alexandria had shattered his plan to make Egypt a dependency. But the Seleucid empire did not thereby sink into the status of a languid client. Antiochus shortly thereafter advertised the vast wealth and resources of his realm at a pageant near Antioch. He proceeded to advance and consolidate Seleucid imperial holdings in the East before his death. Complex maneuverings and fierce rivalries within the royal house plagued the Syrian kingdom in the following decades. Ptolemy VI of Egypt, for example, sponsored two successive contenders for the crown in Antioch from the late 150s through the mid 140s, thus neatly reversing the scheme of Antiochus IV, who had hoped to have his own appointees in Alexandria twenty years before. The various intrigues fell afoul of fortune or failed through miscalculation. But there is little sign of active interference by Rome.[17]

Egypt might seem more beholden to Rome, as Popillius Laenas' mission had saved it from Seleucid overlordship. In addition, for the twenty years following the end of the Third Macedonian War, the brothers Ptolemy VI Philometor and Ptolemy VIII Euergetes II were engaged in a power struggle and repeatedly went to Rome or sent their supporters to gain senatorial backing for their aspirations. But Rome never went beyond verbiage and embassies. Euergetes' schemes got him nowhere, and Philometor gained the upper hand by evading or ignoring rather than adhering to senatorial decrees. The latter even succeeded in annexing Coele Syria and claiming a double diadem in Antioch as ruler of both "Asia and Egypt" shortly before his death in 145. He obviously felt no restraint from Rome. Far from behaving like a client of the western colossus, the king of Egypt installed his own clients in power.[18]

In the year following Pydna, the only drastic break with the past came in Macedon itself (and in the neighboring region of Illyria). The Romans terminated the Antigonid monarchy, created four independent republics, and imposed harsh economic sanctions upon the land. Even here, however, the measures did not amount to the installation of Roman rule. The republics would be governed by their own constitutional and administrative machinery. Macedonians rather than Romans ran the iron and copper mines, and the gold and silver mines were reopened a decade after Pydna. The nation would now pay half its taxes to Rome, whether on a temporary or a permanent basis. But the other half would finance the new regimes in the Macedonian republics, clearly intended as enduring governments. The westerners evidently planned to stay home.[19]

The settlement held for almost twenty years. Roman "hegemony" was felt only lightly during that period. Greek states pursued conventional objectives and fought out traditional feuds. The various players in these games frequently sought Roman assistance and regularly claimed Roman friendship, expecting it to enhance their political standing. A connection to Rome could be a source of pride and a means of intimidation. But the parties to these seemingly interminable disputes pursued their own foreign policies, exploiting Roman pronouncements when useful, ignoring them when unsuitable. They had learned not to expect direct interference.[20]

The breakdown came suddenly and surprisingly. Few, if any, foresaw it. In 150 Andriscus, a Macedonian pretender, claimed to be a son of Perseus and announced his intention to restore the Antigonid monarchy. He won shocking success, swiftly gained control of Macedon, and even threatened Thessaly in an attempt to realize the ancient ambitions of his supposed ancestors. Andriscus apparently exploited strong passions among the people, a deep disappointment with the artificial republics, and, in some circles at least, a longing for a revival of the monarchy. Rome, as usual, preferred diplomacy first, then sent a single legion under a praetor. Only after a humiliating loss at the hands of Andriscus' supporters did the Romans move out in force. In 148 they inflicted a crushing defeat upon the pretender.[21] This time Macedonian liberty would not receive even lip service. The Romans erected no new administrative structure, but they would henceforth regularly dispatch praetors and proconsuls to protect the Macedonian borders and maintain a Roman presence. Tribute would now be permanent. And a new chronological era was instituted, its starting point fixed in the year 148.[22]

Similar shock waves hit Greece shortly thereafter. Here too the initiative did not come from the Romans. The age-old quarrel between Sparta and the Achaean League in the Peloponnese set events in motion. The Achaeans had long enjoyed Roman indifference and assumed that it would continue as they coerced a disaffected Sparta back into the league. But the Romans refused to be disregarded any longer. When envoys from the senate received a rude reception in Corinth, Rome's patience snapped. Since Roman forces were already in Macedon and the new arrangements there could be upset by turmoil in Greece, the Romans decided to suppress that turmoil and to make an example of Corinth. The army of L. Mummius completed the job in 146: the sack of Corinth and the subjection of Achaea to Roman authority. A new dating era began here as well, to start from the fateful year of 146.[23]

In retrospect the establishment of Roman hegemony seems fated and inescapable. Common practice frames the history of this era by the series of wars, from the First Macedonian War through the Achaean War, as if the period witnessed a repeated display of Roman firepower and the steady encroachment of Roman authority over the Hellenistic East. Contemporaries may well have had a different perspective. Major conflicts were separated by long stretches of relative peace (notably between 189 and 171 and between 168 and 148) during which conventional Greek politics resumed without Roman interference, and the wars were triggered by rivalries internal to the Greek world and usually fought out to implement Greek objectives. The patterns of continuity characterize the era better than do the dramatic changes.

Of course, the shadow of Rome loomed over the Hellenic world. The awesome might of its army reminded the Greeks more than once of its dominant presence in the Mediterranean. Greek leaders, dynasts, kings, and pretenders repeatedly called upon the Romans to bestow favors, support their aims, and curb their enemies – all the while know-ing that the chances for concrete assistance were remote. On the whole, they got gestures, embassies, and words. And, for the most part, they wanted nothing more. It was preferable to parade a Roman connection than to harbor a Roman army.

Rome installed no system in the Greek world during this period. On the contrary, its statesmen and leaders preferred to adapt Greek con-ventions that would be familiar, comfortable, and fruitful. One finds this feature in Roman behavior again and again. The Republic refrained in general from concluding formal treaties of alliance with Greek states on the model of the pacts that existed with Italian communities. The latter specified military obligations and bound the partners in a com-mon enterprise. By contrast, the Romans entered into few enduring agreements in the East, and when they did, Hellenic precedents usually prevailed.[24] This held, for instance, in the military alliance with Ae-tolia in 211, whose provisions conceded any territorial acquisitions in advance to the Aetolians, following along the lines of other Aetolian treaties. Greek models also account for subsequent alliances with Achaea and Rhodes, whose terms were conventional formalities, not expected to be carried out to the letter. Later treaties with small and insignifi-cant cities in the Greek East constituted mere tokens of benevolence, nothing resembling a systematic network of Roman alliances.[25]

The more common agreements were informal and extralegal. Pacts of *amicitia* required no documents and involved no fixed com-mitments. They could arise from any number of circumstances, from military collaboration to a mere exchange of embassies. As a diplomatic instrument, *amicitia* proved especially convenient, for its flexibility al-lowed it to provide a pretext for intervention or an excuse for restraint, as conditions dictated. But far from preparing a path for Roman domi-nance, the institution corresponds directly to conventional Greek prac-tice, found in a variety of agreements among Hellenic states, whether peace treaties, arbitral compacts, exchanges of citizenship, or guarantees of asylum.[26] The peace of Apamea in 188, for instance, establishing a "friendship for all time" between Rome and Antiochus III, adopted a formula familiar from Hellenistic compacts – and one that continued to be used within and among Greeks long after the advent of Rome (Polyb. 21.43.1; Livy 38.38.2; cf. Polyb. 4.52.6, 25.2.3).

One should consider in this context even an institution regarded as quintessentially Roman: the mutually reinforcing concepts of pa-tronage and clientage. It has often been claimed that Rome exercised hegemony over the Greek East by extending the patronage system that operated in the social sphere to the international scene, thus creating a *patrocinium* that brought protection to and expected allegiance from "client-states."[27] Of course, the Romans anticipated gratitude for benefits bestowed and expressed indignation at states that failed to show it. But there was nothing distinctively Roman about that. Hellenistic kings too provided favors to cities and showed irritation when they were unappreciated. In the very era of the supposed Roman hegemony, cities and states continued to pay homage to Hellenistic princes and other beneficent patrons and to receive benefactions from them. For smaller states that needed association with larger powers, Rome could be one among several patrons. The island of Delos exemplifies the Hellenic practice of collecting multiple patrons: the Delians dedicated crowns to Perseus, Eumenes, and Prusias (*IDelos*, 449A, lines 14–23). Nor did matters change much on this score in the post-Pydna era. A wide range of cities in Asia Minor and the Aegean instituted cults, games, festivals, and statues to honor Eumenes II and his successor Attalus II in the 160s and 150s. One can find similar actions addressed to rulers of Cappadocia, Pontus, Syria, and Egypt. The kings, for their part, vied for the affections of Hellenic communities, as when several contended to provide favors for Rhodes. Eumenes was especially successful at this game, described by Polybius as eclipsing all other kings in the bestowal of benefits upon Greeks (32.8.5). Rome did not spread an Italian *clientela* system to the Greeks. The practice had a solid Hellenic foundation.[28]

The years from the late third to the mid second century witnessed an increasingly conspicuous role for Rome in the affairs of the Greek East. But it is misleading to refer to the development as the application of a Roman empire or hegemony. In fact, the institutions, traditions, and practices of the Greeks provide the real structure for understanding the relationship between the Republic and the Hellenic states. Romans utilized the institutions and adopted the phraseology of Greeks in concluding treaties, establishing "friendships," engaging in arbitration, spreading propaganda, and fitting into a network of patron-client relationships. The Greeks did not succumb to a Roman system; they supplied the framework, which the Romans could then apply to their own purposes.

After the mid second century, acquisitions of territory in the East came with greater frequency. Yet the concept of "empire" in anything like the modern sense of the term remained foreign to Roman modes of thought. The Romans erected no administrative structure into which annexed territories fit as "provinces" and took their place as units of a composite organization. For the Romans, *imperium* continued to mean the display of authority, not the imposition of governance.[29] And it is striking to note that acceptance of responsibility for certain regions of the eastern world, even after 146, came in no formulaic fashion, nor from monolithic motives like greed for gain or lust for expansion. Ad hoc circumstances, unplanned and often unforeseen, prevailed.

Attalus III, ruler of Pergamum, willed his kingdom to Rome, a fact revealed in 133 after his death. The Romans, notably, showed little eagerness to take up the legacy. Uncertainty reigned in western Asia Minor. A certain Aristonicus, allegedly a member of the royal line, emerged as claimant to the Pergamene throne. Upheaval and warfare followed in the region. The Romans, as often, sent only a delegation in 132 to investigate the situation. No Roman army went to Asia until 131, and then evidently more out of concern for a deteriorating situation and the potential of many states quarreling over disputed territory than to claim an inheritance. Pacification came only in 129, and the settlement that ensued hardly suggests a zeal for absorbing the region into a Roman system. Most of the cities and territory formerly under Pergamene sway were actually given away to Rome's allies or left autonomous. The "province of Asia" constituted little more than what had been the western region of the Pergamene kingdom.[30] Roman generals would henceforth be sent to police the area. But even the exaction of revenues may have applied only to certain communities within it, the practice of collection by tax-farming companies (*publicani*) did not begin for another seven years (a practice installed for domestic political reasons by C. Gracchus), and no sign of excessive exploitation surfaces for another twenty years after that.[31] Both legacy and uprising had come unexpectedly, and subsequent arrangements took place in piecemeal fashion, not as part of a considered scheme to advance empire.

For the Roman senate, the affairs of Anatolia stayed well off the top of the agenda. The princes of states like Bithynia, Pontus, and Cappadocia engaged in time-honored intrigues, with hardly a glance at the new suzerain of the former Attalid kingdom. Rome's reentry into Asia Minor by force came in unanticipated fashion in the 90s. The energetic and ambitious monarch of Pontus, Mithradates VI, flexed his muscles in the region through dynastic manipulation and military aggression. The king maintained diplomatic relations with Rome and more than once yielded to Roman requests, but the disruption in the region grew increasingly worrisome. At some point in the 90s, the senate instructed the propraetor L. Cornelius Sulla (the future dictator), currently assigned to Cilicia, to intervene with an army and to install (or restore) the ruler of Cappadocia, which involved some fighting and a setback to Mithradates' aims. But the Roman action, as so often, came in ad hoc fashion. Sulla had not been assigned Cilicia for this purpose. The show of force seems impromptu. And Mithradates preferred concession to confrontation (Just. 37.4–38.2; Plut. *Sulla*, 5).[32]

Matters got more serious at the end of the decade. Mithradates, together with his allies, drove the rulers of Bithynia and Cappadocia out of their realms and placed his own nominees on those thrones. The Pontic king refrained from threatening the Roman province of Asia or even regions like Pamphylia and Cilicia. But the deposed monarchs, unsurprisingly, turned up in Rome, prompting a Roman commission under M'. Aquillius that demanded their restoration. The senate, it appears, expected no resistance: Aquillius came without an army. The restoration of the kings occurred through a minor show of force by a small number of troops gathered from the province of Asia and elsewhere. Mithradates again did not contest the decision, exhibiting no interest in a war with Rome (App. *Mithr.* 10–11; Just. 38.3–5). But a crisis supervened when Nicomedes, recently placed on the Bithynian throne, invaded the territory of Mithradates, perhaps at the prodding of Aquillius but certainly not on orders from the Roman senate. Mithradates still avoided a militant posture and sought redress from the Roman officials in Asia. He got a characteristically ambiguous reply, but no redress. The Pontic king, shrewdly calculating that Rome was embroiled in the Social War in Italy, retaliated by invading Cappadocia. Overwhelming the Roman force in Asia that attempted in vain to stymie him, Mithradates gained a decisive victory, then followed it up with drastic and dramatic steps. He regained Bithynia, established supremacy in much of Anatolia, captured and executed Aquillius in grisly fashion, and, most stunningly, overran the Roman province of Asia (App. *Mith.* 11–21; Just. 38.5.8–10; Cass. Dio, fr. 99.1–2; Livy *Per.* 76–7).[33]

The events must have come as a shock and surprise in Rome. A war with Mithradates could hardly have been part of a Roman expansionist blueprint. The senate had contented itself with the legacy of Attalus, and it surely did not want to provoke an armed clash in Anatolia when its hands were full with the Social War in Italy. Aquillius may have been overeager to press the cause of Roman nominees, but he had reason to expect that Mithradates would back off, as he had on previous occasions. This time, however, the Pontic king, aware of Rome's commitments elsewhere, confident in his substantial naval superiority, and perhaps presuming that the Romans had no abiding interest in the area, moved ahead with ruthless belligerence. His assault on the province of Asia at last brought a Roman declaration of war. Mithradates responded in

88 with a wholesale massacre of Romans and Italians dwelling in the region (App. *Mith.* 22–3; Flor. 1.40.7–8; Livy *Per.* 78).

The clash may have stemmed from miscalculations on both sides, but the consequences led to a profound shift in the Roman attitude toward the East. Mithradates' authority and popularity spread rapidly beyond Asia Minor to Greece and Macedonia. Rome could not endure such international humiliation. Full-scale war ensued. The armies of Rome under Sulla's command delivered decisive blows to the Pontic king in Greece, another Roman force pressed him in Anatolia, and Mithradates agreed to a submissive peace in 85.[34] The terms of the peace of Dardanus are, on the face of it, quite striking. Mithradates had to yield all territories conquered, to deliver up prisoners captured, and to pay a stiff indemnity. But he could retain his own kingdom of Pontus and even obtain acknowledgment as a friend and ally of Rome – remarkably lenient terms for someone who had trampled on Roman holdings and butchered Romans and Italians in the thousands (App. *Mith.* 55; Plut. *Sulla*, 22). It is also noteworthy that Sulla restored the ousted kings of Bithynia and Cappadocia to their thrones rather than extend Roman governance there or elsewhere. The agreement may have taken this form in part because Sulla had bigger fish to fry in Italy and did not wish to be bogged down further in Asia – indeed it never did receive formal ratification in Rome. Yet those provisions demonstrate that Rome still refrained from widening its sphere of occupied land. On that score, continuity prevailed.

On a deeper level, however, important changes took hold. Sulla levied heavy exactions upon those communities of Asia Minor that had worked on Mithradates' behalf, creating grave hardships and stimulating the influx of Roman tax gatherers and moneylenders. In other cities, even when autonomy was awarded and benefits bestowed, the Roman presence was much more conspicuous and the expressions of gratitude more effusive, indications that the power of the western nation would take increasingly concrete and consistent form in the East. There would be no repetition of the embarrassments inflicted by Mithradates.[35]

The growing exhibition of Roman authority in the East, especially given the continued presence of a chastened but still powerful Mithradates, was bound to generate further friction. The senate or its representatives had not yet struck a satisfactory or well thought through balance between Roman interests and traditional structures in that part of the world. A new clash of arms erupted between Mithradates and Roman forces in 83, not long after Sulla's departure, over a buildup of Pontic forces and a dispute on the arrangements in Cappadocia. Further tensions followed through increased Roman military involvement against piracy in Cilicia that spilled over into incursions on the mainland within Mithradates' sphere of influence.[36] Four Roman legions now stood in Asia Minor, although no stable policy seems to have undergirded their presence. The so-called Third Mithradatic War emerged out of the uncertainties of the situation, the absence of a clear agenda, unfulfilled ambitions, and mutual suspicions. Mithradates formed a link with Rome's formidable foe in Spain, Sertorius. And when the Bithynian throne fell vacant in 74, having been willed to Rome by its last ruler, the Romans this time took up the inheritance without hesitation. Mithradates leaped into the fray and occupied the land. The result was a conflagration that well outstripped in length and extent any previous Roman engagement in the East – and left that region changed forever.

L. Licinius Lucullus led Roman forces against Mithradates for seven long years. The general not only drove his opponent out of Pontus and out of Anatolia altogether but forced him to take refuge with his ally Tigranes in Armenia. There the relentless Lucullus pursued him as well, invading and ravaging that distant land and capturing its major cities, by far the furthest Roman advance into the East.[37] Whether Rome had formulated any clear objectives remains questionable.

Events both in Asia and at home eclipsed any long-range planning. Lucullus soon lost control of matters. He had been circumspect in endeavoring to set aright some of the financial hardships that had befallen the Greeks of Asia Minor at the hands of rapacious Roman financiers. But the slippery Mithradates eluded his grasp. The king managed to return to Pontus and to gain a victory over Roman troops there, while Lucullus' forces became increasingly war-weary and restive. The long, drawn-out campaigns, plus politics in Rome, brought about the replacement of Lucullus in 67, depriving him of the fruits of his conquests. Rome's most celebrated general waited in the wings. Pompey "the Great" received a sweeping command to eradicate piracy in the Mediterranean in 67, and in the following year a law of the people awarded him the task of conducting the war against Mithradates and Tigranes. The Armenian ruler yielded within the year, placing his diadem at Pompey's feet. Mithradates, remarkably enough, continued to dodge and to resist for three years, succumbing only to intrigues within his own family. The plots of his son drove him to suicide in 63. Pompey, in the course of that time, did not limit himself strictly to his mandate. The great general not only extended Roman authority in Anatolia and Armenia but undertook campaigns in the Caucasus, occupied Syria, and moved forces into Judaea.[38] Rome, for the first time in its history, seemed on the brink of a sweeping and wholesale settlement of the eastern Mediterranean.

Settlement indeed there was. And Pompey's came far closer to a comprehensive imposition of a Roman system than had ever been attempted. Yet it is noteworthy and revealing that the structure that emerged was fundamentally a patchwork. In Asia Minor, Bithynia had already been annexed a decade before as a legacy from its last ruler, and Pompey now added Pontus to it to form a combined province. But elsewhere in Anatolia local princes and dynasts continued to hold sway, including the lightweight king of Cappadocia, restored by Pompey to his throne.[39] Even Mithradates' treacherous son controlled a principality of his own in the Crimea with Pompey's blessing. Armenia remained in the hands of the now docile Tigranes. By contrast, Pompey rejected the claims on the Syrian throne by current scions of the Seleucid line and transformed Syria into a Roman province, lest it fall a prey to surrounding peoples. Yet, in the neighboring nation of Judaea, where he also faced a violent conflict between dynastic rivals, Pompey sided with one of the parties, routed the other with an assault on the Temple in Jerusalem, and installed one of the claimants as high priest rather than impose Roman garrisons or governance. If Pompey had some systematic design in mind, there is little sign of it.

Even the new provinces appear to have enjoyed a combination of Roman and local administration. Pontus and Bithynia were divided into political districts that possessed governing authority over lands that had once been royal holdings. Roman tax revenues expanded substantially, and the *publicani* would soon take full advantage – although it is unclear whether the contracts were let in Rome or locally.[40] But there was no neat schema of taxing provinces while leaving autonomous rulers untaxed. In Judaea, for instance, the high priest governed, but the state paid a regular tribute to Rome, a practice that may have applied to some other, but surely not to all, dynasts and monarchs.

In short, the victories of Pompey, building on the achievement of Lucullus, represented a dramatic shift in the level of Roman involvement in the East. There would henceforth be garrisons, troops, and tribute on a steady basis in selected places. No more complete withdrawal or indifference. Yet the "empire" remains an elusive, perhaps misleading, concept. The dispositions that followed the Mithradatic wars reflect that same piecemeal, ad hoc extemporaneity that had characterized Roman actions in the East from the start. An *imperium Romanum* was clearly discernible in the age of Cicero. But it constituted a motley assemblage of improvised arrangements and a segmented exercise of

Roman authority, not a demarcated territory, a tidy structure, or even a describable entity. Flexibility and adaptability remained throughout the hallmarks of the Roman experience in the East.

NOTES

1   Lintott 1993, 22–32.
2   Gruen 1984, 272–381; Errington 1989a, 94–106; a different view in Rich 1984, 126–80.
3   Gruen 1984, 382–98; Meadows 1993, 40–60.
4   Gruen 1984, 441–7.
5   Hammond 1988, 420–43; Errington 1989b, 261–8.
6   Cf. Ferrary 1988, 58–88.
7   Will 1982, 166–78.
8   Badian 1964, 112–39; Will 1982, 178–204; Gera 1998, 73–89.
9   Will 1982, 204–6.
10   Hammond 1988, 468–87.
11   Gruen 1984, 403–19; Hammond 1988, 490–512.
12   Gruen 1984, 505–14.
13   Hammond 1988, 512–63.
14   Gruen 1984, 517–20.
15   Hansen 1971, 120–45; Gruen 1984, 573–92; Habicht 1989, 332–4, 373–5; Gera 1998, 191–205.
16   Berthold 1984, 195–215.
17   Gruen 1976, 73–95; Will 1982, 344–5, 365–79; a different interpretation in Habicht 1989, 350–65; Gera 1998, 205–22.
18   Gruen 1984, 692–711; Lampela 1998, 139–95.
19   Gruen 1984, 425–9; Hammond 1988, 563–9.
20   Will 1982, 385–93; Gruen 1984, 429–31, 518–20; Derow 1989, 319–21.
21   Morgan 1969, 422–46.
22   Kallet-Marx 1995, 11–41.
23   Kallet-Marx 1995, 42–96.
24   Gruen 1984, 13–53. Ferrary (1990, 217–35) sees a more complex evolution.
25   Gruen 1984, 731–44; Hammond 1988, 601–10; Derow 1991, 261–70.
26   Gruen 1984, 69–76.
27   Badian 1958, passim; Errington 1971, passim.
28   Gruen 1984, 158–200; Rich 1989, 119–35.
29   Kallet-Marx 1995, 18–29.
30   Sherwin-White 1984, 80–92; Kallet-Marx 1995, 97–108.
31   Kallet-Marx 1995, 109–22.
32   Various reconstructions by Sherwin-White 1984, 102–11; McGing 1986, 72–9; Kallet-Marx 1995, 239–50; Pastor 1996, 56–80.
33   Sherwin-White 1984, 111–27; McGing 1986, 79–88, 108–12; Hind 1994, 143–9; Kallet-Marx 1995, 250–9; Pastor 1996, 81–103.
34   Keaveney 1982, 78–109; Sherwin-White 1984, 132–42; McGing 1986, 108–31; Hind 1994, 149–64; Pastor 1996, 109–76.
35   Kallet-Marx 1995, 264–90.

36 Sherwin-White 1984, 149–58; McGing 1986, 132–7; Kallet-Marx 1995, 292–6; Pastor 1996, 191–9.
37 Sherwin-White 1984, 159–85; McGing 1986, 145–63; Keaveney 1992, 75–98; Sherwin-White 1994, 233–48; Pastor 1996, 217–57.
38 Seager 1979, 44–52; Greenhalgh 1980, 101–46; Sherwin-White 1984, 186–218; McGing 1986, 163–7; Sherwin-White 1994, 248–65; Kallet-Marx 1995, 311–25; Pastor 1996, 257–86.
39 Sullivan 1990, 30–58.
40 Marshall 1968, 103–9; Badian 1972, 99–100; Greenhalgh 1980, 147–65; Sherwin-White 1984, 226–34; 1994, 265–70; Kallet-Marx 1995, 323–34.

PART 4

ROMAN CULTURE

12: LITERATURE IN THE ROMAN REPUBLIC

Elaine Fantham

✑

By the chronology of Varro, the greatest scholar of the Ciceronian and Augustan age, Rome's republic was 250 years old, and the city itself over 500, before the first literary event in its history. Until the third century, Romans seem to have used stylized language only for the formulae of religion and the law, and literacy was probably limited to the tiny elite who provided the city's priests, legal experts, and politicians. Thus, when literature was publicly welcomed at Rome, it was in a form that had been transferred from Greek culture by a Greek from South Italy; there was drama, which could be performed for a largely illiterate audience, and epic, which could be recited to them.

Despite this delayed flowering, drama and epic developed rapidly at Rome. And before the Republic degenerated into autocracy, poetry, oratory, and expository prose reached a level of achievement equal to the acknowledged greatness of Augustan literature. By 35 B.C. Romans not only heard but also read Latin prose and verse in virtually every genre except the novel; all other literary forms were already represented in the society in which Virgil and Horace, the oldest major poets of the principate, became adult.

Because literacy was so limited,[1] there was a significant time lag between the generations of successful public poetry for mass audiences and the development of personal poetry under Hellenistic influence. Comedy faded after Terence, and tragedy failed with the death of Accius shortly after 90 B.C.; in turn, hexameter poetry expanded beyond epic to take on other material. Satire, first developed by Lucilius, was largely neglected for two generations, while epigram, lyric, iambi, and elegy waited until after 65 B.C. to be developed by Catullus and the neoterics. Although public oratory became prominent during the second century, lacking only the practice of written record, genres of prose intended for private reading such as historiography, biography, and philosophy had not yet reached maturity when Cicero wrote works in the nonpolitical genre of philosophy in the years of Caesar's dictatorial power. Apart from the many-sided eloquence of Cato the Elder, orator, historian and author of a practical manual on farming, no Latin prose has survived in any substantial form that was written or spoken before the time of Cicero, Caesar, and Varro. Yet both the variety and the fragmentary state of texts from the first 150 years of the Republic prevented even Friedrich Leo from carrying his great history of Roman literature beyond the age of Sulla.[2] Early Roman poetry remains a field for specialists,[3] and most students meet only authors from the next generation, the age of Cicero and Caesar, Lucretius and Catullus.

Literary history is usually discussed in terms of the rise and fall of genres, and I shall try to follow their development without creating misleading discontinuities as a result of treating them in three slightly overlapping sections. These sections cover the extended age of public literature, drama and epic, to the death of Accius c. 85 B.C.; the two generations of early personal poetry and memoirs, from Lucilius' satires (after 140 B.C.) to the death of Sulla; and the last republican generation, from Cicero's first surviving speech in 79 to the first works of history[4] preserved complete, namely, the monographs written by Sallust, a contemporary of Catullus and a supporter of Caesar.

THE INTRODUCTION OF LITERATURE INTO ROMAN PUBLIC LIFE

When Cicero looked back to the first landmarks of oratory at Rome in his *Brutus: On Distinguished Orators*, he made his starting point an excerpt from Ennius' historical epic praising the popular eloquence of a consul of 204 B.C. Cicero may have favored this text because it honored the power of an orator over the public, but this year also provided important synchronizations for the beginnings of Roman poetry and prose. As Cicero notes, in 204, Cato was quaestor and the poet Naevius died. Cicero gives death dates for other poets, like Plautus (184 B.C.), but only for Ennius does he offer both a date of birth (239) and of death (169, after Ennius presented his last play, *Thyestes*). Confident of his own original genius, Ennius rewrote Roman literary history by claiming to be an inaugurator and denigrating the achievements of his predecessors.[5] Cicero, however, acknowledges the importance of the two poets who preceded Ennius, Naevius and Livius Andronicus, and goes back a year before Ennius' birth to Rome's earliest literary performance, of the first Latin adaptations of a Greek tragedy and comedy by Livius Andronicus for the victory games of 240 B.C.

Livius was a Greek from the theatre-loving city of Tarentum, probably a prisoner of war from the first Roman capture of the city in 272, who lived as a teacher and perhaps as domestic translator in the noble household of the Livii and who gave public readings of Greek poets. He composed a Latin version of the *Odyssey* in the old accentual Italian verse known as Saturnian, either to draw on the echoes of folk verse or simply because Greek dactylic verse was so difficult to reproduce in the heavy new language.[6] But when the magistrates commissioned Livius to adapt the Greek dramas, he actually composed them in a simplified version of Greek dramatic meters. Only a few lines survive of the epic and of the two dramas.

For the many who had no opportunity to learn to read, tragedies and comedies could ease the unfamiliar poetic diction with the pathos or humour of actors. Livius, who is said to have acted in his own plays, is last heard of as the poet commissioned to compose a thanksgiving hymn for the Roman people after the victory at the river Metaurus in 207 B.C.

Did the dramatic festivals continue to take place every year? Ennius' immediate predecessor, Naevius, produced his first adaptation of Greek drama in the 230s, but there are not enough titles of tragedy or comedy from both Livius and Naevius together to have met regular demand over twenty years. The Campanian Naevius is a more vivid figure in Roman memory. More adventurous than Livius, he composed original plays on Roman themes and also his own Roman epic, the *Bellum Punicum*. Although this epic chronicled the war in which he himself had fought, it included a flashback linking the Trojan legend of Aeneas with the foundation of Rome. Naevius opened in Homeric fashion, invoking the muses as "sisters nine, daughters of Jupiter" (*novem Iovis concordes filiae sorores; Bellum Punicum*, ROL II 1). Fragments preserved by commentators on the *Aeneid* show that Naevius portrayed the flight of Aeneas and Anchises with their wives from Troy; he included sacred prophetic books used by Anchises, a magic ship made by Mercury for Aeneas, and a great sea storm off Africa. It is much less certain whether the person who gently questions Aeneas about his flight (ROL II 19–20) is Queen Dido, and it is unlikely that there was any romance between them. Like Livius, Naevius wrote epic in Saturnian meter, but he adapted Greek plays into simplified versions of Greek meters: iambic trimeters for dialogue and lyric meters for choral odes and monodies (solo song).[7] His tragic titles, such as *The Trojan Horse* and *Hector's Departure*, reflect knowledge of the *Iliad* and a strong identification with Rome's Trojan past. We can read Roman as well as Homeric values in Hector's "I am glad to be praised by you, father, a man himself praised" (*Trag.* 17), and in Naevius' lost national dramas on Romulus and the contemporary defeat of a Gallic chief in single combat by Marcellus at Clastidium.[8]

Livius Andronicus' Latinized Greek comedies were soon forgotten, but Naevius seems to have had a gift for comic description. One of the longest fragments to survive is a portrait of a Tarentine dancing girl seducing her male customers (*Com.* 74–79). Unlike Livius Andronicus, Naevius did not receive any official commissions. His patron Marcellus had already died ignominiously in an ambush (208 B.C.) when Naevius attacked the powerful Metelli in inopportune free speech. "We shall speak with free tongues at the games of Liber the liberator," he proclaimed, then added, "It is Rome's fate that the Metelli become consuls." The Metelli supposedly retorted in a verse threatening him with a thrashing and may have thrown him in prison. Another excerpt (*Com.* 69–71) seems to be a popular protest contrasting the licence enjoyed by comic slaves on stage with the suppression of free speech at Rome.

The epitaph attributed to Naevius claims that the Italic *Camenae* would mourn him because after his death "men at Rome forgot how to speak the Latin tongue" (ROL II 154). With Ennius, who was a speaker of Oscan, Greek, and Latin from Calabria, Hellenic education dictated a certain scorn for old-fashioned *Camenae* and a cultivation of the new role of *poeta* (Greek *Poiêtês*), devotee of the Muses on Olympus and successor of Homer. Ennius seems to have divided his poetic manifestos between Book 1 of his *Annales*, in which he dreamed that Homer appeared to him and hailed him as a reincarnation, and a programmatic introduction to Book 7, which belittled Naevius' Saturnian meter as the primitive meter of woodland spirits. In contrast he claims to be the first *dicti studiosus* (Greek *philologos*) at Rome to ascend the Muses' crags, a man versed in *sapientia* (Greek *sophia*) who now dared to open up the springs of new inspiration.[9] Certainly he enriched Latin epic with a vocabulary that gave dignity and power to his Greek-style quantitative hexameters. Without his *Annales*, there could have been no Roman epic, at least until a poet of equal pride, innovative genius, and erudition had appeared, one who could have made the breakthrough that can be recognized even in Ennius' fragments, the "fractured limbs of a poet" honoured by Horace.[10]

It is generally assumed that Ennius did not begin writing until at least a decade after the Hannibalic War, since surviving excerpts relating to the war are quoted from Books 8 and 9, roughly in the middle of the fifteen originally intended. This would have left six further books to cover the contemporary wars against Macedon and Antiochus of Syria, but the plan must have been open-ended, as he later added three more. Like Naevius, he saw no problem in treating modern engagements like those glamorized by history.

Even in Cicero's time, knowledge of Ennius' *Annales* was uneven. Roman sentiment cherished his tale of Rome's foundation more than any other sequence, although Pyrrhus' invasion of Italy and the struggle with Carthage also kept a hold on the national imagination. Ennius' artistry can best be conveyed by considering what survives of his narrative of the life and death of Romulus. First he presents the mysterious dream of Ilia, daughter of Aeneas, which Ennius is now thought to have substituted for a direct account of her rape by Mars. She is weeping and terrified by her nightmare:

> Child of Eurydice, whom our father loved, strength and life are now ebbing from all my body. For a handsome man seemed to ravish me through the pleasant willow thickets and river banks and strange places. So after that, dear sister, I seemed to wander slowly tracking and seeking you, yet not able to grasp you in my breast: no path directed my foot. Then my father seemed to call me in these words: 'my daughter, you must first suffer hardships, then good fortune will return to you from the river.' When he had spoken, sister, my father suddenly withdrew and did not let me see him, though I longed for him, and I stretched out my hands to the blue temples of heaven, weeping and calling him in a loving voice. My dream has barely left me, sick at heart.
> (*Annales* 1.36–50 Skutsch = ROL I 36–50)

When the twins are exposed to die by the Tiber, Ennius conveys the approach of the she-wolf with bouncing alliteration: *campum celeri passu permensa parumper* ("sweeping the ground with loping step"; 67 Sk. = ROL I 72–4). He also includes a Homeric council of the gods at which Jupiter grants Mars immortality for his son.

But the most powerful set piece describes the ceremony at the foundation of the city (72–91 Sk. = ROL 80–100). The competing twins take up augural positions at nightfall on two peaks of the Aventine, there to await the sunrise. The poet increases tension by evoking the anxiety of the future Roman people, their audience, and comparing it to the excitement of a contemporary crowd at the start of a chariot race in the nearby Circus Maximus. He will infuse the same pathos and suspense into Romulus' final disappearance, evoking the people's longing as they lament: "O Romulus, godlike Romulus, what a guardian the gods begot in you for our country. O father, O begetter, O blood born of the gods. It was you who brought us forth into the light of day"(105–9 Sk. = ROL I 118–21). Later they are comforted with the message that "Romulus is now passing eternity with the gods who begot him."

It would be misleading to neglect Ennius' account of his own times; even in the later books he exploits divine and infernal intervention, such as that of his unforgettable spirit of discord, "the woman clad in warrior's cloak of hellish body, mixed of rain and fire, air and heavy earth" who "breaks down the iron doorposts of war" (220–21 Sk. = ROL I 260–1). The poet adapts Homeric vignettes of heroes in battle, the felling of forests, storms, and a divine intervention recalled by Virgil: "Now Jupiter smiled and all the sunlit breezes, smiled with the smile of almighty Jupiter."[11]

Ennius does not neglect politics. He celebrates Fabius Cunctator, who "restored the state of Rome single-handedly by his skilful delaying; he in no way put gossip ahead of our survival" (363–4 Sk. = ROL I 360–61), and he gives eloquent speeches to Pyrrhus and Appius Claudius (183–90, 199–200 Sk. = ROL I 186–93, 194–5). A long description of a general's confidential associate (268–86 Sk. = ROL I 210–27) may be a self-portrait, though it cannot be surely assigned to any context. Ennius is perhaps the first man and artist that we feel we know in Roman literary history,[12] but scholars have been distracted by his poetic claims of a Hesiodic or Callimachean encounter with the muses and his dream of being a second Homer, and we have failed to celebrate his narrative power and to acknowledge his continued presence in both Lucretius and in Virgilian epic.

Ennius also wrote a national drama, *Sabinae*, about the Sabine women reconciling their Roman husbands with their fathers, and more than twenty tragedies, many adapted from Euripides. Enough survives of his *Medea* and *Iphigenia at Aulis* to show that he could both stay close to his Greek model and deviate from it. Thus the opening of his *Medea* actually "corrects" the nurse's outcry in Euripides by restoring the chronological order to her bitter recall of the launching of the Argo. And though his lines can usually be identified with the text of Euripides, Ennius may change tone or thought, converting Medea's apology to the Corinthian women for appearing in public outside her home into an excuse for being a foreign exile. In *Iphigenia* he introduces a soldiers' chorus and uses it to voice reflections on the evil of idleness drawn from a different tragedy – Sophocles' *Iphigenia*. The pathos of Ilia' dream is matched by the almost operatic laments of Andromache and excerpts from the mad scenes of Alcmaeon and Cassandra, quoted by Cicero.[13] Ennius may have been greater as a poet than as a playwright, but he determined the direction of tragedy adopted by his nephew and successor Pacuvius and by the last serious tragic poet Accius.

Roman critical tradition distinguished Pacuvius for his learning and Accius for his lofty tone (Hor. *Epist.* 2.1.50). Certainly Pacuvius enriched Latin with new forms of abstract nouns and compound adjectives. He also had the erudition to choose unusual plots, often in romantic settings: several plays, like *Medus* and *Chryses*, extend the myths treated by his uncle Ennius or import new complications into the plots of his Greek models. He specialized in scenes of pathos, confused identity, and poignant recognition at the point of disaster, such as in *Antiope*, *Atalanta*, and *Iliona*. Accius, in contrast is more rhetorical, excelling in struggles for power like that portrayed in the *Armorum iudicium* (about the contest between Ajax and Odysseus for the arms of Achilles) or the revenge drama *Atreus*. This latter was his most famous play because of its grim curses and gruesome alliteration, as in

> *Iterum Thyestes Atreum adtrectatum advenit;*
> *iterum iam adgreditur me et quietum suscitat.*
> *Maior mihi moles, maius miscendumst malum,*
> *qui illius acerbum cor contundam et comprimam*

("again Thyestes approaches to attack Atreus; again he assails and rouses me when I am at peace. I must contrive a mightier mass, a greater grief, to crush and cramp his bitter heart" ROL II 163–6). Besides being renowned for his power to convey anger and hatred, Accius was much quoted for sayings like Atreus' "*Oderint dum metuant*" ("Let them hate me so long as they fear me"; ROL II 168). Some fifty years younger than Pacuvius, Accius produced plays between 130 and 86 B.C. He also earned a name for his critical writings on language and literary history.

PLAUTUS AND TERENCE

The twenty-one more or less complete comedies of Plautus[14] and the six of Terence invite more critical analysis than quotation, since texts and translations are easily available. Between them the productions of Plautus and Terence covered just over fifty years, from 211 (*Miles Gloriosus*) to Terence's last play *Adelphoe* in 160 B.C.

Plautus sometimes and Terence always acknowledge their Greek models, and Terence offers a partial description of his method of adaptation in his prologues. In the nineteenth century, before any papyri of Menander were deciphered, scholars often approached the texts as mines from which to unearth traces of the lost Greek comedies. But the discovery of Menander's *Dyskolos* and scenes from several other plays has shown that Greek new comedies were not always as refined as later moralists suggested and that they varied considerably in level of decorum. The last act of *Dyskolos* is horseplay little different from the finale of Plautus' *Stichus* or *Persa*, and Plautus' *Casina*, based on an original by Diphilus, has enough violence in common with the scenes from Diphilus that Terence inserted into his version of Menander's *Adelphoe* to justify accepting the rowdy scenes in Plautus' *Rudens* as part of Diphilus' original Greek comedy.

Instead of excavating Plautus' text to recover the Greek originals, we have learned to explore and analyze the Roman elements and allusions that Plautus contributed, his verbal virtuosity, and his glorification of the slave (or parasite) intriguer. Interest has shifted away from the respectable, sex-free plays like *Captivi* and *Trinummus*, once favoured for use in schools, towards plays of impersonation and cross-dressing like *Casina*, *Persa*, and *Bacchides*, which contain lively female roles, as well as other comedies that exploit metatheatrical humor and the intriguing slave as poetic creator.[15] The finest of these is *Pseudolus*, produced for the Megalesia of 191 and combining intrigue, improvisation, and disguise. It pits against each other the splendid exhibitionists Pseudolus and Ballio, each with their virtuoso arias, at the head of an all male cast. As is typical for this genre, the intriguing slave and villainous pimp dominate the action, while the stern father is subordinated, and the young lover whose problems trigger the intrigue disappears from the end of the play; this play has no female roles.

The discovery of a papyrus from Menander's *Disexapaton*, the original of *Bacchides*, led to a new understanding of how Plautus could rework act divisions in his models,[16] and interest in multiculturalism and "the other" has caused scholars to restudy Plautus' *Poenulus*. Modern concern with slavery and gender has also brought new sociological approaches to Roman comedy.[17] There has also been renewed interest in Plautus' staging and his three levels of musical and metrical complexity: unaccompanied dialogue, highly rhythmic longer verse, and lyric solos and duets in multiple metres. The effect of combining these levels must have been like a modern musical or comic opera.[18]

Increasing knowledge of Greek new comedy has also made scholars more alert to Terence's techniques of adaptation and to the difference in tone between his more sedate comedies like *The Self-Tormentor* and *The Mother-in-Law* (*Hautontimorumenos* and *Hecyra*) and the more lively and farcical *Eunuch* (*Eunuchus*) and *Phormio*. Our concern with women's rights has led to a higher valuation of *Hecyra*, in which the citizen males unite in misjudging the virtuous mother-in-law and generous courtesan. Like *The Self-Tormentor*, *Hecyra* is focused on judging individual moral failure and success, whereas the others are plays of intrigue, featuring more "Plautine" soldiers, parasites, debauched fathers, and termagant matrons.

While palliata comedy (set in Greek cities) was upstaged after the death of Terence by the relatively short-lived togata (set in Rome or Italy), and a revival of the Atellane farces, it was mime, finally established at the annual games of Flora in 173 B.C., that came to dominate the stage at Rome. Though mime, originally with improvised dialogue, was briefly made respectable in the scripted mimes of Publilius Syrus and Laberius, these literary texts – like the gentleman author Laberius – did not survive the domination of Julius Caesar:[19] what flourished instead were sex-farces (exploiting actresses, dressed and undressed) and the uninhibited exhibitionism of the flamboyant pantomime dance artists.

THE TRANSITION TO PERSONAL PROSE AND POETRY

Contemporary with Ennius, and briefly his patron, was Cato the Elder, consul, censor, and versatile author. He deserves our attention as the author of *Origines*, the first historical work in Latin, which traced the origins of Rome from the Trojan settlement to Latium and the growth of other Italian cities from their heroic foundations to his own time. Cato refused to record natural disasters and religious portents or to name successful generals, and his history, like his speeches, strongly reflects his own personality; he even included two of his policy speeches, both on Rome's relations with other peoples. The first (in Book 5) defended the Rhodians for attempting to arbitrate between Rome and Macedon in 167, when Rome was clearly winning, and in it Cato warned the Romans how unpopular their imperialism had become. The second (in Book 7) denounced a Roman commander before the assembly for massacring a Spanish tribe.[20] From a literary point of view, the motivation or truth of Cato's charges is unimportant. What matters is to find a Roman presenting his own political actions in written form for a reading audience. Unlike Cato's original speeches, historical writing was not based on an oral genre, and by publishing these speeches, Cato helped Roman oratory to earn a written form. But though there were serious Latin historians in the next generation, the genre of memoirs would arise only in the early first century, with the memoirs of Aemilius Scaurus and Rutilius Rufus.[21]

A far more significant innovation was the verse satire of Lucilius, a nonpolitical friend of Scipio Aemilianus and a member of his intellectual circle. Poems called *Saturae* were attributed to Ennius, and some brief fragments survive, but not enough to determine their range of content. Thus, Lucilius' *Satires* – personal reflections sometimes couched as letters, sometimes as anecdote, sometimes taking the form of literary and grammatical criticism – appear to have initiated a new Roman genre that had no Greek model. Roman writers offered more than one derivation for the term but agree on its association with a medley; thus Lucilius' first satires were not hexameter poems such as we read in Horace and his successors. Lucilius began with what are now numbered as Books 26–30, composed in dramatic meters, like the tragedies that several fragments clearly parody. He also parodied the programmatic claims and Homeric forms of Ennian epic:[22] both the council of the gods committing his enemy Lentulus Lupus to Hades in Book 1 and the satirical account of Scaevola's prosecution of the Hellenizing Albucius in Book 2 show that Lucilius's later hexameter satires mixed political invective with literary and rhetorical parody. Lucilius claimed (ROL III 635) that he was writing not for learned men like Persius but for educated laymen like Scipio's friend Laelius; his tone generally resembles cultured or relaxed conversation, whose natural setting was a dinner party. And this should be imagined also as the setting of the first Latin erotic epigrams, quoted by Aulus Gellius from the circle of the philhellene Lutatius Catulus.[23] These poets in their different ways foreshadow Horatian satire and the hendecasyllables and short elegiac epigrams of Catullus.

THE LAST GENERATION OF REPUBLICAN POETS: LUCRETIUS AND CATULLUS

Around 60 B.C. Catullus and Lucretius emerge as great but antithetical poets. Though both are associated with the Epicurean politician Gaius Memmius (praetor 58 B.C.) as patron, there is no evidence that either poet knew the other and virtually no evidence at all for the life of

Lucretius and the date of composition of his *De rerum natura*. A letter written by Cicero to his brother in 54 B.C. (*Q. Fr.* 2.10) praises the (presumably complete) poem for its inspiration and artistry, but most critics assume that Lucretius began work on his six books (of 8,000 lines) somewhat earlier than Catullus, whose datable poems can be grouped between 60 and 54 B.C. Lucretius was passionately committed to persuading his readers of the validity of Epicurus' teachings on physics and meteorology, on the interrelation of the human mind and body, and on the nature of human perception and behavior. Epicurus himself had dismissed mythology as nonsense and poetry as useless for, if not obstructive to, understanding the atomic structure of the physical universe, and he had taught that the gods were perfect untroubled beings, unconcerned with rewarding human piety or punishing human sins. His goal was to school his followers in a serene life free of emotion, whereas Lucretius' great poem focuses on liberating men from fear of death or divine anger rather than on instilling a way of life. But even as he reiterated his admiration for the divine mind of Epicurus and his role as mankind's savior from error, Lucretius deliberately chose to compose his work in verse to charm his readers into concentrating on the complexities of the atomic theory and Epicurus' materialist explanation of perception. In his own imagery, men are like children who need to be persuaded to drink bitter medicine by the doctor's trick of smearing the cup with the honey of the Muses (1.936–50). Their childish fears must be cured before they can live properly (6.35–8), and his arguments establishing how men are born, have their physical and mental existence, and die are intended to save them from psychological anguish and allow them to achieve a life of serenity. His strongest gesture of divergence from his own Epicurean professions comes immediately, in the splendid opening "Hymn to Venus," which not only celebrates the goddess as source of animal and human fertility but depicts her as embracing Mars in a vivid visual image of their mythological love-making, then invokes her as a spirit of peace, begging her help in opposing the strife associated with Mars' domain of warfare. This scene from the famous Olympian adultery recounted in Demodocus' song in Book 8 of the *Odyssey* is usually treated by critics as allegory or as the embodiment of the Greek philosopher Empedocles' creative forces of love and strife, since the scene of divine love is followed by Lucretius' famous denunciation of *religio* as misconceived fear of the gods. This false religion drove Agamemnon to sacrifice his own daughter to appease Artemis: "so great a mass of woes did religion impose upon men" (1.101). Although Lucretius focuses his positive teaching on the material universe, his work contains a fierce satirical depiction of the recurring civil conflicts caused by Roman ambition and greed.

The carefully argued analysis of the nature of perception in Book 2 is followed by a detailed consideration of the human mind and heart. Scientific arguments for the mortality of the soul in Book 3 culminate in a section of direct address that sarcastically denounces the human folly of clinging to life, like greedy banqueters from love of material pleasure or superstitious fear of torment after death. In Book 4, a psychologically based analysis of dreams climaxes in the poet's most bitter, almost abusive, repudiation of *eros*, romantic love, as a destructive delusion. The sheer virulence of his descriptions of desire led to the myth that the poet had been maddened by a love philtre and had taken his own life. The resemblance between Lucretius' account of other men's passion and Catullus' obsessive description of his own enslavement to his Lesbia suggests that Roman wealth and leisure had brought the privileged classes of society a new emotional abandonment.

Readers are usually less familiar with the fifth and sixth books of the poem. After hymning the benefactions given to man by Epicurus, the poet explains the nature of wind and storm, and he outlines the development of human society under the positive pressure of desire and its progress in language, music, and the arts despite the destructive nature of war (5.925–1457). Here too readers have been shocked by a surreal passage imagining the horror of warfare if man had tamed wild beasts for combat in the battle line instead of fighting them (5.1308–40). In Book 6, as in Book 5, a relatively calm beginning leads to what seems to have been the planned end of Lucretius' poem, his version (6.1138–286) of Thucydides' Athenian plague narrative (2.47–54). The poet, like the historian, describes this as an evil so great it destroyed loyalty and cooperation within the family and society itself – a grim but unmistakable finale to this world poem.

I cannot convey here the paradoxical interplay of beauty and functionalism in Lucretian poetry; the poet had both to coin equivalents for Greek scientific concepts and to convey a complex nonintuitive argument, but despite the heaviness and at times prosaic nature of his verse, Lucretius honoured poetry and presented himself as the successor to Homer and Ennius, with a theme (the superhuman transformation of nature) comparable to any heroic warfare. He saw the letters of the alphabet as elements giving meaning and beauty to language, just as the atoms themselves give shape and viability to "the nature of things," the whole world around us (2.1013–22). As a poet he exploited every kind of play on sound and sense to beguile the ears of his public – assonance, patterned repetition of emphatic words and phrases, vivid compound adjectives, and even more vivid images. Unfortunately, only some of this emerges in translation. Here is his praise for the heroic courage of Epicurus:

> A Greek mortal man first dared to raise his eyes and was first to confront this fear. Him neither the rumor of the gods nor their thunder nor the threatening rumble of heaven silenced, but aroused his fierce valour of spirit all the more, so that he longed to be first to break through the tight barriers of the gates. (1.66–71)

Translation can perhaps convey the imagery, if not the sound patterning, of his description of the coming of spring:

> But the shining grain rises up and branches grow green on the trees, they themselves grow and are loaded with off-spring; this is how our own tribe and that of wild creatures is nourished, how we see happy cities flowering with children, and the branch-bearing woods singing all around with new birds; how wild beasts and cattle give their bodies repose on happy pastures and gleaming white moisture seeps from their swollen udders; how frolicking new stock plays with wobbling limbs over the grass, their fresh new minds dizzy with undiluted milk. (1.252–61)

Like mother's milk, the Muses' honey of Lucretius' poetry exhilarates the listener and compensates him for the intellectual demands of Epicurean science.

What has been preserved as the single book of Catullus' poetry actually seems to incorporate three poetry books: the sixty "occasional" poems, mostly in lines of eleven syllables (*hendecasyllabi*, 45.1); the eight longer poems (61–8); and almost fifty poems in elegiac meter (69–116). Catullus used hendecasyllables, the seesaw pure iambic meter, and elegiacs alike to convey friendship and encouragement to Calvus (50, 53, and 96) and to Caecilius and Cinna (35, 95), his intense personal passion for Juventius (24, 48, 81, and 99) and for Lesbia, and his political and poetic hatreds. He compresses his scorn for Caesar into a mere distich (93) but repeatedly attacks Caesar's prefect Mamurra (*Mentula* = "Big dick,"; 29, 94, 95, 114, 115); he shoots hendecasyllables in mockery of the poor writers Suffenus (22) and Volusius (36) and men with nasty social habits like Thallus (12, 25) and Egnatius (39). There has never been a lack of admirers for the "Lesbia cycle"[24] and the elegiac expression of Catullus' passion; he can compress depth and complexity into only two lines, as in poem 85: *Odi et amo: quare id faciam fortasse requiris; nescio sed fieri sentio et excrucior.* ("I hate and love; perhaps you seek to know why I do so? I know not, but I feel it happening, and suffer agonies.") On the other hand, a longer and more complex poem like 76 is rightly seen as an early case of true elegy. The short poems also include what we might call pure lyrics, either in meter or in feeling: the celebration of his yacht (4, *phaselus ille*) and his beloved Sirmio (31), the hymn to Diana (34) and the two Sapphic odes, and poem 51 on love's dizzy blend of ecstasy and misery translated from Sappho's Greek. Poem 11 was created by Catullus to send a message to Lesbia by two dubious friends, renouncing his love because of her promiscuous betrayals. This poem of shifting mood and colours opens with the friends' protestations that they will go anywhere for his sake, and the poet answers them with a plain request for a humble favor: "report to my girl a few unkind words" (*non bona dicta*). After a stanza that describes her sexual tricks in the crudest language, his final words revert to Sappho's imagery to evoke the frail flower of his love now trampled underfoot.

Catullus is too often read when we begin Latin, before we can take in the highly wrought longer poems. First come two wedding poems: 61 is a real-life wedding narrative and epithalamium composed in Greek lyric meter for Catullus' friends Torquatus and Aurunculeia, and 62 is a choral exchange between boys and girls exhorting the bride to transfer her allegiance to her new groom. Then comes a long poem in exotic galliambics, narrating how Attis (depicted as a youth from the gymnasia of Hellenistic city culture) is sent mad by Cybele and castrates himself in the wilderness. It pivots around Attis' lament when he returns to sanity, and it ends with the poet's own prayer to Cybele never to send her madness upon him. Central in this group is the miniature epic "Wedding of Peleus and Thetis," which sets in a frame of legendary happiness the tragic desertion of Ariadne by Theseus on Naxos and her rescue by Dionysus. The imagery and sound-play of this poem reach a new level for Roman poetry of sheer beauty and vivid contrasts; its narrative dazzles with shifting pace and time sequences. A description of the wedding coverlet blossoms into the Ariadne sequence, moving backwards and forwards in time from her passionate lament and denunciation of Theseus (in some ways parallel to the lament of Attis) to his father's death and then returning to the clamorous epiphany of Bacchus. The theme of the wedding of Peleus and Thetis resumes, culminating in two virtually independent poems, the song of the Fates foretelling the life and death of their child Achilles and the poet's own distancing of this golden age through a damning account of present-day violations of all bonds of love and kinship.

Poem 66 (introduced by 65, a covering letter to the orator Hortensius) translates a courtly elegy by Callimachus. Callimachus incorporated this homage to his patron Queen Berenice into the *Aitia*, his four-book collective poem that became a model for the learned poetry of Catullus and the Augustan poets. The elegy is spoken by the lock of hair that Berenice dedicated in the temple of Aphrodite for her new husband's safe return; the lock explains how it has been transformed into a new constellation, and Catullus seems to have added, on his own initiative, an account of how this inaugurated a custom for young brides.[25] Most important for Roman elegy, however, is 68, his grateful recall of an intimate meeting with his mistress, described like something between a bridal night and an epiphany. Within this poem Catullus' two great loves, for his brother, dead in the Troad, and for his unlawful beloved, are interwoven with a lament for Troy's destructive war and for the loving Laodamia, separated from her bridegroom, the first Greek hero to die at Troy. This chain of interconnected sorrows is linked by vivid and extraordinary imagery as one theme glides into another, and the poem ends with the poet's resolve to endure Lesbia's infidelities as Juno swallowed the many infidelities of Jupiter himself. In this as in the shorter elegies, the poet submits to his mistress and presents his unsanctioned love as a sacred bond resembling marriage. The lover's ideology shaped by Catullus becomes a generic commonplace of Augustan elegy, but the lyricism and mythologizing of this poem reach a height of passion found again only in Propertius' finest elegies.

CICERO AND SALLUST

So far we have surveyed the development of poetic genres during the Republic. What about prose genres? Does historiography count as literature? Does oratory? After all, historiography is a narrative form strongly akin to fiction. Indeed, it was traditional for Hellenistic Greek historians not only to compose fictional speeches to suit the context but to systematically imitate the form and thought-patterns of tragedy. But artistic historical writing was slow to develop in Latin. After Cato the Elder's strikingly innovative work on early Roman and Italian history, Coelius wrote a colourful monograph on the Hannibalic War, but his work, like the histories of his successors, is lost except for brief quoted excerpts.

We can read the concise (if tendentious) history of Rome before 450 B.C. incorporated by Cicero in his second book, *De republica*, but the first self-contained historical books to survive are the two monographs of Sallust composed after the death of Caesar.

It is more difficult to make a case for considering oratory as literature, since it was both an oral and a pragmatic activity, governed by judicial or political motives. But its artistry was highly appreciated by a Roman audience sensitive to the rhythm and sound of prose as well as to the techniques of persuasion, and it reached its high point with the work of Cicero in the last generation of the Republic. Cicero singles out Cato in his history of Roman oratory as the first Roman to preserve his own oratory by inserting two major policy speeches into his own historical narrative.

Cicero categorizes Roman oratory as either political, delivered before senate or assembly, or judicial; judicial oratory is again divided into speeches in civil litigation or before the essentially political criminal courts (*Quaestiones perpetuae*). But all the best-known speeches served a political purpose. Thus Cato's "On Behalf of the Rhodians" was a deliberative speech to the assembly, but his denunciation of the commander Sulpicius Galba for violating the rights of a Spanish tribe was probably judicial, delivered before a popular court.

It seems that Cicero's teacher, L. Licinius Crassus, may have been the first orator to circulate political speeches in writing, whether for political purposes or to serve as a model for informal pupils like Cicero.[26] Because of the social and civil wars that troubled the 80s, Cicero's own career began quite late, with a criminal defense speech for Roscius of Ameria, accused by jealous cousins of murdering his father during the period of Sullan domination, and a civil lawsuit in which he represented Quinctius against his business partner. But the court case that made his name was virtually his only appearance for the prosecution, when he accepted the brief of the Sicilian provincials to prosecute the influential and corrupt governor C. Verres. Of the seven surviving speeches connected with the case, only the first two, a speech disputing the claims of a rival prosecutor, Caecilius, and his speech in the first session (*actio*), were delivered in court. The five long powerful indictments of the second *actio* were composed to replace the actual court proceedings, which involved massive interrogation of damning witnesses. These "speeches," then, were written for readers, not a court audience, and they remained models of every kind of invective for future orators. Cicero advised orators to compose their speeches carefully in writing before delivering them, and the texts of about forty speeches survive, edited after the event to take account of unforeseen elements in their reception or the relative ignorance of readers. Two surviving orations, one judicial, one senatorial, were composed only to be read: a defense of Milo, which Cicero either failed to deliver or composed after Milo's conviction in 52, and the second of his attacks on the consul Mark Antony in August/September 44, after the death of Caesar. With his tenure of the consulship, however, Cicero felt he had earned recognition as a statesman, and in 60 B.C. he wrote to Atticus (*Att.* 2.1.3) asking for his professional help in publishing a retrospective body of ten speeches from his consulship. About half of these were addressed to meetings of the people (*contiones*), and readers can still compare at least the language, if not the style of delivery, in which Cicero presented the successive crises of Catiline's attempted uprising to the popular audience (*In Catilinam* 2 and 3) and to his peers in the senate. The same comparison can be made between his speeches of thanks to the senate and to the assembled Roman people after his recall from exile in 57, or between two speeches of encomium: his advocacy to the people of the extraordinary command awarded to Pompey in 66 (*De imperio Gnaei Pompei*) and his support in the senate for the prolongation of Caesar's extraordinary command in Gaul in 56 (*De provinciis consularibus*). The people included both rich and poor. The business class was best moved by economic issues, the humbler craftsmen and shopkeepers were more alarmed by talk of arson within the city or thrilled by military glory, so naturally these relatively short speeches stressed Cicero's own tireless devotion to their interests and his faith in the immortal gods. As for the senate, Cicero may call it a wise body of advisors (*sapiens consilium; De or.* 2.333), but he knew the senators to be influenced by a variety of partisan interests that must be conciliated.

In the lawcourts, Roman career orators usually made their debut as prosecutors, like Cicero's brilliant pupil Caelius, but avoided the offense inherent in speaking for the prosecution once they were launched. Their speeches were not courtroom speeches as we know them but public orations in the open forum before a large jury and an inquisitive and partisan crowd (engaged in a favourite form of public entertainment). Three defense speeches in particular appeal to us for their reflection of Roman culture: a speech on behalf of the citizen status of the poet Archias (*c.* 66 B.C.), in which Cicero went out of his way to praise poetry for immortalizing its subject and inspiring posterity to emulate heroic deeds; a speech on behalf of Licinius Murena against charges of winning his election by bribery, in which Cicero set up a brilliant contrast between the popular appeal of a successful general like Murena and the narrower reputation of a legal expert like his defeated rival;

and finally the defense of his pupil Caelius. In Caelius' trial for public violence, Cicero was the third and final speaker, after Caelius himself and Publius Crassus. It was his role to dispel Caelius' bad reputation as a debauchee, and he made brilliant use of the relaxed morality of comedy and mime and of *prosopopoeia* ("impersonation") to turn the accusations against Caelius' ex-lover Clodia and to present him as the innocent victim of an older woman's spite.

Cicero saw the Athenian politician Demosthenes as his model, not only for the technical brilliance of his oratory, but for his patriotic role in rallying the Athenians to defend their liberty against Philip of Macedon. It was in imitation of Demosthenes that, in 60 B.C., he prepared his corpus of consular speeches and also that he gave the name "Philippics" to fourteen speeches against Mark Antony in his last year of life. But his first theoretical work, the dialogue *De oratore*, composed after he had been virtually excluded from independent politics in 55, reveals a knowledge of Greek prose writers well beyond Demosthenes. Cicero's thought was shaped by the very Platonic ideals he ostensibly resisted, and he based his theory of education on the rhetorical teaching of Aristotle and the orator Isocrates, who had developed rhythmic and balanced periodic prose in his largely written "speeches." The dialogue itself is a superb evocation of civilized Roman conversation between older and younger generations, illustrating the different rhetorical excellences and common basic principles that he attributed to his teacher, Licinius Crassus, and to the great judicial orator Marcus Antonius. What survives of Cicero's next dialogue, the political treatise *De republica*, set in the circle of Scipio Aemilianus in the weeks before his sudden death, shows that this too re-created an idealized version of Rome's recent past. The sixth book of this treatise, which was preserved separately as "The Dream of Scipio," offered a counterpart to Plato's "Vision of Er" in its imaginative vision of the universe and the happy afterlife promised to true patriots and heroes. One other political dialogue, *De legibus* ("On the Laws"), was not published in Cicero's lifetime.

Under the domination of Caesar, Cicero turned to different aspects of philosophy: epistemology (*Academica*, now partly preserved in its first edition and partly in its reedition), ethics (*De finibus*, "On the Ends of Good and Evil"), and religion (*De natura deorum*, "On the Nature of the Gods"; *De divinatione*, "On Foretelling"; *De fato*, "On Fate"). These works represented the doctrines and points of view of the predominant philosophical schools – the Epicureans, the Stoics, and the sceptical New Academy, to which Cicero himself subscribed. But the most influential of his prose works were those he wrote last: two short dialogues named for their protagonists and themes (*Cato Maior*, a positive description of old age, and *Laelius*, in which Aemilianus' best friend speaks of the ethics of friendship) and two long works of popular ethics. The consolatory *Tusculan Dialogues*, written for his own age group, are Stoic in outlook, arguing against the fear of death and pain, providing encouragement to avoid distress, anger, and other passions, and finally supporting the notion that virtue was by itself sufficient for a happy life. The *Tusculans* aim at literary appeal and are enriched by vivid illustrations from Roman tragedy or Cicero's own verse translations (which have survived only in the excerpts included in his prose treatises).

But where the *Tusculans* were designed to comfort, Cicero's last work, *De officiis* ("On Obligations"), was intended to advise his son how to behave like a gentleman. He added to Panaetius' two books outlining principles of social duty a third independent study of how to choose between conflicting obligations. Few of Cicero's thousand-odd letters were ever intended for publication as works of literature, but we may except the letter (*Fam.* 5.12) sent to the amateur historian Lucceius in 55, inviting him to compose a monograph on Cicero's consulship, exile, and restoration. The letter, which Cicero asked Atticus to circulate, gives his ideas of the literary form – complete with a tragic hero and his vicissitudes – that he envisaged for a historical monograph. But this was the only prose genre in which Cicero did not compose. The lucid if sanitized narrative of the monarchy in Book 2 of *De republica* is too brief to be judged as historical literature. When Cicero explains in the preface to *De legibus* (1.5–9) why he had not tried to compose history, his claim that he lacked the time for proper historical writing masks a more powerful and more general deterrent – the risk of writing history in the current political circumstances.

Only after Caesar's death, under the triumviral regime represented in Italy by Octavian, were Rome's first surviving historical monographs published by a former radical politician, Sallustius Crispus. Sallust's early retirement may have resulted from Caesar's death or from his own dubious political record. Certainly this explains his elaborate self-justification in the preface of his *Bellum Catilinae*, and it adds a personal motive to his generic claims for the importance of historical writing as a service to one's country (*Cat.* 1–4, *Jug.* 1–4). But Sallust's grandiose generalizations about the life of the mind are little more than traditional clichés intended to provide a kick-start to his outline of early Roman history. The merits of his vigorous archaic diction, his deliberately rough-hewn sentences, and his partisan ideology should be balanced against a certain journalistic crudity and superficiality. Sallust's Rome may be polarized in black and white, but he had the enterprise to convert recent history into coherent narratives. The *Bellum Catilinae* is the most frequently studied, and it is striking for its portrayal of its anti-hero Catiline, of the antithetical Cato (Uticensis), and of Caesar.

It is arguable, however, that the *Bellum Jugurthinum*, probably written before 40 B.C., is a more vivid demonstration of Sallust's talents.[27] In this work he is not writing about contemporaries and so is perhaps freer to create character, but here too he justifies his theme in terms taken from Rome's internal politics. He has chosen to record this war

> because it was a great and terrible war with many shifts of
> success, and because this was the first occasion of real oppo-
> sition to the arrogance of the nobility, a conflict which threw
> all divine and human affairs into confusion and reached such
> a pitch of folly that (only) war and the ravaging of Italy put
> an end to the political partisanship. (*Jug.* 5.1–3)

After setting the stage with a prehistory going back over a century, Sallust shines a bright light on the usurper Jugurtha's exploitation of elite friends at Rome and the failure of senatorial leaders to protect King Adherbal with his damning statement that "the whole city was for sale and would quickly go under if it found a buyer." The narrative is diversified by vivid if inaccurate geographical and anthropological excurses on Africa (17–19) and the treacherous Syrtes (78) and by the inclusion of two major speeches: that of the new radical consul Memmius (31) before the central figure of Marius is gradually introduced into the military narrative and the speech of Marius on his election, voicing the manifesto of the political outsider (*novus homo*, 85). Marius' achievements are balanced by those of his former commander Metellus "Numidicus" (43–83) and future rival Sulla (95–113). This monograph meets the criteria proposed by Cicero's critical description of the Hellenistic historical monograph to Lucceius, with its focus on the rise and fall of a prominent individual (Jugurtha and Marius, however, end up competing as protagonists). The rhetorical power of the speeches also explains why the best preserved excerpts from the completed books of Sallust's *Historiae*, those covering 78–68 B.C., are speeches and letters: the harangues of Lepidus (1.55), the conservative Cotta (2.47), and the radical tribune Licinius Macer (3.48), and Philippus' address to the senate (1.77). The supposed letters, Pompey's threatening dispatch from Spain (2.98), and the savage exposé of Roman policy in Mithradates' letter to Arsaces have all the power of speeches. Mithradates' letter, surely fictitious, achieves some of the astringent tone of Cato's defense of the Rhodians or Tacitus' Calgacus, but it was a bold step to imagine communications between these eastern rulers. Although Sallust's excursus on Sicily survives only in fragments (4.24–8), it nonetheless shaped both Virgil's and Lucan's account of Sicilian geography. For all his mannered imitation of the archaic diction of Cato and the disillusioned worldview of Thucydides, Sallust also demonstrated originality as an architect and a memorable vigour in both narrative and speech.

Roman comedy outlived the end of its creativity, as theatrical libretti became literary texts (and in Terence's case school texts), while the tragedies were eclipsed by the Augustan dramas, regrettably lost even before they were succeeded by Senecan tragedy. Both Catullus' intense miniature epic poem and Lucretius' monumental scientific account of atoms and humanity would be overwhelmed by the achievements of Virgil and Ovid. Roman oratory would never regain the variety and power of Cicero, but philosophy was renewed in Latin by Seneca, though Greek remained its natural medium. History, as we have seen, had still to reach its full development. Sallust's immediate successor, Livy, had a very different experience and outlook, and pursued a radically different project, almost in opposition to Sallust. It was the more remote Tacitus who became Sallust's true and more brilliant heir.

I have said nothing here of Virgil, whose earliest poetry collection, the *Eclogues*,[28] was contemporary with Sallust's work, or of Horace's *Epodes* and *Satires*, written in the 30s, because I view these poets as detaching themselves from the dead Republic. Elegy and lyric, which had barely surfaced during the Republic, would now blossom in the new climate of the Augustan Age. If the period of the Republic was a time of assimilation and of attempts by Roman writers to match the literature of Greece, the Age of Augustus and the early Empire would see the maturation of a national literature confident in its Roman roots and strong enough to generate both the literary and humanist Renaissance and the later Age of Enlightenment.

NOTES

1 Harris 1989, 173: "three . . . factors prevent us from thinking that more than 10% of the population . . . [in late republican Rome] was literate." Other subsequent estimates are more generous.

2 Leo 1913.

3 The best critical survey is that of Gratwick (1982), which can now be supplemented by Conte (1995).

4 Caesar considered his narratives of the Gallic and civil wars not histories but *commentarii*, supposedly objective war reports.

5 Cf. Goldberg 1995; Hinds 1998.

6 Livius' *Odyssia* was probably an abridgment, like the later *Ilias Latina*. Livius may not have intended it as a school reader, but it was still being used in schools when Horace was a child.

7 Whereas the Greek iambic trimeter maintained a rhythmic difference between the first and second foot of each metron, Latin iambics struggled with the lack of short syllables and allowed the substitution of long syllables and other variants in every foot but the final iamb of the verse.

8 Naevius' play may have been composed for Marcellus' triumph, but these Roman plays were more probably performed at votive or funeral games.

9 *Annales* Book 1.1–15 Skutsch = ROL I 1–13; Book 7.206–7, 208–10 Sk. = ROL I 231–5, 229–30. See Hinds (1998) on Ennius' treatment of his predecessors.

10 *Disiecti membra poetae* (Hor. *Sat.* 1.4.60) presupposes a broken statue, not an injured person. By Horace's day, the Romans were imitating Greek practice, which had long honoured poets with statuary.

11 446–7 Sk. = ROL III 450–1. The lines are quoted by Servius as a model for the description of Jupiter's smile in *Aen.* 1.254.

12 Cf. Goldberg 1995, chap. 3–4.

13 *Andromache* fr. XXVII Jocelyn = ROL I 91–108; *Alcmeo* XV Joc. = ROL I 30–7 (*Cassandra*); *Alexander* XVII and XVIII Joc. = ROL I 38–48, 59–79.

14 These are generally understood to be the plays confirmed as Plautine by Varro (twenty-five were identified as authentic by Varro's teacher Aelius Stilo; see Gell. 3.3.12). Only the first eight plays were known in the Renaissance – in fact until the nineteenth-century rediscovery by Studemund of a palimpsest that contained *Menaechmi* to (the first part of) *Vidularia*.

15 On *Pseudolus*, see Wright 1975.

16 Handley 1968.

17 Fantham 1975; Konstan 1983; McCarthy 2000.

18 On women and slaves, see Fantham 1975; Konstan 1983; on performance and music, see Segal 1968; Slater 1985; Moore 2000.

19 For Laberius' humiliation when Caesar forced him to perform in his own mime, see Suet. *Caes.* 39 and Macrob. *Sat.* 2.6.6–7.

20 Parts of Cato's speech for the Rhodians are preserved by Gellius (6.3.14–39); for the attack on Sulpicius Galba, see Cic. *Brut.* 89 and Gell. 13.25.15

21 For Scaurus, see Cic. *Brut.* 112. Rutilius, cited by Cicero and Gellius, may well have written his memoirs in Greek, as we know Sulla did.

22 Cf. Lucilius ROL III 1061, 1064: the council of the gods is a travesty of Ennius' divine council, which decides the deification of Romulus.

23 See Quinn 1999; Courtney 1993.

24 This usually denotes 2, 3, 5, 6, 7 in hendecasyllables, 8 in a special "limping" iambic meter, and 11 in Sapphics.

25 Since Callimachus' elegy (Pfeiffer fr. 110, also printed at the end of the OCT Catullus) is known only from a damaged papyrus, we cannot be sure he did not offer the same exhortation to brides.

26 Cicero speaks of Crassus' speech in support of Caepio's jury law as "virtually our teacher" (*Brut.* 163).

27 See McGushin 1977, 1987; Paul 1984.

28 We often forget that *Eclogae* means "*selected* poems." Both this and the alternative title *Bucolica* ("Herdsmen's Songs") are Greek.

APPENDIX: REPUBLICAN POETS AND PROSE WRITERS

Dates of birth and death marked with a question mark are approximate; works that survive only in excerpts are enclosed in brackets.

Livius Andronicus (290?–after 207) (*Odyssia*, tragedies, comedies from 240).

Naevius (274?–204) (*Bellum punicum*, tragedies, comedies from 235).

Plautus (254?–184) twenty-one comedies.

Ennius (239–169) (*Annales*, tragedies, assorted shorter poems).

Cato (234–149) *On Agriculture*, (speeches, *Origines*).

Pacuvius (220?–130) (tragedies).

Terence (186–159) six comedies.

Lucilius (180?–102) (satires).

Accius (170?–86) (tragedies, literary criticism).

Varro (113–27) *On the Latin Language, On Agriculture*, (scholarly works).

Cicero (106–43) speeches, dialogues, philosophical works, letters, (poetry).

Caesar (100–44) Commentaries on the Gallic and civil wars.

Lucretius (94?–55?) *On the Nature of the World*.

Sallust (85?–35?) *Catiline, Jugurtha*, (*Histories*).

Catullus (84?–54?) poems.

13: ROMAN ART DURING THE REPUBLIC

Ann L. Kuttner

∾

A t issue in a short survey of republican art is the lack of many longer ones, as if there were no art to be discussed. The opposite is true: for nearly half a millennium, the Latin cities, Rome preeminent among them, expressed themselves both intensely and fluently, with art, architecture, and landscape architecture, private and public, in coins and engraved gems, metal and stone images, mosaic and painting, in the brilliantly modeled terracottas of houses and public buildings. Later Roman ages cherished, recorded, and imitated that patrimony and held in respect the memory of the leaders who put art into their cities – even the memory of those who created it, including that interesting generation of early republican nobles who made monumental paintings. But how was that art "Roman"? This chapter offers one concise but nuanced partial response to this question. What follows is an attempt to explore some of the distinctive variety and characteristics of republican art, stressing its public functions for Roman society. (For help in understanding the discussion of Rome's monuments and architecture, consult Fig. 19, which consists of a map of the entire city and a detailed view of the center of the city.)

The sardonic comments of Virgil, Cicero, and Horace – made at the very end of the Republic – that Greek visual art was a non-Roman achievement have misleadingly shaped modern views. In fact, these men elsewhere praised specifically Roman art commissions, which we know were in the "international" styles of their eras, the mimetic art techniques and the styles, formulated in Greek centers, that were, from the sixth century B.C. onwards, the common currency of most cultivated Mediterranean art. Similarly, moralizing and satirical authors frequently commented on societal decadence stemming from new modes

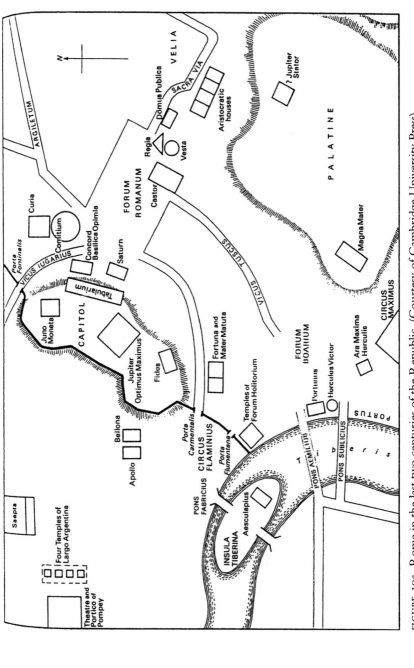

N

ARGILETUM

VELIA

SACRA VIA

? Jupiter Stator

Domus Publica

Aristocratic houses

PALATINE

Regia

Curia

Vesta

Comitium

FORUM

Porta Fontinalis

VICUS IUGARIUS

ROMANUM

Castor

Concord

Basilica Opimia

Saturn

Magna Mater

Tabularium

TUSCUS

Juno Moneta

CAPITOL

Jupiter Optimus Maximus

Fidus

VICUS

Fortuna and Mater Matuta

CIRCUS MAXIMUS

Bellona

Porta Carmentalis

Temples of Forum Holitorium

FORUM BOARIUM

Apollo

Porta Flumentana

CIRCUS FLAMINIUS

Portunus

Herculus Victor

Ara Maxima Herculis

PONS FABRICIUS

PORTUS

Saepta

Four Temples of Largo Argentina

PONS AEMILIUS

T i b e r i s

PONS SUBLICIUS

Aesculapius

INSULA TIBERINA

Theatre and Portico of Pompey

FIGURE 19a. Rome in the last two centuries of the Republic. (Courtesy of Cambridge University Press)

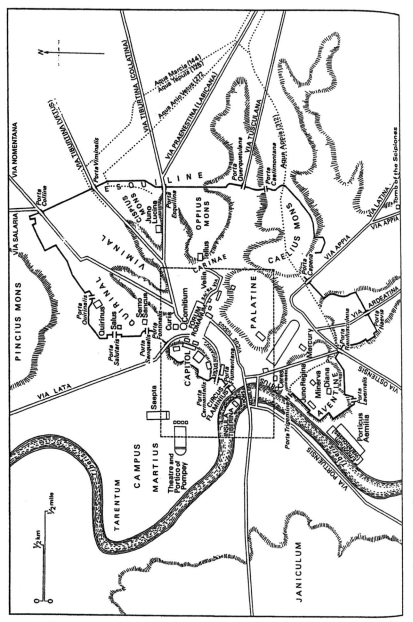

FIGURE 19b. (*Continued*)

of consumption made possible when Rome plundered other, sometimes Greek, states beginning in the third century. Our most important source, Pliny the Elder, lacking other evidence, admirably tried to date republican art habits, which fascinated him, by datable triumph inventories and building inscriptions from the age of conquest. (He was often wrong.) Modern art history jumped from such comments to an assumption validated by no ancient text – that "Greek" meant a Greek style as opposed to a Roman one. But the genre of the sardonic is universal to "Roman" discourse on anything that Romans cared for, and the kind of systematic art history one reads in Pliny itself only arose in the late third century B.C., at the Library of Pergamum. Early on, the Greeks had an idea of a Greek literary mastery, but they aimed at seeing subjects of literature (religion, myth) as transnational, transethnic. Indeed, the "Greek" myths and gods were naturalized in non-Greek Italy so early that from at least 500 B.C. their images seemed to represent local knowledge of universal fact – and of local fact too, like Hercules' support of primeval Rome. Only relatively late was there a perception that visual art mastery was a Greek genius by comparison to the arts of others, guaranteed by a succession of master artists. Roman experience of "Greek" art went back to the earliest days of Greek settlement in the West. Whatever the last generations of the Republic meant by a novel or alien Greekness in the visual arts, the remains prove that it was something about the sociology of art and not about the look of things.

The "master artist" was a social construct, separate from and not necessary to the value placed on art making. This kind of "art history" and the curatorship, collecting, and tourism based on it redefined the status of the "Greek artist" and his products around the Mediterranean, with the result that the status of unsigned art – very common in non-Greek Italy – also had to be renegotiated. The Etrusco-Latin artists' habit of not signing (although the remains clearly document local Italian methods), what often seem more primitive styles for their day in stone relief sculpture, and the fact that archaeologically durable figural wall-fresco only comes in fashion in the first century B.C. have led to the opinion that the Romans, before they could fashion sophisticated images, had to wait for the age of the Greek master artists and for the use of marble (common only from the second century on and not quarried in Italy until c. 50–40 B.C.). Those who hold this common opinion forget that the genres of monumental painting and bronze-work usually do not survive archaeologically, although Romans narrated how they had flourished in the Republic; they also overlook the always stylish monumental terracottas, which were either ignored in Roman sculpture surveys or relegated to Etruscan studies, though scholars now realize that they often ornamented Roman colonies and cities under Roman power. The many vernacular monuments have suggested, too, that there were distinctive Italic and/or plebeian popular styles that express class and ethnic identity. It is true that in the Italo-Roman sphere, people far down on the social ladder seem to have felt the right and the need to make monuments and images; Greek art was more often produced for wealthier persons by more expensive artists. But "primitivism" and manneristic or expressionistic style in Hellenistic-era republican Italy is often a feature of subordinate ornaments to bases and buildings; it is not so apparent in the luxury arts or in the evidence we have for bronze sculpture and monumental painting.

Scholars now realize that in sophisticated Greek zones like Asia Minor much production in analogous relief genres shows similar "primitive" traits. Such simplified styles are not the early phases of a more developed art but rather the very refined stylization of sophisticated strategies employed in obedience to rules of genre and intended to produce a visually competent ensemble for a larger monument. Thus, the friezes of the Monument of Aemilius Paullus are analogous in their simplifications to the contemporary Amazon friezes of the temple of Artemis at Magnesia, because both friezes were the physically elevated banding of an architectonic form made to be legible from a distance and to create a satisfyingly ornamentalized texture like a molding pattern. Roman stone bases of the Republic, which once held sophisticated statues, display similar stylistic strategies that would have assisted a collage of visual rhetorics; seeming simplicity could also rhetorically evoke an air of antiquity and of authentic local or virtuous character.

Patrons picked subjects and locations, and it was these that set styles. Indeed, Romans often saw patrons as "authors" of art and architecture; they were no more wrong than those who thought only of artists. In portraits, for instance, it has long been clear that patrons always demanded that local and immigrant artists, as well as the artists of the eastern Mediterranean who produced Roman commissions there, make for them veristic images of lined, thoughtful, even grimly concentrating mature and aged persons. Similarly, designers were made to adapt and so to renew international canons for Doric, Corinthian, or Ionic architecture for locally distinctive arcaded and arched forms and for basilica, temple, and house types. And painters, too, were forced to think up decoration for the exterior walls of monuments – again

a Latin, not a "Greek," format – and in the late Republic to develop to an extreme the architectural illusions and painted prospects of
"Second Style" fresco and devise novel figure-painted room systems.
By the late fourth century B.C., Rome and the greater Latin cities were
dominant economically and politically, and artists immigrated there as
to any wealthy (Greek) center. By staying and working, they joined a
local art environment.

One characteristic of Roman art was the use of forced contrasts
between different modes. At the Tomb of the Scipios, for instance,
fine naturalistic portrait statues once graced the fashionably formatted
Hellenistic façade, but its podium carried old-style history painting. In
addition, the tomb complex imitated ancient Etruscan rock-cut tombs
in its form, and many inscriptions of the sarcophagi inside combined
contemporary calligraphy with archaic language forms. An eclectic mix
of old and new styles, like that in single portrait images in the late Republic, produced a kind of didactic commentary based on knowledge-
able appreciation of the accumulated image landscape of the Greek and
Italian sanctuary and forum. Take, for instance, the famous bronze head
we call "Brutus." This is not a fifth-century image but rather a third-
or second-century one. It successfully conveys a person of old, austere Roman mores while using modern middle republican (Hellenistic)
strategies of surface realism and of address to the spectator. (The subject
has turned his head to gaze at his viewers.)

Similarly, the late republican temple of Neptune was executed in
cutting-edge Hellenistic modes but was adapted to carry out a Roman
podium temple format. It contained an entire parade of Thetis and her
nymphs riding tritons through the implied waves; by everything we
know of late republican cult statues (and many inserted marble heads
survive), the Neptune around whom these baroque figures disported
would have had the grave, static quality of Hellenistic classicism. When
the second-century immigrant Greek master Scopas made the relief, he
was asked to make a stunning experiment in multi-figure sculpture, a
sort of instant version of the high-relief effects of the Pergamum Great
Altar, along with sculpture sequences for an interior space, something
he would never have been free to do by a conventional Greek commission. The agenda of this commission, to let the person entering the
temple feel immersed in an ocean world, must have shaped the mode
of expression. Like the emphatically decorated house and temple interior, the habit of creating ensembles defines the Roman agenda for art
and space in culturally distinctive ways. Just as the Romans tended to

FIGURE 20. Republican temples at the Largo Argentina. (Photo Kathleen Moretto Spencer)

cluster their manubial temple dedications, as, for example, at the Largo Argentina (Fig. 20) to make programmatic ensembles near and around the triumphal staging ground of the Circus Flaminius, so they tended to build up images in "groups." These groupings begged for translation by analogy, partly to other forms of "stored representation." Thus the Esquiline tomb was visually equivalent to a clan archive room, and a villa's court, garden, or room for sculptures or paintings (*pinacotheca*) recalled sanctuary assemblages.

Roman practice expanded the Hellenistic Greek interest in forms of participatory realism, in which spectators collaborated with images in space and time. People liked to imagine that they were with the figures in the moment and in the place they could see (and they were fascinated by depictions of landscape and architectural settings). We well understand how the informative, even emotionally moving, new images carried in triumphs let viewers in Rome feel that they too could go where the armies had gone. By Pompey's day, we know, Romans were even "spying on" the last moments of their enemies' lives. Pompey showed emotional, vivid paintings of the suicides of Mithradates and his wives and children. Octavian showed effigy images, as for a staged tragedy, of the dying or dead Cleopatra, whose suicide no Roman had seen. Participatory realism in a fictional world well characterizes the first-century B.C. "Second Style" architectural and figure frescoes in house rooms as well as the reconstructed programs of mythologized sanctuary gardens like Fulvius Nobilior's second-century precinct of Hercules and the Muses and Pompey's first-century portico for Venus Victrix.

We know how fundamental to Roman thinking of all kinds were the linked ideas of the monument (*monumentum*), of memory, and of the impact of case-example and message (*exemplum*). We also know how Roman language arts of all kinds aimed to make a monument too, and to make a hearer or reader "see." Many different styles and formats embodied the *exemplum*. The vivid dramatic and epic stories or watchful divine groups on temple pediments were *exempla* encouraging or monitory for a whole community. The stories and images in the house might relax, in a description of this or fantastic worlds, but they might be *exempla* too, intended to provoke discussion of Roman values and aspirations, the tensions of human relationships, and the *domus* and its relation to the world. The core value of *pietas*, respect for the gods, the city, and the clan, expressed itself in art and in looking after art. It is good, however, to remember that the voice of the *exemplum* might be funny, sardonic, and witty as well as sober or religious, and it is also good to remember that pleasure, in due proportion, was also a public good to be encouraged. Beauty had its own utility: to give pleasure, to ennoble didactic and commemorative projects, and also to make them seem worth preserving. The very finely made image or building seduced the public for its own preservation.

Effective and excellent design assisted the impact that all images aspired to have. The more that message mattered, the more did the effectiveness of its delivery matter. Romans wished to be moved strongly by their images from a very early date – moved in the same way that they were by oratory or drama. And images let them imagine that the representations were reacting to *them*. That public portraits watched you, judged you, we see invoked in Cicero's speeches; extant art places this practice at the beginning of the Republic. Its oldest civic icon, miraculously preserved, is in an ancient style (*c.* 500–480 B.C.?), mimetic enough still to evoke response. The bronze Lupa Romana stands with legs braced to protect the now lost babies at her dugs, like a living version of the cave where she first stood, swinging her head sharply and showing her teeth at you, who approach her (Fig. 21). Were you dangerous

FIGURE 21. The "Lupa Romana" ("Capitoline Wolf"), hollow-cast bronze, fifth or fourth century B.C. The Roman Wolf suckling infants Romulus and Remus (the infants are fifteenth-century additions by Pope Sixtus IV). (Photo *DAIR* 70.652, Singer)

to your vulnerable baby ancestors like their wicked uncle? Or were you going to join the humble shepherd Faustulus or the good-hearted whore Acca Laurentia as a pious helper? At the Lupercal cave, under the original fig tree, the Lupa brought you into history on the spot where it transpired. In the early Republic, the Ogulnii made a replica of this statue for the Capitolium (and perhaps the Forum); one can see how the image acquired further meanings by now standing in the very heart of the places where Romans prayed for, and decided, their own current fate. Thus, in 63 B.C., anxious about the threat of civil war posed by Catiline, Cicero could write, shuddering, of the melting of one of the babies of the Capitoline group by lightning as a portent for the destruction of the Republic.

Similarly, it is clear how Romans decided to understand the Dionysiac images that stood in their public spaces, the ancient Marsyas (Fig. 22) and even more ancient Vortumnus. (No Greek city made civic icons of satyrs in this way.) One of their founding myths was of a primeval Roman landscape governed by satyr-kings and nymphs. Instead of bringing panic, these beings welcomed, protected, even loved

FIGURE 22. "Anaglypha Traiani," Hadrianic marble parapet frieze (burning of tax records), showing Forum Romanum (left), the "ficus Ruminalis," and the ancient statue of Marsyas. (Photo *DAIR* 68.2785, Felbermeyer)

the founder of Rome's religious and civic landscape, the sponsor too of its first images, good King Numa. Rome's temple of Liber stressed that he was a loving husband to an apotheosized human, Libera (Ariadne); their shrines, next to those of Ceres, upheld public order for all in the city. For a people with such national myths, a house whose art made it Dionysiac (standard around the Greco-Italic Mediterranean from early on) could be in harmony with civic values, not separate from or hostile to them. So, too, the importance of the theater to a Roman city's formal and religious celebrations affects the reading of theatrical motifs in a house, as it does scenes "from tragedy" in public arts. The corpus of republican art motifs from myth and religion, even when shared with a wider (Greek) world, needs to be reviewed always in local sociological contexts and in the light of the accumulated visual environment that conditioned patrons and viewers.

You will say, "What will this *monumentum* do for me? – well, we are laboring at *res Romanas*" (Cic. *Att.* 4.17.7). So a senator to an *eques* in 54 B.C.

Cicero's interest in the arts was shared in many letters to his close friend Atticus, his brother Quintus, and others. His letters also show how an interest in the arts bound together powerful political allies such as Pompey and Caesar. Often Cicero urgently conveys a dedication to an esthetic agenda, with great precision about physical arrangement, and seeks to give the absent correspondents the flavor of how things would look to them if only they could be present. In a letter to Atticus, Cicero reports that Paulus has just repaired his clan basilica on the Forum, making it a "most magnificent work." What more do you want to know? he asks (evidently Atticus wrote asking for just such art news). Well, he says, nothing is more glorious than what Caesar's friends, Oppius and I, are up to. That monumental project (Forum Julium) you used to go on about so enthusiastically, saying that we could open wide the Forum's capacity and elaborate public space all the way to the Atrium Libertatis? It's costing a fortune, it couldn't be done for less with private funds. But we are achieving a most glorious thing: for in the Campus Martius we're putting up a Saepta of marble for the voting assemblies, and we'll roof it, and we'll ring it with a towering porticus so it takes in a thousand paces. Also, it's right alongside the Villa Publica . . . .

This epistolary chat, referring to long-standing conversations on similar topics, is like the one that Varro (*RR* 3.2) depicts himself holding with a cohort of fellow magistrates, taking time out from the elections in the Villa Publica's gardened square, sitting on its benches amid statues and paintings to talk about – what else? – their own and their friends' decorated villas. Cicero, in the trial of Verres, might have spoken in protective mockery of his Sicilian Greek clients' attachment to their urban markers and personal art treasures, but "art speak" was the normal mode of his own Romans, too. The word picture of the Saepta's design is like the visual miniature of the Villa Publica on the coins struck by Fonteius Capito somewhere in the years 59–55 (*RRC* 429/2). The miniature, which shows a two-storied porticus arcaded below, colonnaded above, clarifies how Caesar's porticus was going to compete with its neighbor. The Basilica Aemilia restoration, we know, was subvented by funds from Caesar as Paulus' political *amicus*. In another case of *amicitia*, Atticus, we believe, had busied himself previously for Cicero's friend Pompey by helping procure art works for Pompey's porticus, near both the Saepta and the Villa Publica. *Amicitia* manifests itself as a transaction with the arts, and mutual interest in public works helps maintain desired or necessary "friendships."

Cicero's letters about house projects differ from the above only in their much greater length and specificity, as if Cicero were taking the friend on an intimate tour. The letters evince both the affection and the collegiality of political caste. (The furious house and art descriptions in the forensic attacks, the *De domo* and the *Verrines*, use similar strategies.) The house letters praise the look of domestic things, too, as a collaborative effort. Quintus far away hears how charming his statues of Greek literati (*palliati*) look as ivy grows around them (Q. *Fr.* 3.1.1). Atticus learns how happily expectant Cicero is about the metal and marble herm-images and the "Megarian statues" that Atticus writes he will dispatch to his friend from overseas (the same role he played for Pompey). And Cicero and Gallus gossip about the garden sculpture sets of other friends (*Fam.* 7.23.1–3), even though Cicero does not want the pretty little Maenads Gallus bought him. ("I do well understand that you acted not just with zeal but with affection for me, because they pleased you – and you're a man I've always believed to be *elegantissimus* in any matter of taste (*iudicium*) – and so you thought them worthy of me.") Friendship manifests in trusting people to send you tasteful things, and true friends can bond over admitted differences of taste, like the playful competition in *Ad Atticum* (4.17) over the magnificence of public projects. Taste matters enough that it is a means and a substance of the exchanges of friendship, in private as in public.

The Roman elite classes bonded with one another by gift exchange and communal building projects as in no other previous Mediterranean culture. Foreign friends caught on fast, giving and loaning artworks to their Roman connections. The most cultured kings and cities showed friendship by lending artists, as the Attalids did for the Cornelii in the second century, but also by obtrusively borrowing Roman forms and designers for their own projects, as in the Attalids' Italo-Roman images (Romulus and Remus, the Catanian Brothers) on their shrine for Queen Apollonis at Kyzikos. Similarly, the Romanizing Seleucid king Antiochus IV hired the Roman Cossutius to build the colossal Athenian temple of Zeus in an Italo-Roman format (the Corinthian order) and brought Cossutius home to work on a whole city quarter in Antioch. The nobles shared their attractive houses around the countryside, as they had long opened their townhouses up to all social classes (friends, subordinates, superiors). In friendship and in competition, the elite caste together must have patronized the same image workshops and architects long before the sources let us know the second-century makers' and patrons' names.

The glory that individuals and clans asserted through their domestic and public constructions and displays was itself shaped by the community, the *res publica*. *Gloria* resulted when other people approved, liked what you showed them. Cicero's correspondence illuminates how elite individuals' public projects had long manifested their personal and political friendships. A century earlier, for instance, when a Lucullus could not get authorization for a full triumph after his Spanish campaign of 151/50 and so could not get the right to dedicate art paid for from booty at his sanctuary of *Felicitas*, his friend Mummius stocked it for him. The plausible pretext was a loan of art to exhibit temporarily; purposefully left there for the temple dedication, the show consequently became a collection of immovable votives – a collection that constituted (says Pliny) Rome's most splendid museum.

Mummius himself is the first known *triumphator* systematically to have shared out art's pleasures around Italy, distributing fine images to Italian cities. He is also the first political figure in the Western world known to have been attacked by political enemies with slurs on his taste in art. The slander mocked Mummius' claims to effective cooperation on Rome's behalf with the Attalids of Pergamum, the allies with whom he had shared the art spoils of Corinth in a very real transaction of friendship expressed through art. (Allegedly the Attalids had had to rescue from Mummius a masterpiece painting carelessly handed to his soldiers to dice upon.) The libel of vulgarity shows that at least some Romans by then thought bungled artistic projects might indicate stupidity in any national project.

By the fourth century B.C. at the latest, artistic sophistication was expected of the upper class, who ought, following Aristotle's rules, consciously to ornament their city. Yet we often misleadingly base our current findings on triumph inventories, which by definition list mostly foreign booty. There are, alas, no equivalent inventories for the continual making of new art. For instance, it is in Pliny's *Natural History* that we read of the amazing new series of marble sculptures of exemplary mothers in the gynecological section of Pompey's portico, not in the accounts of Pompey's triumph displays, nor in the inventory of old art in the "art history" chapters. In the East, archaeology shows, Roman commanders did just what they would have done at home, which is to say commission enormous monuments, portraits, and temple ornaments and insert them into older sequences of buildings and statues. The Monument of Aemilius Paullus is a famous case, among the many still to be fully explored. This is a classic instance in which local (Greek) carvers were employed, but to make a monument with no Greek parallel: a lofty marble pier with a band of historical relief, a precise sculptured image of a particular battle, under the (lost) bronze equestrian statue. At that time, the technology, perhaps even the will, to make action equestrian figures in bronze was the expertise of the Romans' Attalid allies (inherited from the Lysippan school). But the elevated "column portrait" was a Roman phenomenon; the analogues are contemporary, commissioned by the Attalids, and stood side by side, though without the Roman genre of the base frieze. Thus, the genre of plinth monuments seems a Roman-Attalid symbiosis.

The idea of sharing the vision of something good to look at is at the heart of late Hellenistic and Roman forms of monument replication.

That idea of replication was key to republican self-identity from its very early days. Generic urban forms like *capitolium*, *curia*, and *comitium* replicated themselves; so did very particular images. The Latin cities shared images of the Lavinian sow; the colonies displayed replicas of the Marsyas of the Forum Romanum as a *signum libertatis*. Cicero's extant letters speak partly to such generic commissions, as do the generic typologies of the art remains. But from the second century on there were also sometimes replicas of identifiable masterpieces with a formal art-historical pedigree, what the sculptor-scholar Pasiteles would have called *opera nobiliora* (the name of his encyclopedic treatise of the early first century B.C.). The Villa of the Papyri is the most famous extant collection of such statues and of the popular late republican herm-images. The statues bear the portraits of historic leaders, thinkers, and writers and the heads of Greek masterpieces. These stress quotation, both by excerpting (in Roman bust style) and by representing Greek cultural leaders, which was a way of proclaiming affiliation to a dead philosopher, for example, and to living companions who admired the same models of thought or action.

Such quotations may also, however, reference Rome, in the way in which Forum replicas did. For there is every chance that their paradigms had moved to the capital beginning with the second-century wars of eastern conquest. The Alexander Mosaic of the 120s is clearly a statement about participation in the eastern wars by a very wealthy Oscan knight who installed this splendid copy of a painting in a special pavilion off the main garden court in the House of the Faun. It would gain all the more resonance by being an image of spoils from those wars, like those Roman honorific portrait replicas of the later Republic based on the Granikos Group (Alexander's cavalry in battle) taken home by the victorious Metellus Macedonicus in the early second century. As another example, houses at the colony of Fregellae, built for veterans of the Syrian Wars, had *atria* containing fine reliefs depicting those campaigns, plainly meant to quote battle narratives made for the victors and on view at Rome. Importing replications of foreign works at Rome would be a way for allied towns and *municipia* to affiliate with the capital and the idea of "Rome"; importing domestic art would be a way of evoking the greatest of museum cities through the contents of one's own private museum.

Already, pictorial monuments of the fourth century B.C. in Rome, Latium, and Etruria clearly replicate other works; the act of quotation entails that patron and viewer share access to the original. The François Tomb at Vulci famously aligns a new portrait of the owner-occupant as a *triumphator* with overt copies of grand public paintings of murder and assassination: the overthrow of the Tarquins, local history painting, and the killing of prisoners at the Tomb of Patroclus. Anti-Roman in sentiment, the ensemble is all the more emulative of the grand painting traditions of Rome. The round bronze boxes (*cistae*) from Praenestine tombs are Latin art objects, found only in Latium and inscribed in Latin. Their finest examples document the character of monumental painting in the age of Fabius Pictor – and of Zeuxis' visit to paint at Kroton. The Ficoroni cist (Fig. 23) is well known for its signature, the first known for an artist from Rome. ("Novios Plautios made me for Dindia Macolnia and her daughter.") The extraordinary elegance of its Argonaut scenes closely adapts a paradigm that is reflected in other works too. Paradigms such as this must have been accessible to the public in famous centers or they would not and could not have been copied so freely.

The common practice of taking home replications of public art to live with them shows that public art was believed to give pleasure as well as to inculcate exemplary knowledge. The many kinds of public places where paradigm works were installed were open to congregation in distinctive ways. Forums and prominent roadside areas were obvious places. But so too were sanctuaries, at those locations and others. The Italic podium temple porch and stair could be used as a tribunal; interiors were used for senatorial meetings or for meetings of friends, who could tip the temple guardian. The fact that paintings and statues were put in the deep temple porches indicates that they could function as a kind of pavilion in their own right. Many masterworks went into temple interiors with the expectation they would be visited even though sacrificial ritual transpired out of doors. By the second century B.C., extensive sanctuary porticos and the gardens in them afforded casual visits of all kinds and offered access to galleries of images. The multivalent uses of temples and their gardened surrounds are analogous to the now recognized multivalent uses of the elite house, which accumulated art that might at any given time serve different ends – to teach, to warn, to frame formal assembly or relaxed congregation. In houses, congregation focused on banquets; in turn, republican silver settings and house frescoes sometimes showcased politicized motifs, public paradigms. For decking such places, the passion to bring back artworks as booty or to buy them up at forced prices from non-Roman communities was a symptom typical of highly urbane cultures, not of boorish ones, as Napoleon's ransacking of Italy to stock the Louvre exemplifies. Even the most personal images were chosen with an eye to public reception. And this is true not just for the open Roman house, with its

FIGURE 23. Ficoroni cista from a tomb at Praeneste, late fourth century B.C. (Photo *DAIR* 80.1582, Singer)

interpenetration of the public and the private and its steadily increasing magnificence. (The Roman house is now so much studied that this chapter refrains from dealing with the subject. Here it is simply noted that late Hellenistic houses generally had elaborate interiors, influenced by palace prototypes, but houses in Sicily and Roman Italy came to be especially ornamented as the Empire grew, to express the stature and map the deeds and predilections of the owners as a spectacle for guests.)

If you were a member of Roman society from at least the third century on, your very individuality was embodied in your chosen image, your signet, which replicated your icon thousands of times as a seal for property and correspondence and as a document guarantor. The poor had glass signets; their betters had precious metal, ivory, and stone ones. The observable fashions in seal types show that people were trying to appeal to one another's eyes. Attested by clusters of meaningful historic scenes in identical compositions or by multiples of elite portraits, shared seal images must sometimes have been the currency of *amicitia*, allegiance, or obedience. In some cases, similarity must have been coded as a good or useful thing in its own right; perhaps shared badges were flashed by members of an officer corps, members of a household, or persons agreeing to a sort of visually coded correspondence, whether as partners, relatives, or employers and agents. (Cheap glass seals would well serve such ad hoc use.) People could use two or more seals for different purposes. The wealthy, certainly, came to collect them by the later Republic, and the seals of the eminent, like Sulla, were well known. Extant republican signets repeatedly emulate coin types. In 56, the relationship was reversed by Faustus Sulla's parallel types, one with the famous signet image his father used, showing him receiving the homage of Bocchus and the submission of Jugurtha (Fig. 24), the other with the seal of Pompey as triple *triumphator* (RRC 426/1, 426/3). The coins' impact depended on the idea that many people had actually seen a sealing from the originals and that many more would have knowledge of them. The coins, indeed, hint that Faustus could use and so further disseminate his father's seal.

Two particular aspects of the Roman image – one iconographic, the other political – speak to its quality of communal address. First, Roman public imagery stressed shared communal experience. Latin, Roman, and Etruscan art distinguished itself from Greek art by its extraordinary attention to "historical images" – unique identifiable events, like particular battles, and generic important ones, like magisterial ceremonies. Historical battle paintings were a Greek genre also, but

FIGURE 24. Silver denarius of Faustus Sulla, Rome mint, 56 B.C.: reverse, Sulla on tribunal receives submission of King Bocchus (left), presenting laurel branch, bound Jugurtha at right, inscribed [Sulla] FELIX. (Obverse, head of Diana, *lituus*, crescent moon, FAUSTUS.) (*RRC* 426/1; photo American Numismatic Society)

documentary historical sculpture of events, in relief, on buildings, or in freestanding groups was not standard Greek practice. Totally local was the attention to civilian and military ritual, parades, and altar groups; standard compositions for these existed from the fourth century onwards, whether for the census, the triumph, or the parley and treaty. Depiction was so common, the desire for it so intense, that already by the fourth century Roman artists had evolved graphically sophisticated visual codes for intensely detailed narratives, as in the famous multiregistered fragment from the Esquiline Tomb, whose expressionistic abbreviation, enlargement, compositional repetition, and stylistic eclecticism from scene to scene permit the telling of a very detailed saga of the Samnite Wars. The vivid abbreviated scenes of voting and audience on Roman coinage later used similar tricks. Some kinds of monument honored a leader by showing him presiding over such a scene. The togate priest and magistrate on the third-century terracotta pediment from the Via San Gregorio heads a sacrificial procession towards divinities for a shrine he must have built; the census on the so-called Altar of Domitius Ahenobarbus of *c.* 100–80 B.C. is centered on a protagonist whose statue stood upon this base (Fig. 25). For individuals, the magisterial processions on second-century Volterran urns (Fig. 26), the audience scenes on late Republic tomb monuments, and the *sella*

FIGURE 25. So-called Altar of Domitius Ahenobarbus, *c.* 110–80 B.C.: statue base front, census frieze panel from the Circus Flaminius; *lustrum* sacrifice at Ara Martis in Campo, censor (head not antique), Mars; *suovetaurilia*, right; military registration left and right (Paris, Louve MA 975). (Sides and back panel, Munich, show wedding of Neptune and Amphitrite and sea-thiasos.) (Photo courtesy of Réunion des Musées Nationaux/Art Resource, NY)

curulis (curule chair) forms often monumentalized for those tombs were means of honoring personal achievement. However, the splendid terracotta equestrian procession that ringed a second-century basilica at Praeneste mirrored the citizenry back to itself, even while incorporating a portrait of the building's donor (Fig. 27).

Trophies of an individual general were "his," but the stacked Roman arms carved in the Doric friezes of basilicas at Cumae and Aquileia, like the shield sets displayed in the Forum Romanum itself, spoke to the citizen soldiers by pointing to their practice, as citizens, of meeting with weapons laid down to deliberate on when to take them up again. On the Monument of Aemilius Paullus at Delphi, the battle frieze under the lost bronze equestrian image of that general did focus attention on his portrait. But it also gave respectful, accurate attention to the tactics and weaponry of the Roman and allied forces defeating Macedonians at the Battle of Pydna. Every man who had been there could see himself praised in art of this kind. In the Esquiline fresco, the generals are bigger than the stylized, close-packed crowds at their heels; remarkable, though, is that the crowds are depicted at all. Triumphal paintings often mirrored the citizen soldiery back to itself, as even the bare extant titles indicate. Roman historical art is overwhelmingly an art about crowd scenes and participatory rituals, intended to energize participatory looking by the living crowd. And it is often, and strikingly, an art about talking – parley, tribunal meetings, priestly prayers. Togate orators and mounted horsemen throw their arms out in direct rhetorical address; the moment is one in which we go silent before the charismatic speaker – but it is also a moment in which the speaker remains ignorant of whether we will freely agree, vote yes or no. When the early Republic called the Marsyas statue in the Forum an icon

FIGURE 26. Knight's urn (alabaster), *c.* 125–75 B.C.: equestrian parade; *lictor* with fasces visible top left; right, preparations for sacrifice, with *victimarius* holding ram or sheep and flute player and lyre player at podium temple (triton? giant? in pediment). London, British Museum. (Photo *DAIR* 40.817)

of citizen liberty, his arm thrown up and head tossed back in free speech were as central to that interpretation as the broken slave-shackles on his ankles. Honorific portraits often occupied assembly places, and in such documentary modes, they made a performative stage for living rituals of communality, just as triumphal images clustered along – and, atop arches, above – triumphal routes (Fig. 28).

A vital early office of the Roman public career functioned partly as an art ministry. *Aediles* decked the Forum and the spectacle zones with temporary displays (in the later Republic at least), and what they used were art loans. These still relatively young politicians and their sponsors could thus advertise connections, and inherited clan ties to communities around the Empire were shown off in loans from friendly foreign entities. From the early third century at the latest, the *aediles* converted fines they levied back into fine bronze and gilt bronze images for the community to look at. Livy usually gives only bare details ("five bronzes to the temple of Ceres"); however, his expanded narrative of the aedileship of the Ogulnii hints at how much this must have contributed to the iconic cityscape. The Ogulnii may well have used fines to make

313

FIGURE 27a,b. Praeneste, terracotta plaques from a monumental frieze with equestrian and ?sacrificial parade, *transvectio equitum*; lictors, horseman. Rome, Museo Nazionale Romano, Antiquarium 115218–19. (Photos *DAIR* 82.967, 82.973, Schwanke)

FIGURE 28. "Tivoli general," from Tibur, Sanctuary of Hercules Victor, c. 100–60 B.C. Heroic scale (now 1.88 m; once c. 2 m); of pieced Greek marble (missing top of head was separately added). Fringed *paludamentum* (general's cloak) around hips, cavalry cuirass with Medusa emblem at side; left hand held a ?sheathed sword, missing right arm was raised to hold lance. (Photo *DAIR* 32.412, Faraglia)

their new Lupa for the Forum Romanum and the new bronze quadriga for the roof of the Capitolium. In any case, their statue commissions were clearly based on accepted aedileship art practices. If this was indeed a proud assertion by the plebeian nobility, it staked out a claim to a place in the nation next to everyone else, by means of nationally significant stories given communally accessible form, at the highest visible point of all Rome and the center of the Forum.

In republican history writing, *luxuria* meant the private hoarding of art, which was condemned on the principle that the pleasures of art ought to be publicly shared. Sumptuary laws were intended to enforce caste egalitarianism and preserve class distinctions, not to denigrate artifice. Overextravagant public gifts, like any other extravagant benefice (including funerary expense), were often suspected of being demagogic tools; art booty was sometimes attacked, not for being art but for being embezzled. Meanwhile, Roman elites gave one another an extraordinarily free hand in choosing the look of nationally commissioned buildings and innovating in the physical and cultic religious landscape. Auctorial inscriptions forever marked buildings as their creators' contribution to the communal vision. Borrowed from occasional Hellenistic royal practice, the habit of putting prominent signatures on building façades in estheticized calligraphic forms permanently influenced the Western tradition. When Rome voted a man the right to a monument, the honorand picked aspects of the monument's design and doubtless supervised the contracting. That gift to him of the pleasure of shaping public pleasure leads us to speak of voted honorifics as the self-fashioning of the person who received them.

The mint masters were sometimes very noble, but ranked lower as magistrates than the *aediles*. For reasons we do not know, in the early 130s they were permitted to vary the national coin types with a free hand, as if choosing their own signets. Much studied are the ways in which moneyers used coin images to look after others' *monumenta* as well as their own achievements, trying to make people remember their own famous ancestors or, later, the projects of their political partners. Although we assume that many of the divinities on Greek and Roman coinage depict cult statues, we tend not to think this through. The only systematic reviews of monuments on coins focus on the easily cataloguable buildings and arches and some honorifics like equestrian statues; but though it is sometimes difficult to guess if a die is an autonomous image or not, clearly many types (including portraits) pictured another public image. This record appealed to common knowledge of another marker; not just a memory record of family and office

FIGURE 29. Silver *denarius* of C. Minucius Augurinus, Rome mint, 135 B.C.: reverse (C. AUG.), two togate officiants approach the Columna Minucia [at the porta Trigemina] – depicted as a tapering, spiraled, or palm-trunk column. Its archaizing "Aeolic" capital bears the statue of "Minucius Augurinus" togate, holding staff in right hand. From the column base stretch the foreparts of two reclining lions, heads upraised. [Column supposed to have been voted by the Roman people for Minucius' grain distributions of 439 B.C.] From the statue's platform dangle objects (?bells). From the lions seem to spring enlarged leafy stalks of wheat. At right stands an unveiled togate augur with *lituus*; at left, a togate figure approaches holding out objects (loaves? patera and ?), stepping up onto an upturned grain measure (*modius*). (Obverse: helmeted head of Roma, ROMA.) (*RRC* 242/1; photo Ashmolean Museum, Oxford)

motifs, it documented communal art as such. The very first year of the new "liberated" coinage sees depictions of Roman images: Veturius' denarius showed the Forum group of Romulus and Tatius sacrificing to make their treaty unifying Sabine arms with Rome; the scene of Faustulus finding the twins Romulus and Remus alludes to a generic public image class if not to a specific picture. (The archaic label, like writing on early paintings, is interesting [*RRC* 234/1, 235/1].) The 135 B.C. denarius (Fig. 29) showing the Columna Minucia (for the moneyer's ancestor [*RRC* 243/1]) is interesting, not just because it depicts a monument and can be used to reconstruct it, but because it describes live spectators. We look at images of people looking at a portrait image – a sophisticated late Hellenistic conceit here turned into a significant communal activity in its own right.

No review of republican art can omit the Roman portrait, distinctive in its uses and aims, settings and iconographies. The frequent use of the very non-Greek bust form privileges the unique skull and hair and face of one individual at one particular moment; all such faces privilege the marks of age as a visual record of experience and status. The lines on Etruscan or Roman faces physically track the exercise of the mind and the achievements and status that such statues document. Roman portraits have active faces, which is to say, active minds; the face focuses, its small muscles bunch and contract, the jaw and mouth set, directing that Roman "glare." Motion created the lines, motion shows them off. This habit of "verism" (something trying to look true) exploited any style that could serve. Certainly in the heartland of the Republic there is a strong regional style offered by local or resident artists. From the time when Rome started to take in many foreign artists in the second century B.C., however, there are also other styles. What counts is the voracious habit in whose service artists from many schools created images they would never otherwise have made. In Greek traditions from the fourth century on, this harsh naturalism was used mostly for the "man of mind," the thinker as poet or philosopher. Romans give men of action this treatment to make the same point – there is shrewd wisdom in this skull, which has seen many years. Republican verism furthers several ends. One is the visceral Roman sense that you are your family, and thus you are your family features, recorded with an honesty that is its own arrogance. Another is that you are you; these portraits aspire to be a record of excellence achieved by the individual – a record created by delineating the features of that visibly unique individual. The third is that these are, truly, historical monuments. They show the face one makes out of the face one is born with; they show the person of whom biographies can be written while still formidably active. (We have very few actually old faces.) Because verism was iconic, the face could sign one way and the body a different way, as on those late Republican portraits that match matured features done in one style to a youthful torso in a different style.

A good way to close this meditation is to draw attention to public life with images. The populace walked under a kind of city in the sky, where roof sculptures, honorific column portraits, and arch groups gave high place to the highly placed. Every rank jostled in the streets to the Forum, where statues clustered especially thick. A distinguishing feature of Rome was the number of its ancient sacred springs and trees, not least in this monumental core. From the forth century or earlier there were conscious efforts to use illusionistic sculpture to depict an

FIGURE 30. Signet-ring intaglio, third or second century B.C., with military oath scene, after the statue group of Romulus and Titus Tatius on the Sacra Via. Vienna, Kunsthistorisches Museum IX.B.899. (Photo by I. Luckert, courtesy of the Kunsthistorisches Museum, Vienna)

event at the place where it had occurred, setting and image together reinforcing memory. Only the most privileged had the right to ancestor masks, but Rome displayed the whole city's ancestral actors, in the form of statues, where everyone could see them. These statues let the modern, living Roman trespass back into time, as far back as the first woodland valley of the satyr kings. Identifications that were anachronistic readings of very old monuments only proved the Roman wish to preserve and to identify. These statues were described by texts, coins, and engraved gems as well as copies in other media, meaningful scenes to a host of persons. The sacrifice group of Romulus and Tatius on the Sacred Way is mentioned directly, for instance, only in the late Roman Servius' monument commentary, but it is depicted on many republican gems (Fig. 30), on important republican coins (Fig. 31), and on imperial silver. By the middle Republic, images of historical Romans came to be deployed in the same way, often configured and placed so that depicted persons permanently could be seen where and how they had significantly acted in life. Hence the premium placed on having one's statue at the politicians' speaking platform (*rostra*). Hence also the use of arches

FIGURE 31. Silver half-stater, Rome mint, 225–212 B.C.: reverse, military oath scene as in Fig. 30, ROMA in exergue. (Obverse, laureate Dioscuri/Janus herm heads.) (*RRC* 28/1; photo American Numismatic Society)

as special bases for statues, as a means, in particular, of showing a chariot or equestrian procession taking a road without actually blocking it.

The intense monumentalization of the republican city over time shows how the community kept its bearings as Roman trade and conquest spread outward, reaching almost unimaginable distances. Replication and generic practice were ways of holding together; another was to have at the city's center places, buildings, images that were irreplaceable, inimitable. For the entire span of the Republic, Roman sociopolitical identity was a major issue. Its agenda took the form of local and regional pride and a sense of superiority to visibly different neighbors. Being Roman meant being either a citizen of the Republic or a noncitizen contributor to Rome's empire – a complex, and, in its world, a highly distinctive sociopolitical organism. The longer the Republic lasted, the more objectified became the idea of the Republic. Although Carthage had nearly as long a run, only Sparta had an equally long one – and the world knew it. In the defensive and aggressive militarist identity of Rome, as also in its commercial identity, "non-Roman" Italians took a full and proud part, whatever their municipal status, whatever set of languages they commanded. As for republican art, it is best defined as any and all artwork that the peoples of the developed Republic made and displayed at home and abroad.

Roman patronage showed two startling extremes. Best known is the imposition of a physical template of rigid consistency, as Roman cities far and wide were stamped with forum and *comitium, atrium* house, *insulae*, Etrusco-Latin podium temple, and capitolium. Yet, at the same time, Romans cultivated visible diversity and individualism in modes for which cultural anthropologists would expect extreme standardization of self-definition (such as in their funerary monuments). Unlike in other ancient city-states, almost all communally relevant projects were delegated to the individual, shaped and signed by the individual, not by a committee, and remained the legacy of his clan. Road, bridge, aqueduct, basilica, curia, sanctuary, theater, circus, and porticus were as individually authored as the private house and garden. Surely, there were constraints on where individuals could put votives and what kinds they could use; more striking is the freedom they had in choosing a dedication and the clear expectation that permission would be routinely granted should someone wish to dedicate on the Capitol or in the Forum. Some contemporaries savagely attacked Lucius Scipio for dedicating a portrait of himself in Macedonian-style royal garb at the Capitolium; however, no one would have thought to stop him or to remove his statue. Each of the shrines stacked up at the Forum Boarium and the Largo Argentina is enjoyably distinctive. This legacy of diversity as an essential Roman characteristic needs very much to be factored into the phenomenon we call "resistance"; some local art forms of the Empire's subjects persisted whereas others did not. In this sense the visual arts do seem to map the resiliency of the Republic as a tightly defined system that nonetheless permitted individual aspiration and invention.

14: Spectacle and Political Culture in the Roman Republic

Harriet I. Flower

∾

uolgo dictum ipsius ferebant, et conuiuium instruere
et ludos parare eiusdem esse qui uincere proelio sciret.

"A saying of his (L. Aemilius Paullus) was commonly repeated:
that a man who knows how to conquer in battle should also know
how to give a banquet and to organize the games."

Livy (45.32.11)

R oman culture was in many ways a culture of spectacle: spectacle
was at the heart of politics and of the Romans' understanding of the identity of their community. Theirs was above all a
visual culture, a culture of seeing and being seen, both on special occasions and in everyday life. Consequently, many actions were essentially
theatrical, and there was relatively much less of what a modern person
would call privacy. Indeed, a person's identity and status took on their
full meaning only in the eyes of his fellow citizens. Repeated spectacles,
which mostly belonged to recognizable types, reinforced Roman ways
of thinking, especially through the power of the example (*exemplum*)
and through the relation of the individual to the precedents established
by traditional norms (*mos maiorum*). This culture of spectacle expressed
the values of the political elite but also served as a vehicle for communication between all citizens, as all participated together in celebrating and
reaffirming the common values, shared goals, and political institutions of
the community. This chapter, using examples involving members of the
ancient patrician family of the Aemilii, explores the various spectacles

that were developed during the Republic and became characteristic expressions of Roman life and politics.

Although many Roman republican spectacles were based on ancient traditions, such as the triumphal processions that derived from earlier Etruscan parades, the nexus of spectacles as a cultural ensemble really emerged at Rome in the later fourth century B.C. The development of spectacle was intimately linked with the rise of the office-holding elite, defined by the sharing of political power between patricians and plebeians. Spectacle took on renewed cultural value at the same time as the visual arts and was also similar to the visual arts in celebrating the achievements and virtues of this new political class. Consequently, spectacle needs to be appreciated as integral to the stability and success of the republican system of government.

At the same time, spectacle was one of the most typical features of life in the city of Rome itself. The topography of the city developed partly in response to increasingly elaborate shows and parades and served as a kind of theatrical stage for these performances. After the end of the Second Punic War, citizens of Rome would have been treated to spectacles that were increasingly frequent and ever more splendid. These spectacles expressed and mediated the many creative tensions between tradition and change in Roman society. Spectacles illustrate for us, as they did for the citizens of Rome, the interlocking of the different spheres of Roman experience. This was true because politics was inseparable from religion, the individual identified strongly with the community as a whole, events abroad had an increasing impact on life at home, and Roman identity was defined by a series of encounters with "the other" in the Mediterranean world and beyond.

The present discussion will look first at the magistrates who organized the various public spectacles and games and then at the events themselves and their venues, before moving on to consider their evolution and function within Roman culture and society during the last three centuries of the Republic. This chapter is especially concerned with the cumulative and combined effects of the various celebrations as a coherent system, representing the Roman community and its place in the world through display and performance within the space of the city itself. The essentially "republican" character and function of the various spectacles is further demonstrated by the fact that so many of them were decisively modified in the time of Augustus, as a direct result of the change to a system of government in which one man (and his family) dominated politics at Rome.

THE ORGANIZERS

It is important to start by noting that virtually every public spectacle in Rome was organized by a magistrate in office at the time of the event. Hence spectacle was closely connected with that coveted year in office and with the fact that each year was also an election year. Helping to defray the cost of public entertainment was a major expense for the magistrate in question but one that was consciously associated with his own status and with his prospects for election to even higher office within the next few years. His role as coordinator and overseer of the event gave him a part to play that was integral to the spectacle itself. Meanwhile, priests, who might exercise similar roles, came from the same elite social background and usually also held magisterial office in their careers.

A magistrate in high office provided his own spectacle in the daily life of the city. As he moved around the streets in his toga with its purple border, the magistrate with *imperium* was accompanied by lictors holding the rods and axes that symbolized his executive power (*fasces*) and by attendants who carried other necessary equipment (including, in the case of curule magistrates, the ivory curule chair he would sit on to give judgments) or who fulfilled secretarial functions. The entourage of the magistrate had its own processional character and was especially visible as it escorted him from his house to the Forum for daily business or to whatever place was being used for a meeting of the senate or for an assembly of the people. Similarly, any special moment in the magistrate's duties tended to take place with maximum associated publicity. One may take special note of the magistrate who was setting out for or was returning from duties in the provinces. Both his departure (*profectio*) and his return (*adventus*) were marked by ceremonies and ideally by crowds of supporters and well-wishers escorting him on part of his journey.

The elite status of the magistrate was conferred by his election to high office. The most exclusive ranks of the office-holding caste were called the *nobiles* (it is from this term that the English word "noble" is derived). The term *nobilis* in Latin has as its original and most basic meaning the concept of being "well known" or "conspicuous." From this original definition, the word then came to be used to describe Rome's leading politicians and also their families, which had been "ennobled" by the service of family members in the highest offices. It is suggestive and striking that the Roman political elite was explicitly defined not in terms of wealth, birth, education, or virtue but in terms of publicity or profile. There was an essential and natural link between the "nobility of office," which emerged after the end of the "Conflict of the Orders," and the role of the spectacles that were the monopoly of these same men. In other words, once elite status was no longer defined purely in terms of birth and family, as it had been for the patricians in the earlier Republic, new modes of self-definition were needed by what represented itself as an aristocracy of merit and achievement. In typically Roman fashion, merit needed to be publicly recognized and the names of leaders needed to be made known to their fellow citizens. Spectacle and public self-representation were as important to the Roman officeholder as to any modern politician seeking election for himself or public support for his party.

THE SHOWS

The spectacles put on by the magistrates were many and varied: an overview of the most important ones will demonstrate this point. Each was subject to its own body of laws and customs. Although the purpose of this chapter is to discuss spectacles in general, not religious festivals in particular, it is worth noting that there were many of them and that their number grew significantly as a result of the expanding empire. From the earliest days of the Republic, religious festivals were celebrated with processions, sacrifices, and races. Pantomime dances to flute music are attested from the mid fourth century onwards. As it was a custom for a conquering general to use his booty to build a new temple, often to thank a deity to whom he had made a vow during his campaign, the building of temples to honor new gods (or old gods under new guises) was a regular occurrence. Each of these temples would then have a special birthday, and the important ones had games and festivals associated with them. A good example is provided by the cult of the Great Mother (Cybele; Livy 29.10–14), which was brought from Asia Minor in 205 B.C. in association with renewed efforts to drive Hannibal out of Italy by taking a Roman army across to North Africa and attacking his hometown of Carthage. This cult, for all its exotic elements, became a feature of the republican city and had important games associated with it, the *ludi Megalenses*. Plays in various genres were performed at this festival, and the steps in front of the temple on the Palatine served as seats for the audience who watched the dramas, commissioned by the presiding magistrate and held in honor of the goddess. Hence, temple festivals offered both some of the very oldest and some of the newest opportunities for community celebration, with parades, sacrifices, games, drama, races, and public holidays in the context of a calendar that had no regularly occurring holy day each week.

It was during the second half of the third century B.C. that theatre was introduced into Rome in imitation of Greek models, initially by playwrights from outside the city who simply translated Greek plays into Latin. Regularly produced genres included tragedy, comedy, and plays on historical subjects (*fabula praetexta*). Soon a tradition of writing original plays in Latin developed, based on both public and private sponsorship of authors. Genres not formally connected to literature also flourished, such as mime, farce, and acrobatics. Public entertainment in the form of performances was closely associated with the official games and state holidays. Hence, all such performances were sanctioned and arranged by the magistrates in office to coincide with specific days in the calendar, at least at some level. The number of such days increased greatly, especially during the second century B.C. Thus Romans experienced a significant change in the level of their culture of performance and entertainment.

From the early second century B.C. onwards, seating at public performances, notably of drama, was arranged by social rank, with the senators seated in the front (Livy 34.44). The decision to introduce this change by law must reflect the senate's perception of the theatre as a political space and of the relationship of members of the audience both to what was on stage and to each other. It is especially striking to see this development well before a permanent theatre on the Greek model was built in Rome. We know from Cicero that the theatre of the late Republic was a highly political arena, offering the audience many opportunities to voice their views, both to individual politicians as they entered or left their seats and in response to the drama on stage. Although many plays were on topics drawn from Greek myth, the Roman audience was in the habit of reacting to lines that seemed applicable to contemporary politics. We can see, then, that the theatre offered a variety of spectacles and of means of communication between different groups in society. The senators had chosen to make themselves especially conspicuous in this setting, and they had also organized the seating in such a way that they could determine which social class was expressing a reaction to what was happening on stage or in the theatre.

Together with the major games and festivals of the gods, the celebration of a triumph after a great military victory was the most characteristic form of Roman spectacle. The triumph was also in essence a religious event, since its climax was the sacrifice of thanksgiving to Jupiter on the Capitol at the main temple of the city (the temple of the

Capitoline triad, comprising Jupiter, Juno, and Minerva). The greatest success that any Roman general could achieve was to celebrate a victory parade, traditionally associated with a war that had ended in the decisive defeat of the enemy. Regardless of which gods the general might have made vows to in battle, the final thanksgiving was offered by him to Jupiter on behalf of the community as a whole. This was the only occasion on which a general was allowed to lead his army into the city.

The procession would form on the Campus Martius north of the city and would enter through the specially designated triumphal gate (*porta triumphalis*). The parade included the soldiers as well as booty and captives from the war and the general himself, who rode in a special chariot. The general was dressed as Jupiter and even had his face painted red to match the color of the statue, which was made of terracotta. After winding its way through the city and the Forum, past many of its major monuments and crowds of jubilant citizens, the procession would make its way up the Capitoline Hill to the temple of Jupiter, where the sacrifice of thanksgiving took place in front of the temple. Afterwards there would be a public address (*contio*), followed by public banquets and feasting. On this occasion, the general would reward his soldiers with military decorations and with monetary gifts, often distributed before the procession started. A triumph validated a victory, the slaughter of the war, and its booty or plunder, for both the general and his army.

The celebration of a triumph was the apex of the public career of any Roman politician, affording him his community's ultimate recognition of his achievements. Few men lived to celebrate more than one. Understandably, access to the right to triumph (i.e., to celebrate a triumph) was carefully controlled by the senate, and competition could be fierce. The senate usually decreed a vote of thanks to the gods (*supplicatio*) for a major military success: such a vote of confidence became a virtual prerequisite for the subsequent granting of a triumph. Because the general could not enter the city after a war without losing his right to triumph, the senate would hold a special meeting outside the city limits, usually in one of the temples on the Campus Martius. There the general would give an account of his successful achievements (*res gestae*) and would submit a formal petition to his peers to grant him the right to triumph. The size of the victory, the attainment of his military objectives, and the number killed on the Roman side were all factors taken into consideration by the senators. Political rivalry might also lead either an individual or a coalition of opponents to try to block a triumph. The debates were often heated and involved an assertion of status and rank by all involved, especially by the general who was making his claim, but also by the senators who were exercising their right to determine his ultimate status and its public representation. Some generals waited years outside the city for a triumph that never came.

It is easy to see that the triumph originally had a decidedly military flavour to it, as the early wars in Italy would often have yielded booty mainly comprising enemy weapons, horses, and other military equipment. As Rome's expanding empire saw her armies travel to distant lands, the triumphs that resulted were very different in character. The booty was to become immense and often included precious metal and jewels, art objects, exotic animals, and people from different tribes and nations dressed in local costumes. In addition, the exploits of the general and his soldiers were represented in increasingly dramatic and didactic ways, by means of paintings showing important moments in the war and maps, models of towns, and labels or placards explaining what was being paraded. Julius Caesar's famous dictum "I came, I saw, I conquered" (veni, vidi, vici) was originally written on a placard for a triumph. In the heyday of the age of conquest in the second century B.C., the residents of Rome could expect to see a triumph about every eighteen months, each naturally vying with the preceding ones to present the most memorable scenes and impressive booty.

An especially famous example is offered by the triumph of L. Aemilius Paullus over the Macedonian king Perseus in 167 B.C. (Polyb. 18.35.4; Livy 45.40; Plut. Aem. 38). Paullus' triumph extended over three days and was the most splendid to have been seen in Rome up until that time. The first day was devoted to a parade of art objects and paintings conveyed on 250 wagons. Paullus had brought the painter Metrodoros from Athens to create the pictures to illustrate his campaign and conquests. The second day's parade consisted of armor and weapons on wagons as well as silver, including coins in jars and individual silver objects, carried in procession by three thousand men. On the third day Paullus himself appeared, preceded by 120 oxen with gilded horns for Jupiter's sacrifice, masses of gold and precious stones, Perseus and his children with their royal equipment and entourage, and 400 gold wreaths presented as gifts to Paullus by the Greek cities. The victorious general was followed by his soldiers, who sang songs, both celebratory and mocking, as was the Roman custom.

Paullus' war booty, the greatest part of which he gave to the public treasury, was so large that the inhabitants of Italy were no longer required to pay direct taxes (tributum) to Rome. Paullus kept for himself only the royal Macedonian library, which he used to educate his sons. He had also celebrated victory games over many days at Amphipolis in Thrace so that he could demonstrate the Romans' new power in the East and make a spectacle of the dissolution of the Macedonian kingdom before envoys from the whole Greek world. His choice of a dual celebration reveals Paullus' understanding of the political role of spectacle for the Roman general (also shown by the saying of his quoted at the beginning of this chapter); it also demonstrates the ultimate importance of a triumph within the city of Rome itself, especially one that included the enemy leader and his family in the parade. While on tour in Greece, Paullus had adapted a monument of Perseus at Delphi so that it now celebrated Paullus with an equestrian statue, a relief showing his victory over Perseus at Pydna, and a Latin inscription claiming credit in his own name (Figs. 32 and 33).

However splendid, a republican triumph rarely lasted more than one day and never more than four; it did, however, give access to many of the status symbols that marked the most successful Romans. It is notable that when statues of living men started to be erected in Rome in the early third century B.C., they nearly all honored men who had triumphed. Even as statues of magistrates proliferated in the middle Republic, they were always associated in some way with the triumph. The same principle is illustrated in the Forum of Augustus, where the series of famous Romans of the past in niches along the sides represented almost exclusively men who had celebrated a triumph. Similarly, the art of Roman painting as a genre developed to illustrate the achievements of Rome's military and political elite, in particular, their conquests and battles. Paintings of military victories were specially commissioned for a triumph but could then be housed permanently in a temple or even in the family home. The scanty surviving fragments of paintings from republican tombs can be connected with such triumphal art. Similarly, the booty of the victorious general was often spent partly on a monument to recall his glory for posterity, either a war memorial (such as a column or an arch) or a new temple. Although the triumph was not necessarily an official prerequisite in each case, there were few Romans who built a major monument or temple who had not also celebrated a triumph. Indeed, the arch erected by Scipio Africanus (Livy 37.3.7) after his great victory over Hannibal not only was placed on the way up to the Capitol, that is, on the triumphal route itself, but seems to have featured statues of the seven members of his family who had celebrated a triumph. The paintings on the façade of the family tomb of the Scipios on the Appian Way seem also to have featured triumphal themes.

The symbolic significance of the triumph for the Roman elite is brought out perhaps most clearly by the fact that for any man who had

celebrated a triumph, that distinction, rather than any of the political offices he had held, marked the apex of his career and defined his ultimate rank in society. Thus, although it is essentially correct to describe the republican political elite as a "nobility of office," ultimate status came not from election to high office by the people in their electoral assemblies but from the celebration of a triumph, in other words from a public recognition of military success while in office. Permission to celebrate a triumph was in practice granted by the senate and was merely ratified by the people in a ceremony that was usually a formality. The dignity accorded to the triumphing general naturally also reflects the essentially warlike ethos of the Roman upper classes and indeed of the whole community. The empire was popular with the common people, and their enthusiastic support seems to have gone to its most prominent builders and most aggressive defenders.

The fact that being permitted to hold a victory parade was the greatest honor that a Roman could achieve leads logically to the subject of the special funerals of Roman magistrates, which were celebrated with great splendor in a highly public and exceptional manner. The best account of such a funeral was written by the Greek Polybius (6.53–4) in the mid second century B.C. in an attempt to explain to the Greek readers of his history what he saw as an essential characteristic of the Roman community. Special funerals of a distinctly public nature were celebrated only for members of Rome's political elite, specifically men who had been elected at least to the office of *aedile*. When such a man died, instead of being buried immediately, as an ordinary Roman citizen would be, his body lay in state in the *atrium* of his house, sometimes for up to a week. Meanwhile, preparations were made for his funeral, and all citizens were invited through public announcements made by heralds. On the day of the funeral, his body would be carried in a procession from his house to the Forum, where his funeral eulogy was delivered from the *rostra*, the platform used by politicians to address the Roman

---

FIGURE 32. Equestrian plinth monument of Aemilius Paullus before the temple of Apollo at Delphi, 168–67 B.C. Reconstruction. The frieze of the "base" (see Fig. 33) under the crowning equestrian bronze statue of Paullus in battle showed the defeat by Roman and allied soldiers of the army of King Perseus of Macedon at the Battle of Pydna, 168 B.C. (white marble, ht. 45 cm; statue plinth, 1.25 × 2.45 m). Marble plinth was originally made for Perseus; inscription: *L. Aimilius L.f. inperator de rege Perse Macedonibus cepet* (Lucius Aimilius, son of Lucius, commander captured [this] from King Perseus [and] the Macedonians). (Reconstruction after E. Künzl, *Der römische Triumph. Siegesfeiern im antiken Rom* [Munich, 1988], Fig. 65)

FIGURE 33a,b. Monument of Aemilius Paullus at Delphi, battle relief with rider-less horse, 168–167 B.C. (Photo Bildarchiv Foto Marburg 135.132, 135.133, 135.134, 135.135)

FIGURE 33c,d. (Continued)

people. The eulogy would be delivered by his son, if he had one, or by another family member, often from a younger generation.

Actors representing the ancestors who had held political office (at least the office of *aedile*) wore wax masks of their faces made specifically to represent them after death. They formed an important part of the procession and walked ahead of the body as it was being carried out. These masks were not "death masks" in the conventional sense but functional masks that could be worn by someone who was impersonating the man as he had appeared during his lifetime. Each actor would wear the garb and be accompanied by the attributes and symbols of the highest political office the individual had held during his lifetime. For many, that would be the office of consul or censor, and actors representing these ancestors would appear in the toga with the purple border or in the all purple toga of the censorship. Each magistrate would be escorted by the appropriate number of lictors (with rods and axes) and other attendants to suggest his rank. The exception was provided by the man who had celebrated a triumph: he would appear in triumphal garb and was often surrounded by whatever props might still be available from his triumph, such as paintings or booty that had been retained by the family. Even items stored in temples might be fetched and paraded again. An actor representing the dead man himself took part in the funeral, joining the illustrious ancestors and walking immediately in front of his own bier.

Once this procession had arrived at the Forum, the "ancestors" all sat on the ivory chairs of office that they had used during their time as magistrates, thus forming a special audience for the funeral oration. During the eulogy, it was not only the life and achievements of the immediately deceased that were described, but also the deeds and renown of each one of the ancestors represented as being present. Because of this inclusion of the ancestors, the funeral of a leading politician functioned as a public event that could be shared by the whole community but also provided an opportunity for the family to celebrate their history over as many generations as they had been prominent in public life. Initially such funerals were celebrated only for men who had themselves been magistrates, but first other male relatives and then, during the last two generations of the Republic, women also came to be honored in this way. After the eulogy, the family accompanied the body outside the city walls for burial in a private ceremony, usually attended only by close family friends. A very small number of the most ancient families, such as the patrician Claudii, had family cemeteries inside the city walls. (These had been established in the very early days of the Republic or even before.)

For the average Roman citizen, such funerals provided a dramatic representation of major personalities and events from Roman history in the context of the role played by the families of the *nobiles* in public life. The life of the politician and hence also his death were public events for the whole community to share. The funeral of a member of an old political family offered the most impressive array of the status symbols of office and rank that could be seen on any occasion in the city. Every year only two consuls held office, but many, including the most famous of past ages, would appear again in the Forum when one of their descendents was being buried. The splendor of these "ancestors" would have been all the more evident because any magistrates in attendance at the funeral would have appeared in mourning. At the same time, the funeral procession was used to recall and even to recreate, at least in part, the triumphs of the past that had been celebrated by earlier family members.

In 160 B.C., at the funeral of Lucius Aemilius Paullus, conqueror of Macedon, the family arranged for his bier to be carried by alternating teams of individuals representing the peoples he had defeated in war, namely, the Spaniards, Ligurians, and Macedonians (Livy *Per.* 46; Plut. *Aem.* 39). Publicity was so good that many people came into the city to see the funeral from various parts of Italy. Diodorus tells us of the actors who had trained specially to represent the ancestors in this funeral (31.25.2). The funeral was accompanied by gladiatorial shows of exceptional lavishness (costing at least 30 talents, according to Polybius [31.28]), as well as by performances of two of Terence's comedies (*Adelphoi* and *Hecyra*). Paullus' funeral allowed spectators to revisit scenes from his two triumphs, which recalled his three areas of foreign conquest, and to share his interest in Greek culture in performance.

A funeral was essentially a competitive occasion, an opportunity for the family to put on a display of recent achievements in the context of their whole history. It therefore provided a prime venue for a family to deploy its "symbolic capital" in public and to stress its strength across the generations at the moment when a leading member had just died. However, that should not obscure the fact that the splendid funerals of the *nobiles*, like their triumphs, simultaneously served to celebrate the glory and values of the political class as a whole and the system of rank conferred by public election to a series of offices. In other words, Roman spectacles expressed the dynamic interplay between competition and cooperation that was so typical of the classic period of the Roman Republic.

Meanwhile, the spectacle of a young family member praising his ancestors and reciting his family's history in what was often his first public speech was in itself a powerful event that suggested the arrival of another generation to carry on the great traditions of the past. Public speech in the Forum and especially from the *rostra* was strictly limited to magistrates in office and to individuals they might call on to speak in front of the people. A funeral provided the only occasion on which a family could designate a speaker and effectively take over the role of a magistrate for the day. We should not, then, think simply in terms of family propaganda being foisted on an unsuspecting public but of a celebration of the past and of its meaning that the family shared with their fellow citizens. There is every reason to believe that the crowds responded actively to the spectacle of the funeral procession, just as they might cheer a triumphant general or react to a play in a theatrical setting. There is some evidence that the actors aimed to give a dramatic impersonation of the ancestors in the procession, including the extemporizing of lines spoken in character to members of the crowd. The use of professional actors to represent the ancestors may have led to a crossover of dramatic styles between the theatre and the funeral. Professional mourners and musicians and a procession of living family members also added to the spectacle. Funerals might include gladiatorial combat (staged mainly at funerals during the Republic), plays on a variety of topics, and banquets provided for the populace by wealthier families.

Although we are unable to trace the exact relationship between the wax masks (*imagines*) used at funerals (none of which survive) and Roman portraits in more permanent media, it seems that a connection must have existed. Roman portraiture during the Republic was often characterized by an interest in creating individualized likenesses and by a focus on the face as expressing the character of the person. When not in use at a funeral, the wax masks were stored in cupboards in the *atrium*, the most accessible reception room of the house. The cupboards were labeled with inscriptions (*tituli*) recording the name of the individual and usually a brief outline of his career. Often the cupboard doors would be closed in order to protect the masks, which were fragile and sensitive to heat, light, and smoke. It seems that the labels were visible even when the doors were closed. On high days and holidays, as well as on days of family celebration, the cupboard doors were opened and the masks were decorated in a festive manner. There is no evidence of cult associated with the masks in the *atrium*. It is notable that families decided not to keep their masks in storage areas that would have made them last longer. Rather the masks were an essential element of the everyday life of the household, both for the family itself and for any visitors who entered the front door, and as such they were able to evoke memories of the funeral processions in which they were used. Also, the masks often appeared in a setting that featured a painted family tree and displays of war booty and portraits in other media. The aristocratic house itself served as a memory space to preserve and to display family achievements, as expressed through the careers of officeholders.

The Setting

As is evident from the discussion so far, the city itself served as the essential backdrop for most spectacles. It is characteristic of the Republic that the Romans built few formal entertainment spaces and long resisted the erection of a permanent stone theatre in the city. The Circus Maximus and the Circus Flaminius were notable exceptions: these racetracks were built because of the risks to spectators and riders during chariot and horse races or events that featured wild animals. The Circus Flaminius was especially associated with the triumph and came to be surrounded by triumphal monuments and temples built by victorious generals. For events of other types, temporary wooden seating was sometimes erected, but spectators were often required to stand. Most of the traditional Roman spectacles were enacted in the public streets and squares of the city. Neither the triumphal route nor the route of the funeral procession was firmly established, and heightened effects could obviously be achieved both by extending processional routes and by passing significant monuments associated with earlier triumphs or family members. In the late fourth century B.C., balconies for spectators (*maeniana*) were added to the Forum, and this makes clear how important it was as a central area of spectacle, a venue for processions, funeral speeches, and gladiatorial combats.

Some places in the city were closely identified with certain spectacles. For example, the temple of the Magna Mater (Cybele) was the site for the plays performed during the *ludi Megalenses* in April. Spectacles were so common, however, that each temple or street might have had its own customary procession or festival. And although the triumphal gate (*porta triumphalis*) always had special significance as the entrance for the triumphing general and his army, other gates also saw solemn entrances and exits of magistrates, religious processions, and funerals. The ubiquity of spectacle demonstrates the essentially Roman sense of permeability between public and private space within the city and even inside the houses of the elite, who traditionally kept their front doors open during the day unless someone had died in the household. Consequently, Roman culture took on its full value in its own context, and that context was provided by the topography of the city of Rome itself.

THE FUNCTION AND DEVELOPMENT OF ROMAN SPECTACLE

Spectacles, therefore, enacted Roman culture within the space and time (calendar) of the city. Their main functions can be described in the following ways. They expressed the roles, values, and hierarchy of the office-holding elite, the *nobiles*. At the same time they created a sense of identity, solidarity, and tradition for the community as a whole. They created and configured the spaces of the city to confer honor on leading individuals and to set up a dialogue between individual leaders (and their families) and the citizens at large. Hence, spectacle enacted the face-to-face quality of Roman life and of political power. Roman memory was defined in particular ways, and the city itself became a memory space for the recalling of the past and for the assertion of its continuing relevance to the life of the whole community. Spectacles reproduced the social and political order in a way that was essentially didactic for all citizens, but especially for the young. Ultimate achievement and prestige could be meaningful only when publicly displayed within the city and through traditional venues and media. Spectacle was central to the expression of competition and cooperation and hence also of the dynamic tension between the two.

Despite the essential role of spectacle in conferring status on the individual, the Republic was always based on the idea that no man should become so preeminent that he dominated the state. In the first century B.C., the increasingly fierce competition between the great generals for precisely such a position of preeminence also expressed itself in terms of spectacle and games. When Marius, during his second consulship in 104 B.C., tried to enter a meeting of the senate in his triumphal costume, he was attempting to gain special recognition from his peers, which they angrily refused to grant him. He was forced to leave the meeting to change his clothes (Plut. *Mar.* 12.5). His ambitions are revealed in a new use of traditional symbols of rank and military success, such as trophies and triumphal images. His rival Sulla was more successful; indeed, Sulla set the precedent for the great military hero who dominated and "restored" the Republic. Sulla's great victory games set new standards for the magnificence of Roman spectacle and for its celebration of one man rather than the success of the community as a whole. Sulla erected his own special victory monuments even as he removed the images and trophies of Marius. He also cultivated Venus as his special protectress. His innovations were later imitated by Pompey and Caesar. Hence, the transgression of republican norms was consistently enacted and experienced through new forms of spectacle – forms that took on their full meaning by virtue of their contrast with what was more traditional within republican culture.

Meanwhile, spectacle had become increasingly linked to the growing empire and to the vast booty that Romans brought home from distant lands. It is a truism of republican history that the essentials of the Roman constitution did not change significantly in response to Rome's increased influence and responsibilities overseas and that this rigidity prevented the government of the city from proving equal to the task of overseeing a world empire. Spectacle, however, was constantly evolving, and in such a way that it acted as a mirror, held up for the inhabitants of the city. In this mirror, they could see a reflection of themselves, their leaders, and their own lives as well as a picture of their empire as it rapidly expanded. In the riches of the empire and its military might, Romans could see the increasing interdependence of wealth and status. The impact of the empire at home was often first felt in the novelties to be seen in the triumphal procession, as each returning general aimed to outdo his predecessors. Hence the Romans' own experience of change and growth was regularly reflected in processions and performances.

The expanding empire had a significant impact on many aspects of Roman culture. A sense of empire, expressed by maps and paintings, was engendered primarily by the triumph. Similarly, foreign peoples and exotic animals were put on show by returning generals at triumphs and in the theatre. The enormous wealth that was pouring into the city and that was to change its lifestyle almost beyond recognition was literally put on show in processions of carts and floats. A general was supposed to put all his booty – money and bullion but also art and luxury items – on show for the public. Roman art itself was influenced by the wide variety of objects and craftsmen that were imported through conquest. At the same time, public spaces in the city and some elite houses became display areas for the captured artistic treasures of conquered cities and kingdoms.

Slaves, primarily prisoners of war captured by Roman armies, were amongst the most important commodities to flood into the city. While not all prisoners would appear in a triumph – many would be sold to slave dealers before the day of celebration – a representative number would be reserved for the parade itself. These prisoners enacted for the Roman public not simply their own defeat and new subservient status in relation to their conquerors but also the changes sweeping through Roman society. Similarly, new religious cults and practices were mainly introduced from conquered areas and as a result of the vows and other religious preferences of the generals. In each case, both the triumph itself and the temples built from the victor's booty were closely linked to his achievements in war. The net result was that the face of the city was completely transformed by the new resources acquired through conquest and by an increasing tendency to appropriate whatever was available.

Meanwhile, the sense of dialogue between the politicians and the people continued to develop within the sphere of spectacle, where the people could express their attitude of cooperation or of resistance to the political elite. Our understanding of the personal glory that the individual general could gain through spectacle must be complemented by an awareness of a more generalized narrative about the manifest destiny of an imperial people under the protection of their powerful gods. Above all, a triumph presented a picture of the victorious as opposed to the defeated, of a Roman "self" conquering a foreign "other," whether Greek or barbarian. Certainly the vast increase in the number and splendor of spectacles in the second century B.C., including games, theatrical performances, and triumphs, was stunning.

THE SUPPORT STAFF

The media used for Roman spectacles were a combination of spoken words, texts, and visual representations. The vehicles were processions and performances of a more or less formal and dramatic kind. Processions involving magistrates were especially notable features common to many public spectacles. All were orchestrated by the magistrates in office or by the priests, with the exception of funerals, which were arranged by the families of the deceased officeholders. It is worth noting that the services of large staffs of professionals, usually of humble social status, were clearly required, often at short notice. Shrines and religious cults would have had their own personnel, while musicians, artists, and performers of all kinds would find seasonal work, according to the festival calendar in Rome and in other Italian cities. The funerals of the elite were contracted out to professional undertakers (*libitinarii*) and were organized by hired foremen (*dissignatores*) who could provide actors, musicians, and professional mourners and had the necessary expertise to stage a major procession through the city, often at no more than a week's notice.

We do not know whether most actors who appeared in funeral processions also performed in plays or whether the undertakers retained their own guild of performers specially trained to represent the ancestors. It seems likely that people, like props, tended to be reused, simply because of the challenges posed by the increasingly ambitious programs of display. In any case, drama could be seen in a variety of contexts, most notably at the regular public festivals, at the funerals of the prominent, and probably also at the dedication of new temples. Genres were not necessarily specific to the occasion, as can be seen from the fact that some comedies of Terence were first seen at funerals. As has already been stressed, the props of a triumph could be reused in a funeral procession, which must eventually have changed the character of funerals to reflect the new sophistication of the triumphs and their increasingly imperialistic and materialistic messages. Comic dancers who appeared at the major public festivals also could be seen in funeral processions. The political elite who put on these spectacles were called upon to negotiate between their own resources and the evolving expectations of the general public in an increasingly competitive arena where their own reputations, and that of their families, could be at stake. In 129 B.C. Quintus Aelius Tubero was not elected praetor after giving a meager banquet at the funeral of his uncle, Scipio Aemilianus (Cic. *Mur.* 75).

SPECTACLE AS AN EXPRESSION OF ROMAN LIFE

The range of meaning and the importance of spectacle in Roman culture are further revealed by the fact that most elements of public display were fully developed well before the advent of equivalent written forms of Latin literature, especially prose. Funeral orations were amongst the first Latin speeches to be published, in keeping with the central role played by oratory in Roman political life. Drama was written primarily for performance, not for a reading public. Historiography was not written by Romans until the early second century B.C., and then initially by senators writing in Greek with a view to reaching an international reading public beyond the city itself. However, the great spectacles of the second century surely influenced literary genres and were in turn shaped by interaction with them, as was also the case with monuments, inscriptions, and the visual arts in general. Any convincing picture of Roman republican culture must try to recapture at least something of the noise, colors, and pageantry of the triumphal procession or the atmosphere of the audience reacting to a play by Plautus as they sat on the steps of the temple of the Magna Mater on the Palatine. Each occasion had its full effect specifically within its original context in the city and through its interdependence with other public media and before what was probably a largely similar audience of citizens who lived in or near Rome itself. Those in public life could reach the most prominent positions and exercise their authority only by repeatedly facing huge crowds and gaining public recognition and acclaim. At the same time, the Roman crowds themselves must have been able to gain some awareness of the often fragile balance between the increasingly fierce aristocratic competition and the traditional societal consensus that was shaping their city and its empire.

Polybius provides a vignette, from the mid second century B.C., of the way spectacle had spilled out into various areas of Roman life and had come to define the situation of the elite (31.26). He gives a brief description of the appearance of Aemilia, sister of Aemilius Paullus and wife of P. Cornelius Scipio Africanus, in the traditional processions of women at religious festivals. She was well known for her entourage of numerous slaves, who carried the magnificent personal effects and equipment, made of silver and gold, that she brought for her own use on religious occasions. Her looks, dress, and style were consciously designed to reflect her status as the wife of the great Scipio, the conqueror of Carthage, and, in effect, each of her appearances in public was turned into a procession that reflected the triumphs of the Scipios and the wealth acquired through empire as it was directly affecting the lifestyle of the conquerors. When Aemilia died in 162 B.C., her adopted grandson Scipio Aemilianus (who was her nephew by birth) gave these items to his own mother Papiria, who had been divorced for a long time and was living in reduced circumstances. Papiria had in fact stopped attending festivals owing to her poverty. Now she reappeared in public with Aemilia's effects and entourage to reassert her status as an aristocratic lady, regardless of the fact that she had no husband at the time. Her inability or unwillingness to participate in the life of the community without the requisite status symbols surely reflects a marked change over what her mother or grandmother would have perceived as the norm, especially during the austere days of the Second Punic War, when displays of luxury were considered unpatriotic and were limited by law. Even for women, the display of status and wealth had become publicly linked to the political achievements and pretensions of their male family members, within increasingly elaborate and sumptuous rituals of spectacle and self-advertisement.

PART 5

⁓

EPILOGUE:
THE INFLUENCE OF THE
ROMAN REPUBLIC

15: THE ROMAN REPUBLIC AND THE FRENCH AND AMERICAN REVOLUTIONS

Mortimer N.S. Sellers

⟳

W hen George Washington gave his inaugural speech as the first president of the United States under the new federal constitution, he asserted that "the destiny of the republican model of government" was "*deeply*, perhaps . . . *finally*, staked on the experiment entrusted to the hands of the American People."[1] A new "Senate" would meet on the "Capitol" hill, overlooking the "Tiber" river (formerly "Goose Creek"), as in Rome,[2] to restore "the sacred fire of liberty" to the Western world.[3] The vocabulary of eighteenth-century revolution reverberated with purposeful echoes of republican Rome as political activists self-consciously assumed the Roman mantle. James Madison and Alexander Hamilton, the primary authors and advocates of the United States Constitution, wrote together pseudonymously as "Publius" to defend their creation,[4] associating themselves with Publius Valerius Poplicola, founder and first consul of the Roman Republic.[5] Camille Desmoulins attributed the French Revolution to Cicero's ideal of Roman politics, imbibed by children in the schools.[6] At every opportunity, American and French revolutionaries proclaimed their desire to reestablish the "stupendous fabrics" of republican government that had fostered liberty at Rome.[7]

The Roman name of "republic" evoked first and above all the memory of government without kings.[8] Roman authors dated their republic from the expulsion of Rome's last king, Tarquinius Superbus, and mourned its fall in the principate of Augustus.[9] As French and American politicians came increasingly into conflict with their own monarchs, they found a valuable ideology of opposition already fully formed in the Roman senatorial attitude towards Caesar and his successors. The guiding principle of this republican tradition, as remembered (for example) by Thomas Paine, was government for the "*res-publica*, the public affairs, or the public good," perceived as naturally antithetical to monarchy and to any other form of arbitrary rule.[10] Paine and other eighteenth-century republicans viewed the individual and collective well-being of citizens as the only legitimate purpose of government. Their rallying cry of "liberty" signified subjection to laws made for the common good, and to nothing and to no one else.[11] Statesmen traced this principle to the frequently cited passage in Livy[12] that attributes the liberty of Rome to Lucius Junius Brutus and to his introduction of elected magistrates into Roman politics, constrained by the rule of law.[13]

American and French republicans thought of themselves as part of a 2,000-year-old tradition originating in Rome. The standard account divided political science between the "ancient prudence," destroyed by Caesar and Augustus, "whereby a civil society of men is instituted and preserved upon the foundation of *common interest*" and the "modern prudence," in force ever since, "by which some man, or some few men, subject a city or a nation, and rule it according to his or their private interests."[14] Republicans fought to restore the ancient prudence, which had ended "with the liberty of Rome."[15] John Adams, the Massachusetts republican (and later president of the United States), credited this analysis to James Harrington, the English commonwealth's-man,[16] who attributed it to Donato Giannotti, the Florentine exile,[17] who had it from Tacitus,[18] in a passage made popular for English and American readers by Thomas Gordon[19] and passed on as a legacy of liberty from generation to generation.[20] The tradition of republican opposition to arbitrary authority in Europe had developed far in advance of the French and American revolutions[21] and strongly influenced political events centuries before new republics emerged on the scene, or nations knew them by that name.[22]

Thomas Hobbes perceived the threat to settled institutions in republican doctrine and blamed the schools and universities for instigating the English Civil War by teaching "*Cicero*, and other writers [who] have grounded their Civil doctrine, on the opinions of the Romans, who were taught to hate Monarchy" and to love republican government, so that "by reading of these Greek, and Latine Authors, men from their childhood have gotten a habit (under a false shew of Liberty) . . . of licentious[ly] controlling the actions of their Sovereigns; and again of controlling those controllers, with the effusion of so much blood; as I think I may truly say, there was never any thing so dearly bought, as these Western parts have bought the learning of the Greek and Latine tongues."[23] Italian, Dutch, and English reformers all appealed to Roman institutions,[24] with enough success that, by the early eighteenth century in Britain, John Trenchard and Thomas Gordon (writing as "Cato") could claim that although "[t]he same principles of nature and reason that supported liberty in Rome, must support it here and everywhere,"[25] Hanoverian England was "the best republick in the world, with a prince at the head of it," being "a thousand degrees nearer a-kin to a commonwealth . . . than it is to absolute monarchy."[26]

"Commonwealth" was simply the English translation of "republic," but the short history and ultimate failure of the self-styled "Commonwealth" of England in the seventeenth century complicated subsequent usage. Although the English commonwealth was denominated "*respublica*" on Oliver Cromwell's state seals,[27] as the American Commonwealth of Pennsylvania was styled in Latin "*Respublica*" in all its early law reports,[28] the word "commonwealth" came to be associated with parliamentary unicameralism during the English Civil War and later with Pennsylvania's famously unicameral constitution of 1776.[29] This made the name of "commonwealth" both "unpopular" and "odious" to many who would have preferred institutions more faithful to the older Roman model of "mixed" republican government.[30] Opponents of the Pennsylvania plan formed what they called the "Republican Society" to advocate the stronger checks and balances of a more truly "republican" constitution.[31]

French republicanism developed its institutions under the strong influence of Benjamin Franklin, who had presided at Pennsylvania's constitutional convention. Franklin represented the United States as ambassador to France from 1776 until 1785, and he secured the translation of the first American state constitutions into French. French opinion had long admired Pennsylvania as a modern Sparta and its founder, William Penn, as the new American Lycurgus.[32] This contributed to a gradual divergence between French republicanism, which looked to Pennsylvania, Sparta, and English Commonwealth authors for its inspiration as much as it did to Rome, and American republicanism, which looked primarily to Rome but also to the British Whig "republican" tradition as it had existed after the Glorious Revolution of 1688.[33] The practical results of these differing attitudes were constitutional first, contributing to French carelessness about the checks and balances of republican government, and cultural second, leading to a greater French emphasis on public virtue than Americans felt would be necessary under the republican form of government.[34]

The problem for would-be republicans, in America as much as in France, was that the Roman Republic itself had ultimately failed. Tacitus, in a well-known passage, described republican government as fragile and evanescent, easier to praise than to practice for long.[35] Tacitus gave a sympathetic presentation of the emperor Galba's argument that the Roman Empire had simply become too large to continue under republican institutions and needed a measure of slavery to survive.[36] Montesquieu made this supposition famous in his *De l'esprit des lois*, which concluded that large republics will inevitably become corrupt and die into despotism.[37] All modern republicans had to face the problem of Rome's failure, but various authors offered different remedies, depending on their circumstances and to some extent on which Roman sources they read (or chose to read). Certain revolutionaries cited Livy to advocate the rule of law.[38] Others followed Plutarch in their emphasis on rural simplicity.[39] Sallust had stressed the dangers of corruption.[40] The question facing modern republicans was this: which "combination of powers in society" would "compel the formation of good and equal laws" and "an impartial execution, and faithful interpretation of them, so that the citizens may constantly enjoy the benefit of them, and be sure of their continuance."[41]

The importance of Rome's republican model for French and American revolutionaries lay in the courage it gave them to contemplate government without a king by providing politicians with a rival set of political institutions opposed to the hereditary principle. Roman republican rhetoric had stressed the importance of the common good, the corruption of kings, the authority of the senate, the balance of the constitution, and the sovereignty of the people.[42] This set the tone for public debate. Agitators disputing pseudonymously in the newspapers called themselves "A Republican,"[43] "Civis,"[44] "Cato,"[45] "Curtius,"[46] "Brutus,"[47] "Publius,"[48] "Cincinnatus,"[49] and so forth. They all struck Roman poses, but what they actually fought over in arms and disputed in print was the power and constitution of the state. The republican revolutions of the eighteenth century sought government for the common good ("republican government") but also sought the constitution best suited to secure government for the common good (the "republican form of government"), which always led them back to republican Rome. Rome's great and lasting contribution to the French and American revolutions consisted not only in political principles but also in a set of constitutional mechanisms designed to secure republican liberty through the fundamental structure of the state.[50]

John Adams, the preeminent American political scientist of his era and author of the Constitution of the Commonwealth of Massachusetts[51] collected in his *Defence of the Constitutions of Government of the United States of America* three volumes of examples and commentaries on the "reading and reasoning which produced the American constitutions."[52] Adams traced "the checks and balances of republican government" back to the "mixed governments" of monarchy, aristocracy, and democracy attempted "with different success" in ancient Greece and Rome.[53] The Greeks never mastered the "checks and balances of free government," to their ultimate cost,[54] but Adams (citing Cicero) reviewed how the Romans had developed institutions to protect freedom and justice through a careful balance and mixture of the different powers of the state.[55] The principal Roman texts cited by Adams in his introduction to define republican government were Cicero's endorsement of the mixed constitution,[56] his prescription for civic "harmony," secured by checks and balances,[57] and his conclusion that republics exist first and above all to serve the common good.[58] Adams supplied all three texts for his readers, both in Latin and in English paraphrase, along with two other excerpts from Cicero's *Republic* reiterating the primacy of the common good over democracy and identifying the common good with justice.[59] "As all the ages of the world have not produced a greater statesman and philosopher united in the same character" than Cicero, Adams concluded, "his authority should have great weight."[60]

Cicero's unrivaled authority in republican politics supported the balancing of powers between three branches of government,[61] very much in the form that it had already evolved in the British colonies of North America in the 150 years before the American Revolution.[62] Americans noticed the parallel, which strengthened their resolve to protect their old institutions against British innovation.[63] They also shared many of Cicero's fundamentally patrician attitudes. American politicians like James Madison drew a sharp distinction between their "republican" pursuit of the common good and the "democratic" tyranny of simple majority rule.[64] The single greatest difference between Roman republican institutions, as Americans remembered them, and America's own (as they hoped) more stable republican constitution was "*the total exclusion of the people in their collective capacity*" from any share in the government of the United States.[65] Americans hoped that by extending the "representative" principle already present in Rome's consuls and senate to other formerly more "democratic" branches of government,[66] they could introduce a "republican remedy for the diseases most incident to republican government."[67] The American House of Representatives would replace Rome's popular assemblies to act, in a sense, as a second senate, helping to defend the people "against their own temporary errors and delusions."[68]

The sixth book of Polybius provided the classical summary of the "republican form of government" that eighteenth-century republicans sought to perfect by modifying the Roman constitution. Polybius' endorsement of limited and divided power stressed a balance between monarchy, aristocracy, and democracy.[69] His modern successors proposed instead the checks and balances not so much of "orders" or "classes" of men as of "offices" held by otherwise equal citizens.[70] The evil to be avoided was "tyranny" or the establishment of any "unlimited power" that some one, few, or many citizens might use to dominate the rest.[71] John Adams provided translations and a summary of Polybius' sixth book in his collection of republican sources,[72] published just in time to be used by delegates at the United States Constitutional Convention.[73] Modern would-be republicans remembered the Roman consuls as having been primarily executive officers; the senate was thought of as having been primarily responsible for finances and declarations of war; and the popular assemblies were understood to have held the power of electing magistrates and approving the nation's laws and wars.[74] They struggled to improve this balance in their own constitutions – as in the United States, where the president was the executive,[75] the Senate ratified all treaties,[76] and the House of Representatives succeeded the Roman popular assemblies in holding final approval over all laws and declarations of war.[77] The aim of the modern republics still remained what moderns thought that it had been at Rome – the maintenance of strong enough political checks and balances so that whenever any branch of the government or people became too "ambitious," the others would unite to control it, thus keeping all public powers within their original bounds, as prescribed by the Constitution.[78] The United States Constitution guarantees to every state in the Union a "republican form of government,"[79] enforced by means of federal power against the states' governments, as in the American Civil War.[80]

French republicans never developed a stable set of political theories or institutions as clear and coherent as those set forth in John Adams's *Defence of the Constitutions of Government of the United States of America* or James Madison and Alexander Hamilton's *Federalist* letters, but they drew on the same Roman sources and came to many of the same conclusions. The Baron de Montesquieu's masterpiece *De l'esprit* des lois (1748) and Jean-Jacques Rousseau's Du contrat social (1762) both preceded the French and American revolutions, and were "scarcely republican" in the eyes of subsequent writers.[81] Nevertheless, both relied heavily on Roman authorities and profoundly influenced American (mostly Montesquieu) and French (mostly Rousseau) republican thought. Anne Robert Jacques Turgot (died 1781) and the Abbé Gabriel Bonnot de Mably (died 1785) had both interpreted American republicanism for French readers without fully endorsing the North American models. Turgot proposed a single all-powerful public assembly and criticized American bicameralism.[82] Mably disliked the American commercial spirit, which he thought would make Americans corrupt.[83] Both men's attitudes reflected a French sense of the "ancients" and "moderns," well summarized by Benjamin Constant in the wake of the French Revolution's collapse into empire. Constant dismissed ancient "liberty" as having required universal subjection to the public will – a will expressed collectively in large public assemblies and under the direction of a public political virtue that modern citizens had lost and could never hope to regain.[84] Montesquieu had doubted that ancient republicanism of this kind could ever survive outside small homogenous cantons.[85] Rousseau reluctantly agreed,[86] adding that democratic assemblies of limited local populations offered the only realistic hope of republican liberty or political justice in this world.[87]

Rousseau's conception of republican virtue and his dogmatism about the necessary corruption of large states set an almost impossible task for French republicans and contributed to the excesses of Maximilien Robespierre and the Jacobin Terror in France. Like Livy and John Adams, Rousseau identified republican government with the rule of law under the sovereignty of the people[88] acting to secure their common good.[89] Rousseau described such public decisions as expressions of the "general will."[90] The people are the "sovereign" authors of the laws that bind them,[91] which makes them "free,"[92] but only so long as the sovereign people legislate collectively in pursuit of their common good.[93] Rousseau differed from other republicans only in his opposition to representation in the popular assembly[94] and his heightened fear of "factions," by which he meant any group, large or small, acting in its own private interest.[95] These views had significant practical implications, however, at least in France. If all laws have to be ratified by democratic assemblies of the people,[96] then the people must become virtuous[97] or mutually reasonable (which is the same thing).[98] Rousseau wrote of changing human nature[99] and believed that good public morals would be necessary to maintain any successful republican government.[100] Yet the French were notoriously corrupt and depraved.[101] This made the maintenance of their virtue an extremely difficult task, perhaps an impossible one, and so, with his French successors, Rousseau supposed that without profound reforms, some peoples (perhaps including the French themselves) would simply remain unfit for republican government.[102] French republicans looked upon public virtue as rare and difficult to maintain.[103] American republicans preferred to believe that by instituting good order they could secure good men.[104]

The history of republican principles in Europe in the centuries preceding the French and American revolutions saw a series of political advances, as scholars, then clerics, courtiers, and kings, steeped in Latin learning, embraced the republican commitment to government for the common good. Some even recognized the desirability of popular sovereignty and mixed or balanced government to secure the common good while at the same time doubting their practicality, given the fallen state of European morals.[105] In his answer to the *XIX Propositions Made by Both Houses of Parliament* in 1642, King Charles I claimed that England was already a mixed and balanced government.[106] The English "Cato" said the same of England under George I,[107] while disavowing the thought that any fully implemented "Republick" would be "practicable" in England's current circumstances.[108] This remained the American position until 1776, after the publication of Thomas Paine's *Common Sense*, which convinced many Americans that the king's "long and violent abuse of power"[109] had finally made it necessary to develop the "republican materials" long embedded in England's mixed and balanced constitution.[110] The French were just as hesitant until the king's flight to Varennes in June 1791, and even then they brought him back and renounced the prospect of a full republic.[111] Politicians denied that they were republicans,[112] although Robespierre did defend the constitution proposed after Varennes as a "republic with a king at the head of it."[113] The French introduced most of the elements of the republican form of government into their constitution in 1791, but they maintained their constitutional monarchy until 10 August 1792.[114]

The French revolutionary model of a republic with a king at the head of it was wholly in keeping with Rousseau's political precepts.[115] Rousseau had always made a strict distinction between the magistrates, who could be hereditary, and the public legislative assemblies, which should include the whole people and constitute the only legitimate sources of law.[116] While Rousseau would have preferred that elected magistrates implement the people's laws,[117] he accepted that sometimes a monarch might govern "legitimately" – that is, in accordance with laws that had already been approved in the public assemblies.[118] Both Montesquieu and Rousseau had suggested that some nations might be or become too large or corrupt to be ruled as republics (as Rome had done) and that monarchs sometimes suited such states better than elected magistrates, despite their well-known injustices.[119] Yet Rome had survived as a republic for many years despite its size. This offered the French some hope.[120] They attempted various stratagems to make the people more virtuous, and Rousseau even considered the institution of slavery, justified as having been the vehicle through which Spartan citizens attained the leisure to give thorough attention to the public good and so properly pursue their deliberative duties in the legislature.[121]

The French republicanism of Rousseau and his disciples differed from its Roman, Polybian, and American antecedents in its general reliance on unanimity in the public assemblies, rather than on checks and balances, to guard against faction.[122] While Polybius, Madison,[123] Adams,[124] and even Montesquieu[125] wrote of using power as a check to power and ambition to counteract ambition, Rousseau turned to mixed government only to protect popular sovereignty, by preventing magistrates from usurping the legislative power of the people.[126] French scholars studied the Roman *comitia* in detail for ideas about how to guide public legislative debate, whether through the use of census classes, through the exclusion of the proletariat, or by instituting a body of censors to guard against the greed, intrigue, and inconstancy of "modern" human society.[127] Montesquieu thought that many proto-republican checks and balances had existed already under the Roman kings.[128] This made it easier to tolerate monarchy, even in a state that understood republican liberty as the primary object of government. Learned Frenchmen thought that Roman liberty had first been lost, not through the agency of kings, but rather when democracy invaded the diplomatic authority of the senate and usurped the magistrates' executive power.[129]

Latin literature and the Roman ethos were not a novelty in 1789. Joseph Addison's *Cato* (1713) and Voltaire's *Brutus* (1730)[130] had promoted a republican sensibility in the theater. Jacques-Louis David's *Oath of the Horatii* (1784) mimicked republican austerity in art. Charles Willson Peale's portrait of William Pitt (1768) shows the prime minister in a toga standing beside a statue of Roman Liberty (with her *pilleus* and *vindicta*) and worshiping at the sacred flame on her altar. Charles Rollin's *Histoire ancienne* (1731–1738) and *Histoire romaine* (1738–1748) fed a ravenous popular demand.[131] A Roman sensibility dominated the architecture,[132] sculpture,[133] and rhetoric of French, English, American, and most European public life, although rarely was an openly "republican" position embraced.[134] What changed in North America in 1776 and in France in 1792 was the public's willingness to believe that republican government would be possible in modern times, with all its checks and balances and without the hereditary principle.[135]

The French republic, when it finally emerged, quickly repeated five hundred years of Roman history in a decade. From a self-styled Brutus (Desmoulins) to the pseudo-Gracchus (Babeuf) and would-be Caesar or Augustus (Bonaparte), French politicians reenacted the evolution and eventual destruction of the Roman Republic in the blood of their own citizens, to the amazement, inspiration, and eventual horror of Europe. The French experience seemed to confirm all the doubts of Tacitus, Montesquieu, and Rousseau that republican government could ever be re-created after Rome, or survive very long if it was. But the United States did survive, and American republicans had predicted the republican failure in France.[136] The French republicans' excesses could be attributed to their inattention to the traditional checks and balances of the republican form of government on the Roman model, or so many surviving republicans believed.[137] Others blamed their inherent corruption as Frenchmen.[138] Like Rome itself, France found an imperial solution to republican anarchy, ignoring checks and balances in favor of a plebiscitary dictatorship, which discredited the republican tradition in Europe for almost a century afterwards.[139]

French advocates of Roman checks and balances appear to have had their chance to make republican government work in the failed constitutions of 1791, 1793, 1795, and 1799, all of which tinkered with limited magistrates, deliberative senates, and representative popular assemblies. In fact, French government seemed to move (in form at least) ever closer to the Roman model – beginning with a constitutional monarchy and unicameral assembly (1791), then replacing the monarch with an executive council (1793), adding a second chamber in the legislature (1795), and finally creating "consuls," "tribunes," and a senate-for-life (1799). In reality, none of the French constitutions ever had a chance to take hold, and the various "Sénatus-consultes" and "Proclamations des Consuls" that made Napoléon Bonaparte a consul for life and eventually emperor, discredited Roman vocabulary for subsequent generations in France.[140] The old republican advocates of checks and balances and liberty now called themselves "liberals" and turned their attention to individual rights.[141] What later French politicians remembered as "republican," for good or ill, were the unicameral expressions of the "general will" made in the manner of Jean-Jacques Rousseau by the National Convention and the Constituent Assemblies,[142] along with Robespierre's vain attempts to inculcate civic virtue on the Spartan model during his own brief ascendancy.[143]

The French and American revolutions changed subsequent conceptions of republican government, and divided the republican tradition, by creating their own inspiring republican narratives to supersede the histories of Rome. Of course, the Roman model remained, so long as students read Cicero, Sallust, Livy, and Tacitus in school,[144] but the American republic now provided a more contemporary example of successful republican government, and one as yet without final failure.[145] The French republican tradition after Robespierre differed from Roman practice mostly in disparaging the senate.[146] When France returned to bicameralism at the end of the nineteenth century, it did so under American influence, against the grain of its own "republican" tradition and without reference to Rome.[147]

The essence of republican government, as French and American revolutionaries in the late eighteenth century knew from the example of Rome, was government for the common good, through the rule of law, under a sovereign people, guided by magistrates that they had elected themselves. The "republican form of government," more respected in the United States than in France but much discussed in both nations, controlled the powers of the magistrates, the senate, and the public assemblies by balancing their responsibilities in the manner of republican Rome. Both France and the United States replaced the direct democracy of the Roman *comitia* with elected representative assemblies, and they denigrated "democracy" generally, as tumultuous, partisan, and ill-conceived.[148] This old opposition between "Roman" republicanism and "Greek" democracy diminished with time as French politicians forgot Rousseau's distinction between the sovereign people and their government.[149] Americans in the southern states also turned to "democracy" in the early nineteenth century, as they embraced French speculation about the benefits of Greek slavery[150] to justify their own slave power in the face of emerging "republican" opposition.[151]

The history and institutions of the Roman Republic gave French and American republicans the courage and vocabulary to pursue their own independence nearly two millennia after Cato's death in Utica extinguished republican liberty in the ancient world.[152] The French and American cry of "liberty" was a call for the equal citizenship under law that Europeans remembered as the final legacy of Rome. French and American politicians had drawn slightly different conclusions from the civil conflicts that ended the Republic – the Americans followed Cicero in strengthening the senate, the French followed Sallust in somewhat weakening its power – but both embraced the Roman aim (as they remembered it) of serving the common good through popular sovereignty, balanced representative government, and the rule of law.

At the end of the American Revolution, after the colonists had defeated the British king (with French help) and earned their nation's independence, the officers of the Continental Army returned, unpaid and unappreciated, to their separate homes and farms. Steeped in the republican ethos, they did not revolt against their mistreatment but took the name of "Cincinnati," after Rome's great general Lucius Quinctius Cincinnatus, who had also returned to his plough after victory and without reward. Their motto recalled their sacrifice and the debt that American liberty owed to Latin education in the schools: *omnia reliquit servare rempublicam.*[153] Modern republicans found both their morals and their constitution in the old republican legacy of Rome.

NOTES

1   George Washington, *The First Inaugural Speech* (30 April 1789), in W.B. Allen, ed., *George Washington: A Collection* (Indianapolis: Liberty Classics, 1988), p. 462.

2   Mocked by Thomas Moore: "Where tribunes rule, where dusky Dari bow, and what was Goose-Creek once is Tiber now." The poem is discussed by Carl J. Richard, *The Founders and the Classics: Greece, Rome and the American Enlightenment* (Cambridge, Mass.: Harvard University Press, 1994), p. 50.

3   George Washington, *First Inaugural*, p. 462.

4   "Publius" [Alexander Hamilton, John Jay, James Madison], *The Federalist: A Collection of Essays Written in Favour of the New Constitution*, 2 vols. (New York. J. and A. McLean, 1788).

5   Letter of James Madison to James K. Paulding, 24 July 1818, in Gaillard Hunt, ed., *The Writings of James Madison*, 9 vols. (New York: G.P. Putnam's Sons, 1900–1910), vol. 8, pp. 410–411.

6   Camille Desmoulins, *Histoire des Brissotins ou Fragment de l'histoire secrète de la Révolution* (1793), in Jules Claretie, ed., *Oeuvres de Camille Desmoulins*, vol. 1, p. 309. See also H.T. Parker, *The Cult of Antiquity in the French Revolution* (Chicago, 1937); Claude Mosse, *L'antiquité dans la Révolution française* (Paris, 1989).

7   "Publius" [Alexander Hamilton], *Federalist*, IX. See M.N.S. Sellers, *American Republicanism: Roman Ideology in the United States Constitution* (Basingstoke, England: Macmillan; New York: New York University Press, 1994); M.N.S. Sellers, *The Sacred Fire of Liberty: Republicanism, Liberalism and the Law* (Basingstoke, England: Macmillan; New York: New York University Press, 1998).

8   William R. Everdell, *The End of Kings: A History of Republics and Republicanism* (New York: The Free Press, 1983).

9   Cornelius Tacitus, *Ab excessu divi Augusti annalium libri*, 1.2; Titus Livius, *Ab urbe condita*, 2.1.1.

10 Thomas Paine, *The Rights of Man*, Part II (1792), in Bruce Kuklick, ed., *Paine: Political Writings* (Cambridge: Cambridge University Press, 1989), p. 168.

11 E.g., Jean-Jacques Rousseau, *Du contrat social* (1762) II.6, ed. Henri Guillemin (Paris. U.G.E., 1973), p. 99.

12 John Adams, *A Defence of the Constitutions of Government of the United States of America*, 3 vols. (London: C. Dilly, 1787–1788), at I. 125.

13 Titus Livius, *Ab urbe condita*, 2.1.1.

14 Adams, *Defence*, at I.126, quoting James Harrington, *The Commonweath of Oceana* (1659). See J.G.A. Pocock, ed., *Harrington: The Commonwealth of Oceana and a System of Politics* (Cambridge: Cambridge University Press, 1992), p. 8.

15 Harrington, *Oceana*, p. 8.

16 Adams, *Defence*, at I.126.

17 Harrington, *Oceana*, p. 8; Donato Giannotti, *Libro della repubblica de' Viniziani*, in Giannotti, *Opere* (Pisa, 1819).

18 Cornelius Tacitus, *Ab excessu divi Augusti annalium libri*, 1.2.

19 Thomas Gordon, *The Works of Tacitus* (London, 1728–1731). See also [John Trenchard and Thomas Gordon], *Cato's Letters: or, Essays on Liberty, Civil and Religious* (1724), Letter 65, *"jura omnium in se traxit,"* in Ronald Hamowy, ed., *Cato's Letters*, 2 vols. (Indianapolis: Liberty Fund, 1995), vol. 1, p. 458.

20 Josiah Quincy's will, written in 1774, left his son "when he shall arrive at the age of fifteen years" Algernon Sidney's works, John Locke's works, and Lord Bacon's works, Gordon's *Tacitus* and Cato's *Letters*. "May the spirit of liberty rest upon him." Quoted in Meyer Reinhold, *The Classick Pages: Classical Readings of Eighteenth-Century Americans* (University Park, Pa.: Pennsylvania State University Press), p. 100.

21 See, e.g., J.G.A. Pocock, *The Machiavellian Movement: Florentine Political Thought and the Atlantic Republican Tradition* (Princeton, N.J.: Princeton University Press, 1975).

22 See, e.g., Zera S. Fink, *The Classical Republicans: An Essay in the Recovery of a Pattern of Thought in Seventeenth-Century England* (Evanston, Ill.: Northwestern University Press, 1945); Caroline A. Robbins, *The Eighteenth-Century Commonwealth's Man: Studies in the Transmission, Development and Circumstances of English Liberal Thought from the Restoration of Charles II until the War of the Thirteen Colonies* (Cambridge, Mass.: Harvard University Press, 1959).

23 Thomas Hobbes, *Leviathan* (1651) II.21, in Richard Tuck, *Hobbes: Leviathan* (Cambridge: Cambridge University Press, 1996), p. 150.

24 See, e.g., Biancamaria Fontana, ed., *The Invention of the Modern Republic* (Cambridge: Cambridge University Press, 1994); H.A.L. Fisher, *The Republican Tradition in Europe* (New York and London: G.P. Putnam's Sons, 1911); Sellers, *The Sacred Fire of Liberty*.

25 Hamowy, ed., *Cato's Letters*, vol. 1, p. 14 (preface).

26 Ibid., Letter 37, vol. 1, p. 262.

27 G. Vertue, *Medals, Coins, Great-Seals, Impressions, from the Elaborate Works of Thomas Simon, Chief Engraver of the Mint to Charles the 1st, to the Commonwealth, the Lord Protector Cromwell, and in the Reign of King Charles the IInd to 1665* (London: 1753), plate XVIII.

28 See, e.g., *Respublica v. Ross*, December Term, 1795, reported in A.J. Dallas, *Reports of Cases Ruled and Adjudged in the Several Courts of the United States and of Pennsylvania*

Held at the Seat of the Federal Government, ed. F.C. Brightly (New York: Banks, 1903), vol. 2, p. 239.

29 *Plan and Frame of Government for the Commonwealth of Pennsylvania* (September 28, 1776) in F.N. Thorpe, ed., *Federal and State Constitutions, Colonial Charters and Other Organic Laws*, 7 vols. (Washington, D.C., 1909), p. 3084.

30 Adams, *Defence*, at I.208.

31 Republican Society, *To The Citizens of Pennsylvania* in the *Pennsylvania Packet*, March 23, 1779, on the first and last pages. See also Benjamin Rush, *Observations upon the Present Government of Pennsylvania in Four Letters to the People of Pennsylvania* (Philadelphia, 1777).

32 See, e.g., Charles de Secondat, Baron de la Brède et de Montesquieu, *De l'espirit des lois* (1748), at I.iv.6, in R. Derathé, ed., 2 vols. (Paris: Garnier, 1973), vol. 1, p. 43. Cf. François Marie Arouet de Voltaire, *Lettres écrites de Londres sur les Anglais et autres sujets* (Basle, 1734).

33 Adams, *Defence*, at I.208. "The Constitution of England is in truth a republic, and has been ever so considered by foreigners, and by the most learned and enlightened Englishman."

34 Ibid., at III.504–505.

35 Tacitus, *Annalium libri*, 4.33.

36 Tacitus, *Historiarum libri*, 1.16.

37 Montesquieu, *De l'espirit des lois*, at I.8.16. Cf. Montesquieu, *Considérations sur les causes de la grandeur des Romains et de leur décadence* (Amsterdam: J. Desbordes, 1734).

38 E.g., John Adams, *Defence*, at I.125: "*Imperia legum potentiora fuerunt quam hominum.*"

39 Charles Lee, *Letter to Robert Morris*, 15 August 1782, in *Lee Papers* (New York: New York Historical Society, 1872–1875), vol. 4, p. 26.

40 See "Sallust and Corruption" in M.N.S. Sellers, *American Republicanism* (New York: New York University Press, 1994), pp. 87–89. For the classical reading of eighteenth-century Americans, see Reinhold, *The Classick Pages*.

41 Adams, *Defence*, at I.128.

42 E.g., Marcus Tullius Cicero, *In M. Antonium orationes Philippicae*, 4.4.8.

43 *New York Journal*, 6 September 1787, in John P. Kaminski and Gaspare J. Saladino, eds., *The Documentary History of the Ratification of the Constitution*, vol. 13, *Commentaries on the Constitution, Public and Private* (Madison, Wis.: State Historical Society of Wisconsin, 1981), p. 137.

44 *Pennsylvania Packet*, 25 June 1787, in Kaminski and Saladino, XIII.144.

45 *New York Journal*, 27 September 1787, in Gaspare and Saladino, XIII.255.

46 *New York Daily Advertiser*, 29 September 1787, in Gaspare and Saladino, XIII.268.

47 *New York Journal*, 18 October 1787, in Gaspare and Saladino, XIII.411.

48 *New York Independent Journal*, 27 October 1787, in Gaspare and Saladino, XIII.486.

49 *New York Journal*, 1 November 1787, in Gaspare and Saladino, XIII.529.

50 See Philip Pettit, *Republicanism: A Theory of Freedom and Government* (Oxford: Oxford University Press, 1997); Maurizio Viroli, *Republicanism*, trans. A. Shugaar (New York: Hill and Wang, 2002).

51 See John Adams, *Report of the Constitution or Form of Government for the Commonwealth of Massachusetts* (1779), in C. Bradley Thompson, ed., *The Revolutionary Writings of John Adams* (Indianapolis: Liberty Fund, 2000), pp. 297–322.

52 Adams, *Defence*, at I.xviii.

53 Ibid., at I.ii.

54 Ibid., at I.iii.

55 Ibid., at I.xvi.

56 Ibid., at I.xvi; Marcus Tullius Cicero, *De re publica*, 2.23.41: "... *statu esse optimo constitutam rem publicam, quae ex tribus generibus illis, regali et optumati et populari, confusa modice ...*"

57 Adams, *Defence*, at I.xvii; Cicero, *De re publica*, 2.42.69: "*ut enim in fidibus aut tibiis atque ut in cantu ipso ac vocibus concentus est quidam tenendus ex distinctis sonis, ... sic ex summis et infimis et mediis interiectis ordinibus ut sonis moderata ratione civitas consensu dissimillimorum concinit.*"

58 Adams, *Defence*, at I.xviii; Cicero, *De re publica*, 1.25.39: "*respublica res [est] populi, populus autem non omnis hominum coetus quoquo modo congregatus, sed coetus multitudinis iuris consensu et utilitatis communione sociatus.*"

59 Adams, *Defence*, at I.xviii.

60 Ibid., at I.xvii.

61 Ibid. "His decided opinion in favour of three branches is founded on a reason that is unchangeable."

62 Sydney George Fisher, *The Evolution of the Constitution of the United States* (Philadelphia: Lippincott, 1897); D. Lutz, *The Origins of American Constitutionalism* (Baton Rouge: Louisiana State University Press, 1988).

63 Adams, *Defence*, at I.xix.

64 "Publius" [James Madison], *Federalist*, X.

65 Ibid., LXIII (Madison's italics).

66 Ibid.

67 Ibid., X.

68 Ibid., LXII.

69 Adams, *Defence*, at I.98.

70 Ibid., at I.93.

71 Ibid., at I.99.

72 Ibid., Letter XXX, at I.169–176.

73 Kaminski and Saladino, *Documentary History*, at XIII.83–85.

74 Adams, *Defence*, at I.171–173.

75 *The Constitution of the United States* (1787), Article II.1.

76 Ibid., Article II.2.

77 Ibid., Article I.8.

78 Adams, *Defence*, at I.175.

79 *The Constitution of the United States* (1787), Article IV. 4.

80 The Republican party cited the guarantee clause in opposition to Southern slavery. William Wiecek, *The Guarantee Clause of the United States Constitution* (Ithaca, N.Y.: Cornell University Press, 1972); William Wiecek, *The Sources of Antislavery Constitutionalism in America, 1760–1848* (Ithaca, N.Y.: Cornell University Press, 1977).

81 See Adams, *Defence*, at I.124.

82 His *Letter to Dr. Price* of 22 March 1778 was published as an appendix to Richard Price, *Observations on the Importance of the American Revolution*, 1785.

83 Abbé de Mably, *Observations sur le gouvernement et les lois des Etats-Unis d'Amérique* (Amsterdam, 1784).

84 Benjamin Constant, *De la liberté des anciens comparée à celle des modernes* (1819) (Paris: Hachette, 1980).

85 Montesquieu, *De l'espirit des lois*, at I.viii.16.

86 Rousseau, *Du contrat social*, at III.1, 15.

87 Ibid., at II.9, III.15.

88 Ibid., at II.6.

89 Ibid., at II.1.

90 Ibid., at I.6.

91 Ibid., at I.7.

92 Cf. ibid. at I.8: "*L' obéissance á la loi qu'on s'est prescrite est liberté.*"

93 Ibid., at II.3.

94 Ibid., at III.15.

95 Ibid., at II.3.

96 Ibid., at II.7.

97 Ibid., at III.4.

98 Ibid., at II.6.

99 Ibid., at II.7.

100 Ibid., at II.12.

101 As Niccolò Machiavelli had famously observed not only of the French but also of the Spanish and the Italians in his *Discorsi sopra la prima deca di Tito Livio* (1517), at I.55.

102 Ibid., at III.8.

103 Ibid., III.4.

104 Adams, *Defence*, at III.505.

105 Machiavelli, *Discorsi*, at I.55. Machiavelli was a major source for the continental preoccupation with virtue as a precondition to any successful republic. See Gisela Bock, Quentin Skinner, and Maurizio Viroli, eds., *Machiavelli and Republicanism* (Cambridge: Cambridge University Press, 1990). On the adoption of republican checks and balances by princes and kings, see Adams, *Defence*, at I.i.

106 Charles I, *XIX Propositions Made by Both Houses of Parliament, to the King's Most Excellent Majestie: With His Majesties Answer Thereunto* (York, 1642), in Joyce Lee Malcolm, ed., *The Struggle for Sovereignty: Seventeenth-Century English Political Tracts* (Indianapolis: Liberty Fund, 1999), pp. 167–171.

107 *Cato's Letters*, preface, at I.15.

108 Ibid., at I.31.

109 Thomas Paine, *Common Sense* (1776), introduction in Kuklick, ed., *Paine*, p. 2.

110 Ibid., chap. 1, p. 6.

111 Patrice Gueniffey, "Cordeliers and Girondins: The Prehistory of the Republic," in Fontana, *Invention*, pp. 86–106; Ran Halévi, "La république monarchique," in François Furet and Mona Ozouf, eds., *Le siècle de l'avènement républicain* (Paris: Gallimard, 1993), pp. 165–196.

112 *Les Révolutions de Paris*, issue of 12–19 June 1790.

113 Maximilien Marie Isidore de Robespierre, 13 July 1791, to the Jacobins, in A. Aulard, ed., *Recueil des documents pour l'histoire du Club des Jacobins de Paris*, 6 vols. (Paris, 1889–97), vol. 3, p. 12.

114 Keith Michael Baker, "Fixing the French Constitution," in *Inventing the French Revolution: Essays on French Political Culture in the Eighteenth Century* (Cambridge: Cambridge University Press, 1990), pp. 250–305.

115 Rousseau, *Du contrat social*, at II.6 (with his notes).

116 Ibid., at I.8.

117   Ibid., at III.5.

118   Ibid., at III.6.

119   Ibid., at III.8.13.

120   Ibid., at III.12.

121   Ibid., at III.15.

122   Ibid., at IV.2.

123   "Publius" [Madison], *Federalist*, X.

124   Adams, *Defence*, at I.132.

125   Montesquieu, *De l'esprit des lois*, at II.11.4.

126   Rousseau, *Du contrat social*, at III.7.

127   Ibid., at IV.4; Montesquieu, *De l'esprit des lois*, at II.11.14.

128   Montesquieu, *De l'esprit des lois*, at II.11.14.

129   Ibid., at II.11.17.

130   Robert L. Herbert, *David, Voltaire, "Brutus" and the French Revolution* (London: Allen Lane, 1972).

131   Hugh Honour, *Neo-Classicism* (London: Pelican, 1968).

132   Giles Worsley, *Classical Architecture in Britain: The Heroic Age* (New Haven, Conn.: Yale University Press, 1995).

133   François de Polignac and Joselita Raspi Serra, *La fascination de l'antique 1700–1770: Rome découverte, Rome inventée* (Paris: Somogy, 1998).

134   See, e.g., Philip Ayres, *Classical Culture and the Idea of Rome in Eighteenth-Century England* (Cambridge: Cambridge University Press, 1997).

135   For the explosion of republican imagery in France after 1791, see Jacque Boineau, *Les toges de pouvoir (1789–1799) ou la révolution de droit antique* (Toulouse: Editions Eché, 1986).

136   E.g., Adams, *Defence*, at I.128–129.

137   Anne Louise Germaine de Staël-Holstein, *Des circonstances actuelles qui peuvent terminer la révolution et des principes qui doivent fonder la république en France*, ed. Lucia Omacini (Geneva: Librairie Droz, 1979).

138   Constant, *De la liberté*.

139   For a recent discussion of the evolution of French views of the republic in this period, see Keith Michael Baker, "Transformations of Classical Republicanism in Eighteenth-Century France," *Journal of Modern History* 73 (2001): 32 f.

140   The documents implementing this transformation are gathered in Dominique Colas, ed., *Textes constitutionnels français et étrangers* (Paris: Larousse, 1994).

141   See Sellers, *Sacred Fire of Liberty.*.

142   Claude Nicolet, *L'idée républicaine en France (1789–1924): Essai d'histoire critique* (Paris: Gallimard, 1982); Serge Berstein and Odile Rudelle, eds., *Le modèle républicain* (Paris: Presses Universitaires de France, 1992).

143   The best discussion of this is still Harold T. Parker, *The Cult of Antiquity and the French Revolutionaries: A Study in the Development of the Revolutionary Spirit* (Chicago: University of Chicago Press, 1937), chap. 11–13, esp. chap. 11, "The Problem of Regeneration."

144   Meyer Reinhold, *Classica Americana: The Greek and Roman Heritage in the United States* (Detroit: Wayne State University Press, 1984).

145   Natalio R. Botana, *La tradición republicana: Alberdi, Sarmiento y las ideas políticas de su tiempo* (Buenos Aires: Editorial Sudamericana, 1984).

146   Nicolet, *L'idée républicaine*, p. 172.

147 See, e.g., Edouard Laboulaye, *Esquisse d'une constitution républicaine suivie d'un projet de constitution* (Paris, 1872); John Bigelow, *Some Recollections of the Late Edouard Laboulaye* (New York: G.P. Putnam's Sons, 1888).

148 E.g., "Publius" [Madison], *Federalist, X*; Rousseau, *Du contrat social*, at III.4.

149 Rousseau, *Du contrat social*, at III.1.

150 Ibid., at III.15.

151 Achille Murat, *A Moral and Political Sketch of the United States of America* (London: 1833). Cf. George Fitzhugh, *Slavery Justified by a Southerner* (Fredericksburg, 1850) in Eric L.McKittrick, ed., *Slavery Defended: The Views of the Old South* (Englewood Cliffs, N.J.: Prentice-Hall, 1963), pp. 42–44. Article IV Section 4 of the United States Constitution, guaranteeing every state in the Union a "republican" form of government, had become the basis on which many abolitionists denied the constitutionality of slavery in the United States. See Wiecek, *Antislavery Constitutionalism*.

152 Joseph Addison's *Cato* was George Washington's favorite play, and he had it performed in 1778 for the American troops at Valley Forge. Garry Wills, *Cincinnatus: George Washington and the Enlightenment* (New York: Doubleday, 1984), pp. 133–137; Carl J. Richard, *Founders and the Classics*, p. 58.

153 Minor Myers, Jr., *Liberty without Anarchy: A History of the Society of the Cincinnati* (Charlottesville: University Press of Virginia, 1983).

TIMELINE

All dates are B.C.

754/3	Traditional date of Rome's foundation
509	Expulsion of the Etruscan kings; foundation of the Republic
494	First tribunes of the plebs elected
451/450	Law of the Twelve Tables
396	Capture of Veii
390/386	Gauls sack Rome
367	Licinio-Sextian laws: sharing of political power between the patricians and plebeians
282–275	War with Pyrrhus, king of Epirus
264	First gladiatorial combat in Rome
264–241	First Punic War
241	Sicily becomes the first Roman province
238	Provinces of Sardinia and Corsica established
225	Gauls invade Italy
219/218	*Lex Claudia* limits commercial activities of senators
218–201	Second Punic War
200–146	Wars against Macedonia and in the East
197	Two Spanish provinces established; Philip V, king of Macedonia, defeated at Cynoscephalae
196	Flamininus proclaims Greece's freedom
190	Antiochus III, king of Syria, defeated at Magnesia
186	Suppression of the Bacchanalian cult in Italy
168	Perseus, king of Macedonia, defeated at Pydna
149	First permanent jury court established
149–146	Third Punic War
146	Destruction of Corinth and Carthage; provinces of Macedonia and Africa established
133	Pergamum bequeathed to Rome by its last king, Attalus III

133–121	Reforms of the Gracchi brothers
129	Province of Asia established
121	Province of Gallia Narbonensis (Provence) established; first suspension of the constitution
112–105	War with Jugurtha, king of Numidia
107	Marius' army reforms
c. 100	Province of Cilicia established
91–87	Social War: all Italians become Roman citizens; Sulla captures Rome
83–82	Civil war
82	Sulla captures Rome
82–79	Sulla controls Rome: restoration of the Republic
75/74	Province of Cyrenaica established
67	Province of Crete established; defeat of pirates
66–63	Pompey in the East
64	Province of Syria established
63	Province of Bithynia and Pontus established; consulship of Cicero; Catilinarian conspiracy
60	Political alliance of Pompey, Caesar, and Crassus
59	Province of Cyprus and province of Illyricum established; consulship of Caesar
58–50	Gallic War
49	Caesar crosses the Rubicon and invades Italy
49–45	Civil war between Caesar and his senatorial opponents (esp. Pompey and Cato)
44	Caesar is named dictator for life; Caesar is assassinated on the Ides of March
43	Triumvirate consisting of Antony, Octavian, and Lepidus; assassination of Cicero
42	Brutus and Cassius die after defeat at Philippi
31	Battle of Actium: Octavian defeats Antony and Cleopatra
27	Octavian "restores the Republic" and takes the name Augustus

BIBLIOGRAPHY

GENERAL WORKS

Alföldy, G. 1988. *The social history of Rome*. Baltimore.

Astin, A., F. Walbank, M. Fredericksen, and R. Ogilvie, eds. 1989. *Rome and the Mediterranean to 133 B.C.* Vol. 8 of *The Cambridge ancient history*. 2nd ed. Cambridge.

Badian, E. 1968. *Roman imperialism in the late Republic*. 2nd ed. Oxford.

Beard, M., and J. Henderson. 1995. *Classics: A very short introduction*. Oxford.

Beard, M., J. North, and S. Price. 1998. *Religions of Rome*. Cambridge.

Beard, M., and M. Crawford. 1999. *Rome in the late Republic: Problems and interpretations*. 2nd ed. London.

Boardman, J., J. Griffin, and O. Murray, eds. 1991. *The Oxford history of the Roman world*. Oxford.

Brunt, P.A. 1988. *The fall of the Roman Republic and related essays*. Oxford.

Claridge, A. 1998. *Rome: An Oxford archaeological guide*. Oxford.

Cornell, T.J. 1995. *The beginnings of Rome: Italy and Rome from the Bronze Age to the Punic Wars (c. 1000–264 B.C.)*. London.

Cornell, T.J., and Matthews, J. 1982. *Atlas of the Roman world*. Oxford.

Crawford, M. 1974. *Roman republican coinage*. 2 vols. Cambridge.

    1993. *The Roman Republic*. 2nd ed. Cambridge, Mass.

    1996. *Roman statutes*. London.

Crook, J.A., A. Lintott, and E. Rawson, eds. 1994. *The last age of the Roman Republic 146–43 BC*. Vol. 9 of *The Cambridge ancient history*. 2nd ed. Cambridge.

Cunliffe, B. 1978. *Rome and her empire*. New York.

David, J.-M. 1996. *The Roman conquest of Italy*. Oxford.

Degrassi, A. 1957. *Inscriptiones latinae liberae rei publicae*. Florence.

Gabba, E. 1976. *Republican Rome: The army and the allies*. Berkeley.

Gelzer, M. 1975. *The Roman nobility*. Oxford.

Gruen, E.S. 1974. *The last generation of the Roman Republic*. Berkeley.

    1984. *The Hellenistic world and the coming of Rome*. Berkeley.

    1990. *Studies in Greek culture and Roman policy*. Leiden.

    1992. *Culture and national identity in republican Rome*. Ithaca, N.Y.

Harris, W.V. 1979. *War and imperialism in republican Rome 327–70 B.C.* Oxford.

Hornblower, S., and A. Spawforth, eds. 1996. *The Oxford classical dictionary*. 3rd ed. Oxford.

Kallett-Marx, R.M. 1995. *Hegemony to empire: The development of the Roman imperium in the East from 148 to 62 B.C.* Berkeley.

Keppie, L. 1991. *Understanding Roman inscriptions*. Baltimore.

Lintott, A.W. 1999. *The constitution of the Roman Republic*. Oxford.

Malcovati, H. 1976. *Oratorum romanorum fragmenta*. 4th ed. Turin.

Walbank, F.W., A.E. Astin, M.W. Fredericksen, R.M. Ogilvie, and A. Drummond, eds. 1989. *The rise of Rome to 220 B.C.* Vol. 7, pt. 2, of *The Cambridge ancient history*. 2nd ed. Cambridge.

Millar, F. 2002. *Rome, the Greek world, and the East: The Roman Republic and the Augustan revolution*. Vol. 1. Chapel Hill.

Nicolet, C. 1980. *The world of the citizen in republican Rome*. Berkeley.

——— ed. 1978–1979. *Rome et la conquête du monde mediterranéen 264–27 av. J.-C.* 2nd ed. 2 vols. Paris.

Rawson, E. 1985. *Intellectual life in the late Roman Republic*. Baltimore.

Scullard, H.H. 1980. *A history of the Roman world 753–146 B.C.* London.

Stambaugh, J.E. 1988. *The ancient Roman city*. Baltimore.

Taylor, L.R. 1949. *Party politics in the age of Caesar*. Berkeley.

THE EARLY REPUBLIC

Adcock, F.E. 1957. "Consular tribunes and their successors." *JRS* 47:9–14.

Alföldi, A. 1965. *Early Rome and the Latins*. Ann Arbor.

Badian, E. 1966. "The early historians." In *The Latin historians*, edited by T.A. Dorey, 1–38. London.

Broughton, T.R.S. 1950–1986. *The magistrates of the Roman Republic*. New York.

Cloud, J.D. 1998. "The origin of *provocatio*." *RPh* 72:25–48.

Cornell, T.J. 1983. "The failure of the plebs." In *Tria corda* (Biblioteca di Athenaeum 1), edited by E. Gabba, 101–20. Como.

——— 1986a. "The formation of the historical tradition of early Rome." In *Past perspectives: Studies in Greek and Roman historical writing: Papers presented at a conference in Leeds, 6–8 April 1983*, edited by I.S. Moxon, J.D. Smart, and A.J. Woodman, 67–86. Cambridge.

——— 1986b. "The value of the literary tradition concerning archaic Rome." In *Social struggles in archaic Rome: New perspectives on the Conflict of the Orders*, edited by K.A. Raaflaub, 52–76. Berkeley.

——— 1995. *The beginnings of Rome. Italy and Rome from the Bronze Age to the Punic Wars (c.1000–264 BC)*. London and New York.

Degrassi, A. 1957–1963. *Inscriptiones latinae liberae rei publicae*. Florence.

Flower, H.I. 1996. *Ancestor masks and aristocratic power in Roman culture*. Oxford.

Harris, W.V. 1979. *War and imperialism in republican Rome 327–70 B.C.* Oxford.

Humbert, M. 1978. Municipium et civitas sine suffragio: *L'Organisation de la conquête jusqu' à la guerre sociale* (CEFR XXXVI). Rome.

Lintott, A.W. 1972. "Provocatio." *ANRW* 1.2:226–67.

Oakley, S.P. 1993. "The Roman conquest of Italy." In *War and society in the Roman world*, edited by J.W. Rich and G. Shipley, 9–37. London.

Raaflaub, K.A. 1986. *Social struggles in archaic Rome: New perspectives on the Conflict of the Orders*. Berkeley.

Richard, J.-C. 1979. "Sur le plébiscite *ut liceret consules ambos plebeios creari*." *Historia* 28:65–75.

Rosenstein, N. 1990. Imperatores victi: *Military defeat and competition in the middle and late Republic.* Berkeley.

Salmon, E.T. 1969. *Roman colonization under the Republic.* London.

 1982. *The making of Roman Italy.* London.

Sherwin-White, A.N. 1973. *The Roman citizenship.* 2nd ed. Oxford.

Staveley, E.S. 1953. "The significance of the consular tribunate." *JRS* 43:30–6.

Walbank, F.W., A.E. Astin, M.W. Frederiksen, R.M. Ogilvie, and A. Drummond, eds. 1989. *The rise of Rome to 220 B.C.* Vol. 7, pt. 2, of *The Cambridge ancient history.* 2nd ed. Cambridge.

Watson, W.A.J. 1975. *Rome of the XII Tables.* Princeton.

Wiseman, T.P. 1979. *Clio's cosmetics.* Leicester.

POWER AND PROCESS UNDER THE REPUBLICAN 'CONSTITUTION'

Alexander, M.C. 1990. *Trials in the late Roman Republic.* Toronto.

Badian, E. 1968. *Roman imperialism in the late Republic.* 2nd ed. Oxford.

 1972. "Tiberius Gracchus and the beginning of the Roman revolution." *ANRW* 1.1:668–731.

 1996a. "*Tribuni plebis* and *res publica.*" In *Imperium sine fine,* edited by J. Linderski, 187–213. Stuttgart.

 1996b. "*Provincia.*" In *Oxford classical dictionary.* 3rd ed., edited by S. Hornblower and A. Spawforth, 1265–7. Oxford.

Bleicken, J. 1981. *Zum Begriff der römischen Amtsgewalt*: Auspicium – potestas – imperium. Göttingen.

Brennan, T.C. 1989. "C. Aurelius Cotta, *praetor iterum* (*CIL* I² 610)." *Athenaeum* 67:467–87.

 2000. *The praetorship in the Roman Republic.* New York.

Broughton, T.R.S. 1951. *Magistrates of the Roman Republic* I. New York.

 1952. *Magistrates of the Roman Republic* II. New York.

 1986. *Magistrates of the Roman Republic* III. Atlanta.

 1991. *Candidates defeated in Roman elections: Some ancient Roman "also-rans."* Philadelphia.

Crawford, M.H. 1974. *Roman republican coinage* I–II. Cambridge.

 ed. 1996. *Roman statutes* I–II. London.

Finer, S.E. 1997. *The history of government from the earliest times* I. Oxford.

Habicht, C. 1997. *Athens from Alexander to Actium.* Cambridge, Mass.

Honoré, T. 1996. "Legal literature." In *Oxford classical dictionary,* 3rd ed., edited by S. Hornblower and A. Spawforth, 838–9. Oxford.

Jocelyn, H.D. 1971. "*Urbs augurio augusto condita.*" *PCPhS* 17:44–51.

Klebs, E. 1893. "Aemilius (68)." In *Realencylopädie der classischen Altertumswissenschaft,* vol. 1, edited by A. Pauly and G. Wissowa, coll. 552–3. Stuttgart.

Linderski, J. 1986. "The augural law." *ANRW* 16.3:2146–312.

 1995. *Roman questions.* Stuttgart.

Lintott, A.W. 1993. *Imperium Romanum: Politics and administration.* London.

 1999. *The constitution of the Roman Republic.* Oxford.

Millar, F. 1998. *The crowd in Rome in the late Republic.* Ann Arbor.

2002. *The Roman Republic in political thought.* Hanover, N.H.

Mommsen, T. 1887. *Römisches Staatsrecht* I. 3rd ed. Leipzig.

Münzer, F. [1920] 1999. *Roman aristocratic parties and families.* Translated by T. Ridley. Baltimore.

Rawson, E. [1975] 1983. *Cicero: A portrait.* Reprint. London.

Rosenstein, N. 1986. "*Imperatores victi:* The case of C. Hostilius Mancinus." *ClAnt* 5:230–52.

Ryan, F.X. 1998. *Rank and participation in the republican senate.* Stuttgart.

Taylor, L.R. 1966. *Roman voting assemblies.* Ann Arbor.

THE ROMAN ARMY AND NAVY

Ager, S. 1996. *Interstate arbitration in the Greek world 337–90 BC.* Berkeley.

Betrand, J.-M. 1989. "À propos du mot *provincia:* Étude sur les modes d'élaboration du langue politique." *Journal des Savants:* 191–215.

Briscoe, J. 1989. "The Second Punic War." In Vol. 8 of *The Cambridge ancient history,* 2nd ed., edited by A.E. Astin, F.W. Walbank, M.W. Frederiksen, and R.M. Austin, 44–80. Cambridge.

Brunt, P.A. 1988. *The fall of the Roman Republic and related essays.* Oxford.

Cornell, T.J. 1995. *The beginnings of Rome: Italy and Rome from the Bronze Age to the Punic Wars (c. 1000–264 BC).* London.

Derow, P.S. 1973. "Kleemporos." *Phoenix* 27:118–34.

———. 1991. "Rome and Pharos." *ZPE* 89:261–70.

Drummond, A. 1989. "Rome in the fifth century II: The citizen community." In *The rise of Rome to 220 BC.* Vol. 7, pt. 2, of *The Cambridge ancient history,* 2nd ed., edited by F.W. Walbank, A.E. Astin, M.W. Frederiksen, and R.M. Ogilvie, 172–242. Cambridge.

Dyson, S. 1985. *The creation of the Roman frontier.* Princeton.

Errington, R.M. 1989. "Rome and Greece to 205 B.C." In *Rome and the Mediterranean to 133 BC.* Vol. 8 of *The Cambridge ancient history,* 2nd ed., edited by A.E. Astin, F.W. Walbank, M.W. Frederiksen, and R.M. Ogilvie, 81–106. Cambridge.

Ferrary, J.-L. 1988. *Philhellénisme et impérialisme: Aspects idéologiques de la conquête romaine du monde hellénistique.* Paris.

Franke, P. 1989. "Pyrrhus." In *The rise of Rome to 220 B.C.* Vol. 7, pt. 2, of *The Cambridge ancient history,* 2nd ed., edited by F.W. Walbank, A.E. Astin, M.W. Frederiksen, and R.M. Ogilvie, 456–85. Cambridge.

Gabba, E. 1976. *Republican Rome, the army and the allies.* Translated by P.J. Cuff. Oxford.

Goldsworthy, A. 1996. *The Roman army at war 100 B.C.–A.D. 200.* Oxford.

Gomme, A.W., A. Andrewes, and K.J. Dover. 1970. *A historical commentary on Thucydides* 4. Oxford.

Hansen, M.H. 1981. "The number of Athenian hoplites in 431 B.C." *Symbolae Osloensis* 56:19–32.

Harris, W.V. 1979. *War and imperialism in republican Rome, 327–70 B.C.* Oxford.

———. 1989. "Roman expansion in the West." In *Rome and the Mediterranean to 133 B.C.* Vol. 8 of *The Cambridge ancient history,* 2nd ed., edited by A.E. Astin, F.W. Walbank, M.W. Frederiksen, and R.M. Ogilvie, 107–62. Cambridge.

Hornblower, J. 1981. *Hieronymus of Cardia.* Oxford.

Kienast, D. 1966. *Untersuchungen zu den Kriegsflotten der römischen Kaiserzeit.* Bonn.

Keppie, L. 1984. *The making of the Roman army from Republic to Empire*. London.

Knox, M., and W. Murray. 2001. "Thinking about revolutions in warfare." In *The dynamics of military revolution 1300–2050*, edited by M. Knox and W. Murray, 1–14. Cambridge.

Mason, H.J. 1974. *Greek terms for Roman institutions: A lexicon and analysis*. Toronto.

McGushin, P. 1992. *Sallust: The* Histories *1 books i-iii*. Oxford.

Millar, F. 2002. "Political power in mid-republican Rome: *Curia* or *comitium?*" In *The Roman Republic and the Augustan Revolution*, 85–108. Chapel Hill. Originally published in *JRS* 79 (1989) 138–50.

Oakley, S.P 1997–. *A commentary on Livy, Books VI–X*. Oxford.

———. 1993. "The Roman conquest of Italy." In *War and society in the Roman world*, edited by J. Rich and G. Shipley, 9–37. London.

Patterson, J. 1993. "Military organization and social change in the late Roman Republic." In *War and society in the Roman world*, edited by J. Rich and G. Shipley, 92–112. London.

Phang, S. 2001. *The marriage of Roman soldiers (13 B.C.–A.D. 235): Law and family in the imperial army*. Leiden.

Pollard, N. 1996. "The Roman army as 'total institution' in the Near East? Dura-Europos as a case study." In *The Roman army in the East* [*JRA* Supp. 18], edited by D.L. Kennedy, 212–27. Ann Arbor.

Rawson, E. 1991. "The literary sources for the pre-Marian army." In *Roman culture and society: Collected papers*, 34–57. Oxford. First published in *PBSR* 39 (1971) 13–31.

Rich, J. 1976. *Declaring war in the Roman Republic in the period of transmarine expansion*. Collection Latomus 149. Brussels.

———. 1993. "Fear, greed and glory: The causes of Roman war-making in the middle Republic." In *War and society in the Roman world*, edited by J. Rich and G. Shipley, 38–68. London.

Richardson, J.S. 1986. *Hispaniae: Spain and the development of Roman imperialism 218–82 B.C.* Cambridge.

Roberts, M. 1967. "The military revolution 1560–1660." In *Studies in Swedish history*, edited by M. Roberts, 195–225. Minneapolis.

Rogers, C.J. 1995. *The military revolution debate: Readings on the military transformation of early modern Europe*. Boulder.

Rosenstein, N. 1990. Imperatores victi: *Military defeat and aristocratic competition in the middle and late Republic*. Berkeley.

Roth, J.P. 1999. *The logistics of the Roman army at war (264 B.C.–A.D. 235)*. Leiden.

Rowe, G. 2002. *Princes and political cultures: The new Tiberian senatorial decrees*. Ann Arbor.

Sabin, P. 1996. "The mechanics of battle in the Second Punic War." In *The Second Punic War: A reappraisal* [Bulletin of the Institute of Classical Studies suppl. 67], edited by T. Cornell, B. Rankov, and P. Sabin, 59–79. London.

———. 2000. "The face of Roman battle." *JRS* 90:1–17.

Skutsch, O. 1985. *The* Annals *of Quintus Ennius*. Oxford.

Taylor, L.R. 1962. "The forerunners of the Gracchi." *JRS* 52:19–27.

Theil, J.H. 1954. *A history of Roman sea-power before the Second Punic War*. Amsterdam.

von Arnim, H. 1892. "*Ineditum vaticanum*." *Hermes* 27:118–30.

Walbank, F.W. 1957–1979. *A historical commentary on Polybius*. Oxford.

———. 1972. *Polybius*. Berkeley.

Watson, A. 1993. *International law in archaic Rome: War and religion*. Baltimore.

THE CRISIS OF THE REPUBLIC

Alföldi, A. 1985. *Caesar in 44 v. Chr. Studien zu Caesars Monarchie und ihren Wurzeln.* Bonn.

Badian, E. 1970. *Lucius Sulla: The deadly reformer.* Sydney.

———. 1972. "Tiberius Gracchus and the beginning of the Roman Revolution." *ANRW* 1.1:668–731.

Barnard, S. 1990. "Cornelia and the women of her family." *Latomus* 49:383–92.

Bauman, R.A. 1992. *Women and politics in ancient Rome.* London.

Bernett, M. 1995. *Causarum cognitio. Ciceros Analysen zur politischen Krise der späten römischen Republik.* Stuttgart.

Bernstein, A.H. 1978. *Tiberius Sempronius Gracchus: Tradition and apostasy.* Ithaca, N.Y.

Bleicken, J. 1998a. "Staatliche Ordnung und Freiheit in der römischen Republik." In *Gesammelte Schriften*, vol. 1, 185–280. Stuttgart.

———. 1998b. "*In provinciali solo dominium populi Romani est vel Caesaris.* Zur Kolonisationspolitik der ausgehenden Republik und frühen Kaiserzeit." In *Gesammelte Schriften*, vol. 2, 722–77. Stuttgart.

———. 1998c. "Gedanken zum Untergang der römischen Republik." In *Gesammelte Schriften*, vol. 2, 683–704. Stuttgart.

Bonnefond-Coudry, M. 1989. *Le sénat de la république romaine de la guerre d'Hannibal à Auguste: pratiques délibératives et prise de décision.* Rome.

Bracco, V. 1979. "Un nuovo documento della centuriazione graccana: Il termine di Auletta." *Rivista storica dell'antichità* 9:29–37.

Bringmann, K. 1977. "Weltherrschaft und innere Krise Roms im Spiegel der Geschichtsschreibung des zweiten und ersten Jahrhunderts v. Chr." *Antike und Abendland* 23:28–49.

———. 1985. *Die Agrarreform des Tiberius Gracchus: Legende und Wirklichkeit.* Stuttgart.

Broughton, T.R.S. 1951–1986. *The magistrates of the Roman Republic.* 3 vols. Cleveland and Atlanta.

Bruhns, H. 1978. *Caesar und die römische Oberschicht in den Jahren 49–44 v. Chr. Untersuchungen zur Herrschaftsetablierung im Bürgerkrieg.* Göttingen.

———. 1980. "Ein politischer Kompromiß im Jahr 70 v. Chr. Die *lex Aurelia iudiciaria.*" *Chiron* 10:263–72.

Brunt, P.A. 1966. "The Roman mob." *Past and Present* 35:3–27.

———. 1988. *The fall of the Roman Republic and related essays.* Oxford.

Burckhardt, L.A. 1988. *Politische Strategien der Optimaten in der späten römischen Republik.* Stuttgart.

———. 1990. "The political elite of the Roman Republic." *Historia* 39:77–99.

Burckhardt, L.A., and J. von Ungern-Sternberg. 1994. "Cornelia, Mutter der Gracchen." In *Reine Männersache? Frauen in Männerdomänen der antiken Welt*, edited by M.H. Dettenhofer, 97–132. Cologne.

Canfora, L. 1999. *Giulio Cesare: il dittatore democratico.* Rome.

Carney, T.F. 1970. *A biography of C. Marius.* 2nd ed. Chicago.

Cavaggioni, F. 1998. *L. Appuleio Saturnino tribunus plebis seditiosus.* Venice.

Christ, K. 2000. *Krise und Untergang der römischen Republik.* 4th ed. Darmstadt.

Collins, J.H. 1972. "Caesar as a political propagandist." *ANRW* 1.1:922–66.

Dahlheim, W. 1977. *Gewalt und Herrschaft. Das provinziale Herrschaftssystem der römischen Republik.* Berlin.

1987. *Julius Cäsar. Die Ehre des Kriegers und der Untergang der römischen Republik.* Munich.

1992. "Die Armee eines Weltreiches. Der römische Soldat und sein Verhältnis zu Staat und Gesellschaft." *Klio* 74:197–220.

David, J.-M. 1992. *Le patronat judiciaire au dernier siècle de la république romaine.* Rome.

1994. *La Romanisation de l'Italie.* Paris.

1997. "La clientèle, d'une forme de l'analyse à l'autre." In *Die späte römische Republik* [*La fin de la république romaine*], edited by H. Bruhns, J.M. David, and W. Nippel, 195–210. Rome.

de Blois, L. 1987. *The Roman army and politics in the first century B.C.* Amsterdam.

Degrassi, A. 1957. *Inscriptiones latinae liberae rei publicae.* Florence.

Deininger, J. 1998. "Zur Kontroverse über die Lebensfähigkeit der Republik in Rom." In *Imperium Romanum: Festschrift K. Christ,* edited by P. Kneissl and V. Losemann, 123–36. Stuttgart.

de Ligt, L. 2001. "Studies in legal and agrarian history III: Appian and the *lex Thoria.*" *Athenaeum* 89:121–44.

Diehl, H. 1988. *Sulla und seine Zeit im Urteil Ciceros.* Hildesheim.

Drummond, A. 1995. *Law, politics and power: Sallust and the execution of the Catilinarian conspirators.* Stuttgart.

Eder, W. 1969. "Das vorsullanische Repetundenverfahren." Ph.D. diss., Munich.

1996. "Republicans and sinners: The decline of the Roman Republic and the end of a provisional arrangement." In *Transitions to empire: Essays in Greco-Roman history, 360–146 B.C., in honor of E. Badian,* edited by R.W. Wallace and E.M. Harris, 439–61. Norman, Okla., and London.

Evans, R.J. 1994. *Gaius Marius: A political biography.* Pretoria.

Ferrary, J.-L. 1997. "*Optimates* et *populares.* Le problème du rôle de l'idéologie dans la politique." In *Die späte römische Republik* [*La fin de la république romaine*], edited by H. Bruhns, J.-M. David, and W. Nippel, 221–31. Rome.

Gabba, E. 1976. *Republican Rome, the army and the allies.* Berkeley.

Gelzer, M. 1959. *Pompeius.* 2nd ed. Munich.

1960. *Caesar. Der Politiker und Staatsmann.* 6th ed. Wiesbaden.

[1912] 1969a. *The Roman nobility.* Translated by Robin Seager. Oxford.

1969b. *Cicero. Ein biographischer Versuch.* Wiesbaden.

Giovannini, A. 1995. "Catilina et le problème des dettes." In *Leaders and masses in the Roman world: Studies in honor of Zvi Yavetz,* edited by I. Malkin and Z.W. Rubinsohn, 15–32. Leiden.

Girardet, K.M. 1996. "Politische Verantwortung im Ernstfall: Cicero, die Diktatur und der Diktator Caesar." In *Lenaika: Festschrift C. W. Müller,* edited by C. Mueller-Goldingen and K. Sier, 217–51. Stuttgart and Leipzig.

2000. "Caesars Konsulatsplan für das Jahr 49: Gründe und Scheitern." *Chiron* 30:679–710.

Greenhalgh, P. 1980–1981. *Pompey.* 2 vols. London.

Grelle, F. 1994. "Centuriazione di Celenza Valfortore, un nuovo cippo graccano e la romanizzazione del subappenino dauno." *Ostraka* 9:249–58.

Griffin, M. 1994. "The intellectual developments of the Ciceronian age." In *The last age of the Roman Republic, 146–43 B.C.* Vol. 9 of *The Cambridge ancient history,* 2nd ed., edited by J.A. Crook, A. Lintott, and E. Rawson, 689–728. Cambridge.

Gruen, E.S. 1974. *The last generation of the Roman Republic.* Berkeley.

Guarino, A. 1979. *Spartaco: analisi di un mito*. Naples.

Habicht, C. 1990. *Cicero the politician*. Baltimore.

Hackl, U. 1979. "Der Revolutionsbegriff und die ausgehenede römische Republik." *Rivista storica dell'antichità* 9:95–103.

Hampl, F. 1979. "Römische Politik in republikanischer Zeit und das Problem des 'Sittenverfalls.'" In *Geschichte als kritische Wissenschaft* 3 (Darmstadt) 22–47.

Hantos, T. 1988. Res publica constituta. *Die Verfassung des Dictators Sulla*. Munich.

Heuss, A. 1995a. "Der Untergang der römischen Republik und das Problem der Revolution." In *Gesammelte Schriften*, vol. 2, 1164–91. Stuttgart.

——— 1995b. "Das Revolutionsproblem im Spiegel der antiken Geschichte." In *Gesammelte Schriften*, vol. 1, 500–71. Stuttgart.

Hillman, T.P. 1998. "Pompeius' *imperium* in the war with Lepidus." *Klio* 80:91–110.

Hölkeskamp, K.-J. 2000. "The Roman Republic: Government of the people, by the people, for the people?" *Scripta Classica Israelica* 19:203–23.

Hopkins, K. 1983. *Death and renewal*. Cambridge.

Hurlet, F. 1993. *La dictature de Sylla: Monarchie ou magistrature republicaine?* Brussels.

Jehne, M. 1987. *Der Staat des Dictators Caesar*. Cologne.

——— ed. 1995. *Demokratie in Rom? Die Rolle des Volkes in der Politik der römischen Republik.* Stuttgart.

Kallet-Marx, R.M. 1995. *Hegemony to empire: The development of the Roman imperium in the East from 148 to 62 B.C.* Berkeley.

Keaveney, A. 1987. *Rome and the unification of Italy*. London.

——— 1992. *Lucullus: A life*. London.

König, D. 2000. "Q. Sertorius. Ein Kapitel des frühen römischen Bürgerkriegs." *Klio* 82:441–58.

Konrad, C.F. 1995. "A new chronology of the Sertorian War." *Athenaeum* 83:157–87.

Levick, B.M. 1982a. "Sulla's march on Rome in 88 B.C." *Historia* 31:503–8.

——— 1982b. "Morals, politics, and the fall of the Roman Republic." *Greece and Rome* 29:53–62.

Lintott, A. 1992. *Judicial reform and land reform in the Roman Republic*. Cambridge.

——— 1994a. "The crisis of the Republic: Sources and source-problems." In *The last age of the Roman Republic, 146–43 B.C.* Vol. 9 of *The Cambridge ancient history*, 2nd ed., edited by J.A. Crook, A. Lintott, and E. Rawson, 1–15. Cambridge.

——— 1994b. "Political history, 146–95 B.C." In *The last age of the Roman Republic, 146–43 B.C.* Vol. 9 of *The Cambridge ancient history*, 2nd ed., edited by J.A. Crook, A. Lintott, and E. Rawson, 40–103. Cambridge.

Mackie, N. 1992. "Popularis ideology and popular politics at Rome in the first century B.C." *Rheinisches Museum* 135:49–73.

Maier, U. 1978. *Caesars Feldzüge in Gallien (58–51 v. Chr.) in ihrem Zusammenhang mit der stadtrömischen Politik*. Bonn.

Malcovati, H. 1976. *Oratorum Romanorum fragmenta liberae rei publica*. 4th ed. Turin.

Marshall, B.A. 1976. *Crassus: A political biography*. Amsterdam.

Martin, J. 1965. *Die Popularen in der Geschichte der späten Republik*. Ph.D. diss., University of Freiburg.

Mastrocinque, A. 1999. *Studi sulle guerre Mitridatiche*. Stuttgart.

Meier, C. 1965. "*Populares*." *RE* Suppl. X:549–615.

——— 1975. "Das Kompromissangebot an Caesar i. J. 59 v. Chr. Ein Beispiel senatorischer 'Verfassungspolitik.'" *Museum Helveticum* 32:197–208.

1982. *Caesar*. Berlin.

1990. "*C. Caesar Divi filius* and the formation of the alternative in Rome." In *Between Republic and empire: Interpretations of Augustus and his principate*, edited by K.A. Raaflaub and M. Toher, 54–70. Berkeley.

1997. *Res publica Amissa: eine Studie zur Verfassung und Geschichte der späten römischen Republik.* 3rd ed. Frankfurt.

Millar, F. 1998. *The crowd in Rome in the late Republic.* Ann Arbor.

Mitchell, T.N. 1979. *Cicero: The ascending years.* New Haven.

1991. *Cicero: The senior statesman.* New Haven.

Mommsen, T. 1874–1875. *Römische Geschichte.* 6th ed. 3 vol. Berlin.

Mouritsen, H. 1998. *Italian unification: A study in ancient and modern historiography.* London.

2001. *Plebs and politics in the late Roman Republic.* Cambridge.

Münzer, F. 1923. "C. Sempronius Gracchus." *RE* IIA:1375–400.

Nicolet, C. 1976. *Le métier de citoyen dans la Rome républicaine.* Paris.

ed. 1983. *Demokratia et aristokratia. A propos de Caius Gracchus: mots grecs et réalités romaines.* Paris.

Nippel, W. 1995. *Public order in ancient Rome.* Cambridge.

Perelli, L. 1982. *Il movimento popolare nell'ultimo secolo della repubblica.* Turin. Reviewed in *Gnomon* 58:154–9.

Pohl, H. 1993. *Römische Politik und Piraterie im östlichen Mittelmeer vom 3. bis zum 1. Jh. v. Chr.* Berlin.

Raaflaub, K. 1974. *Dignitatis contentio. Studien zur Motivation und politischen Taktik im Bürgerkrieg zwischen Caesar und Pompeius.* Munich.

Rawson, E. 1975. *Cicero: A portrait.* London.

1994. "Caesar: Civil war and dictatorship." In *The last age of the Roman Republic, 146–43 B.C.* Vol. 9 of *The Cambridge ancient history*, 2nd ed., edited by J.A. Crook, A. Lintott, and E. Rawson, 424–67. Cambridge.

Rubinsohn, W.Z. 1993. *Die großen Sklavenaufstände der Antike: 500 Jahre Forschung.* Darmstadt.

Ryan, F. 2001. "Knappe Mehrheiten bei der Wahl zum Konsul." *Klio* 83:402–24.

Schulz, R. 2000. "Zwischen Kooperation und Konfrontation: Die römische Weltreichsbildung und die Piraterie." *Klio* 82:426–40.

Seager, R. 1979. *Pompey: A political biography.* Berkeley.

1994a. "Sulla." In *The last age of the Roman Republic, 146–43 B.C.* Vol. 9 of *The Cambridge ancient history*, 2nd ed., edited by J.A. Crook, A. Lintott, and E. Rawson, 165–207. Cambridge.

1994b. "The rise of Pompey." In *The last age of the Roman Republic, 146–43 B.C.* Vol. 9 of *The Cambridge ancient history*, 2nd ed., edited by J.A.Crook, A.Lintott, and E. Rawson, 208–28. Cambridge.

Sherwin-White, A.N. 1973. *The Roman citizenship.* 2nd ed. Oxford.

1984. *Roman foreign policy in the East 168 B.C. to A.D. 1.* London.

1994. "Lucullus, Pompey and the East." In *The last age of the Roman Republic, 146–43 B.C.* Vol. 9 of *The Cambridge ancient history*, 2nd ed., edited by J.A. Crook, A. Lintott, and E. Rawson, 229–73. Cambridge.

Sion-Jenkis, K. 2000. *Von der Republik zum Prinzipat. Ursachen für den Verfassungswechsel in Rom im historischen Denken der Antike.* Stuttgart.

Stockton, D. 1979. *The Gracchi.* Oxford.

Strasburger, H. 1942. "Optimates." *RE* XVIII:773–98.

    1982a. "Concordia ordinum." In *Studien zur Alten Geschichte*, vol. 1, 1–82. Hildesheim.

    1982b. "Caesar im Urteil seiner Zeitgenossen." In *Studien zur Alten Geschichte*, vol. 1, 343–421. Hildesheim.

Syme, R. 1939. *The Roman revolution*. Oxford.

    1964. *Sallust*. Berkeley.

Tatum, W.J. 1999. *The patrician tribune: Publius Clodius Pulcher*. Chapel Hill.

Taylor, L.R. 1962. "Forerunners of the Gracchi." *JRS* 52:19–27.

Thommen, L. 1988. "Das Bild vom Volkstribunat in Ciceros Schrift über die Gesetze." *Chiron* 18:357–75.

    1989. *Das Volkstribunat der späten römischen Republik*. Stuttgart.

Timpe, D. 1962. "Herrschaftsidee und Klientelstaatenpolitik in Sallusts *Bellum Jugurthinum*." *Hermes* 90:334–75.

Vogt, J. 1955. "*Homo novus*: Ein Idealtypus der römischen Republik." In *Gesetz und Handlungsfreiheit in der Geschichte*, edited by J. Vogt, 81–106. Stuttgart.

Von der Mühll, F. 1906. *De L. Appuleio Saturnino tribuno plebis*. Ph.D. diss., University of Basel.

von Ungern-Sternberg, J. 1970. *Untersuchungen zum spätrepublikanischen Notstandsrecht: Senatus consultum ultimum und hostis-Erklärung*. Munich.

    1982. "Weltreich und Krise. Äussere Bedingungen für den Niedergang der römischen Republik." *Museum Helveticum* 39:254–71.

    1988. "Überlegungen zum Sozialprogramm der Gracchen." In *Sozialmassnahmen und Fürsorge: Zur Eigenart antiker Sozialpolitik*, edited by H. Kloft, 167–85. Graz.

    1998. "Die Legitimationskrise der römischen Republik." *Historische Zeitschrift* 266:607–24.

Ward, A.M. 1977. *Marcus Crassus and the late Roman Republic*. Columbia, Mo.

Weinstock, S. 1971. *Divus Julius*. Oxford.

Welwei, K.-W. 1996. "Caesars Diktatur, der Prinzipat des Augustus und die Fiktion der historischen Notwendigkeit." *Gymnasium* 103:477–97.

Wiseman, T.P. 1971. *New men in the Roman Senate 139 B.C.–A.D. 14*. Oxford.

    1994a. "The Senate and the *populares*, 69–60 B.C." In *The last age of the Roman Republic, 146–43 B.C.* Vol. 9 of *The Cambridge ancient history*, 2nd ed., edited by J.A. Crook, A. Lintott, and E. Rawson, 327–67. Cambridge.

    1994b. "Caesar, Pompey and Rome, 59–50 B.C." In *The last age of the Roman Republic, 146–43 B.C.* Vol. 9 of *The Cambridge ancient history*, 2nd ed., edited by J.A. Crook, A. Lintott, and E. Rawson, 368–423. Cambridge.

Yakobson, A. 1999. *Elections and electioneering in Rome: A study in the political system of the late Republic*. Stuttgart.

Yavetz, Z. 1979. *Caesar in der öffentlichen Meinung*. Düsseldorf.

UNDER ROMAN ROOFS: FAMILY, HOUSE, AND HOUSEHOLD

Andreau, J., and H. Bruhns, eds. 1990. *Parenté et stratégies familiales dans l'antiquité romaine*. Rome.

Bradley, K.R. 1991. *Discovering the Roman family: Studies in Roman social history*. New York and Oxford.

1993. "Writing the history of the Roman family." *CPh* 88:237–50.

Burguière, A., C. Klapisch-Zuber, M. Segalen, and F. Zonabend, eds. 1996. *Distant worlds, ancient worlds.* Vol. 1 of *A history of the family.* Cambridge.

Champlin, E. 1991. *Final judgments: Duty and emotion in Roman wills, 200 B.C.–A.D. 250.* Berkeley.

Clarke, J.R. 1991. *The houses of Roman Italy 100 B.C.–A.D. 250: Ritual, space, and decoration.* Berkeley, Los Angeles, and Oxford.

Clauss, M. 1973. "Probleme der Lebensaltersstatistiken aufgrund römischer Grabinschriften." *Chiron* 3:395–417.

Corbier, M. 1991a. "Divorce and adoption as Roman familial strategies (Le divorce et l'adoption 'en plus')." In *Marriage, divorce, and children in ancient Rome,* edited by B. Rawson, 47–78. Canberra and Oxford.

1991b. "Constructing kinship in Rome: Marriage and divorce, filiation and adoption." In *The family in Italy from antiquity to the present,* edited by D.I. Kertzer and R.P. Saller, 127–44. New Haven and London.

Crook, J. 1967a. *Law and life of Rome.* London.

1967b. "*Patria potestas.*" *CQ* n.s. 17:113–22.

1986. "Women in Roman succession." In *The family in ancient Rome: New perspectives,* edited by B. Rawson, 58–82. Ithaca, N.Y.

Daube, D. 1969. *Roman law: Linguistic, social and philosophical aspects.* Edinburgh.

Dixon, S. 1985. "The marriage alliance in the Roman elite." *Journal of Family History* 10:353–78.

1988. *The Roman mother.* London and Sydney.

1991. "The sentimental ideal of the Roman family." In *Marriage, divorce, and children in ancient Rome,* edited by B. Rawson, 99–113. Canberra and Oxford.

1992. *The Roman family.* Baltimore and London.

1997. "Continuity and change in Roman social history: Retrieving 'family feeling(s)' from Roman law and literature." In *Inventing ancient culture,* edited by M. Golden and P. Toohey, 79–90. London.

Dupont, F. 1992. *Daily life in ancient Rome.* Translated by Christopher Woodall. Oxford.

Eyben, E. 1980–1981. "Family planning in Graeco-Roman antiquity." *AncSoc* 11/12:5–82.

1991. "Fathers and sons." In *Marriage, divorce, and children in ancient Rome,* edited by B. Rawson, 114–43. Canberra and Oxford.

Flower, H.I. 1996. *Ancestor masks and aristocratic power in Roman culture.* Oxford.

Gardner, J.F. 1997. "Legal stumbling-blocks for lower-class families." In *The Roman family in Italy: Status, sentiment, space,* edited by B. Rawson and P. Weaver, 35–53. Oxford.

1998. *Family and* familia *in Roman law and life.* Oxford.

Gardner, J.F., and T. Wiedemann. 1991. *The Roman household: A sourcebook.* London.

Garnsey, P., and R.P. Saller. 1987. *The Roman Empire: Economy, society and culture.* London.

George, M. 1997. "Repopulating the Roman house." In *The Roman family in Italy: Status, sentiment, space,* edited by B. Rawson and P. Weaver, 299–319. Oxford.

Hales, S. 2000. "At home with Cicero." *GaR* 47:44–55.

Haley, S.P. 1985. "The five wives of Pompey the Great." *GaR* 32:49–59.

Hanson, A.E. 1999. "The Roman family." In *Life, death, and entertainment in the Roman Empire*, edited by D.S Potter and D.J. Mattingly, 19–66. Ann Arbor.

Harris, W.V. 1982. "The theoretical possibility of extensive infanticide in the Graeco-Roman world." *CQ* n.s. 32:114–6.

———. 1986. "The Roman father's power of life and death." In *Studies in Roman law in memory of A. Arthur Schiller*, edited by R.S. Bagnall and W.V. Harris, 81–95. Leiden.

———. 1994. "Child-exposure in the Roman Empire." *JRS* 84:1–22.

Hopkins, K., and G. Burton. 1983. "Political succession in the late Republic." In *Death and renewal*, edited by K. Hopkins, 31–119. Cambridge.

Humbert, M. 1972. *Le remariage à Rome. Étude d'histoire juridique et sociale*. Milan.

Kaser, M. 1938. "Der Inhalt der *patria potestas*." *ZSS* 58:62–87.

———. 1971. *Das römische Privatrecht*. 2nd ed. Vol. 1. Munich.

Kertzer, D.I., and R.P. Saller, eds. 1991. *The family in Italy from antiquity to the present*. New Haven and London.

Lacey, W.K. 1986. "*Patria potestas*." In *The family in ancient Rome: New perspectives*, edited by B. Rawson, 121–44. Ithaca, N.Y.

Laslett, P., and R. Wall, eds. 1972. *Household and family in past time*. Cambridge.

Martin, D.B. 1996. "The construction of the ancient family: Methodological considerations." *JRS* 86:40–60.

Moreau, P. 1986. "Patrimoines et successions à Larinum au Ier siècle av. J.-C." *Revue historique du droit français et étranger* 64:169–89.

Nevett, L. 1997. "Perceptions of domestic space in Roman Italy." In *The Roman family in Italy: Status, sentiment, space*, edited by B. Rawson and P. Weaver, 281–98. Oxford.

Parkin, T. 1992. *Demography and Roman society*. Baltimore.

———. 1999. "Clearing away the cobwebs: A critical perspective on historical sources for Roman population history." In *Reconstructing past population trends in Mediterranean Europe (3000 B.C.–A.D. 1800)*, edited by J. Bintliff and K. Sbonias, 153–60. Oxford.

Patterson, J.R. 2000. "Living and dying in the city of Rome: Houses and tombs." In *Ancient Rome: The archaeology of the Eternal City*, edited by J. Coulston and H. Dodge, 259–89. Oxford.

Rawson, B. 1986. "The Roman family." In *The family in ancient Rome: New perspectives*, edited by B. Rawson, 1–57. Ithaca, N.Y.

———. ed. 1986. *The family in ancient Rome. New perspectives*. Ithaca, N.Y.

———. 1991. *Marriage, divorce, and children in ancient Rome*. Canberra and Oxford.

Rawson, B., and P. Weaver, eds. 1997. *The Roman family in Italy: Status, sentiment, space*. Oxford.

Saller, R.P. 1984. "*Familia, domus*, and the Roman conception of the family." *Phoenix* 38:336–55.

———. 1986. "*Patria potestas* and the stereotype of the Roman family." *Continuity and Change* 1:7–22.

———. 1994. *Patriarchy, property and death in the Roman family*. Cambridge.

———. 1997. "Roman kinship: Structure and sentiment." In *The Roman family in Italy: Status, sentiment, space*, edited by B. Rawson and P. Weaver, 7–34. Oxford.

1999. "*Pater familias, mater familias*, and the gendered semantics of the Roman household." *CPh* 94:182–97.

Saller, R.P., and B.D. Shaw. 1984. "Tombstones and Roman family relations in the principate: Civilians, soldiers and slaves." *JRS* 74:124–56.

Salway, B. 1994. "What's in a name? A survey of Roman onomastic practice from *c.* 700 B.C. to A.D. 700."*JRS* 84:124–45.

Shaw, B.D. 1984. "Latin funerary epigraphy and family life in the later Roman Empire." *Historia* 33:457–97.

1987. "The age of Roman girls at marriage: Some reconsiderations." *JRS* 77:30–46.

1991. "The cultural meaning of death: Age and gender in the Roman family." In *The family in Italy from antiquity to the present*, edited by D.I. Kertzer and R.P. Saller, 66–90. New Haven and London.

2001. "Raising and killing children: Two Roman myths." *Mnemosyne* 54:31–77.

Syme, R. 1987. "Marriage ages for Roman senators." *Historia* 36:318–32.

Thomas, Y. 1984. "*Vitae necisque potestas*: Le père, la cité, la mort." In *Du châtiment dans la cité: Supplices corporels et peine de mort dans le monde antique*, 499–548. Rome.

1996. "Fathers as citizens of Rome, Rome as a city of fathers (second century B.C. – second century A.D.)." In *Distant worlds, ancient worlds*, vol. 1 of *A history of the family*, edited by A. Burgière, C. Klapisch-Zuber, M. Segalen, and F. Zonabend, 228–69. Cambridge.

Treggiari, S. 1991a. *Roman marriage*: Iusti coniuges *from the time of Cicero to the time of Ulpian*. Oxford.

1991b. "Divorce Roman style: How easy and how frequent was it?" In *Marriage, divorce, and children in ancient Rome*, edited by B. Rawson, 31–46. Canberra and Oxford.

1991c. "Ideals and practicalities in matchmaking in ancient Rome." In *The family in Italy from antiquity to the present*, edited by D.I. Kertzer and R.P. Saller, 91–108. New Haven and London.

Wall, R., J. Robin, and P. Laslett, eds. 1983. *Family forms in historic Europe*. Cambridge.

Wallace-Hadrill, A. 1994. *Houses and society in Pompeii and Herculaneum*. Princeton.

Watson, A. 1967. *The law of persons in the later Roman Republic*. Oxford.

1971. *The law of succession in the later Roman Republic*. Oxford.

1975. *Rome of the XII Tables: Persons and property*. Princeton.

Wiseman, T.P. 1987. "*Conspicui postes tectaque digna deo*: The public image of aristocratic and imperial houses in the late Republic and early Empire." In *L'Urbs. Espace urbain et histoire (Ier siècle av. J.-C. – IIIe siècle ap. J.-C.)*, 393–413. Rome.

WOMEN IN THE ROMAN REPUBLIC

Bauman, R.A. 1992. *Women and politics in ancient Rome*. London and New York.

Beard, M. 1995. "Re-reading (Vestal) virginity." In *Women in antiquity*, edited by R. Hawley and B. Levick, 166–77. London and New York.

1999. "The erotics of rape: Livy, Ovid and the Sabine women." In *Female networks and the public sphere in Roman society*, edited by P. Setälä and L. Savunen, 1–10. Rome.

Bradley, K.R. 1991. *Discovering the Roman family*. Oxford.

Brouwer, H.H.J. 1989. *Bona Dea*. Leiden.

Corbier, M. 1991. "Divorce and adoption as Roman family strategies." In *Marriage, divorce and children in ancient Rome*, edited by B. Rawson, 47–78. Oxford.

Cornell, T., and K. Lomas, eds. 1997. *Gender and ethnicity in ancient Italy*. London.

Culham, P. 1982. "The lex Oppia." *Latomus* 41:786–93.

———. 1986. "Again, what meaning lies in colour!" *ZPE* 64:235–45.

Delia, D. 1991. "Fulvia reconsidered." In *Women's history and ancient history*, edited by S.B. Pomeroy, 197–21. Chapel Hill.

Dixon, S. 1983. "A family business: Women's role in patronage and politics at Rome 80–44 B.C." *C&M* 34:91–112.

———. 1984. "*Infirmitas sexus*: Womanly weakness in Roman law." *TvR* 52:343–71.

———. 1988. *The Roman mother*. Norman, Okla.

———. 1992. *The Roman family*. Baltimore.

Fantham, E. 1991. "*Stuprum*: Public attitudes and penalties for sexual offenses in ancient Rome." *EMC* 10:267–81.

Fantham, E., H.P. Foley, N.B. Kampen, S.B. Pomeroy, and H.A. Shapiro, eds. 1994. *Women in the classical world*. Oxford.

Flower, H. 2002. "Rereading the *Senatus Consultum de Bacchanalibus* of 186 B.C." In *Oikistes: Studies in constitutions, colonies, and military power in the ancient world offered in honor of A.J. Graham*, edited by V.B. Gorman and E.W. Robinson, 79–98. Leiden.

French, V. 1987. "Midwives and maternity care in the Greco-Roman world." In *Rescuing Creusa*, edited by M.B. Skinner, 69–84. Lubbock, Tex.

Gardner, J.F. 1986. *Women in Roman law and society*. Bloomington, Ind.

Glinister, F. 1997. "Women and power in archaic Rome." In *Gender and ethnicity in ancient Italy*, edited by T. Cornell and K. Lomas, 115–27. London.

Hallett, J.P. 1984. *Fathers and daughters in Roman society*. Princeton.

———. 1977. "*Perusinae glandes* and the changing image of Augustus." *AJAH* 2:151–71.

Hänninen, M.-L. 1999a. "The dream of Caecilia Metella: Aspects of inspiration and authority in late republican Roman religion." In *Female networks and the public sphere in Roman society*, edited by P. Setälä and L. Savunen, 29–38. Rome.

———. 1999b. "Juno Regina and the Roman matrons." In *Female networks and the public sphere in Roman society*, edited by P. Setälä and L. Savunen, 39–52. Rome.

Hawley, R., and B. Levick, eds. 1995. *Women in antiquity: New assessments*. London and New York.

Hemelrijk, E.A. 1999. *Matrona docta*. London and New York.

Hillard, T. 1989. "Republican politics, women, and the evidence." *Helios* 16:165–82.

———. 1992. "On the stage, behind the curtain: Images of politically active women in the late Roman republic." In *Stereotypes of women in power*, edited by B. Garlick, S. Dixon, and P. Allen, 37–63. Westport, Conn.

Hodos, T. 1998. "The asp's poison: Women and literacy in Iron Age Italy." In *Gender and Italian archaeology*, edited by R.D. Whitehouse, 197–208. London.

Hopkins, K. 1965. "Contraception in the Roman Empire." *Comparative Studies in Society and History* 8:124–51.

Joshel, S.R., and S. Murnaghan, eds. 1998. *Women and slaves in Greco-Roman culture*. London and New York.

Kertzer, D.I., and R.P. Saller, eds. 1991. *The family in Italy from antiquity to the present.* New Haven.

King, K.L., ed. 1997. *Women and goddess traditions.* Minneapolis.

Kleiner, D.E.E. 1992. "Politics and gender in the pictorial propaganda of Antony and Octavian." *EMC* 36:357–67.

Marshall, A.J. 1990. "Roman ladies on trial." *Phoenix* 44:46–59.

Mustakallio, K. 1999. "Legendary women and female groups in Livy." In *Female networks and the public sphere in Roman society*, edited by P. Setälä and L. Savunen, 53–64. Rome.

Murray, O. 1994. *Sympotica.* Oxford.

Nielsen, M. 1999. "Common tombs for women in Etruria: Buried matriarchies?" In *Female networks and the public sphere in Roman society*, edited by P. Setälä and L. Savunen, 66–115. Rome.

Phillips, J.E. 1978. "Roman mothers and the lives of their adult daughters." *Helios* 6:69–80.

Pomeroy, S.B. 1975. *Goddesses, whores, wives, and slaves.* New York.

——— ed. 1991. *Women's history and ancient history.* Chapel Hill.

Rathje, A. 1994. "The Homeric banquet in central Italy." In *Sympotica*, edited by O. Murrary, 279–88. Oxford.

Rawson, B., ed. 1991. *Marriage, divorce and children in ancient Rome.* Oxford.

Rei, A. 1998. "Villains, wives, and slaves in the comedies of Plautus." In *Women and slaves in Greco-Roman culture*, edited by S.R. Joshel and S. Murnaghan, 92–108. London and New York.

Richlin, A. 1997. "Carrying water in a sieve: Class and the body in Roman women's religion." In *Women and goddess traditions*, edited by K.L. King, 331–74. Minneapolis.

Riddle, J.M. 1991. "Oral contraceptives and early-term abortifacients during classical antiquity and the Middle Ages." *Past and Present* 132:3–32.

Saller, R.P. 1991. "Corporal punishment, authority, and obedience in the Roman household." In *Marriage, divorce and children in ancient Rome*, edited by B. Rawson, 144–65. Oxford.

——— 1994. *Patriarchy, property and death in the Roman family.* Cambridge.

——— 1998. "Symbols of gender and status hierarchies in the Roman household." In *Women and slaves in Greco-Roman culture*, edited by S.R. Joshel and S. Murnaghan, 85–91. London and New York.

Scullard, H.H. 1981. *Festivals and ceremonies of the Roman Republic.* Ithaca, N.Y.

Sebesta, J.L., and L. Bonfante, eds. 1994. *The world of Roman costume.* Madison.

Setälä, P., and L. Savunen, eds. 1999. *Female networks and the public sphere in Roman society.* Rome.

Skinner, M.B. 1983. "Clodia Metelli." *TAPA* 113:273–87.

——— ed. 1987. *Rescuing Creusa: New methodological approaches to women in antiquity (Helios* 13). Lubbock, Tex.

Spaeth, B.S. 1996. *The Roman goddess Ceres.* Austin.

Staples, A. 1998. *From good goddesses to Vestal virgins.* London and New York.

Treggiari, S. 1976. "Jobs for women." *AJAH* 1:76–104.

——— 1991. *Roman marriage.* Oxford.

Whitehouse, R.D., ed. 1998. *Gender and Italian archaeology.* London.

THE REPUBLICAN ECONOMY AND ROMAN LAW: REGULATION, PROMOTION, OR REFLECTION?

General

De Martino, F. 1979. *Storia economica di Roma antica.* Florence.

De Neeve, P.W. 1984. *Colonus: Private farm-tenancy in Roman Italy during the Republic and the early Principate.* Amsterdam.

Duncan-Jones, R. 1990. *Structure and scale of the Roman economy.* Cambridge.

Erdkamp, P. 1998. *Hunger and the sword: Warfare and food supply in Roman republican wars (264–30 B.C.).* Amsterdam.

Finley, M.I. 1985. *The ancient economy.* 2nd ed. London.

Forte, F. 1999. *Il pensiero antico greco-romano e cristiano.* Vol. 1 of *Storia del pensiero dell'economia pubblica.* Milan.

Frayn, J.M. 1993. *Markets and fairs in Roman Italy: Their social and economic importance from the second century B.C. to the third century A.D.* Oxford.

Harris, W.V., ed. 1993. *The inscribed economy: Production and distribution in the Roman Empire in the light of* instrumentum domesticum. Ann Arbor.

Joshel, S.R. 1992. *Work, identity, and legal status at Rome: A study of the occupational inscriptions.* Norman, Okla.

Kloft, H. 1992. *Die Wirtschaft der griechisch-römischen Welt. Eine Einführung.* Darmstadt.

Laurence, R. 1997. Review of *Metropolis and hinterland: The city of Rome and the Italian economy, 200 B.C.–A.D. 200,* by N. Morley. *JRS* 87:286–7.

Moatti, C. 1993. *Archives et partage de la terre dans le monde romain (IIe siècle avant – Ier siècle après J.-C.).* Rome.

Morley, N. 1996. *Metropolis and hinterland: The city of Rome and the Italian economy, 200 B.C.–A.D. 200.* Cambridge and New York.

Nicolet, C. 1988. *Rendre à César: économie et société dans la Rome antique.* Paris.

Quilici, L., and S. Quilici Gigli, eds. 1995. *Agricoltura e commerci nell'Italia antica.* Rome.

Rauh, N.K. 1993. *The sacred bonds of commerce: Religion, economy and trade society at Hellenistic Roman Delos, 166–87 B.C.* Amsterdam.

Scheidel, W. 1995. *Grundpacht und Lohnarbeit in der Landwirtschaft des römischen Italiens.* Bern.

Silver, M. 1995. *Economic structures of antiquity.* Westport, Conn.

Specific

Aberson, M. 1994. *Temples votifs et butin de guerre dans la Rome républicaine.* Rome.

Andreau, J. 1987. *La vie financière dans le monde romain: Les métiers de manieurs d'argent (IVe siècle av. J.-C. – IIIe siècle ap. J.-C.).* Rome.

Andreau, J. 1999. *Banking and business in the Roman world.* Cambridge.

Aubert, J.-J. 1994. *Business managers in ancient Rome: A social and economic study of* Institores, *200 B.C.–A.D. 25.* Leiden.

1999a. "La gestion des *collegia*: aspects juridiques, économiques et sociaux." *CCG* 10:49–69.

1999b. "Les *institores* et le commerce maritime dans l'empire romain." *Topoi* 9:145–64.

2001. "The fourth factor: Managing non-agricultural production in the Roman world." In *Economies beyond agriculture in the classical world*, edited by D.J. Mattingly and J. Salmon, 90–111. London and New York.

Forthcoming. "Dead bodies and entrepreneurship." In *Papers in memory of M.W. Frederiksen*, edited by E. Lo Cascio and W.V. Harris.

Barlow, C.T. 1978. *Bankers, moneylenders and interest rates in the Roman Republic*. Ph.D. diss., University of North Carolina.

Carlsen, J. 1995. Vilici *and Roman estate managers until* A.D. *284*. Rome.

Colonna, G. 1990. "Città e territorio nell'Etruria meridionale." In *Crise et transformation des sociétés archaïques de l'Italie antique au Ve siècle av. J.-C.*, 7–21. Rome.

Cornell, T. 1995. *The beginnings of Rome: Italy and Rome from the Bronze Age to the Punic Wars (1000–264 B.C.)*. London and New York.

Crawford, M.H. 1974. *Roman republican coinage*. Cambridge.

——— ed. 1996. *Roman statutes*. London.

D'Arms, J.H. 1970. *The Romans on the Bay of Naples: A social and cultural study of the villas and their owners from 150 B.C. to A.D. 400*. Cambridge, Mass.

——— 1981. *Commerce and social standing in ancient Rome*. Cambridge, Mass. and London.

de Ligt, L. 1993. *Fairs and markets in the Roman Empire: Economic and social aspects of periodic trade in a pre-industrial society*. Amsterdam.

——— 1999. "Legal history and economic history: The case of the *actiones adiecticiae qualitatis*." *TR* 67:205–26.

——— 2001. "Studies in legal and agrarian history III: Appian and the lex Thoria." *Athenaeum* 89:121–44.

De Martino, F. 1982. "*Lex Rhodia*." In *Diritto privato e società romana*, 72–147. Rome. Originally published in *Rivista del diritto della navigazione* 3 (1937) 335–47; 4 (1938) 3–38, 180–214.

Dyson, S.L. 1992. *Community and society in Roman Italy*. Baltimore.

Gargola, D.J. 1995. *Lands, laws, and gods*. Chapel Hill.

Greene, K. 1986. *The archaeology of the Roman economy*. Berkeley and Los Angeles.

Harl, K.W. 1996. *Coinage in the Roman economy, 300 B.C. to A.D. 700*. Baltimore.

Harris, W.V. 1999. "Demography, geography, and the sources of Roman slaves." *JRS* 89:62–75.

Howgego, C. 1992. "The supply and use of money in the Roman world 200 B.C. to A.D. 300." *JRS* 82:1–31.

Lafon, X. 2001. Villa maritima: *Recherches sur les villas littorales de l'Italie romaine (IIIe s. av. J.-C. – IIIe s. ap. J.-C.)*. Rome.

Lintott, A. 1992. *Judicial reform and land reform in the Roman Republic*. Cambridge.

Lo Cascio, E. 1994. "The size of the Roman population: Beloch and the meaning of the Augustan census figures." *JRS* 84:23–40.

Morley, N. 2001. "The transformation of Italy, 225–28 B.C." *JRS* 91:50–62.

Nicolet, C. 2000. "Economie, société et institutions au IIe siècle av. J.-C.: De la lex Claudia à l'*ager acceptus*." In *Censeurs et publicains: Economie et fiscalité dans la Rome antique*, 19–43. Paris. Originally published in *Annales E.S.C.* 35:871–94.

——— 2000. *Censeurs et publicains: Economie et fiscalité dans la Rome antique*. Paris.

Peppe, L. 1981. *Studi sull'esecuzione personale* I. Milan.

Percival, J. 1976. *The Roman villa: A historical introduction*. London.

Poma, G. 1989. "*Il plebiscito Genucio ne fenerare liceret* (Liv., VII, 42, 1)." *RSA* 19:67–91.

Rathbone, D.W. Forthcoming. "The control and exploitation of *ager publicus* in Italy under the Roman Republic." In *Tâches publiques et entreprise privée*, edited by J.-J. Aubert.

Roth, J.P. 1999. *The logistics of the Roman army at war, 264 B.C.–A.D. 235*. Leiden.

Rotondi, G. [1912] 1966. *Leges publicae populi romani*. Reprint. Hildesheim.

Rougé, J. 1966. *Recherches sur l'organisation du commerce maritime en Méditerranée sous l'Empire romaine*. Paris.

Rouveret, A. 2000. "*Captiva arma*: guerre, butin, économie dans les cités de Grande Grèce et de Campanie du Ve siècle à l'expédition de Pyrrhus." In *Économie antique: La guerre dans les économies antiques*, edited by J. Andreau, P. Briant, and R. Descat, 83–102. Saint-Bertrand-de-Comminges.

Savunen, L. 1993. "Debt legislation in the fourth century B.C." In Senatus populusque Romanus: *Studies in Roman republican legislation*, edited by U. Paananen, 143–59. Helsinki.

Scardigli, B. 1991. *I trattati Romano-Cartaginesi*. Pisa.

Scheidel, W. 1999. "The slave population of Roman Italy: Speculations and constraints." *Topoi* 9:129–44.

——— 2001. "Roman age structure: evidence and models." *JRS* 91:1–26.

Smith, J.T. 1997. *Roman villas: A study in social structure*. London.

Tarpin, M. 2000. "Le butin sonnant et trébuchant dans la Rome républicaine." In *Économie antique. La guerre dans les économies antiques*, edited by J. Andreau, P. Briant, and R. Descat, 365–76. Saint-Bertrand-de-Comminges.

Tchernia, A. 1986. *Le vin de l'Italie romaine: essai d'histoire économique d'après les amphores*. Rome.

Tchernia, A., P. Pomey, and A. Hesnard, eds. 1978. *L'épave romaine de la Madrague de Giens (Var)* (*Gallia* suppl. 34). Paris.

Waelkens, L. 1998. "Nexum et noxalité." In *Le monde antique et les droits de l'homme*. *Actes de la 50e session de la Société internationale F. De Visscher pour l'histoire des droits de l'antiquité, Bruxelles, 16–19 septembre 1996*, edited by H. Jones, 89–94. Brussels.

Wallinga, H.T. 1996. "Official Roman washing and finishing directions: *lex Metilia fullonibus dicta*." *RHD* 64:183–90.

Wyetzner, P.S. 1995. "The social and cultural contexts of Roman sumptuary intervention." Ph.D. diss., University of California, Berkeley.

——— 2002. "Sulla's law on prices and the Roman definition of luxury." In Speculum iuris: *Roman law as a reflection of social and economic life*, edited by J.-J. Aubert and A.J.B. Sirks, 15–33. Ann Arbor.

Zehnacker, H. 1990. "Rome: Une société archaïque au contact de la monnaie (VIe–IVe siècle)." In *Crises et transformations des sociétés archaïques de l'Italie antique au Ve siècle av. J.-C.*, 307–26. Rome.

ROMAN RELIGION

Aberson, M. 1994. *Temples votifs et butin de guerre dans la Rome républicaine*. Rome.

Bakker, J.T. 1994. *Living and working with the gods: Studies of evidence for private religion and its material environment in the city of Ostia (100–500 A.D.)* (Dutch Monographs on Ancient History and Archaeology 12). Amsterdam.

Barton, T. 1994. *Ancient astrology*. London.

Beard, M., J. North, and S. Price, 1998. *Religions of Rome. 1: A history. 2: A sourcebook.* Cambridge.

Belayche, N., A. Bendlin, et al. 2000. "Römische Religion (1990–1999)." *Archiv für Religionsgeschichte* 2:283–345.

Bendlin, A. 2000. "Looking beyond the civic compromise: Religious pluralism in late republican Rome." In *Religion in archaic and republican Rome and Italy: Evidence and experience*, edited by E. Bispham and C. Smith, 115–35, 167–70. Edinburgh.

Bernstein, F. 1998. Ludi publici. *Untersuchungen zur Entstehung und Entwicklung der öffentlichen Spiele im republikanischen Rom* (Historia Einzelschriften 119). Stuttgart.

Cancik, H. 1986. "Rome as sacred landscape: Varro and the end of republican religion in Rome." *Visible Religion* 4/5:250–65.

Cecamore, C. 1995. "Il santuario di Iuppiter Latiaris sul Monte Cavo: spunti e materiali dai vecchi scavi." *BCAR* 96:19–44.

Cole, S.G. 1995. "Civic cult and civic identity." In *Sources for the ancient Greek city-state* (Acts Copenhagen Polis Centre 2), 292–325. Copenhagen.

Comella, A. 1981. "Tipologia e diffusione dei complessi votivi in Italia in epoca medio- e tardo-repubblicana: contributo alla storia dell'artigianato antico." *MEFRA* 93:717–803.

Cramer, F.H. 1954. *Astrology in Roman law and politics* (Memoirs of the American Philosophical Society 37). Philadelphia.

Dumézil, G. 1970. *Archaic Roman religion.* 2 vols. Chicago.

Erskine, A. 2001. *Troy between Greece and Rome: Local tradition and imperial Rome.* Oxford.

Fenelli, M. 1975. "Contributi per lo studio del votivo anatomico: i votivi anatomici di Lavinio." *ArchCl* 27:206–52.

Forsén, B. 1996. *Griechische Gliederweihungen: Eine Untersuchung zu ihrer Typologie und ihrer religions- und sozialgeschichtlichen Bedeutung* (Papers and Monographs of the Finnish Institute at Athens 4). Helsinki.

Gatti Lo Guzzo, L. 1975. *Il deposito votivo dell'Esquilino, detto di Minerva Medica.* Florence.

Gladigow, B. 1970. "*Condictio* und *inauguratio*: ein Beitrag zur römischen Sakralverfassung." *Hermes* 98:369–79.

Gustaffson, G. 1999. *Evocatio.* Uppsala.

Liebeschuetz, J.H.W.G. 1979. *Continuity and change in Roman religion.* Oxford.

Linderski, J. 1986. "The augural law." *ANRW* II.16.3:2146–312.

MacBain, B. 1982. *Prodigy and expiation: A study in religion and politics in republican Rome* (Collection Latomus 177). Brussels.

Malaise, M. 1972. *Les conditions de pénétration et de diffusion des cultes égyptiens en Italie* (EPRO 22). Leiden.

Mansfeld, J. 1999. "Theology." In *The Cambridge history of Hellenistic philosophy*, edited by A.A. Keimpe, 452–78. Cambridge.

Moatti, C. 1997. *La raison de Rome: naissance de l'esprit critique à la fin de la République.* Paris.

——— ed. 1998. *La mémoire perdue: recherches sur l'administration romaine.* Rome.

Orlin, E.M. 1997. *Temples, Religion, and politics in the Roman Republic.* Leiden.

Pailler, J.-M. 1988. Bacchanalia: *la répression de 186 av. J.-C. à Rome et en Italie: Vestiges, images, tradition* (Bibliothèque des écoles françaises d'Athène et de Rome 270). Rome.

Rawson, E. 1985. *Intellectual life in the late Roman Republic.* London.

Rosenberger, V. 1998. *Gezähmte Götter: das Prodigienwesen der römischen Republik* (HABES 27). Stuttgart.

Rüpke, J. 1990. Domi militiae: *die religiöse Konstruktion des Krieges in Rom*. Stuttgart.

　　1995a. *Kalender und Öffentlichkeit: die Geschichte der Repräsentation und religiösen Qualifikation von Zeit in Rom (RGVV 40)*. Berlin.

　　1995b. "*Fasti*: Quellen oder Produkte römischer Geschichtsschreibung?" *Klio* 77:184–202.

　　1995c. "Wege zum Töten, Wege zum Ruhm: Krieg in der römischen Republik." In *Töten im Krieg* (Schriften des Instituts für Historische Anthropologie 6), edited by H. v. Stietencron and J. Rüpke, 213–40. Freiburg.

　　1996. "Charismatics or professionals? Analyzing religious specialists." *Numen* 43:241–62.

　　2001. *Die Religion der Römer*. Munich. Forthcoming as *The religion of the Romans: An introduction*. London: Polity Press.

　　2002. "*Collegia sacerdotum*: Religiöse Vereine in der Oberschicht." In *Raum und Gruppe: Religiöse Vereine in der römischen Antike* (Studien und Texte zu Antike und Christentum 13), edited by U. Egelhaaf-Gaiser and A. Schäfer, 41–67. Tübingen.

Scheer, T.S. 1993. *Mythische Vorväter. Zur Bedeutung griechischer Heroenmythen im Selbstverständnis kleinasiatischer Städte* (Münchener Arbeiten zur Alten Geschichte 7). Munich.

Smith, J.Z. 1998. "Religion, religions, religious." In *Critical terms for religious studies*, edited by M.C. Taylor, 269–84. Chicago.

Stuckrad, K. v. 2000. "Jewish and Christian astrology in late antiquity: A new approach." *Numen* 47:1–40.

Szemler, G.J. 1972. *The priests of the Roman Republic: A study of interactions between priesthoods and magistracies* (Collection Latomus 127). Brussels.

Taylor, L.R. 1942. "The election of the *pontifex maximus* in the late Republic." *CP* 37:421–4.

Versnel, H.S. 1981. *Faith, hope and worship: Aspects of religious mentality in the ancient world* (Studies in Greek and Roman Religion 2). Leiden.

Wiseman, T.P. 1992. "Lucretius, Catiline, and the survival of prophecy." In *Historiography and imagination: Eight essays on Roman culture*, 49–67, 133–9. Exeter.

　　2000. "Liber: myth, drama and ideology in republican Rome." In *The Roman Middle Republic: Politics, religion, and historiography c. 400–133 B.C.* edited by C. Bruun. Rome. 265–99.

Wissowa, G. 1912. *Religion und Kultus der Römer* (HbdA 5,4). 2nd ed. Munich.

Ziolkowski, A. 1992. *The temples of mid-republican Rome and their historical and topographical context* (Saggi di Storia antica 4). Rome.

ITALY DURING THE ROMAN REPUBLIC 338–31 B.C.

Andreau, J. 1983. "À propos de la vie fiancière à Pouzzoles: Cluvius et Vestorius." In *Les 'Bourgeoisies' municipales italiennes aux II^{ieme} et Iere siècles av. J.-C.*, edited by M. Cébeillac-Gervasioni, 9–20. Paris and Naples.

Arthur, P. 1991. *Romans in northern Campania*. London.

Barker, G., and T. Rasmussen. 1998. *The Etruscans*. Oxford.

Bradley, G.J. 1997. "Iguvines, Umbrians and Romans: Ethnic identity in central Italy."

In *Gender and ethnicity in ancient Italy*, edited by T.J. Cornell and K. Lomas, (Accordia Specialist Studies on Italy 6), 53–68. London.

Brown, F. 1980. *Cosa: The making of a Roman town*. Ann Arbor.

Brunt, P.A. 1971. *Italian manpower*. Oxford.

Carandini, A. 1985. *Settefinestre: una villa schiavistica nell'Etruria romana*. Bari.

Carter, J.C. 1998. *The* chora *of Metaponto: The* necropoleis. Austin.

Castrén, P. 1975. Ordo Populusque Pompeianus: *Polity and society in Roman Pompeii.* Rome.

Coarelli, F., and A. La Regina. 1984. *Abruzzo Molise* (Guide archeologiche Laterza 9). Bari.

Cornell, T.J. 1995. *The beginnings of Rome*. London.

Cotton, M.A. 1979. *The late republican villa at Posto, Francolise*. London.

Crawford. M.H. 1995. *Roman statutes*. London.

D'Arms, J.H. 1984. "Upper class attitudes towards *viri municipales* and their towns in the early Roman Empire." *Athenaeum* 62:440–67.

Dench, E. 1995. *From barbarians to new men*. Oxford.

De Polignac, F., and M. Gualtieri. 1991. "A rural landscape in western Lucania." In *Roman landscapes: Archaeological survey in the Mediterranean region*, edited by G. Barker and J.A. Lloyd, 194–203. London.

Desy, P. 1993. *Recherches sur l'économie apulienne au IIe et au Ier siècle avant notre ère*. Brussels.

Giardiana, A., and A. Schiavone, eds. 1981. *Società romana e produzione schiavistica: L'Italia: insediamenti e forme economiche*. Rome and Bari.

Greco, E. 1981. *Magna Grecia*. Guide Archaeologica Laterza 12. Bari.

Hatzfeld, J. 1912. "Les Italiens residants à Delos." *BCH* 36:1–218.

1919. *Les trafiquants Italiens dans l'orient Héllenique*. Paris.

Herring, E., and K. Lomas, eds. 2000. *The emergence of state identities in Italy in the 1st millennium B.C.* London.

Holleran, C. 2002. "The development of public entertainment venues in Rome and Italy." In *"Bread and circuses": Euergetism and municipal patronage in Roman Italy*, edited by T.J. Cornell and K. Lomas, 46–63. London.

Holloway, R.R. 1994. *The archaeology of early Rome and Latium*. London.

Hopkins, K. 1978. *Conquerors and slaves*. Cambridge.

Humbert, M. 1978. Municipium et civitas sine suffragio: *l'organisation de la conquête jusqu'à la guerre sociale*. Rome.

Jongman, W. 1988. *The economy and society of Pompeii*. Amsterdam.

Jouffroy, H. 1986. *La construction publique en Italie et dans l'Afrique romaine*. Strasbourg.

Keaveney, A. 1987. *Rome and the unification of Italy*. London.

Laurence, R.M. 1994. *Roman Pompeii: Space and society*. London.

Lloyd, J.A., N. Christie, and G. Lock. 1997. "From the mountain to the plain: Landscape evolution in the Abruzzo: An interim report on the Sangro Valley Project (1994–5)." *PBSR* 65:1–57.

Lomas. K. 1993. *Rome and the western Greeks, 350 B.C.–A.D. 200: Conquest and acculturation in southern Italy*. London.

1996. *Roman Italy, 338 B.C.–A.D. 200: A sourcebook*. London.

2002. "Euergetism and urban renewal in Italy, 90 BC–AD 100." In *Euergetism and municipal patronage in ancient Italy*, edited by T.J. Cornell and K. Lomas, 28–45. London.

Morel, J.P. 1981. *Céramique campanienne: les formes.* Rome.

Morley, N. 1996. *Metropolis and hinterland: The city of Rome and the Italian economy, 200 B.C.–A.D. 200.* Cambridge.

Oakley, S.P. 1995. *The hill-forts of the Samnites.* London.

Patterson, J.R. 1987. "Crisis, what crisis?: Rural change and urban development in imperial Appenine Italy." *Papers of the British School at Rome* 42:115–46.

 1991. "Settlement, city and elite in Samnium and Lycia." In *City and country in the ancient world,* edited by J. Rich and A. Wallace-Hadrill, 147–68. London.

Pedley, J.G. 1990. *Paestum.* London.

Pobjoy, M. 2000. "Building inscriptions in republican Italy: Euergetism, responsibility and civic virtue." In *The epigraphic landscape of Roman Italy,* edited by A. Cooley, 77–92. London.

Potter, T.W. 1987. *Roman Italy.* London.

Rawson, E.D. 1991. "The Ciceronian aristocracy and its properties." In *Roman culture and society: Collected papers,* 204–22. Oxford. Originally published in M.I. Finley, ed., *Studies in Roman property* (Cambridge, 1976).

Rich, J. Forthcoming. "Treaties, allies and the conquest of Roman Italy." In *War and peace in ancient and medieval history,* edited by P. de Souza and J. France, Cambridge.

Salmon, E.T. 1965. *Samnium and the Samnites.* Cambridge.

 1969. *Roman colonisation under the Republic.* London.

Sherwin-White, A.N. 1973. *The Roman citizenship.* 2nd ed. Oxford.

Small, A.S. 1991. *Gravina: An Iron Age and republican settlement in Apulia.* London.

Tchernia, A. 1988. *Le vin de l'Italie romaine: essai d'histoire économique d'après les amphores.* Rome.

Terrenato, N. 1997. "The Romanisation of Italy: Global acculturation or cultural bricolage?" In *TRAC 97: Proceedings of the 7th Theoretical Roman Archaeology Conference,* 20–7. Oxford.

 1998. "*Tam firmum municipium*: The Romanization of Volaterrae and its cultural implications." *JRS* 88:94–114.

 2001. "Introduction." In *Romanisation in Italy and the West: Comparative issues in Romanisation,* edited by N. Terrenato and S. Keay, 7–16. Oxford.

Toynbee, A.J. 1965. *Hannibal's legacy.* Oxford.

Veyne, P. 1990. *Bread and circuses: Historical sociology and political pluralism.* Translated by B. Pearce. London.

Wilson, A.J.N. 1966. *Emigration from Italy in the republican age of Rome.* Manchester.

Wiseman, T.P. 1971. *New men in the Roman Senate, 139 B.C.–A.D. 14.* Oxford.

Zanker, P. 1998. *Pompeii: Public and private life.* Cambridge, Mass.

ROME AND CARTHAGE

Brunt, P.A. 1971. *Italian manpower 225 B.C.–A.D. 14.* Oxford.

Caven, B. 1980. *The Punic Wars.* London.

Cornell, Tim 1996. "Hannibal's legacy: The effects of the Hannibalic war on Italy." In *The Second Punic War: A reappraisal* (*BICS* suppl. 67), edited by T. Cornell, B. Rankov, and P. Sabin, 97–113. London.

Frank, T. 1928. *The Cambridge ancient history.* 1st ed. Cambridge.

Gibbon, E. 1910. *The decline and fall of the Roman Empire.* Everyman's Library. London.

Goldsworthy, A. 2000. *The Punic Wars.* London.

Harris, W.V. 1979. *War and imperialism in republican Rome.* Oxford.

Hoyos, B.D. 1998. *Unplanned wars: The origins of the First and Second Punic Wars.* Berlin and New York.

Lazenby, J.F. 1978. *Hannibal's war.* Warminster.

1996a. *The First Punic War.* London.

1996b. "Was Maharbal right?" In *The Second Punic War: A reappraisal* (*BICS* suppl. 67), edited by T. Cornell, B. Rankov, and P. Sabin, 39–47. London.

Liddell Hart, B.H. 1992. *Scipio Africanus: Greater than Napoleon.* London. Originally published in London in 1926 as *A greater than Napoleon: Scipio Africanus.*

Proctor, D. 1971. *Hannibal's march in history.* Oxford.

Rankov, B. 1996. "The Second Punic War at sea." In *The Second Punic War: a reappraisal* (*BICS* suppl. 67), edited by T. Cornell, B. Rankov, and P. Sabin, 49–57. London.

Toynbee, A.J. 1965. *Hannibal's legacy.* Oxford.

ROME AND THE GREEK WORLD

Badian, E. 1958. *Foreign clientelae (264–70 B.C.).* Oxford.

1964. *Studies in Greek and Roman history.* New York.

1972. *Pubicans and sinners: Private enterprise in the service of the Roman Republic.* Ithaca.

Berthold, R. 1984. *Rhodes in the Hellenistic age.* Ithaca, N.Y.

Derow, P.S. 1989. "Rome, the fall of Macedon, and the sack of Corinth." In *Rome and the Mediterranean to 133 B.C.* Vol. 8 of *The Cambridge ancient history,* 2nd ed., edited by A.E. Astin, F.W. Walbank, M.W. Fredericksen, and R.M. Ogilvie, 290–323. Cambridge.

1991. "Pharos and Rome." *ZPE* 88:261–70.

Errington, R.M. 1971. *The dawn of empire.* London.

1989a. "Rome and Greece to 205 B.C." In *Rome and the Mediterranean to 133 B.C.* Vol. 8 of *The Cambridge ancient history,* 2nd ed., edited by A.E. Astin, F.W. Walbank, M.W. Fredericksen, and R.M. Ogilvie, 81–106. Cambridge.

1989b. "Rome against Philip and Antiochus." In *Rome and the Mediterranean to 133 B.C.* Vol. 8 of *The Cambridge ancient history,* 2nd ed., edited by A.E. Astin, F.W. Walbank, M.W. Fredericksen, and R.M. Ogilvie, 244–89. Cambridge.

Ferrary, J.-L. 1988. *Philhellénisme et impérialisme.* Paris.

1990. "Traités et domination romaine dans le monde hellénique." In *I trattati nel mondo antico: Forma, ideologia, funzione,* edited by L. Canfora, M. Liverani, and C. Zaccagnini, 217–35. Rome.

Gera, D. 1998. *Judaea and Mediterranean politics, 219 to 161 B.C.E.* Leiden.

Greenhalgh, P. 1980. *Pompey, the Roman Alexander.* London.

Gruen, E.S. 1976. "Rome and the Seleucids in the aftermath of Pydna." *Chiron* 6:73–95.

1984. *The Hellenistic world and the coming of Rome.* Berkeley.

Habicht, C. 1989. "The Seleucids and their rivals." In *Rome and the Mediterranean to 133 B.C.* Vol. 8 of *The Cambridge ancient history,* 2nd ed., edited by A.E. Astin, F.W. Walbank, M.W. Frederiksen, and R.M. Ogilvie, 324–87. Cambridge.

Hansen, E.V. 1971. *The Attalids of Pergamum.* 2nd ed. Ithaca, N.Y.

Hammond, N.G.L. 1988. *A history of Macedonia.* Vol. 3. Oxford.

Hind, J.G.F. 1994. "Mithridates." In *The last age of the Roman Republic, 146–43 B.C.* Vol. 9 of *The Cambridge ancient history,* 2nd ed., edited by J.A. Crook, A. Lintott, and E. Rawson, 129–64. Cambridge.

Kallet-Marx, R. 1995. *Hegemony to empire: The development of the Roman* imperium *from 148 to 62 B.C.* Berkeley.

Keaveney, A. 1982. *Sulla: The last republican.* London.

1992. *Lucullus: A life.* London.

Lampela, A. 1998. *Rome and the Ptolemies of Egypt: The development of their political relations, 273–80 B.C.* Helsinki.

Lintott, A.W. 1993. Imperium Romanum: *Politics and administration.* London.

Marshall, A.J. 1968. "Friends of the Roman people." *AJP* 89:39–55.

McGing, B.C. 1986. *The foreign policy of Mithridates VI Eupator, King of Pontus.* Leiden.

Meadows, A.R. 1993. "Greek and Roman diplomacy on the eve of the Second Macedonian War." *Historia* 42:40–60.

Morgan, M.G. 1969. "Metellus Macedonicus and the province Macedonia." *Historia* 18:422–46.

Pastor, L.B. 1996. *Mitridates Eupator, rey del Ponto.* Granada.

Rich, J.W. 1984. "Roman aims in the First Macedonian War." *PCPS* 210:126–80.

1989 "Patronage and international relations in the Roman Republic." In *Patronage in ancient society,* edited by A. Wallace-Hadrill, 119–35. London.

Seager, R. 1979. *Pompey: A political biography.* Berkeley.

Sherwin-White, A.N. 1984. *Roman foreign policy in the East, 168 B.C. to A.D. 1.* London.

1994. "Lucullus, Pompey, and the East." In *The last age of the Roman Republic, 146–43 B.C.* Vol. 9 of *The Cambridge ancient history,* 2nd ed., edited by J.A. Crook, A. Lintott, and E. Rawson, 229–73. Cambridge.

Sullivan, R.D. 1990. *Near Eastern royalty and Rome, 100–30 B.C.* Toronto.

Will, E. 1979. *Histoire politique du monde hellénistique 323–30 av. J.C.* 2nd ed. 2 vols. Nancy.

LITERATURE IN THE ROMAN REPUBLIC

Courtney, E. 1993. *The fragmentary Latin poets.* Oxford.

Fantham, E. 1975. "Sex status and survival." *Phoenix* 29:44–72.

Goldberg, S. 1995. *Epic in republican Rome.* Berkeley.

Handley, E.W. 1968. *Menander and Plautus: a study in comparison: an inaugural lecture delivered at University College, London.* London.

Harris, W.V. 1989. *Ancient literacy.* Cambridge, Mass.

Hinds, S. 1998. *Allusion and intertext.* Cambridge.

Kenney, E.J., and W.V. Clausen. 1982. *Latin literature.* Vol. 2 of *The Cambridge history of classical literature.* Pt. 1, "The early Republic." Cambridge.

Konstan, D. 1983. *Roman comedy.* Ithaca, N.Y.

Leo, F. 1913. *Geschichte der römischen Literatur.* Berlin.

McCarthy, K. 2000. *Slaves, masters, and the art of authority in Plautine comedy.* Princeton.

McGushin, P. 1977. C. Sallustius Crispus, Bellum Catilinae: *a commentary.* Leiden.

1987. *Sallust. The conspiracy of Catiline: a companion to the penguin translation of S.A. Handford.* Bristol.

Moore, T.J. 2000. *Plautus and his audience.* Austin.

Paul, G.M. 1984. *A historical commentary on Sallust's* Bellum Jugurthinum. Liverpool.

Quinn, K. 1999. *The Catullan revolution.* Cambridge.

Sallust. 1992–1994. *The Histories,* 2 vols. Translated and with commentary by P. McGushin. Oxford.

Segal, E. 1968. *Roman laughter*. Cambridge, Mass.
Slater, N.W. 1985. *Plautus in performance*. Princeton.
Wright. 1975. "The transformations of Pseudolus." *TAPA* 105:403–16.

Bibliographical Note

For literacy and its role in conditioning the development of literature at Rome, see W.V. Harris, *Ancient literacy* (Cambridge, Mass., 1989). Most modern discussions of early Roman literature still depend on the pioneering history of F. Leo, *Geschichte der römischen Literatur* (Berlin, 1913). See now A.J. Gratwick, *Cambridge history of classical literature*, vol. 2, *Latin literature* (Cambridge, 1982), part I; also G.B. Conte, *Latin literature* (Baltimore, 1995). Texts and translations of Livius, Naevius, Ennius, Pacuvius, Accius, and Lucilius are collected in *Remains of old Latin*, edited by E.H. Warmington, vols. 1–3 (Cambridge, Mass., 1935–1940). There are separate editions of Ennius' *Annales*, by O. Skutsch (Oxford, 1968), and of his tragedies, by H.D. Jocelyn (Cambridge, 1967). S. Goldberg's *Epic in republican Rome* (Berkeley, 1995) is an accessible study of Roman epic from Livius to Cicero. For Ennius' rewriting of literary history, see now S. Hinds, *Allusion and intertext* (Cambridge, 1998).

On Roman comedy, see D. Konstan, *Roman comedy* (Ithaca, 1983). On Plautus, see E. Segal, *Roman laughter* (Cambridge, Mass., 1968); N.W. Slater, *Plautus in performance* (Princeton, 1985); and T.J. Moore, *Plautus and his audience* (Austin, 2000). Good recent studies on Lucretius are *Myth and poetry in Lucretius* by M. Gale (Cambridge, 1995) and *Science and thought in Lucretius* by D. Sedley (Cambridge, 1997). K. Quinn's study *The Catullan revolution* has now been updated with a preface by C. Martindale (Cambridge, 1999); on Catullus in his social setting, see T.P. Wiseman, *Catullus and his world* (Cambridge, 1985), and also *Cinna the poet and other essays* (Leicester, 1974). No one book does justice to Cicero's works, but *Cicero: A portrait* by E. Rawson (London and Ithaca, 1967) provides a balanced survey in the context of his career; see also *Cicero the philosopher*, edited by J. Powell (Oxford, 1998). Syme's monumental study *Sallust* (Berkeley, 1964) is now supported by good editions and commentaries on *Jugurtha* by G.M. Paul (Liverpool, 1983) and on the *Histories* by P. McGushin (Oxford, 1994). *Roman literary culture from Cicero to Apuleius* by E. Fantham (Baltimore, 1999) aims to provide a continuous account of the transition from literature in the society of the last "republican" years under Caesar's domination to the triumviral and Augustan periods.

ROMAN REPUBLICAN ART IN CONTEXT

Journals

American Journal of Archaeology. Contents and abstracts online at
    http://www.ajaonline.org/
Bryn Mawr Classical Review. Online journal at
    http://ccat.sas.upenn.edu/bmcr/
College Art Association Reviews. Online journal at
    http://www.caareviews.org/contents.html
Journal of Roman Archaeology. Online contents for issues and supplements at
    http://www.JournalofRomanArch.com/

Reference Works

Aufstieg und Niedergang der römischen Welt (ANRW, 1982). Berlin and New York. See esp. vol. II.12.1.

Lexicon iconographicum mythologiae classicae (LIMC, 1981–). Zürich. See sections *"pars occidentalis"* for Etruscan and Roman myth and religion images, and see main (Greek) entries with Italian proveniences, and with dates from third century onwards. There is an online bibliography search engine at http://www.rzuser.uni-heidelberg.de/~m99/limc/

Lexicon topographicum urbis Romae (LTUR, 1993–2000), Eva Margareta Steinby, ed. Rome.

The Princeton encyclopedia of classical sites (PECS, 1976), R. Stillwell, W.L. MacDonald, and M. Holland McAllister, eds. Princeton. Online at the Perseus Project (also generally useful) at http://www.perseus.tufts.edu

Classical Studies Search Engines

The Stoa Consortium, http://www.stoa.org/finder/showlinks?kws=Augustus+Caesar for Diotima, *BMCR, ZPE, ANRW,* ANS-Library, Gnomon Thesaurus bibliography, Perseus, OhioLink, *Suda.*

The *Database of Classical Bibliography,* joint website of *DCB* (vols. 40–63, 1969–1982) and *Année Philologique* (vols. 64–71, 1983–2000), http://web.gc.cuny.edu/dept/CLASS/dcb.htm

Books and Articles

Andreae, B. 1972. *The art of Rome.* New York.

Beard, M., and J. Henderson. 2001. *Classical art from Greece to Rome.* Oxford.

Bergmann, B. 1995. "Greek masterpieces and Roman recreative fictions." *HSPh* 97:79–120.

Bergmann, B., and C. Kondoleon, eds. 1999. *The art of ancient spectacle* (Studies in the History of Art 156; Center for Advanced Study in the Visual Arts, Symposium Papers 34). Washington, D.C.

Bianchi Bandinelli, R. 1970. *Rome, the center of power, 500 B.C. to A.D. 200.* Translated by P. Green. New York.

Bodel, J. 1997. "Monumental villas and villa monuments." *JRA* 10:5–35.

Brendel, O. 1979. *Prolegomena to the study of Roman art.* New Haven.

1998. *Etruscan art* (Pelican History of Art). 2nd ed. New Haven.

Clarke, J. 1991. *Houses of Roman Italy, 100 B.C.–A.D. 250: Ritual, space, and decoration.* Berkeley.

Coarelli, F. 1977. "Public building in Rome between the Second Punic War and Sulla." *PBSR* 45:1–23.

1996. *Revixit ars: arte e ideologia a Roma, dai modelli ellenistici alla tradizione repubblicana.* Rome.

De Caro, S. 1994. *Il Museo archeologica nazionale di Napoli. Guida alla collezione: I mosaici: La Casa del Fauno.* Naples.

De Grummond, N., and B. Ridgway, eds. 2000. *From Pergamon to Sperlonga: Sculpture and context.* Berkeley.

Denti, M. 1991. *I Romani a nord del Po: archaeologia e cultura in età repubblicana e augustea* (Biblioteca di archeologia 15). Milan.

Feldherr, A. 1998. *Spectacle and society in Livy's History.* Berkeley.

Frazer, A., ed. 1998. *The Roman villa*: Villa urbana (University Museum Monograph 101, Symposium Series 9). Philadelphia.

Gazda, E. 1995. "Roman sculpture and the ethos of emulation: Reconsidering repetition." *HSPh* 97:121–56.

Gruen, E. 1992. *Culture and national identity in republican Rome*. Chap. 3, "Art and civic life" (84–130), and Chap. 4, "Art and ideology" (131–82). Ithaca, N.Y.

Henig, M., ed. 1983. *A handbook of Roman art: A comprehensive survey of all the arts of the Roman world*. Ithaca, N.Y.

Hofter, M.R. 1988. *Kaiser Augustus und die verlorene Republik: eine Austellung im Martin-Gropius-Bau, Berlin, 7. Juni – 14. August 1988*. Mainz.

Kent, J.P.C. 1978. *Roman coins*. London.

Kleiner, D. 1992. *Roman sculpture*. New York and London.

Koeppel, G. 1982. "The grand pictorial tradition of Roman historical representation during the early Empire." *ANRW* II.12.1:507–35.

Kozloff, A.P., D.G. Mitten, and S. Fabing. 1988. *The gods delight: The human figure in classical bronze. The Cleveland Museum of Art, November 16, 1988 – January 8, 1989*. Cleveland.

Kuttner, A. 1995. *Dynasty and empire in the age of Augustus: The case of the Boscoreale cups*. Berkeley.

——— 1998. "Prospects of patronage: Realism and *romanitas* in the architectural vistas of the 2nd style." In *The Roman villa*: Villa urbana (University Museum Monograph 101, Symposium Series 9), edited by A. Frazer, 93–108. Philadelphia.

Ling, R. 1991. *Roman painting*. Cambridge.

Massa, F.P. 1992. *Iconologia e politica nell' Italia antica: Roma, Lazio, Etruria dal VII al I secolo a.C.* (Biblioteca di Archaeologia 18). Milan.

Pollitt, J.J. 1986. *Art in the Hellenistic age*. New York.

——— 1978. "The impact of Greek art on Rome." *TAPA* 108:155–74.

——— 1983. *The art of Rome c. 753 B.C.–A.D. 337: Sources and documents*. Cambridge.

——— 1997. "Rome, the Republic and early Empire." In *The Oxford history of classical art*, edited by J. Boardman, 217–96. Oxford.

——— 2000. "The phantom of a Rhodian school of sculpture." In *From Pergamon to Sperlonga*, edited by N.T. De Grummond and B.S. Ridgway, 92–110. Berkeley.

Richardson, L. 1992. *A new topographical dictionary of ancient Rome*. Baltimore and London.

Simon, E. 1986. *Augustus: Kunst und Leben in Rom um die Zeitenwende*. Munich.

Smith, R.R.R. 1991. *Hellenistic sculpture: A handbook*. London.

Steingräber, S., ed. 1986. *Etruscan painting: Catalogue raisonné of Etruscan wall paintings*. New York.

Strong, D.E., and D. Brown, eds. 1976. *Roman crafts*. London.

Strong, D.E., J.M.C. Toynbee, and R. Ling. 1988. *Roman art*. 2nd ed. London.

Torelli, M. 1999. *Tota Italia: Essays in the cultural formation of Roman Italy*. New York.

——— 1982. *Typology and structure of Roman historical reliefs*. Ann Arbor.

Tuchelt, K. 1979. *Frühe Denkmäler Roms in Kleinasien: Beiträge zur archäologischen Überlieferung aus der Zeit der Republik und des Augustus*. Tübingen.

Wallace-Hadrill, A. 1994. *Houses and society in Pompeii and Herculaneum*. Princeton.

Wiseman, T.P. 1987. *Roman studies: Literary and historical*. Liverpool and Wolfeboro, N.H.

——— 1998. *Roman drama and Roman history*. Exeter.

SPECTACLE AND POLITICAL CULTURE IN THE ROMAN REPUBLIC

Beacham, R.C. 1991. *The Roman theatre and its audience.* London.

Bernstein, F. 1998. Ludi publici. *Untersuchungen zur Entstehung und Entwicklung der öffentlichen Spiele im republikanischen Rom.* Stuttgart.

Ferrary, J.-L. 1988. *Philhéllenisme et impérialisme: aspects idéologiques de la conquête romaine du monde hellénistique de la seconde guerre de Macedoine à la guerre contre Mithridate.* Rome.

Flower, H.I. 1996. *Ancestor masks and aristocratic power in Roman culture.* Oxford.

Goldberg, S.M. 1998. "Plautus on the Palatine." *JRS* 88:1–20.

Gruen, E.S. 1990. *Studies in Greek culture and Roman policy.* Leiden.

    1992. *Culture and national identity in republican Rome.* Ithaca, N.Y.

Hölkeskamp, K.-J. 2001. "Capitol, Comitium und Forum. Öffentliche Räume, sakrale Topographie und Erinnerungslandschaften der römischen Republik." In *Studien zu antiken Identitäten,* edited by S. Faller, 97–132. Würzburg.

Hölscher, T. 2001. "Die Alten vor Augen. Politische Denkmäler und öffentliches Gedächtnis im republikanischen Rom." In *Institutionalität und Symbolisierung. Verstetigungen kultureller Ordnungsmuster in Vergangenheit und Gegenwart,* edited by G. Melville, 183–211. Cologne.

Künzl, E. 1988. *Der römische Triumph. Siegesfeiern im antiken Rom.* Munich.

Moore, T.J. 1994. "Seats and social status in the Plautine theatre." *CJ* 90:113–23.

Nicolet, C. 1976. *The world of the citizen in republican Rome.* Berkeley.

Rawson, E. 1981. "Chariot racing in the Roman Republic." *PBSR* 51:1–16.

    1985. "Theatrical life in republican Rome and Italy." *PBSR* 53:97–113.

Shatzman, I. 1975. *Senatorial wealth and Roman politics.* Brussels.

Wallace-Hadrill, A. 1990. "Roman arches and Greek honours: The language of power at Rome." *PCPS* 216:143–81.

Wiedemann, T. 1992. *Emperors and gladiators.* London.

Wiseman, T.P. 1998. *Roman drama and Roman history.* Exeter.

Ziolkowski, A. 1992. *The temples of mid-republican Rome and their historical and topographical context.* Rome.

INDEX

✑